{ The Long Ago Lake }

Mill Lake was a perfect lake.

The Long Ago Lake

A Child's Book of Nature Lore and Crafts

written by
MARNE WILKINS
illustrated by Martha Weston

Sierra Club Books / Charles Scribner's Sons
San Francisco / New York

The Long Ago Lake was edited and prepared for publication at The Yolla Bolly Press, Covelo, California, under the supervision of James and Carolyn Robertson during the fall and winter of 1977. Production staff: Gene Floyd, Loren Fisher, Joyca Cunnan, Diana Fairbanks, Jay Stewart.

Manufactured in the United States of America

1 3 5 7 9 11 13 15 17 19 MD/C 20 18 16 14 12 10 8 6 4 2
1 3 5 7 9 11 13 15 17 19 MD/P 20 18 16 14 12 10 8 6 4 2

Library of Congress Cataloguing in Publication Data

Wilkins, Marne.
The long ago lake.

SUMMARY: The author recollects her childhood summers in the Wisconsin Lakes district and the nature lessons her family learned from their Indian friends. Nature crafts projects are included.
1. Natural history — Outdoor books — Juvenile literature.
2. Natural history — Wisconsin — Juvenile literature.
3. Handicraft — Juvenile literature.
[1. Natural history — Wisconsin. 2. Nature craft. 3. Handicraft.]
I Title.
QH48.W48 1978   500.9'775 [B]   77-18173
ISBN 0-684-15614-8
ISBN 0-684-15613-X pbk.

For Liz and Muff and theirs.
To Al and Peg.

TABLE OF CONTENTS

A Long Time Ago
page 11

⸂ Part One ⸃

Water: Worlds, Wonder, Knots, and Pots
page 25

❧ Part Two ❦

❧ Part Three ❦

❧ Part Four ❦

Lore and More
page 139

More Books to Read
page 157

Index to Crafts
page 159

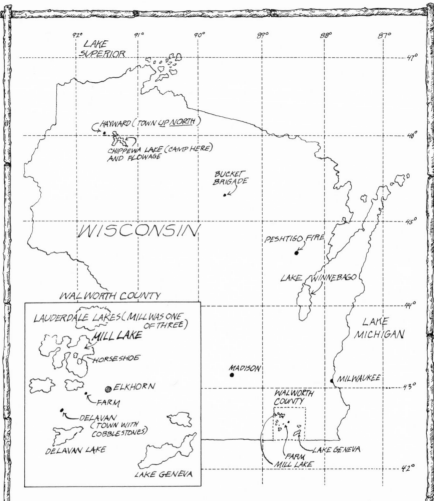

The stories and anecdotes in this book took place mostly when I was a girl in Wisconsin. I lived in a small town, but spent part of the year at my grandfather's farm, part of the year at the family house at Mill Lake, and a month each summer at the secret lake *up north*. Here is a map that shows where these places are. Now you know why streams and lakes were so much a part of our lives. We were surrounded by them.

{A Long Time Ago}

ONCE, A LONG TIME AGO, I was a young girl. I had a brother and three boy cousins, and we all grew up together. Our home was located in a small Wisconsin town which was surrounded by dairy farms, wood lots, and lakes. In the summertime we cousins and our mothers and fathers and grandparents all moved to the lake. Our lake, Mill Lake, was a very old one made when the glaciers pushed the land in Wisconsin around during the Ice Age. It was supplied with fresh water from many beautiful springs and from trickling little streams. The lake had a good flow of water to its outlet, and the Indians had built a mill there to grind grain many years before white settlers ever knew where Wisconsin was. Mill Lake was a perfect lake, and my cousins and brother and I would scrap with anyone who argued any other was better. Even though we loved Mill Lake, we looked forward to the month of August when we left it for awhile. It was then that we stuffed the family cars with everything needed to keep us warm and for catching fish, and we drove *up north*. We had a secret place and secret friends.

Shall I tell you? Well, my uncle is a fisherman, and he never gives up trying to find the best place to fish and the best way to do it. Michigan, Minnesota, and Wisconsin have a

11

particular fish called a *muskie* that lives in northern lakes. Every year many huge muskies are caught and weighed to see which state produces the biggest fish. When my uncle was a young boy, he made friends with some Chippewa Indians who lived in the northern corner of Wisconsin. They told him of a hidden lake where he would be able to catch all the fish he could imagine — especially muskies. They invited him to their home and led him to that lake. They gave him permission to camp and fish there and that is where he took us. His Indian friend had children, too, and they became our friends.

We cousins always knew we had found the right trail to the Indians' secret lake because there was a giant lodgepole pine tree at the edge of the camp, and it could be seen from a long way. We scrambled out of the loaded cars as soon as they stopped and raced to the tree. Up we climbed to see who could reach the top first. One year we discovered we were getting *big*. No sooner had we reached our favorite sitting branch, which was large enough for all of us to sit on, than it snapped, and we tumbled out of the pine, bouncing, scraping, and crashing into a heap at the bottom in the merciful duff. The Chippewa boys had heard us arrive and were standing at the edge of the woods, holding their sides from laughing so hard! They instantly made up for it, though, by helping us gather a pail full of blueberries which my aunt then made into a pie and baked next to an open fire down by the lake.

Preparing the camp was a job we did carefully. We always made it so that when we left for home at summer's end, it was hardly possible to know anyone had been there. That way our camp stayed a special, secret, and wild place. When the ice was thick, the Indians would saw blocks of ice which they shared with us. We carefully dug holes and packed them with sawdust to keep the ice from melting and to keep the fish we caught cool and safe from bears.

{How to Make a Reflector Oven}

Materials needed: sheet metal or heavy-duty aluminum foil, tin shears.

The kind of blueberry pie Aunt Gladys made was a one crust version baked in a roasting pan lid. My mother and aunt were wizards at cooking during all kinds of weather and in all conditions. The two Coleman stoves were set up behind a big tarp against rain or wind, and most of our camp meals featured some product from their fires. Of course these stoves had ovens, but the oven we liked best was a simple reflector.

A successful reflector oven requires:

(1) A good steady hot-bedded fire.

(2) A way to mount your baking pan off the ground in front of the reflector.

(3) Shiny material to reflect the heat of the fire onto your baked goods.

Reflectors can be made of rock that is thoroughly heated but other materials work too. Sheet metal or tin is cut into a piece that is 2 feet by 2 feet and folded in the middle. A hole is punched in each of the four corners large enough to hold a coat hanger wire which is poked through and bent to pull the two halves together to form an angle.

If sides are needed, the original piece of metal is cut 4 feet long across the top half and 2 feet along the bottom. Then cut the side triangle down to the center fold. This should make a triangle about 12 inches by 12 inches by 17 inches from the top to the center fold.

The baked goods are placed on a rack of some kind so they are off the ground and between the reflector oven and the hot bed of coals. The reflector is adjusted, so that the heat from the fire is reflected onto the baked goods.

The whole oven can also be made by using heavy-duty aluminum foil bent over sticks for a frame. We like to carry foil on camping trips instead of other cooking utensils. There always seems to be a forked stick which, when covered, can be just the kind of pan you want to use.

FOR A REFLECTOR WITH SIDES:
4 FEET
TIN
2 FEET
4 CORNER HOLES
2 FEET
FOLD IN SIDES AND BOTTOM
ATTACH CORNERS WITH WIRE THROUGH HOLES

BEND FOIL OVER STICKS

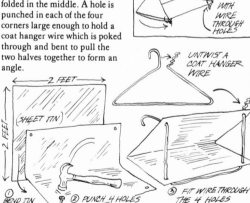

UNTWIST A COAT HANGER WIRE

2 FEET
(SHEET TIN)
2 FEET
① BEND TIN IN HALF
② PUNCH 4 HOLES
③ FIT WIRE THROUGH THE 4 HOLES

MOVE REFLECTOR CLOSER TO FOOD FOR MORE HEAT

We tumbled out of the pine, crashing into a heap.

Fires were built on the sandy beach. And boxes holding food and gear were either hung by rope or lashed to trees to keep them away from animals.

⇥[Outdoor Wisdom]⇤

I have found out since growing up that no matter what kind of outdoor living you do, there are certain things you need to know. I have camped in snow, in high mountains, in deserts, along streams, and on islands, in crowded public campgrounds, and in wild, scary forests. Now I live in the wooded mountains of Northern California on a little ranch a long way from the small town and lake and farms where I grew up. Our Chippewa friends and my life in all these places have taught me so many tricks and habits to make living and camping out-of-doors enjoyable and interesting that I would like to share them with you.

First, there are two big, important habits that people can spend all their lives trying to learn well. It's true! And they will seem so simple you'll probably laugh, but — just the same — they come before anything else. The first is the habit of *seeing* what you look at. The Indians know that habit better than anybody and our Chippewa friends taught us what they could. It was hard to learn, though.

I'll tell you an example. Recently I was describing to a friend a beautiful fresh hide a man had given me to tan for leather. I was pleased with the pretty markings and had already begun to work on it. The friend asked me if the hide was prime. First, I was surprised and then I felt pretty stupid. I had not really *seen* that hide. I had looked only at the markings. Of course, anything but a newborn calf would not be a very good hide in the summer, so I hurried home to look. But luckily enough, the inside was snowy white and unmarked by any stains or streaks. It was a prime hide. I had

15

spent several hours scraping and salting that side of the hide, but I never did really *see* it. It's strange, isn't it? Sometimes it is hard to *see* what you look at. In the out-of-doors, it is so important that sometimes it not only saves you a whole lot of trouble, but maybe even your life.

The other habit you need to learn to be a really good outdoor person is to *be ready*. That means having your food planned; you tools sharp, clean, and safe; and your gear in good condition. To me, it means even more than that; it means *being ready* to do the most important things. *Being ready* means when somebody says, "Let's go fishing," I not only know where my pole is, but I know how to fish, too. My dad understood that. He used to put a pail in the backyard for us to practice casting into. If we were *ready*, we could hit the water in the pail every time. Then when we did go fishing, we could cast our lure into the water right by a lily pad or stump so that a wise, worthy fish might think it was just exactly what he wanted for dinner that day. *Be ready*, and you will know what knot to use when you want to tie a packsaddle onto a horse. *Be ready*, and if you need to start a fire during a rainstorm you can do it. If you go too far from home, and it gets dark too early, *be ready* to find your way home with the help of the stars.

Learning to *be ready* will teach you many things. You can enjoy learning the knots for making nets and securing loads, and how to lash and whip rope, or how to tell time by the sun, or when a storm is approaching by the clouds and the feel of the wind. You can practice listening to sounds and warnings all around you. For example, do you know what the ground squirrel is scolding about? And why? Is it a snake after quail eggs? Or a hawk overhead? Why is the blue jay squawking so loudly? Is he worried? About what? Listen to the trees. Often you can tell by the changing sounds what the weather is doing. Rocks tumbling onto a mountain path in little trickles can be a warning that an animal just scurried away above

16

⁌How to Tie Some Useful Knots⁋

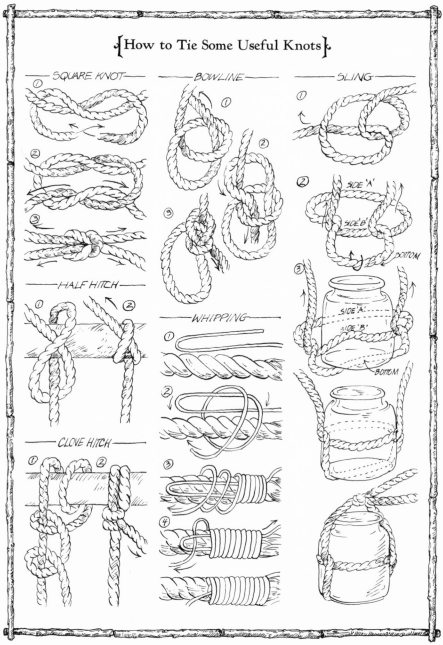

SQUARE KNOT

BOWLINE

SLING

HALF HITCH

WHIPPING

CLOVE HITCH

SIDE 'A'
SIDE 'B'
BOTTOM

SIDE 'A'
SIDE 'B'
BOTTOM

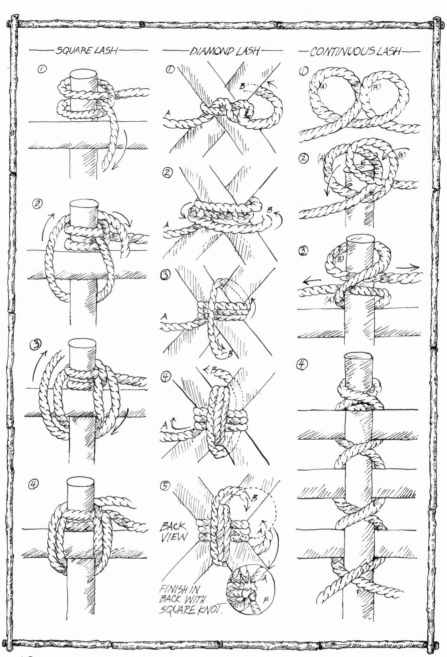

SQUARE LASH

① ② ③ ④

DIAMOND LASH

① ② ③ ④ ⑤

BACK VIEW

FINISH IN BACK WITH SQUARE KNOT.

CONTINUOUS LASH

① ② ③ ④

18

you, or it may mean that a bigger slide started somewhere higher up. *Be ready* to see the little rocks and read what they can tell you. *Be ready* to know what animals live near you and how they live, so you won't hurt them in their homes, and they won't accidently hurt you either. You can learn to read tracks and how to *see* nests and burrows, too. Many animals leave droppings, or scats, that tell us who they are and what they have eaten. In some scats, you will see feathers, pellets, down, or broken eggshells, if you practice looking.

{Ghost Owl and Mountain Cat}

There is a wonderful man named Dr. Allen, an ornithologist at Cornell University, who loves birds and has told us many things about them. He has made records of bird sounds, and they have helped me to learn more about birds I couldn't recognize before. Now each evening about five o'clock I hear an owl conversation. The owls talk back and forth, calling across several hills. By listening to Dr. Allen's recording, I finally decided which owl it was that I could hear.

One night our family saw what appeared to be a huge flying ghost sailing and swooping toward some trees where our chickens were roosting. We were *ready*. We knew from listening and comparing with Dr. Allen's recordings that some rare great horned owls lived nearby, and that someday they would tire of catching mice and try a nice fat hen instead. We turned a bright lantern right at the hen's tree and away the owl soared. He was huge, but we were *ready* for his visit, and so we saved our hen.

Up north at the secret lake, we used to listen to the loons laugh and call. Their sound was so spooky we shivered. We soon learned that it was when they didn't call that we should be afraid. When they hid, we should do the same! Back down

19

Preparing the camp was a job we did carefully.

at Mill Lake, we would be gliding along in a canoe when suddenly all chatter among the red-winged blackbirds would stop. We stoped and listened, too, Then we saw that mink had come down to hunt by the water or that hawks were flying too close.

One time my own little girl and I were hiking on a high cliff trail. Going around a ledge, we came to a high overhang making a space like a cave. We had already noticed what seemed to be the fresh tracks of a mountain cat, and we had decided just how we would leave that trail in a hurry if we had to. Sure enough, right there in that cave was a freshly killed rabbit, a perfect mountain-cat lunch; but there was no cat! We just knew that cat was in a safe place watching us. We were *ready,* and we left the trail as we had planned to, so the cat didn't have to be afraid of us stealing its lunch; and we had nothing to fear, either.

Besides *being ready* and learning to *see,* some other important skills and habits have to do with eating and sleeping. Whenever we find ourselves out-of-doors, different conditions determine how we do those two things. Learning to prepare, carry, and store food and gear, and to make a comfortable place to sleep can be a pretty sizable task out-of-doors. Other know-how has to do with finding your way, sometimes by the stars, sometimes by a compass, or sometimes by reading tracks or maps. And more has to do with finding ways to help people, animals, and plants, and learning new things from them. There is no end to all the things we can learn about and do outdoors!

21

{ Part One }

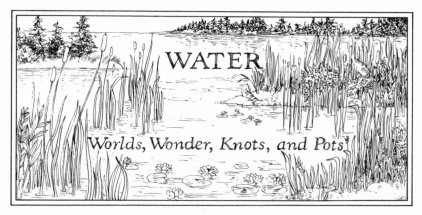

WATER

Worlds, Wonder, Knots, and Pots

AY or early June was when we moved to Mill Lake for the summer. As soon as we arrived, we cousins all ran down the hill to the water. That started our annual inspection tour. In the whooping and shouting and excitement, one of us would always slip and roll most of the way down, barely stopping in time at the breakwater. Bob would balance on the rocks at the edge of the lake and, more times than I can count, would lose his glasses in the icy water. The rest of the day we invented ways to fish for them without getting wet. At least once that day somebody would come and insist that our energies were needed for unloading supplies. But after making sure that the big tins of marshmallows and cartons of graham crackers were stored on their top shelves, we found more important things to do.

We hung the swings and hammocks. We checked the boathouse for swallow nests, the pier for ice damage, and grandfather's peony bed for a proper supply of ants. Grandfather's father had brought the first peonies to our town when he came from England. Grandfather insisted that ants were necessary to help the peony buds to open. Since his peonies were always spectacular, he was no doubt right.

25

{How to Make a Rush Mat}

Materials needed: cattail (bulrush) leaves, masking tape, scissors.

Gather young cattail rushes (leaves) and dry them, out of the sun. When you are ready to weave, dampen and wrap them in a towel. Use 18 rushes, each about 1 inch wide and 30 inches long for the long side and 14 rushes about 26 inches long for the short side.

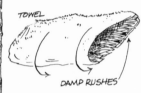

TOWEL

DAMP RUSHES

Cut the bottom end to the same shape as the top end with scissors. Now lay the long rushes out flat, side by side, with no space in between. You can keep them in place with a piece of masking tape across the ends.

FIRST RUSH : OVER FIRST, THEN UNDER

SECOND RUSH : UNDER FIRST, THEN OVER

To begin weaving your mat, start at one side with a short rush and work opposite the direction of the long rushes. Put the short one first *over* then *under* the 18 long rushes. The next short rush is placed beside the the first short rush, but it starts by going *under* the first long rush, then over, under, over, under.

Leave 6 inches sticking out at the top and bottom of the mat and at each end. These are turned back and woven into the other weaving so that the edge of the mat has a solid finish instead of a loose, wiggly one.

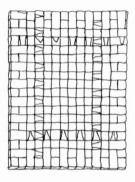

If you want to make a square mat, use rushes that are all the same length. If you want to make a thicker one, use two layers and weave them as one.

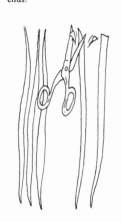

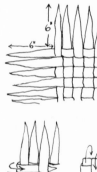

6"

6"

How many different kinds of water can you think about? Rushing streams, big rivers, lakes, reservoirs, ponds, oceans, lagoons, and many more? Then do you think about beaches and swamps and marshes and cliffs and caves and jettys and bogs and currents and riptides and quicksand and sunburn? And what about shells and weeds and sand and fleas and jiggers and nests and turtles and pollywogs and bullfrogs and lily pads and beavers and bears? Do you think about swimming? Sailing? Canoeing or speedboating? Water-skiing or scuba diving or surfing? What about fishing? Do you need a pole, a net, a trap? Do you use bait, a lure, a fly?

No matter what kind of water or where it is, there is one rule to know from the start. The rule is that we must treat water with respect. One false move, one little breath taken at the wrong time, and water can be a very dangerous place. Mostly water is wonderful, full of adventure and teeming with living things and great beauty. It is a world for enjoying, if you remember that one rule.

⁘{ The Horseshoe }⁘

One of the most perfect worlds at the lake was the part known as the Horseshoe — because of its shape, I suppose. It had slow-moving water and bogs and lily pads and frogs and turtles. It had rushes and sand bars, perfect for secret picnics. A canoe or raft could slide around all day without being noticed in the busy world there. In spring the rushes could be pulled up for tasty roots, more delicious than any potato! When the rush leaves were dry, they could be used to weave pretty mats and pads for grandma's table. We had contests to see who could pull the longest lily stem without tipping the canoe over, and we enjoyed presenting our gorgeous trophies for bouquets at home. No one ever tired of their beauty.

(*Text continued on page 30.*)

27

{How to Make a Rope Swing}

Materials needed: ¾-inch or thicker cotton rope, rubber tire (optional).

A sturdy ¾-inch cotton rope of the sort used for leading horses is the safest for this swing, because cotton won't burn when it slides over hands and knees. Other ropes may be stronger and weather better, but they burn and stretch.

The rope is simply slung over a high but strong tree branch and fastened with a clove hitch. (See Knots page 17.) Overhand knots are tied at intervals down its length, giving a grip for feet and hands and making quick climbing and swinging an adventure. You can put the overhand knots in before you tie your rope to the branch.

We also had swings made of rope that was tied to a rubber tire and one great swing that was made from a saddle tied in such a way that when you mounted the saddle, you rode a mildly bucking bronco.

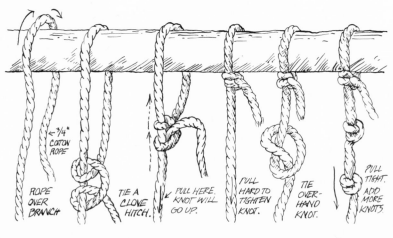

←¾" COTTON ROPE

ROPE OVER BRANCH

TIE A CLOVE HITCH.

PULL HERE. KNOT WILL GO UP.

PULL HARD TO TIGHTEN KNOT.

TIE OVER- HAND KNOT.

PULL TIGHT. ADD MORE KNOTS.

We hung the swings and hammocks.

One summer a dredge came to "clean out" the Horseshoe to make room for more swimmers and boats. Now there isn't a lily anywhere — or a bulrush either.

There was a stream which fed the lake that went through a farm, and the farm pasture came right down to the edge of the lake. The stream had thick grass growing down over its edges and all kinds of creatures lived in the sheltered world under that grass. We made dams that created ponds, and we watched as young turtles grew up in them. They were our summer family and we gave them names and built houses for them out of rock and willow sticks.

One thing I learned there about water was that it always wants to get under things, and it always moves to somewhere if it can.

It was a shock to me to learn that the Indians used baskets to cook in — even to boil water in. I knew people who couldn't even cook in nice steel kettles, but cooking in a basket I thought must be magic. Only later did I discover the secrets. To cook the food in baskets, the Indians used rocks which had been heated in the fire, then dropped into the basket of food or water. But how did they keep water from getting out the holes? I have learned since then that water also goes into air spaces in certain materials like clay and wood and grass and causes them to swell and become larger. People have put this knowledge to use, letting the water itself make holes and seams grow tight. That is how a wooden barrel works. It is also one way a basket can be made to hold water. This is how rawhide leather can be made strong and how wood can be shaped into curves that are unnatural to it.

Another thing that happens when water goes into material like clay is that once it fills up all the air spaces, it sometimes starts going on through. An Indian person I know irrigates his garden with clay pots, just like all his people did before him. He makes a nice big pot out of clay that is porous. That means it has a lot of air spaces. The pot is then fired until it is

30

{ How to Make a Clay Pot }

Materials needed: clay — earthenware (can be dug up or bought), large spoon, cloth.

Pots may be made in several different ways or in combinations. They are either built by hand or thrown on a potter's wheel. This clay pot is hand built and requires no tools, except perhaps a spoon. It is made by the coil method. Make up the clay to be moist enough to handle and shape without it sticking to your hands. Then work the clay roughly, to get all the air holes out of it.

Pinch off a handful and begin to roll between the palms of your hands to form a snakelike strip. As the strip becomes longer, put it on a smooth surface and roll it until it's of the same thickness along its full length, as thick as a finger, about ½ inch. Make several strips and keep them damp by covering them with a wet cloth.

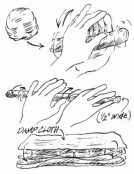

DAMP CLOTH   (½" wide)

The bottom may be made by patting a piece of clay to a round with a thickness of 3/8 inch and a diameter of about 4 inches.

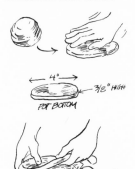

4"   3/8" HIGH   POT BOTTOM

WATER BETWEEN LAYERS   (BOTTOM)

The coils are then wound around the base, adding water to join the coils to each other. One coil is added on top of another in this manner until the desired height and shape are made. To make a smooth surface, the clay from the top coil is gently pulled down onto the coil below it by thumb pressure. This results in a sure seal between the coils but is still

USE OPPOSITE PRESSURE

not smooth. To smooth, wet the clay until the surface feels creamy and use the back of a spoon to shape the clay into a smooth surface.

When working a pot, it's necessary to use *opposite* pressure. This means that as you work on the outside surface, you put equal pressure on the inside surface just opposite the place you are working. This helps prevent losing the shape as you work. Shape the pot by adding shorter or longer coils to make wider or narrower places in the pot.

When you get to the top, moisten the edge of the top clay coil and flatten it into a smooth

WET TOP COIL, SMOOTH FLAT   WET POT   SMOOTH SIDES WITH SPOON BACK

surface. Put the pot to one side to dry until it is leather hard. Then clean off rough places and pare (or cut) the bottom if it seems too thick, especially where it joins the coils. Let it dry thoroughly before firing.

How to Fire a Clay Pot at Home

Materials needed: firewood, brick, pebbles, clay pot.

There are two methods for firing without a kiln. One is in the fireplace and the other is out-of-doors.

I try to thoroughly warm the pot before firing it in the fireplace. This allows me to start with a bed of hot coals and ashes instead of a cold fireplace.

The pot may be set on a brick in the middle of these. You may want to mount your pot on a few small, flat pebbles placed on the brick to allow some circulation under the pot.

Now carefully build a fire of fine, hot-burning wood over your pot. Add more wood as the fire requires, building up as much heat as possible, while keeping as little fire as you can balance. Try to keep the temperature even for two hours or more. It is best to do the firing at night because this allows the pot to cool in the fireplace overnight.

Take it out in the morning, carefully removing debris and ashes. A dry paint brush will clean off the ash dust. If your

clay did not contain too much iron, your pot will probably be very satisfactory for many uses.

A high iron content tends to make pots brittle and difficult to handle. Often you can tell at a glance by the sparkle and very red look of the fired clay if it has a lot of iron. Near my home, the natural potting clay that can be dug up is green, brown, or yellow, but all three fire to a deep terra cotta red — iron!

Open firing outside is similar to a fireplace but allows more flexibility. The traditional pottery of many countries is fired out-of-doors, and there are great variations in technical skills from crude to excellent. The Japanese have carried the quick-fire outdoor method to extreme refinement, and it is known as the *raku* method.

A simple firing outside can be done over a pit or on level ground. In either case, the pots are carefully arranged in a pile of fuel with as little surface touching between them as is possible while still achieving a steady stack. Lightweight sticks are heaped on the pottery and kindled, and the fire is encouraged and tended for about two hours.

Warming the pots is a good idea, and a separate little smoldering fire can be made and kept going for this. Old pieces of broken pottery can be placed on top of the stack for some protection against cool drafts.

The main idea is to get as much heat and circulation evenly around the pots as possible. Finishing is the same as with fireplace firing.

Bernard Leach, who wrote *A Potter's Book*, relates that he saw Nigerians heap dry grass on the embers at the end of a firing to prevent breakage from drafts. This is probably a good idea, as it is important in firing to bring the heat up gradually and cool it down gradually too. A draft of air that is a different temperature could easily crack the pot.

hard. Sometimes holes are added around the sides but not always. The pots are then buried at measured spaces throughout the garden, but the tops show just above ground. When they are filled with water, the water seeps slowly out through the holes and through the clay and feeds the garden plants nearby. When the pots are empty, the gardener knows it is time to water again, so he fills the pots. Many places in our country have good clay soil that can be made into nice pottery. It's not surprising that the remains of very ancient pots and different methods for making them can be found nearly everywhere.

People have always tried to find ways to store and carry water, and their inventions are as different as can be. Once when I was a little girl and on a visit to New Mexico, I was given a ten-gallon hat. I didn't really believe that the cowboy hat was supposed to be named for how much water it carried; however, years later, I discovered that my tall hat did indeed hold a big drink for me and my horse. I was glad for it too!

It is important to know how to carry water and keep it cool because it is not always possible to be near good, safe drinking water. People who do long hours of work out-of-doors have come up with some beautiful methods. One of them is the practice of covering bottles or canteens so as to insulate them against sun or body heat. There are many ways to do this, from simply wrapping wet canvas or blanket material around water containers to the elegant and traditional demijohns which are made of knots or wicker closely covering the form of the bottle or canteen. Some of the most interesting demijohns are those made by sailors — always good knot makers — for their stored bottles of fresh water.

One time I tried and tried to find a person who could show me how to make a demijohn and had almost decided it was a lost art. Then I met a wonderful old German sheepherder who had been a sailor when he was a young man. He lent me a book on knots and in it were pictures of demijohns and

33

descriptions of the knots used for each! To my surprise, they were the most common knots, but made so tightly and neatly that they seemed different. The finishing touch on these was the top, which was a cork with a handle made out of a lovely shell. When I told my friend what I had found in his book, he became interested and showed me some other grand knots from his sailoring days.

There seems to be no end to the usefulness of knots and the different ways you can make them. Can you believe that the very same knots are used for making dainty necklaces and dress trimmings as are used for tying big loads onto trucks? The difference is the size of the material used, from fine cord to thick rope.

It wasn't long after this that I had a sick ewe, and my same friend came to help me with her. He saw that she needed to be raised into a standing position and between us we quickly rigged up a fine sling using a simple combination of broomsticks, gunny sacks, and a good rope.

When you live on a ranch or farm or if you like to spend a lot of time camping and hiking, sooner or later you will want to know how to make a litter. Litters are second cousins to slings because they are designed to move big loads. As with slings, you can use litters for raising an animal or a person or a load. But you can also carry the load because a litter is movable.

❧{Mother and the Snakes}❧

Have you ever become too tired when you have spent a day or a vacation by the water? It's the very best tiredness there is. At the lake I would lie for long hours, face down, looking through the pier boards and watching the schools of fish and the muskrat who lived under there. If I became too hot, I would slide off into the water and squish along to the

34

{How to Make a Demijohn}

Materials needed: seine twine or jute, bottle, scissors.

There are many ways to cover bottles. The easiest way is to start by covering the bottom itself and working out and then up. This consists of putting on a series of half hitches.

Begin by making a length of chain and hitching the ends together to make a small circle as shown. Then tuck the starting end under, and with the other end make hitches around the knot circle through the loops of the chain that is already there.

When you reach the edge of the bottle, pull your knots up, and keep them tight to make the turn. Then continue knotting up the sides of the bottle. When the hitches begin to come close

5.

REPEAT UNTIL CHAIN IS THE DESIRED LENGTH

6.

together as the bottle tapers, skip a loop at intervals.

Finish by weaving the end into the knotting. If the cord begins to fray while you are working, you can rub a piece of beeswax along the length of it. As you run out of twine, add more by tying on a new piece and either bury the knot or incorporate it into the hitches.

TO ADD ROWS TO CHAIN:

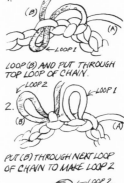

/.

(B)

(A)

LOOP 1

LOOP (B) AND PUT THROUGH TOP LOOP OF CHAIN.

2.

LOOP 2
LOOP 1

(B)

(A)

PUT (B) THROUGH NEXT LOOP OF CHAIN TO MAKE LOOP 2

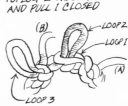

3.

LOOP 2
LOOP 1

(B)

(A)

PUT LOOP 2 THROUGH LOOP 1 AND PULL 1 CLOSED

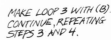

(B)

LOOP 2
LOOP 1

(A)

LOOP 3

MAKE LOOP 3 WITH (B). CONTINUE, REPEATING STEPS 3 AND 4.

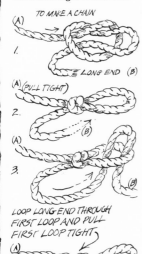

TO MAKE A CHAIN

(A)

/.

LONG END (B)

(A) (PULL TIGHT)

2.

(B)

(A)

3.

(B)

LOOP LONG END THROUGH FIRST LOOP AND PULL FIRST LOOP TIGHT

(A)

4.

(B)

REPEAT

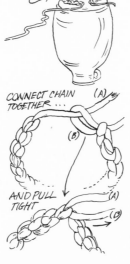

MAKE CHAIN INTO A CIRCLE TO FIT ON BOTTOM OF BOTTLE

CONNECT CHAIN TOGETHER ... (A)

(B)

AND PULL TIGHT

(A)

(B)

WHEN BOTTLE BOTTOM IS COVERED, GO UP SIDES

35

{How to Make a Litter or Travois}

Materials needed: two poles, a blanket.

Two poles slipped through coat sleeves and the coat wrapped around and buttoned can make an emergency carrier. Another carrier that two people can manage is one made by using two strong poles laid side by side about 2 feet apart and on top of the middle third of a blanket or tarpaulin.

One side of the blanket is folded over a pole toward the middle; the second pole is placed over the blanket edge; and then the other third of the blanket folds over all, so it is three thicknesses of blanket and two poles.

Each person carrying holds the pole ends, and if the load being carried is a person, the rule is to carry feet first except uphill.

A one-man litter is made so that one end is dragged on the ground. It can be made by lashing either two poles together at one end or by putting a third pole across the end. The blanket or tarpaulin is then mounted like the two-man carrier, or it can be tied at the four corners, if the load is light enough.

This kind is easiest to use where it is sandy, like the beach. It makes a good emergency carrier for gear you find just too heavy when you're all sunburned and tired out.

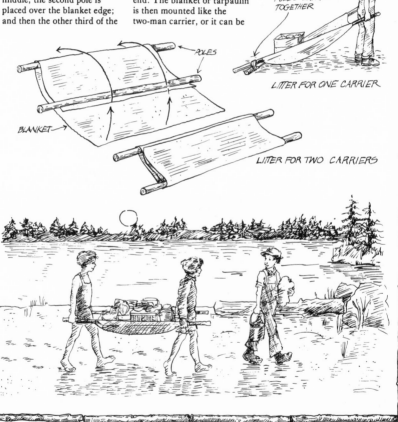

POLES

POLES LASHED TOGETHER

LITTER FOR ONE CARRIER

BLANKET

LITTER FOR TWO CARRIERS

boathouse. Soft crabs and clams lived there, and there were great spiders to poke at. If the swallows were nesting at the boathouse, we stayed out. We didn't even put our boat away because swallows ruled there, and no one was allowed to enter without getting pecked!

Another cousin came from Texas to visit in the summer. He taught me how to catch snakes because he collected them. We learned about all the snakes that lived around us at the lake, where their homes were, and what they ate. I was going to make a collection too, but I wasn't much of a scientist. One day I found three nice snakes, but I was in a hurry to go swimming, so I wrapped them snugly in a bandanna and put them into my dresser drawer. The next thing we all heard was a yowl and a crash! My unsuspecting mother had opened my drawer to put the laundry away, and the three snakes were there to greet her. She fainted dead away! That ended my collection, but after my cousin went home, I mailed him three special snakes in a carefully made cage-box. He wrote and thanked me for *the* snake, and that was how I learned that king snakes eat other snakes — even rattlers. Since my "Texas cousin" summer, I have continued to see snakes. They are probably some of the most beautiful creatures on earth.

The little pools that you can find around the rocky places at the edges of lakes and streams and oceans are often treasure troves. Some of them are like old junkyards because of the empty shells and bits of bones and lures that float into them and stay trapped there. These pools are exquisite miniature worlds, and hours can be spent watching all the wiggling, busy things going on. The colors are often spectacular in these pools because of the weeds that grow in them. Twice I have seen the sapphire blue snake there. It is like finding the rarest and most costly jewel. In gold country the pools are where gold nuggets, which are heavy, settle under rocks until the next high water comes to the creeks.

37

No one was allowed to enter the boathouse without getting pecked.

At Mill Lake there were special pools created by the springs and bogs. The springs that fed the lake bubbled up in one little bay, and each spring was surrounded by boggy things that were half floating weed and half land. If we were feeling brave and rowdy, we would take a canoe paddle and shove it against the mass. The mass would part and move, but then it would come right back again. That was spooky and it wasn't hard to imagine all kinds of mysterious things under there. The plants in bogs are strange. Bogs are one place where you can even find several kinds of plants that eat insects for nourishment.

Sometimes pieces of the bogs broke loose and floated off until they snagged on a shallow place to become surprise islands! I was always a little afraid to get on one to explore. One time, when we arrived at camp up at the secret lake a bog island settled against our secluded beach. It was a rather large one with a couple of trees on it. One day my brother and cousins climbed one of those trees and rocked back and forth until the bog actually started to make waves. I was sure I'd never see them again and ran, wailing, up the hill for help!

The crystal clear water of the springs plus their bubbling created pockets of scoured sand, and the sun shone down in these pockets, lighting them and making them more beautiful than anyone could describe. Nothing lived in those pockets of very cold spring water, but the areas around them teemed with life, and there we caught big orange-bottomed turtles and slippery frogs and water spiders.

⌠Indian Secrets⌡

Our Chippewa friends told us about lake bottoms and some of their mysteries, which are pretty dramatic in glacier country like our part of Wisconsin. When the glacial ice

(*Text continued on page 43.*)

39

⟨How to Make Bone and Shell Jewelry⟩

Materials needed: bones, deer antlers, clam shells, hack saw, awl or ice pick, emery cloth, hand drill, coping saw.

Bone may be used either uncooked or cooked. A beef or ham bone works well. It must be cleaned of all grease, sinew, marrow, and flesh. To do this, scrape and then wash it thoroughly with detergent. Rinse and boil the bone in clean water or soak for a few days in warm water. Wood ash may be stirred into the water when soaking; the ash acts as a mild bleach. Dry the bone and cut it with a fine-toothed saw to the shape you want to use.

SCRAPE BONE CLEAN

WOOD ASH WARM WATER

RINSE BONE. SOAK IN WARM WATER A FEW DAYS. (ADD WOOD ASH AS A BLEACH)

A friend made a fine fleshing tool for me using a bone chewed on by a neighbor's dog and left, bleaching in the sun. It was a shank bone, hard as a rock, clean and hollow.

It fit my hand perfectly, so he cut the bottom edge into many

sawlike teeth. It is a fine tool for cleaning hides.

Small bones, such as bird bones, may be strung on a fine thong into patterns combined with beads and shells. Chicken bones that are cooked should not be used as they are too soft. Animal bones may be polished with sandpaper or emery cloth, carved with designs to look like ivory, and used for pendents, bolo ties, or buttons.

I like to keep a supply of bone buttons for the garments that I weave. Deer antlers make good

HACK SAW

BONE

AWL, FOR CARVING DESIGN (ICE PICK WOULD WORK)

EMERY CLOTH TO POLISH BONE

buttons. Every once in a while I find one that has been shed in the woods, or a hunter friend will give me one to use.

Saw through the antler to the thickness desired, just as you would saw frozen sausage. An antler button is usually less than a ¼ inch. Polish the piece with pumice or emery cloth, and drill two or four holes for sewing the button on.

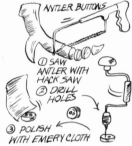

ANTLER BUTTONS

① SAW ANTLER WITH HACK SAW ② DRILL HOLES
③ POLISH WITH EMERY CLOTH

Clam shells make nice buttons too. They can be easily sawed into a small, round shape. Drilling sometimes splits them, but if you work carefully, holes can be made.

CUT CLAM SHELLS WITH COPING SAW.

Deer and elk antlers are treasured teething devices for puppies. One time a friend gave me some elk buttons for Christmas. When we came to the tree on Christmas morning, things were in shambles. Our collie had smelled the buttons and ransacked the packages until he found them. He must have remembered his puppy days. To me the buttons looked and smelled just like regular ivory ones!

40

I was almost sure I'd never see them again.

{How to Make a Tom-Tom}

CUT 2 CIRCLES FOR TOP AND BOTTOM

(COULD BE RAWHIDE, INNER TUBE RUBBER, CHAMOIS OR SHEEPSKIN.)

③

PUNCH HOLES 1 INCH FROM EDGE IN EACH CIRCLE.

⑤ LACE TOP AND BOTTOM TIGHTLY, LIKE THIS

RAWHIDE THONG

⑥ KNOT THONG. TAP KNOT FLAT.

Materials needed: a hollow log or container; rawhide, chamois, sheepskin or inner tube rubber; lacing.

An Indian drum can be made from many things such as oatmeal boxes or nail kegs with the top and bottom covered with rubber inner tubing or even heavy paper.

If you can find a hollow log about a foot in diameter, cut a section out of it about 14 inches long, clean it out, and scrape any loose bark from the outside.

CLEAN OUT HOLLOW LOG

SCRAPE OFF LOOSE BARK ①

14"

The top and bottom may be made of rawhide, chamois, sheepskin, or inner tube rubber. Cut two pieces; one for the top and the other for the bottom. Cut the piece large enough so that some of the material folds down over the sides about 2 to 3 inches.

Lay the circles out flat, and punch holes around the circle at even spaces, 1 inch from the edge.

Put one piece on the floor; place the hollow wood on top of this. Put the second circle over the top. Using a leather shoe-lace thong, lace the two circles together, going from top to bottom in a zigzag (one up, one down). Keep the lacing as snug as possible. The thong will stretch over the wood sides, making a triangle pattern.

④

2" or 3"

When you knot the thong at the end, take a mallet or hammer and tap the knot flat. When it is all laced and secure, thoroughly soak the top and bottom leathers and thong with water and allow to dry. They should be quite tight. If not, wet them again or adjust the lacing. Flattening the knots of the leather thong will keep them tight.

⑦

SOAK TOP, BOTTOM, AND THONG WITH WATER....

....WHEN LEATHER DRIES, IT WILL STRETCH TIGHT.

scraped the land, it cut through layers of soil and water. Sometimes what appears to be a bottomless lake is the result of those cuts, which actually connect two or more lakes by underground rivers. The Indians told us that objects which were lost in one lake sometimes were found in another because of those underground waterways. They used to know all the best places for finding treasures, and they made beautiful jewelry and beads and buttons from polished shells, horns, and bones that they had found.

While we shared many hours with those friends and with their help learned about the woods and lakes *up north,* there were some things we were never a part of and never shared. In the bark and log cabins of the Indian village, we had seen beautiful decorated buckskin ceremonial dresses. Head-pieces, breastplates, and drums were all made and kept for special events. We were friends, yet we never went at night to the village events where those special, decorated garments were worn. Sometimes in the nearest town there were programs in the park which were supposed to be true Indian dances, but I am sure they were not. The garments used in the park dances were different, but also pretty.

I can remember the very first time I heard that village ceremony. A body of water causes sounds and voices to carry farther than the same sounds would carry over land. I had been tucked snugly into my bedroll for the night and was sleeping soundly. Suddenly I became aware of a sound I had never heard before. The moon was bright in the sky. It was reflecting on the water so the whole world was brilliant in its silver light. I first wondered if the sound was an animal that makes a special noise on such a night, and I shivered with a cold feeling brought on by fear of what is unknown. My eyes strained, peering into the light and shadows. Gradually my ears sorted out the sounds. *Tom-toms!* I had made and played with tom-toms, but to me they were just play drums. These were the real thing. Voices began to separate from the

43

I could hear the sounds of the ceremony clear and resounding.

drums, and I could hear a chant. It was all from another world; the Indian world we could never enter. That was a world known only to them and their ancestors. All I could do was sink back into my blankets and be glad we were friends, that the warpath days were over, and that water was near us so I could hear the sounds of the ceremony, clear and resounding and never to be forgotten.

{ Part Two }

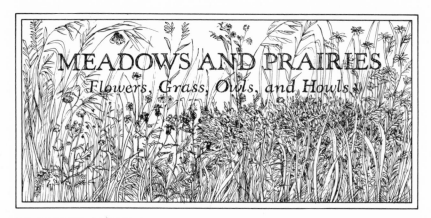

MEADOWS AND PRAIRIES
Flowers, Grass, Owls, and Howls

Y brother and cousins and I used to have long and serious debates about what we thought was the best place in the world. The boys usually claimed a place in the woods or by a lake was, but I almost always defended the meadows — deep, grassy, flowering meadows — springtime meadows, summertime or anytime meadows.

On the first day of May each year, my whole family headed for the meadows to gather flowers for our May baskets. We had made little baskets in advance and had precious friends to whom we gave our buttercups, shooting stars, and lilies. The tradition was to leave a basket on the doorstep, ring the bell, then run. If your friend caught you, you were kissed! Besides those adventures, we took May baskets to old people who couldn't get out to join us and to sick friends, too. May Day was a happy day, marking the end of winter snow and cold and promising warm spring and summer days to come.

For all the creatures who had been living under snow-heaped thickets or in burrows and nests underground, sunny May meant having grass and tender shoots and roots to eat. For birds it was a hectic time of declaring territories and getting settled and building new nests.

49

The meadows and prairie land that surrounded our spring-fed, natural lakes were a wonderful world. As I grew up I learned that meadows and prairies extend clear across our country with vast expanses opening up in the West. I learned there are many kinds of meadows too, but all prairies and meadows are wide open. You can run and stretch and shout and fill yourself with sunshine and air, and you can see and see and see — up and down and all around. Cows and horses and sheep use them for pastures; birds and small animals makes nests and burrows in them. Little streams feed them and carve them; and solitary, monumental trees decorate them like sculptures. Wild meadows and prairies have deer, antelope, and elk in them; and I have seen herds, startled by a sudden sound, run like the wind and never stop as far as I could see. Our own meadows, where I live now, welcome our colts and lambs and are sunshiny, grassy, perfect new worlds for them.

The edges of meadows make prime hiding and nesting places. They have thickets of wild rose briar, willows, berries, and sometimes even lumpy places with big rocks, which provide lookouts for birds and animals and forts for boys and girls.

⌐Soggy Bogs⌐

Marshes are found between meadows and lakes, ponds and streams. Back home, some of our marshes had peat bogs in them. We were always concerned that they would start burning. They did this once in awhile, because in the decaying process so much heat was given off that a fire sometimes started by itself. Marshes are just the opposite of meadows. They aren't open at all. Instead of being able to run and run, you must pick your way carefully, always with a fear that you might make a mistake and so fall into the tangly, watery

{How to Build a Birdhouse}

Materials needed; nails, 2 inches of ¼-inch dowel, screw eye, 46-inch piece of 1-x-6-inch lumber.

All over the country people build birdhouses to attract birds to their gardens for their songs and company, and for help catching insects which harm the garden. Birds, like people, have certain ideas about what a proper house should provide, and one of the most important features of all is the size of the entrance opening.

The most well-known are: house wrens — 7/8 inch; white-breasted nuthatches — 1 1-1/4 inches; woodpeckers — 2 inches; martins and tree swallows — 2 inches; house finches — 2 inches; and chickadees — 1 1/8 inches. Robins like a more open place than a house. They will come to a roost that has only two sides. Some birds, such as martins, enjoy living in colonies like apartment dwellers; others would rather be alone.

One time I watched and listened as a wren and a goldfinch argued about a piece of wool the wren had tried to stuff into a house. Later he chose another house and abandoned the wool as well as the original house. However, when a goldfinch decided to take the wool, the wren "said" no.

All morning they carried on a chirping argument. Finally they moved to a neutral corner of the yard, and there the wren perched, never taking his eye off the goldfinch, as the goldfinch flew back, snatched the wool, and stuffed it quickly into his nest in a rose bush. Then the wren sang his little raspy banjo song and went on about his business.

I think it is important for birdhouses to have a sturdy perch under their entrance as birds very often bring food only to the door and thrust it in to the nesting mate; or else they land, look around, and then enter.

The entrance must face opposite prevailing winds, if possible. One of the most crucial times in a bird's life is the moment it leaves the nest. If the nest is in a birdhouse, other predator birds often have noticed the action as the house swings when the wriggling babies grow and become noisier and noisier. You can know when to help by paying attention. Parent birds must coax their babies to come out, and you will notice a very different, insistent note in their calls. Also, they don't dive into the house with food when they are calling like that.

If you have placed the house so that it is safe from animals who steal from nests, your next concern would be placing it

where new babies have the best chance to land safely and to get away entirely before being captured. Hanging the house from a slippery wire several feet off the ground is good insurance against cats, and having low bushes nearby for hiding and perching in when the young first try their wings, shields against jays and mockingbirds.

Birds are good housekeepers and will try to keep their nests clean, so houses should be large enough for them to move about in, but not so large that they have to bring in all outdoors to fill it for nesting. A wren house can be about a 7-inch cube, or even a bit larger. Birds need air, so it isn't necessary to be an absolutely perfect carpenter! Use sturdy wood that won't collapse under the weather.

A house may be made from one 1-by-6-inch board that is 46 inches long. The pieces measure as follows: front — 6-by-7 inches; back 6-by-9 inches; two sides 6 inches wide with one

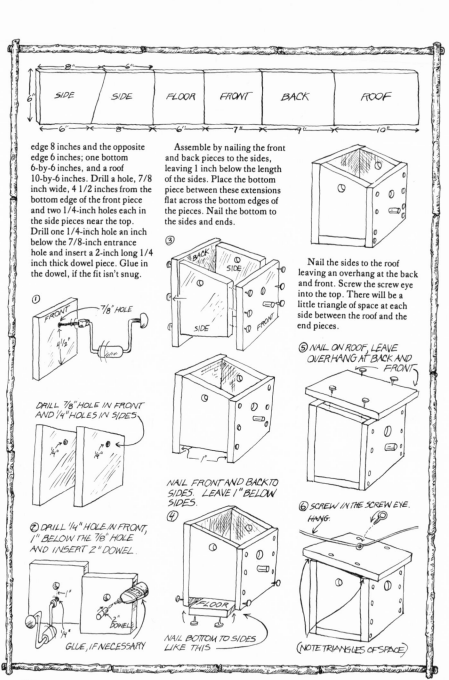

SIDE	SIDE	FLOOR	FRONT	BACK	ROOF

8" 6"

6"

6" 8" 6" 7" 9" 10"

edge 8 inches and the opposite edge 6 inches; one bottom 6-by-6 inches, and a roof 10-by-6 inches. Drill a hole, 7/8 inch wide, 4 1/2 inches from the bottom edge of the front piece and two 1/4-inch holes each in the side pieces near the top. Drill one 1/4-inch hole an inch below the 7/8-inch entrance hole and insert a 2-inch long 1/4 inch thick dowel piece. Glue in the dowel, if the fit isn't snug.

Assemble by nailing the front and back pieces to the sides, leaving 1 inch below the length of the sides. Place the bottom piece between these extensions flat across the bottom edges of the pieces. Nail the bottom to the sides and ends.

Nail the sides to the roof leaving an overhang at the back and front. Screw the screw eye into the top. There will be a little triangle of space at each side between the roof and the end pieces.

① FRONT 7/8" HOLE 4 1/2"

DRILL 7/8" HOLE IN FRONT AND 1/4" HOLES IN SIDES.

1/4" 1/4"

② DRILL 1/4" HOLE IN FRONT, 1" BELOW THE 7/8" HOLE AND INSERT 2" DOWEL.

1" 2" DOWEL 1/4"

GLUE, IF NECESSARY

③ BACK SIDE FRONT SIDE

NAIL FRONT AND BACK TO SIDES. LEAVE 1" BELOW SIDES.

1"

④ FLOOR

NAIL BOTTOM TO SIDES LIKE THIS

⑤ NAIL ON ROOF, LEAVE OVERHANG AT BACK AND FRONT.

⑥ SCREW IN THE SCREW EYE. HANG.

(NOTE TRIANGLES OF SPACE)

52

places all around. They are important hiding and fishing areas for many kinds of birds and small animals, and some, like pack rats and muskrats, live in them luxuriously. Pack rat houses get bigger every year as new apartments are built on top of the ones from last year. Other animals move into the older parts, and sometimes loons build their nests on top of the whole structure. When you poke into them, there is no end to what can be found: shiny buttons, pop-bottle lids, shoelaces. One time I found a spool of metal thread I thought I had lost forever.

In springtime and early summer, meadows are colorful with their flowers and bright, flitting birds building nests in the grass and swaying on weed stalks as they perch there to sing. Once at the lake, in the tangle of vines and berries that made the edge between marsh and meadow, the wild canaries came in a sudden migration and made me think the thicket was alive with dancing golden fairies. The variety of birds found there is one of the riches of meadow life. Of course, that is true about forests and trees, too, but the great game birds like the quail, pheasant, and grouse and the exquisite songbirds like the goldfinches and warblers choose meadows and streams and grain fields. Groups of burrowing owls can be found near dusk, turning their heads to pretend they aren't there when you come upon them.

People have always enjoyed birds being a close part of their lives; keeping them in cages and aviaries, stuffing and mounting them, and even creating imitation songbirds using music boxes for their songs. I have always had a pet canary. One of my earliest experiences with a sick pet was when my canary caught pneumonia. He was my treasure and I nursed him carefully. Nevertheless, he died as sick birds most often do. Since that time I've learned more about how to help birds when they are sick and also how to keep them well. Canary birds can live for a long time, but most birds have an extremely short life in the wild.

53

We headed for the meadows to gather flowers.

I very often find a bird that has died for some unknown reason, and I have learned how to preserve them. My first effort was the result of thinking I wanted to become a great surgeon. I found a dead owl at the foot of a huge pine tree and dissected it with a pair of crude kitchen scissors. My father was very cross and told me I had no right to do that to the owl, dead or alive. He was right. I'd only made a bad job and didn't learn anything, except that owls have more feathers than anything else. Eventually I found someone who could teach me. As with so many crafts, I discovered the main ingredients for doing a good job were patience, practice, and the proper tools.

There are two kinds of mounts for birds. One is the beautiful exhibition mount which is an imitation of the creature in real life; the other is the museum mount meant for observation and study. This is the one found in all natural history museums and good biology classes.

Beautiful Treasures

Another beauty who shows up in summertime meadows is the butterfly. Sometimes you're lucky enough to find a caterpillar making its sticky preparations for becoming a butterfly. You can visit each day and watch it change. A great day is when you see the newly hatched butterfly unfold wet wings and stand to dry in the sun. Butterflies don't have very long lives and often you can find perfect butterflies that are dead for no apparent reason. I began a collection of those a long time ago.

My cousin's father was Walter P. Taylor, a renowned naturalist, and he had taught his family some special skills and attitudes. *Collecting,* he felt, meant being orderly, selective, and purposeful; whereas *gathering* frequently resulted in taking more than you require and can lead to waste and even harm to a species. He encouraged me to take only what I needed for study or for completing and filling out a group subject, and then only if such an activity could not be accomplished without taking specimens. Many things can be learned and enjoyed right in the out-of-doors without being taken home at all. This is probably one of the best ways for all of us to be able to see and enjoy the countryside, helping to take care of it for the others who will come after us.

The number and variety of insects found in meadows are beyond imagination. Some of the most interesting are the hordes that come out to eat and live at night! A good trick for catching moths is to use a light. They will come to it, especially a hanging lantern, and if you place a bed sheet or white paper underneath the lantern, you can pick up your choice as it falls. Mounting them, especially the beautifully colored butterflies and moths, can be done so that they look like a painting. Sometimes people make whole miniature scenes using dried grass, twigs, and flowers, and then they mount their choice butterflies or moths in the scene, just as they saw them in nature.

There are many ways to save the flowers and leaves for such displays. Some flowers grow naturally so that they last without being treated at all. These belong to the everlasting family and are strawlike to touch. Others need your help to keep their color and shape. But most of these flowers can be saved perfectly with a little care. Even fluffy dandelions and thistles can be saved by delicately spraying a light lacquer or hair spray over them.

One of the oldest and most useful ways to preserve flowers is to use sand. The sand must be fine and well-worn so its grains have no sharp edges to cut the fragile flower petals. Hobby stores now sell a special packaged material called *silica gel* for this purpose, with directions for using it. Just the same, many parts of our country have perfect sand and by careful sifting and feeling, you can often find enough to use.

How to Make a Field I.D. Kit

Materials needed: file cards, unlined, 5-by-7 inches; clear contact paper (hardware store); two rubber bands; mat board or rigid cardboard.

This field identification system was devised by Vincent Roth, director of the Southwest Research Station that the American Museum of Natural History maintains in Portal, Arizona. People journey from all over the world to study and do research there and this has proved to be a worthy, handy tool for beginners and professionals alike.

The kit is assembled as follows: (1) mat board, (2) approximately 50 file cards, (3) mat board, (4) rubber bands around all to keep secure and work as a press. Specimens collected are placed between cards allowing a blank card between two that enclose a specimen.

Notations can be made on the specimen card at that time or soon after finishing the collecting and identifying. Allow time for the specimen to dry

thoroughly, and then cover it with clear contact paper. File the completed cards and add new clean ones to your minipress. This press may be conveniently carried in a pocket.

When you start doing things like saving beautiful insects and shells and flowers, you can bring your attention to the whole world of nature in a way that you may never have experienced before. This is a good way of practicing to *see*.

⟨Learning from the Birds⟩

When you learn to *see*, it isn't hard to find out what's been going on in the meadow. Snakes leave a diagonal mark in the dust, telling where they've been. Birds and mice leave scratchy looking places. Grass piled up a bit unnaturally often has a hole poked into a side of the pile that leads to a nest or a burrow. Feathers on the ground can tell us who has been there and why. Sometimes a depression means a bird will have just taken a dust bath, but if there are broken feathers, then that bird was probably some animal's dinner.

Tracks and nests are storytellers if we can *see* what we look at. Meadows have hundreds and hundreds of living places in them, and if you sit still and look closely, you'll almost lose count of the animal villages and houses you can see. Start with anthills, gopher towns, and spider and insect caves. Next count the mice nests and snake holes and badger burrows and rabbit forms and ground nests belonging to birds.

It gives me the shivers when I see dune buggies or motorcycles zipping *through* meadows and deserts instead of on designated trails. I know the drivers can't see such things as the mother kildeer running away, limping, to lead intruders away from her young in their nest. A week later that same elegant lady bird strides proudly along with her young who look like miniature striped fluff balls on toothpick legs teetering along behind her. Well, *no one* who had seen her would wreck her house, I'm sure. But her nest is just a

(*Text continued on page 62.*)

One time I found a spool of thread I thought was lost forever.

{How to Preserve Flowers and Leaves}

DRIED FLOWERS

Materials needed: sand, coffee can, spoon, fine watercolor brush.

Sift some sand into a box or container such as a coffee can that can be tightly closed. Place

① SAND — SIFT A LITTLE SAND INTO CAN

CLOSE-FITTING LID

your flowers on this sand so they don't touch one another, and then sift and spoon small amounts of dry sand in and around each flower until each is completely covered.

Now the hard part; seal them off with the lid and wait!

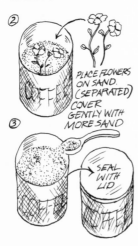

② PLACE FLOWERS ON SAND. (SEPARATED) COVER GENTLY WITH MORE SAND

③ SEAL WITH LID

Sometimes it takes several days, but the silica, which is the drying part of sand, will absorb the moisture and finally your flowers will be dry and ready to use.

It's a good idea when you take them out of their sand to let them rest in the air, lying on top of the sand for a while.

④ GENTLY REMOVE SAND AND FLOWERS. LET FLOWERS REST ON SAND.

Sometimes the sand leaves a film of dust on the petals and leaves, but this can be brushed off with a *fine* watercolor brush. Be gentle so that the flowers won't break.

Cornmeal and borax are both usable materials for drying, but sand is the old standby. Great Salt Lake sand is the very best but can't be shipped or taken out of Utah anymore.

⑤ DUST OFF ANY REMAINING SAND USING A VERY FINE (TINY) WATERCOLOR BRUSH.

PRESSED FLOWERS

Materials needed: paper towels, press or heavy book, mounting paper, white glue, watercolor brush.

Another favorite way to preserve flowers is to press them and then make pictures using the dried flowers. There are two tricks in doing this. They are: (1) How to press the flowers so they keep their color and shape, and (2) How the flowers are mounted when they are dried. For the first, study the flower in nature and try to place it on the pressing paper so that when it is stiff and dry, it still looks like it's in a natural position. Remember that once it is dry, you can't tug and pull the stem or leaf into a position you'd like.

Keeping the color sometimes seems to be a matter of luck. One thing I know that makes a difference is the time in its cycle that the flower is picked. If possible, it's much better to select a blossom just as it reaches its full maturity, or better, just before, so long as you can still keep the form you want.

Press the flowers between fine, clean paper. If you don't have a press put the papers under a big book or a stack of

FINE, CLEAN PAPER

FLOWER

books. When ready to mount, use white glue thinned with water and paint it carefully on one side of your pressed flower. Use as little glue as possible and a fine brush. Handle with care and don't move the flower once you have put it in place as the glue will smear. If you feel clumsy it might be easier to pick up your flower with tweezers.

THIN WHITE GLUE WITH WATER

VERY FINE BRUSH

PAINT GLUE ON ONE SIDE OF DRIED FLOWER (HOLD WITH TWEEZERS)

GLUE FLOWERS TO PAPER OR BOARD

—PRESERVED LEAVES—

Materials needed: glycerin, water, jar.

Leaves alone are so different on each tree! Like flowers, some leaves dry by themselves and stay pretty. Big bouquets of several kinds together are beautiful. One way to dry them makes them turn a rich caramel color, and they last for many years. All you do is place the stems or branch just as you would in a vase, only instead of water, put them in a mixture of one part glycerin and two parts water. You can buy glycerin at a drugstore.

FILL VASE WITH ONE PART GLYCERIN, 2 PARTS WATER

GLYCERIN

WATER

WATER

They should stand for about six weeks, and after that they are sturdy and don't need anything. They last long enough and are so useful that you become well acquainted with their shapes and character.

LEAVE IN LIQUID FOR 6 WEEKS

simple saucer shape, open and exposed among pebbles and rocky places. It is hard to see and so easy to destroy.

Each family of birds makes its own kind of nest, but each nest, even so, is different from every other. Many birds never use the same nest again even though they may return to the same tree or bush every year. Some do return to their nests, so we don't collect those unless we're sure they've been abandoned for more than one season.

Orioles make some of my favorite nests. I just can't believe some of the extravagant oriole nests I have found. I like to imagine how nice it would be to be a baby oriole snug in such a swinging cradle. At our house now, the oriole nests are made with hair stolen from horses' tails, and they are lined with layers of sheep's wool, but I have found oriole nests made from other things. Nylon fishing line is a favorite material, and I even have one made completely of Christmas tinsel.

Once I tried making a bird nest. I had imagined that might be how people learned to weave, but it was impossible for me to do, even though I have fingers to use. All birds can do is tug and pull with their beaks. There is one thing birds do that I can do, and it really works. Most bird nests are made of some material that is woven around and around, then lined with softer stuff in the middle. If you take long strands of grass and work them into a coil of loose braid, this coil can be placed in a chicken nest and kept there for a long time, while the middle part gets changed and cleaned when necessary. Even old grass hay works well for the braided part.

Grasses are the staple material of meadows and prairies. Where there is a good supply of water, the grasses grow graceful and luxurious; they are short and stubborn where the countryside is dry. Most grass is good food and is very important to many creatures. It is also beautiful. If it is deep, the wind makes it ripple so it looks like ocean waves. Grass may have a blossom time that gives color to acres and acres.

62

{ How to Make a Grass Handle and More }

Materials needed: grass, water, cloth, string or raffia, scissors.

Grasses grow so abundantly in all parts of our country that it's difficult to believe that they exist today as a mere token of what they originally were. The destruction of the grasses which flourished on this continent is one of the sad stories in our history as inhabitants, and worse, one we are still perpetuating.

Perhaps as you search for grass to use in this project, you will be noticing grasses in a way that causes you to appreciate for the first time the natural beauty and grace and luxury of them, to say nothing of the health and life grasses provide for so many creatures, including ourselves.

Placing pretty dried grass between two pieces of wax paper (wax side toward the grass) and then pressing with a medium hot iron makes a pretty picture or decoration.

Pads for placing under hot dishes, planters, and coasters can be made, if a coil about the size of a finger is wound around in flat circles and sewn together snugly. These can be dyed pretty colors, too.

Some grasses may be cut in early summer and hung upside down to dry while still green, and others are best cut in the fall when mature. These latter are usually golden or white, like

ivory. All must be thoroughly dry before using. They may be coiled and used to make baskets in the same way pine needles are used. If used for baskets, split grass or raffia is used for sewing

or wrapping the coils. Often though, baskets and pots require handles which can be made from many materials, and grass is one which is appropriate and strong, giving a good effect. The grass handle may be wrapped or twisted or braided.

To make a braided handle, soak the grass to be used for half an hour in cool water, then remove to a towel to keep it damp for working. Arrange the grass fibers side by side. Divide the grass into three groups and tie each end off using string. Leave a short length of string on each and tie these onto a hook. Tightly braid the three hanks to the length of the desired handle plus 4 inches.

① DIVIDE GRASSES AND TIE ENDS TO HOOK

② BRAID GRASS

KEEP BRAIDING TIGHT

③

ADD GRASS AS YOU BRAID, TO LENGTHEN

BRAID LENGTH OF HANDLE, PLUS 4"   4"

(RUBBER BAND TO HOLD)

If a loop exists on the pot or basket for mounting the handle, slip the braid through it from the top side; make a loop and bring the braid back on itself. Wind split grass or raffia tightly around both thicknesses of braid covering the end for a nice finish.

④

⑤

USE SPLIT GRASS OR RAFFIA

Bring the end of the raffia down through the grass, burying the end and then cutting it off very close to the braid. The braid may be worked flat or round, but the character of the grass used should determine which would be best.

TUCK END OF RAFFIA INTO BRAID — CUT OFF CLOSE TO BRAID

⑥

There is one place near my home that sometimes looks for all the world like a lake because of the blue flowers that bloom there. Grass is also useful. It can be made into things — all the way from dolls to teapot handles to pictures!

⊰[Red Rock Land]⊱

Meadows and prairies were formed in different ways so they have different things in them. In some places I know, meadows are made by old lakes that have become filled with soil over many years. Where I grew up, they were mostly made in places where land was cleared of trees by pioneer settlers in the early days of our country. They were also made by glaciers which scraped the land bare there. In some places the glacier dumped soil and rocks. In other places it scraped and exposed the rock. The rock in Wisconsin was usually granite or limestone. There were beautiful limestone cliffs and caves and quarries all around our countryside. The granite was equally beautiful, of many different colors, and it made fine building material.

My grandfather built granite chimneys and fireplaces in several homes. I was proud, knowing people thought they were worth driving many miles to see. One of our duties as children was to remove rocks from meadows when we came upon them, and another was to tell grandfather whenever we spotted a beautiful red rock. Red granite was considered special. To this day I cannot pass a red rock without wanting to pack it along home. The red rocks we found would be worked into a chimney or wall, and that way we learned to see how rocks could be made to fit together. Some of the best stonemasons worked in our part of Wisconsin, and their work is still there to see: perfectly cut rectangles of granite laid up in walls with the fit so flawless nothing had to be added to make them stick together.

{How to Make a Tassel Doll}

Materials needed: grass, string or yarn, scissors.

Grass dolls, like their cousins made from cornhusks, are made entirely from grass. They can be made like little tassels or complete with arms and legs and garments. They must be worked with dry grass which has been moistened.

A tassel doll is made by looping a hank of grass in half and tying the loop about an inch from the top as securely as possible. This tied place becomes the neck. Now carefully maneuver the grass until the loop above the tie is a complete round, and the grass hangs in an even fullness below the tie.

Trim the hank with scissors to a length of 3 inches below the tie, and then pick up two small bunches from opposite sides. Pull these out at right angles from the trimmed hank and tie them an inch from the end. Trim to ½ inch from the tie. These are the arms.

This simple little doll can be varied by using a slightly longer hank and making a tie for a waist after the arms are made. If a man is desired, simply tie the part below the waist into two parts leaving about an inch for the feet. If the amount of grass is too bulky for his legs, snip some of the excess out irregularly from the center of each section so that the mass becomes thinner, but the long, uncut pieces are on the surface.

A face may be embroidered on the top loop ball, and a string can be threaded through from under the neck tie out the top and back down through the neck and knotted, leaving a loop at the tip for hanging the doll as an ornament.

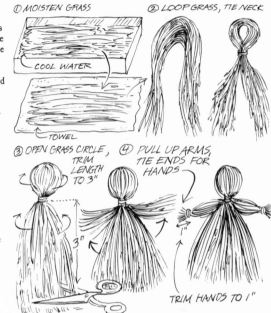

① MOISTEN GRASS
COOL WATER
TOWEL

② LOOP GRASS, TIE NECK

③ OPEN GRASS CIRCLE, TRIM LENGTH TO 3"
3"

④ PULL UP ARMS, TIE ENDS FOR HANDS
1"

TRIM HANDS TO 1"

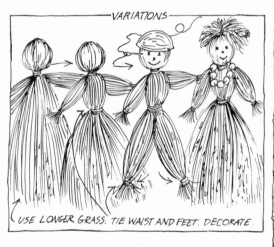

— VARIATIONS —

USE LONGER GRASS. TIE WAIST AND FEET. DECORATE.

Our meadows and streams had many, many small rocks called cobblestones. Laid close together and flat, they were used to pave streets and walks and to make walls. But I hated them! Our town had a rivalry with a nearby town. To me and my cousins, our town seemed perfect and everything the other town did seemed a mistake. Their cobblestone street was an example. It was slippery in winter, caused unsure footing, and made my ears hurt so badly, I cried when our car rattled over the rough paving. I only learned after I was grown that the town had saved its old cobblestone street as a remembrance of a victory over mud and dust.

Inns and mills were frequently built of cobblestones and they became landmarks. My grandmother always pointed to one, so old it was going back to the earth, that her father had stayed in on his journeys to Milwaukee for supplies. It was a 45 minute journey for us when we were kids but for him, a pioneer, it had taken two days. He and his family had settled in southern Wisconsin and started a village named Westville. Now it is all gone except for a few stone foundations which show where the buildings had been.

Our breakwater at Mill Lake was made of rock, and it was so solidly built by my grandfather that our land never washed away behind it. This didn't seem as important to me as having a cement breakwater like some other people had. Ice always broke the cement and made little quiet pools where frogs and turtles grew their young. Grandfather finally relented and built another wall out into the shallow water, making a long lagoon. There we planted lilies and other pretty water plants.

Rock walls make one of the most beautiful settings for plants. The plants can be grown in little dirt pockets or against the wall itself, which makes a perfect background. Of course, the sight of a well-made rock wall stretching across a green meadow and off into the distance is probably the most elegant sight of all!

{The Runaway}

Then there are horses. Horses are another reason I think meadows are the best places. Horses and meadows just "go" together.

For me, one of the best days each summer was when I rode my fine standardbred horse, David, from our farm where he had spent the winter to Mill Lake where he lived in a pasture by our cottage. During the winter I used to walk or ride my bike the mile and a half to the farm to take care of David and ride him along the country roads and through the fields. When summer came, it was time to move him to Mill Lake. The best way was to ride there, and it meant an all-day trip over countryside we seldom traveled. We didn't go on the highway. Instead, we meandered on a safer but longer course through lanes where we opened and closed gates so cows wouldn't get into the corn. We rode across broad open fields and through scrub woods. We crossed pretty streams and swam small ponds. David was a good swimmer, and it must have been a treat for him to sink all the way into those cool ponds and make his way lazily to the other side. He was a calm but spirited horse, and I considered him my best friend in the world.

One summer day when David and I were well on our way to the lake, we were trotting along on a narrow gravel road and a bad thing happened. Weeds and grass along the roadside were not sprayed or mowed down like they often are today, and we were enjoying the smell of sweet clover and brushing against the blue blossoms of the chicory. We passed an especially dense stand of grass. All of a sudden we disturbed a hobo in his grassy hiding place, and he threw a sharp rock. It stung and surprised my horse. In one motion David reared onto his hind feet and reversed his direction, starting to travel at top speed. My knapsack and lunch

68

We meandered through lanes.

⟩{How to Build Rock Walls}⟨

Materials needed: rock hammer, drill or grinding chisel, wedges, rocks.

Most important is to develop a good eye for a good rock and that comes from practice. After deciding upon a project, the weight of tools you will need for the rock project must be determined. Heaving big rocks requires big tools to match. And fitting rocks together sooner or later requires some tools to break the rocks to the shapes needed. For actually working on the rocks, you will need a rock hammer, a drill or grinding chisel, and wedges. For big rocks the task of removing the rock and taking it to the wall-building site means extra planning and figuring out ways to dig the rocks up and pull them or haul them to where you want them.

Rocks very often have little hairline cracks, crevices where moss grows, or a line of another material such as quartz. Any such place is a likely one to try splitting the rock. The main reason for splitting a rock is to make a flat surface or if you suspect an unusual inside surface.

If there is no obvious place to begin a split you need, you can try making a scratch and then with even pressure tap along the length of the scratch several times. Sometimes this will cause a crack, and then you can hammer a wedge into it. If it stays stubborn, holes can be drilled in a line and then wedges put into

the holes, but that is really a long, hard, hard job. Remember that when you hit a rock, even along a crevice, chips of rock may fly, so be careful of your eyes.

Laying up the rock is another job that takes practice. Whether your job is a wall or a walk, it is important to plan and make a good bed for the rocks to rest on. Besides a clean, level bed — slightly below the surrounding surface — some drainage should be provided. This can be done either by sloping the bed or by digging a separate ditch next to the bed and filling it with gravel.

Try to have a big supply of rock at hand when you build, because it often takes several tries to find a rock that just fits.

SITE FOR ROCK WALL

PEBBLES IN DRAINAGE DITCH → LOWERED, LEVEL BED

Rock walls can be built by casually piling up rocks, usually round, into a continuous pile. Sometimes posts can be sunk at intervals and topped by rails.

METHOD I

(CUT-AWAY VIEW)

Another way to work with round rock is to build two walls side by side and pour dirt, sand, or mortar between them as you raise the height of the walls.

METHOD II

The most substantial and beautiful walls are made with flat rock, sometimes cut to fit. They are laid up so that two rocks fit over one, then one over two. This gives great strength to the wall even when the ground shifts underneath from moisture or cold.

METHOD III

scattered to the far winds, and I only guessed what had happened when I heard the high cackle of a laugh as we sped by the man in the grass. When David reared, I lost my seat but, instead of being thrown clear, my foot caught in the stirrup. I was left to bounce and be dragged along by that foot. Somehow after minutes of scraping and crashing, I did manage to grab that foot and then the leather just above the stirrup. I rode all the way back to the barn hanging on for dear life to that piece of leather looking, I imagine, like a little laundry bag on the side of a horse. David didn't even stop when we came to the barn. He cantered right in and slid to a stop in his own straw-filled stall. Only then was I able to get out of that awful position, undo the girth, and let the saddle fall. My parents had always insisted I wear boots and long sleeves and pants when I rode, so even though my clothing was tattered, I was still in one piece. David's beautiful mahogany coat was covered with foam, his sides were heaving, and all I could think of was *founder,* the dread crippling that horses sometimes suffer after such an overheating. It would mean walking and walking him, preferably in a cool stream. Who could do that? My leg was so bruised that I knew I'd have to cut the boot to get it off! Finally I decided on a compromise and found a big tub that I could fill with cold water. It was painful for both of us; but I managed to soak all his legs thoroughly, and by evening I was sure he was out of danger. The farmer came in from the fields to milk, and I begged him to take me home. He did and then it was my turn to soak — in the lake.

Later my grandfather hauled David out to the lake in a stock truck, and we had good rides together. That was the summer I gained permission to ride bareback! David seemed to know things were different, and instead of teasing and playing his usual game of running off unless I had a sugar lump or corncob to offer, he came to me nuzzling and standing quietly by the fence so that I could mount easily. We

71

became better friends than ever, and when it was time to leave that summer to go *up north,* it was especially hard for me to say good-bye.

⊰[Belgians and Buffalo Chaps]⊱

I am sure the horses I grew up with influenced my liking for meadows and prairie land. We always had a horse around to ride. My father's father was a blacksmith, and he had a huge horse that he rode with both my brother and me perched behind him. Sometimes we rode to nearby farms where he would repair some machinery, and we would visit with the farmer's wife and play with the children. Sometimes this meant a hike out across a meadow to a stream for gathering watercress or blackberries.

My other grandfather raised purebred Belgian draft horses. They were wonderful. Our favorite was Molly. She was so ample that we cousins could all ride her at once. Her colts were famous, and we spent hours and hours teaching them to lead, wading through deep pasture grass to the far corners of their meadows just to be with them. They nuzzled and nickered and loved us. And we loved them. When fair time came, the Belgians went into the show circuit and won prizes of gold cups and colorful ribbons. Sometimes there would be too many competitions scheduled for the same hour. Then grandpa would allow one of us children to lead one horse through its paces while he showed another. We put cots in their stalls at the fairgrounds and slept there to make sure nothing happened to our animals. They trusted us and we trusted them. Just the same, we did have to learn their ways. Surprising them is one of the surest ways to get into trouble with horses, and we all had experiences learning that lesson.

One time we had a young and spirited horse that was ideal for children because he was bigger than a pony but not huge

72

⤜How to Make a Bird Feeding Station⤛

Materials needed: scrap wood and lumber, hammer, nails, saw, wooden molding, hurricane glass or juice can, birdseed.

Bird feeding stations may be anything from a clean slab of sidewalk where food is given regularly to expensive posts filled with attractively decorated structures. The Audubon Society and Ranger Rick Magazine are good sources for ideas and information about birds and their habits and requirements.

One time when my father was confined to bed with two broken legs, we consulted the Audubon Society for ideas about feeding stations and developed several successful arrangements that kept birds near the house and dad's window outlook for much of the year.

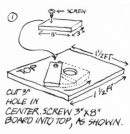

CUT 3" HOLE IN CENTER. SCREW 3"×8" BOARD INTO TOP, AS SHOWN.

Now, we have a meadow station, and it is the one we like best. The top and bottom are made of two 1½-foot squares. The top piece has a 3-inch hole cut out of the center and a piece of 1-by-3-inch wood cut 8 inches long is screwed into the top of the square so that it can swing to either cover the hole or be moved to the side.

The bottom square is fitted with a triangular-shaped piece

of wood across its center length. The piece is about 2 inches high and 4 inches across the triangle base and 1½ feet long.

Two sides are nailed to the base piece, the triangle piece, and the top piece. They are 10 inches long and 3 inches wide, 1 inch thick.

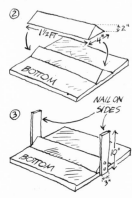

NAIL ON SIDES

Molding is nailed around the bottom piece on the top side of it so the seeds won't scatter too much, and the whole thing is screwed into the post. After many years use, we discovered that putting an extra base piece on the post was a good idea as it gave the screws more bite.

A straight-sided hurricane glass or chimney is balanced on top of the middle of the triangle

④ INSERT HURRICANE GLASS INTO HOLE

NAIL SIDE TO TOP

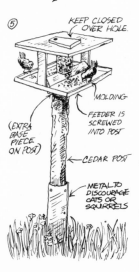

KEEP CLOSED OVER HOLE.

MOLDING

FEEDER IS SCREWED INTO POST

(EXTRA BASE PIECE ON POST)

CEDAR POST

METAL TO DISCOURAGE CATS OR SQUIRRELS

and its top fits in the circle top but not above it.

The worst thing that can happen with this feeder is to leave the top piece off the hole after you have filled the hurricane glass with seed. The seed not only can be ruined, but small birds go right down into the glass and sometimes can't get out. This feeder doesn't put out too much seed at one time, and it does make it available for many days.

We had a horse that decided bird seed was choice food. She discovered that she could break the glass or tip it off and have her fill. We found a juice can that worked to replace the glass, but it wasn't as handy as we couldn't see how much seed we had left. If squirrels or cats rob your feeder, a can or some sheet metal can be nailed around the post. They often can't — or won't — climb past it.

The horse was bug-eyed at the strange creature on his back.

like a full grown horse. We were all proud of his shiny black coat and dainty ways and took every opportunity to show him off. The summer we got him, my uncle came to visit from *out west,* and he brought us a present — a pair of chaps like cowboys wear. Of course they were a curiosity in Wisconsin, but such leather coverings are ideal for riding the sage and brush ranges farther west. But these chaps were not ordinary. They were made of buffalo skin, and the long curly fur had been left on them so that they were dramatic and showy. My brother was the first to try them on, and he immediately mounted our pretty black horse. It was a sight to see, but not for long! The horse was bug-eyed at the strange monster on his back and made a quick decision; he took off from a dead stop to a dead run, but the faster he ran, the more the spectacular chaps flapped and the more shouting sounded behind him. My brother's blond head was all that could be seen of him amidst the flying black mane and huge furry black chaps. He disappeared over a grassy knoll and, guessing where the little horse was headed, the rest of us hurried by a short cut as fast as we could to the Horseshoe at the marshy end of the lake. Sure enough! There they were. My brother was frozen with fright and looked like he was bolted to the saddle. The horse had apparently decided that the only way to fix his problem was to drown it, so into the water he lunged and plunged. It was no easy chore for our grownups to capture him and calm him down. And, as far as I know, they may have left those buffalo chaps at the bottom of the lake! I never saw them again.

My brother and cousins used to argue that just knowing all the life of the meadows — the birds and plants and insects — and having meadows for horses and pastures and rocks wasn't enough to make them the best place over forests and lakes. For them that may have been true. But remember I said meadows are *magic?* They really are. They have an aura, especially when the moon is full. It isn't a mist; it's a

{Everlasting Flowers}

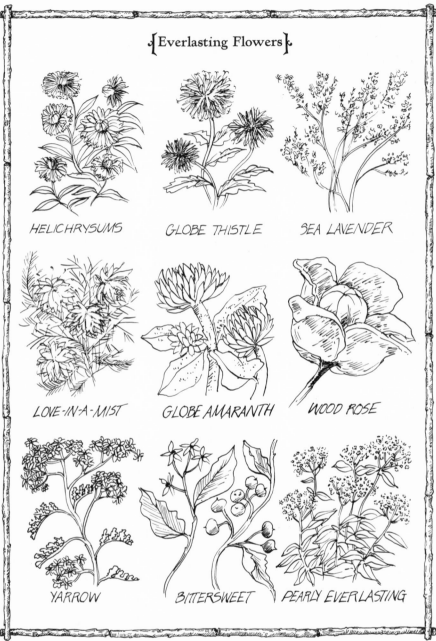

HELICHRYSUMS · GLOBE THISTLE · SEA LAVENDER

LOVE-IN-A-MIST · GLOBE AMARANTH · WOOD ROSE

YARROW · BITTERSWEET · PEARLY EVERLASTING

silver stillness that makes believable all the tales you've ever heard about leprechauns, fairies, elves, and princesses. Meadows are special places for special spirits, and if you share that belief, then the life in the meadows will take you in and you can be a part of it.

I have sat still as a stone and watched while rabbits formed a circle and danced. Our black rabbit, Dunkle, left his unlatched cage to make friends with meadow jack rabbits, and I watched their ritual of welcoming this unusual visitor. He later left his cage forever to live with them. Sometimes we still see him hopping along behind a jack rabbit, looking like an undersized shadow.

We have sat at night surrounded by coyotes yapping their curiosity and howling in fun to each other. One silver night, mother fox came and paraded her family of kits for us to admire. She was proud and her glorious pelt rippled and shone in the special light. Later when the kits were older, we listened to her teaching them to hunt. She had one stationed on a nearby hill, one in a gulch, and one down the meadow lane. She barked in her rasping way and they yelped in answer. The whole meadow seemed alive with foxes! My big collie settled close to me. We both listened and watched. The magic of the silver meadow was at work.

{ Part Three }

FORESTS AND TREES

Seeds, Pods, Needles, and Leaves

ONE time, after I had come to live in California, my grandfather came to visit. He had grown up in Germany near the Black Forest, but he came to America when he was seventeen years old and then went straight to Wisconsin where many of his countrymen were settling. I was the first of his grandchildren to leave Wisconsin, and he came to visit me because he wanted to know in his heart that California was a good place for me. We toured the steep hills in San Francisco and admired all the famous views.

One day I decided that he really should see California's redwood trees, and we drove out to a park in Marin County. To my astonishment my sturdy grandfather wept when he saw those trees, and all the words he could say were, "This is a *real* wald." (Note: *wald* is the German word for forest.) The forests he had known in his youth in Germany were all magnificent, well-managed, and maintained. They proclaimed mystery, treasure, glory, wealth, and power to all the world. Such forests, familiar to every child who has read *Grimm's Fairy Tales* or *Hansel and Gretel,* were grandfather's idea of what a forest should be; woods that last and shelter wildlife for all time.

When we stood on the floor of that quiet redwood grove, the sun shone through the trees in thin rays and seemed a weak contrast to the huge trees. Their still and awesome strength recalled the ultimate power of trees everywhere. My mind was filled with reflections about the forests and trees I had known, just as grandfather was caught up by all of his memories.

When I was a little girl, my grandfather showed me a picture. This picture hung in the county courthouse, which was in the middle of a park. The park was in the middle of our town, and our town was in the middle of our county! The picture was taken of that same place at the time the site for the town was being selected. The town was named Elkhorn because a magnificent rack of elk's horns had been found lying right there where the picture was taken. In the picture, the only things to be seen were trees and lakes. There were eight lakes right by the town and endless trees. Now this town is busy and surrounded by magnificent prairies and farms and golf courses. The elk have disappeared. There is little fishing in the nearby lakes because it is unsafe to sit in a fishing boat while speedboats whiz by. The waters are polluted and native weeds have been removed. The wood lots on farms have gradually been changed to fields, and I find myself wondering: Don't we all still need woods and trees?

Like all plant life, trees are our living companions, but they are more than that to me. Trees and forests stand for something else; they are living witnesses to the years man has been on the earth. Just imagine the stories some trees could tell! In places where man has cooperated with the trees, life continues to flourish for him. Growing trees for fruit and cutting trees for lumber can go on for many centuries when man harvests his tree-companions carefully. My grandfather's native countryside in Germany showed that. Where man becomes greedy and thoughtless, or when he treats forests carelessly, deserts and floods have resulted. What is now

{How to Make Things Using Seeds and Pods}

Materials needed: seeds, pods, feathers, bones, needle, thread. Optional: beeswax, sandpaper, knife, hand drill.

We had seeds and pods of every description. Kernels of corn were some of the handiest. Grandpa grew some ornamental corn for its color, but kernels of plain, dried field corn can be strung into long bead necklaces too. If dyed a soft turquoise color, they resemble Egyptian paste-ceramic beads and can be mixed with other seeds on a nice linen string in all kinds of arrangements. All you do is thread a sturdy darning or embroidery needle with string, linen thread, monofilament, or fine wire, and poke the needle through the seed.

It's up to you what part of the seed you poke because that determines how it will hang from the thread. Generally, corn is strung through the middle, but other seeds can be effective hung from their tops, or, if they are flat, placed side by side with smaller ones in between and strung as a unit.

If the seed or kernel is too brittle and wants to break, put a few in a dish and pour boiling water over them. Leave them a few minutes until they become soft, but not until they start puffing up. Waxing the thread with beeswax makes it stronger, and it slips through seeds more easily too.

BRITTLE SEEDS   BOILING WATER

→ REMOVE BEFORE THEY PUFF UP.

BEESWAX TO MAKE THREAD STRONGER.

Feathers and bones can be added for variation or used by themselves. Bones may be cleaned by scraping with a knife and then placing them in the sun to bleach. Ant hills make a perfect place to put them, because anything you missed the ants will clean for you; so will wasps.

RAW BONE →

(ANT HILL)

Bones can be cut or drilled and polished with sandpaper, emery cloth, pumice, or cloth. Rubbing them with fine oil gives a finished polish and shine.

Buckskin thong makes a good combination with feathers and bones. Cut into fine strips, it can be used as thread in some projects. The Indians used sinew, which was tough and strong.

Seeds and grains and pods can be arranged into very colorful and interesting pictures simply by gluing a surface and placing the seeds on it. Tiles can be made somewhat the same way, using seeds and hobby plastic that can be baked in an oven.

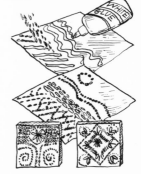

the Sahara Desert, for example, was once a forest. In many countries rivers periodically run out of control in the winter or spring because of deforested hills.

I have thought about this country. From what I have been taught of early America, forests here once appeared unending. Even though many of our native forests have been cut, the variety of forests in our country is still astonishing. Some of the more unusual and rare stands have been saved in our national and state parks. Small patches of cactus trees, date palms, giant sequoias, bristlecone pines, redwoods, preglacial hardwoods, and even petrified forests remain for us to remember how the land once was.

I have visited many of our remaining forests, places such as the swamps in our South with stands of cypress, azaleas, and Spanish moss. I love seeing the high mountains and the timberline trees that grow in the highest mountains bent from winter snow packs, shaped and twisted by their environment. Have you seen a pine tree poke through a rock and insist upon its right to grow right there? Have you chuckled, as I have, at the stingy oak, hanging onto its leaves longer than any other trees around when fall tells of the coming winter?

Did you know that in the spring, if the ash leafs out after the oak, the summer will be wet? That if the willow leaves are cupped and gray, rain is on the way? An old-timer once told me, "The chestnut — he knows." He meant that the chestnut knew not to leaf out before all danger of frost was over. Trees in danger of drought often overproduce seeds to make sure that at least the species has a chance to survive even if they themselves die. The redwood sends out thousands of extra shoots when it is wounded.

Trees are so much a part of our lives that they are a part of our everyday language, too. We say someone is as sturdy as an oak or willowy. We say something is as easy as falling off a log. "Clearing the woods" was a phrase I knew from early childhood. Abraham Lincoln grew up and lived not too far

84

∮How to Make Shakes and Posts∮

Materials needed: froe, mallet or maul, wedge, wood (preferably cedar).

Learning to use the offerings of the woods and fields is an important lesson, not only in how to see them better, but also for making things we need and making them well. Not so long ago, nearly all boys and men knew how to split rails, fence posts, and shakes. Those log cabins that stood for so many years, abandoned in clearings by pioneer settlers, usually had fine shake roofs to protect the beams and rafters from the weather.

It takes a good eye and lots of practice to know when a tree will make good, straight-grained shakes or will split straight enough for fence posts. Cedar trees are the kind traditionally used for wooden shakes and shingles and good split fence posts.

The Chippewas used bark from the big virgin trees to build their homes and protect them from winter cold. The Potawatomis by Mill Lake used the great grasses, but with the log cabin came sod roofs and then split-wood shakes.

Shakes are made from lengths of wood which can be cut square or left round. A wedgelike blade called a *froe* is hit into the top of the piece at the width wanted for the shake. A mallet or sturdy club is used to tap the froe down the length of the wood piece, which is usually from 1½ to 2½ feet long. A tap and a twist, a tap and a twist, and the shake pops off. It is stacked to one side, and the froe put at the next space. Many pieces can be popped out of one piece of wood.

SUPPORT FOR WOOD TO BE SPLIT

MALLET

FROE

TAP AND TWIST.

REPEAT.

Splitting shakes is a little like splitting firewood. It takes practice to see the beginning of a split in a piece of wood to be made into firewood. Standing the piece on end, deciding where to land the blow of the axe, and then hitting that place cleanly, results in a satisfying *snap* and two pieces of firewood!

Sometimes pieces are still too large and need to be split again; or sometimes a piece is too stubborn to split with the axe. Then a wedge is used. Stand the steel wedge in the end of the wood — in a crack if one appears. A couple of good blows on the wedge with a maul will usually break the wood open.

You may "soften" the wood for splitting by knocking it several times on the end with the maul. Soon a crack will appear. Sometimes it has to be finished with an axe.

Splitting lengths of wood for pickets is about the same as for shakes, but smaller blocks are used. Splitting wood for posts is done with the wood horizontal instead of upright; on its side rather than its end. Wedges are started in the round, spaced a little distance from one another. Usually two are enough for a fence post length. Drive first one wedge and then the other and, if necessary, finish the split with an axe or a splitting maul.

Heartwood is the best to use for posts. It can often be found in a downed tree that was burned or broken and left, so that the newest layers of wood have begun to rot away.

{How to Make Prints}

Materials needed: paint or block-printing ink, leaves, nutshells, buttons, potatoes, carrots, wooden frame, cotton organdy, roller or brayer, cardboard, paper.

Leaves and pods can make beautiful designs. At Christmas I make my own wrapping paper, sometimes drawing scenes on tissue, but often mass-producing designs.

There are many things that can be used for printing repeat designs, such as buttons, or patterns cut in potatoes or carrots. Nutshells are a favorite and can be filed down smoothly, inked, and printed to make interesting designs. Walnut or hickory nuts are good.

INK PAD OR PAINT OR BLOCK-PRINTING INK→

Another way to make repeat designs is to arrange several leaves or seeds across the paper or cloth; then spatter tempera paint or block-printing ink over the leaves with a toothbrush which has been dipped in ink or paint and then brushed with a finger causing a spatter.

SPATTER PAINT WITH TOOTH-BRUSH

A roller, or brayer, can be inked and rolled over the leaves, or a piece of screen can be placed over them and then paint brushed over that. You can also take the inked leaves and put them, ink side down, on paper and roll over them. Each gives a different kind of print.

INK

USE THE INKED LEAVES

CLEAN ROLLER

A simple screen can be made by using a frame and tacking and stretching coarse cotton organdy to it on one side. This side must make a flat surface. The screen is wet after being tacked and allowed to dry.

Now paint, about as thick as glue, can be poured into one end of the back side of the frame. The frame is placed on top of the leaf and the paper, and the paint is drawn across the screen.

For pulling the paint, a piece of cardboard may be cut to the width of the frame or a rubber squeegee can be used. Paint is squeezed through the holes and covers the paper below. Lift the screen off and then lift the leaf off the paper.

More leaves or seeds can be added after that paint dries, as can other colors. If using more than one color, start with the lightest and work toward dark.

① ATTACH CLOTH ② WET CLOTH

BOTTOM (TAPE)

③

LEAVES THICK PAINT

④

CARDBOARD

⑤

from our lake country. When he was a boy, he was just like many other rail-splitters around home. The log cabins made famous in Lincoln stories were the kind of houses built in Sweden. When Swedish people came to America, they began building their native log houses here too. It was a perfect solution. Log cabins were good houses and they used trees that were being cleared from the land anyway to make way for farms. Log cabins can still be found standing all across our country. Many old ones are still being used. One of the secrets that makes them last is having a good roof. Even when they were abandoned by a farmer moving to more promising land farther west, the sturdy cabins stood for many years, if the roof was sound.

A Log Cabin Adventure

In my town there was an empty cabin that no one had torn down. It stood at the back of a yard next door to my grandmother's house. When we grew old enough to be Girl Scouts, I thought the girls in our troop should have a meeting place. We got together and asked her neighbors if we could use that cabin. It hadn't been used for a long time, but the owner said if we cleaned it up and cared for it, we could use it.

We were lucky because someone had built a solid wooden floor in it, so we didn't have to worry about the coldness of an earth floor in winter. We swept, washed, and polished. We put new plaster in between the logs and patched broken shingles on the roof.

Finally one day, we thought everything was perfect. Outside the front door we planted a little garden with flowers, and we had made a table and benches inside for our meetings. When it was all done, we invited our mothers to a party. It was a chilly fall day, so we decided at the last minute to make it a real christening by lighting a fire in the fireplace. After we had read poems and sung our favorite songs, the big moment arrived. We lit the fire and it took off in a true scoutlike blaze. But instead of having a nice cheery fire, we suddenly found ourselves enveloped in a smoke cloud that had backed down the chimney and covered everyone and everything with black soot. Our eyes burned and itched. We coughed and choked and everyone ran outside. Soon the cloud of smoke even smothered the little fire. We looked up the chimney to find out what had gone wrong. After much poking and a lot more soot, we found the problem: an ancient, abandoned squirrel's nest was stuck up the chimney. It was so big it had blocked off the opening so that no smoke or air could draw through! We filled a gunny sack with stones, tied a rope to it, and lowered it into the chimney from the roof top. By raising and lowering and swinging it, we managed to knock the nest out along with the dirt and chimney soot. We decided after that to clean the chimney every year before building our first fire!

Next, we did a careful search of all the nooks and crannies outside the cabin and under it. Fixing up the inside hadn't been enough. We discovered that a family of skunks had lived under the house and that raccoons had enjoyed coming into the house for the winter. We located the coons' secret entrance under a pole rafter and blocked it up. We had another party when everything was finished, and by that time everyone we invited knew it was a *very special* log cabin.

⟨Snowballs and Robins' Eggs⟩

Our house in town was built out of an old horse barn. The kitchen room was added on. Where that addition jutted out, there was a huge snow apple tree. I think they are called snow apples because of the clean white flesh of the fruit under the bright red skin. Besides the apples and shade which the tree gave, it showered us with pink blossoms in a sweet blessing

88

We suddenly found ourselves enveloped in a smoke cloud.

{How to Make a Lashed Table}

Materials needed: six poles, rope for lash (clothesline).

Cut four poles 3 feet long each. Use a diamond lashing knot (see Knots page 18) to fasten two together, making an X for each end of the table. A pole cut the length of the table is then square lashed to the top inside of the X poles, fitting the ends as closely as possible.

Another two poles 2½ feet long are cut to fit across the top of the long poles at each end. Use a square lash to join. This is the key pole. It supports the top and it keeps the table from collapsing. A top may be made of planks or a smooth-surface door or a piece of plywood.

This same X and cross pole design can also be used to construct benches and small tables.

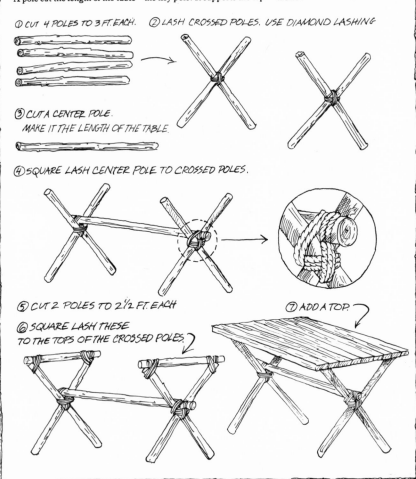

① CUT 4 POLES TO 3 FT. EACH.   ② LASH CROSSED POLES. USE DIAMOND LASHING

③ CUT A CENTER POLE.
MAKE IT THE LENGTH OF THE TABLE.

④ SQUARE LASH CENTER POLE TO CROSSED POLES.

⑤ CUT 2 POLES TO 2½ FT. EACH

⑥ SQUARE LASH THESE TO THE TOPS OF THE CROSSED POLES.

⑦ ADD A TOP.

90

every spring. Each year at that time my father would move my big wooden doll house outside under the tree and hang out swings on our favorite branches.

In winter we used the apple tree for a lookout station. It was a perfect tree for climbing. Nearby, we had a snow fort in our yard, which we made solid by carefully pouring water over the walls on the coldest nights so they would freeze. There were similar forts in the yard next door and in several others all along the path to our school. Going to school on those winter days was high adventure, and our apple tree was an important post along the route.

Sometimes bully boys would make iceballs instead of snowballs or put a rock inside a snowball. Then there was a big fight that would have made everybody late for school except for one thing. The man in charge of ringing the school bell rang it from inside a tower and from up there he could see almost the whole town. On the days that we were delayed, he just kept ringing the bell a few more times. He had grown up using the same path to the same school, and he knew exactly what was happening.

The other tree by our house grew next to my bedroom window. It was a maple. A robin family came to nest there every year and as long as we lived there, I could count on seeing those blue eggs in the spring nest. That tree was part of a long row of maples that grew along the main road through town. In the fall the maple trees drop beautifully colored leaves, and we would make mounds of them that were many times taller than we were. Then we jumped into the mounds and played and got buried and lost in the weightless mass of color.

In summer, when we moved to grandfather's cottage at Mill Lake, we would awaken each morning to the drilling of red-headed woodpeckers on the trees. Sometimes their tapping made a roar on the metal downspouts, but most often it was a brrrruuum as holes were bored in a hardwood tree

The squirrels performed daring feats of leaping from tree to tree.

where they stored what seemed like millions of acorns. My grandfather often left hickory trees standing when they died. They seldom fell and when they became hollow, they provided homes from top to bottom. Small animals, such as raccoons, lived in the bottom, and birds, like flickers, woodpeckers, owls, and wood ducks, lived in the higher hollows. Birds like to have dead trees, called snags, to light upon. They provide a clear place to watch from.

I was taught by my family to care for our trees and to manage them so that there would always be lots of trees. Like so many people in Wisconsin, our family had farms, and every farm needed a wood lot. This was not only because we used wood for cook stoves, heaters, fence posts, and rails; it was also because of the other life that the trees supported. Rabbits, grouse, pheasant, and quail all needed the trees too. Owls hunted rodents, and squirrels buried their acorns, so we didn't have to plant any.

How we loved to watch squirrel games in the big old oaks and maples. The squirrels were very good at their own versions of tag and hide and seek. Daring feats of leaping from tree to tree and fast scrambles up and down and in and out were all part of the action. They were great beggars and robbers, too. They teased us and we teased them back. I remember one big gray squirrel who used to come to us for handouts of walnuts. A whole tree of walnuts was nearby, but he liked the fun of coming to us. Once we gave him a lemon instead of a walnut. He sneaked it away and sat down to eat it, picking it up in his front paws as he prepared for a big dinner. We watched him take a bite, pause, and then with all his strength and both paws, throw the lemon as far as he could and run away, scolding us at the top of his voice. All the while we shrieked with laughter.

Trees for windbreaks are another important feature of that area. Sometimes they are called shelter belts. The main idea is to give protection from the prairie winds which in winter

cause giant snowdrifts, and in summer make topsoil blow off
newly planted fields. The loss of good topsoil, caused first by
clearing the woods and later by cultivation, is a sad part of
the history of this country. In Wisconsin two additional forces
acted on the land. One was the action of the prehistoric
glaciers and the other was fire: prairie grass fires and forest
fires.

Caught in a Ring of Fire

On the very same day that Mrs. O'Leary's cow started the
famous Chicago Fire, there was a forest fire in Wisconsin.
Because of the Chicago Fire publicity, hardly anyone has
ever heard of the Peshtigo Fire, but it was the largest forest
fire in history and one of the worst fires of any kind. In that
sparsely settled country, there was no way to stop it, and it
raged out of control, burning whole counties and making
thousands of people and animals homeless.

It seems like people feared fire more in those days. One
time when we were driving on our way north, we were called
to a stop at the edge of a small town. We had been enjoying
the drive alongside a trout stream, but when the man hailed
us to stop, we knew something terrible was wrong. He asked
us to help the town in a bucket brigade! Everyone who could
furnish a bucket or lift one was needed. Our grownups fell
into the line of people who were passing the water-filled
buckets in a steady flow from the stream to a fire that had
started at the edge of town. It was a sobering business, and I
felt very helpless and small, just like the small forest creatures
must have felt as they watched.

Another time, while we were in camp *up north*, we began
to notice that the animals and birds in the forest around us
seemed restless. A fawn and doe bounded straight through
camp, scarcely noticing where they were. We were amazed!

{How to Make a Wooden Spoon}

Materials needed: a 12- to 14-inch piece of wood, jackknife, sandpaper, a gouge, wax or oil, saw.

The first thing to learn in doing any project which uses a jackknife is a respectful attitude toward your knife. If you have this attitude, then you aren't likely to injure yourself or anyone else, and your knife will always be ready to work for you. The basic care of any knife can be put into a few simple rules. I have eight stitches in my left index finger which help me to remember the rules, but it's better to learn before you hurt yourself.

(1) Choose a knife that's the right size for the job you are going to do.

(2) Keep your knife clean, honed sharp, and oiled.

(3) Use your knife as a knife. Blades are not screwdrivers or can openers, and knicks in blades cause uneven handling, which can be dangerous.

(4) Place an open knife down flat, not on its edge.

(5) To pass an open knife to another person, give the handle first.

Select a piece of wood, which is thoroughly dry, with long clear grain. It can be from the family woodpile or it can be from a lumberyard. The piece should be trimmed into a block about 12 inches long and 3 inches thick and square. Use pine or a hardwood.

Sketch the spoon shape on the length of the block; the long grain should run the length. Saw away the part of the block around what will be the handle, and roughly saw the shape of the spoon bowl.

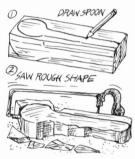

① DRAW SPOON

② SAW ROUGH SHAPE

Using the jackknife, whittle down the piece left for the handle and shape it into the bowl. Move the knife away from you toward the bowl.

Now whittle the sides gradually to shape the bowl. Turn it upside down and shape the bottom. The gouge should be used just for the inside of the bowl. Gouges are best used along the grain of the wood (with the grain).

③ SHAPE HANDLE

④ SHAPE BOWL SIDES

⑤ SHAPE BOTTOM

Start at the handle end and, working away from you, gouge toward the center of the bowl, away from the handle. Gradually move around the bowl until it appears necessary to gouge from the tip end of the bowl. Repeat for the second half, gouging as much with the grain as possible, until a uniform thickness is achieved for the whole bowl.

⑥

USE SPOON GOUGE TO CUT INSIDE OF BOWL.

Sand the whole spoon until it feels smooth enough to use. Polish it with wax or soak it in warm vegetable oil.

⑦ SAND SMOOTH. WAX OR SOAK IN VEGETABLE OIL.

Almost any wood which is hard enough to stand wear and tear makes a good spoon. My treasure for many years was one I inherited and used many times each day. It was made of bird's-eye maple. Finally it became so thin that it simply broke in two. Often the shape of a piece of wood itself suggests the shaping of the spoon bowl and handle. Making spoons is a hobby you can enjoy all your life and one that will always give pleasure to others, too.

Finally, some friends from the Indian village came by and said they thought there was probably a fire. They were going to scout it out. Before long they returned and with them was a forest ranger. He asked us how long our supplies would last and reported that we were completely cut off from any road out of the area. The village and our camp were encircled by a forest fire! It wasn't close, but it made escape impossible.

The villagers and animals had been unable to detect the nature of the fire because it was burning in a circle, and there was no clue as to its direction. No one could judge where it was coming from or where it was going. The ranger hurried away saying he would return when he could let us know how to leave camp safely.

Well, this was one time I learned about *being ready!* The days dragged on. The sky became a sickening yellow. The skittering and chattering of the chipmunks and birds made us all nervous. I made excuses to stay in our tent. Games of cards and some books we had brought suddenly seemed very interesting. My mother and father held quiet conversations with my aunt and uncle. I know now they were solemnly making plans. If we were really trapped, the Chippewas knew how to get out by old waterways that their ancestors had used. This would be risky, but possible. The adults made two plans for the exact moment when they knew we must act. One was to leave the camp by car and the other was by boat, leaving our car and tents for the fire to burn.

At last one day my uncle's Chippewa friend came running into camp. He called, "C'mon!" and we did! We all knew our jobs and did them instantly. He told us to bring our car. Everything not absolutely necessary for everyday use had already been packed. We quickly dismantled the rest of the camp and were fleeing after the dust of his jalopy in what must have been record time.

We followed along, going on trails we had never known. Soon we came to an open road. Around us were smoldering

96

woods, charred fallen trees, and flickering fires. Blinking in the dust and smoke, our Indian friend waved us to go in a certain direction, and we went with a grateful gesture and a good-bye. The road was strewn with flaming debris. We were uncertain. After driving a few miles, we came to fire fighters who explained that there was an unexpected, temporary break in the fire due to a shift in wind and the "back" fires the Indians had started at just the right places. "Back" fires are constructed up ahead in the path of a forest fire in hopes of burning back all the fuel the original fire would have fed upon. When the original forest fire burns up to the place where the back fire was, there is no more fuel to burn and the forest fire is cut off. The Indians knew how to do this and had protected their lands for many years, but no one can make a defense against some things that people will do. We later heard that some crazy person had set that fire.

{ Wild Creatures and Us }

One of the excitements in approaching our camping spot by the lake was going over narrow strips of land which connected one section of forest to another, with water in between. Whole forests, drowned by the flooding for a power station, were under that water. It was called the Chippewa Flowage, named after the Chippewa River that flowed through it. The giant dead trees had become lookout stations for herons, kingfishers, and other birds who nested near there.

One time we heard a screech and wild cries in the sky and stopped to watch a whole battle take place between an eagle and a heron. The eagle and the heron were both fishing, but the eagle had glided too far into the heron's territory. We knew where the eagle's nest was — bigger every year — but had not seen the heron's nest. It turned out to be almost

97

under the place where they were fighting, so that must have been the reason for the fight. To our surprise, the heron won and the eagle went away. The eagles had been long gone from the lake and farm areas of southern Wisconsin, as had most of the herons; so seeing them was a sure sign we really were *up north!*

Another sign was the gray wolf. We would sing around the campfire late at night, and once in a great while we could see the eyes of the wolf glowing in the light at the edge of the woods that surrounded our camp. Many animals love the sound of music and will make great efforts to listen to it. Wolves are very sociable, so it wasn't surprising to have them come. It seemed so natural that even if they howled, it wasn't frightening.

I was usually dividing my sleepy attention anyway. Our nightly campfires were a joy and a worry because of the lumpy tree toads. They loved campfires. Each night they hopped as close as they dared, sometimes landing right *in* the fire. When that happened, there would be a flurry and a scuffle to make a rescue. Sometimes there were also tears when we were too late.

Kangaroo mice came out to play at that time, too, and if we sat still or snuggled down quietly, they sometimes came and did a jig on our blankets. In silhouette against the firelight, they looked like giants.

The Chippewa boys showed us how to make slingshots and how to use them. They never used guns and didn't need to. Being on a reservation, their lives were not regulated by the game laws. Instead, they still followed their traditional practices. Small game, such as squirrels and some birds, were sources of daily food as they always had been. The boys were never without a slingshot, and they could hit a moving target with such an effortless motion that it was hard to see anything happening. We never hunted with slingshots, but we did have great contests trying to hit the bull's-eye on a target. We

98

The tree toads loved campfires.

How to Make Casts of Tracks

Materials needed: tin can, water, plaster of paris, oil, felt-tip pen.

Casting is simple to do. It is a matter of casting twice and being careful. Don't lose the track by overcasting and make sure the second cast has no place to lock onto the first.

After finding a track, mix plaster of paris in a can filled with enough water to cover the track. Always add the plaster to the water. Do not stir yet.

When no more will settle to the bottom, stir to mix. Build a small wall of mud around the cast an inch high and pour the plaster ¾ inch deep into this. It will set quickly.

If the track appears too fragile, use a thinner mix gently at first. When this begins to set, the thicker mix may be poured on top.

① *FIND A TRACK YOU WANT TO CAST*

② *ADD PLASTER TO WATER*

PLASTER OF PARIS

WATER INSIDE

③ *ONLY STIR WHEN NO MORE PLASTER WILL SETTLE TO BOTTOM.*

④ *BUILD MUD WALL*

1 INCH HIGH

⑤ *POUR IN PLASTER MIXTURE TO 3/4 INCH.*

The cast will not appear as you saw the track, so a reverse one is made. Oil your first cast well and trim off any rough edges. Make a wall or use a throwaway container and put your cast in it, face up.

⑥ *WHEN DRY, LIFT OFF MOLD*

⑦ *OIL WELL*

OIL

TRIM ROUGH EDGES

MOLD

Now cover the well-oiled cast with another layer of plaster. When this hardens, discard the wall or container and pry the two casts apart — carefully. If you've done a good job, the casts should come apart easily.

⑧ *PLACE TRACK-UP IN BOX*

The new cast will be the mold of what you saw. Mark on the back of this cast information about the track: where you found it, when, what the weather was like, *who* it belongs to.

⑨ *POUR IN MORE PLASTER MIXTURE*

⑩ *WHEN DRY, SEPARATE HALVES.*

FINISHED CAST →

Tracks can also be "collected" by making careful drawings in a notebook along with information. As you see the same animal tracks, you become familiar with the patterns shown when the animal is running. sitting, walking, or hunting. This can be a fascinating way to learn the habits of your neighboring animals.

100

became good enough shots to feel like we had protection for ourselves when we carried a slingshot in our pockets.

The Chippewa boys were such good shots that one day my aunt asked them if they would get a bunch of bullfrogs for us. The boys were enthusiastic and started off toward the bogs. Suddenly, one of them came back and asked my aunt why she wanted the frogs. She said, "To eat, of course." To our surprise, the boy turned slightly green, and his eyes practically popped out of his head. He said, "Well! I've *heard* of people who eat snakes and frogs, but I've never *seen* one before!" And away he ran.

The boys not only refused to bring any frogs, but they didn't come to visit for a few days, either. When they did, one of them happened to shoot a chipmunk but only wounded it. Then it was our turn to be upset. We made a box for it and nursed it until its broken leg was well. My dad explained to us all that not everybody values life in the same ways. He said that it was all right to be different from each other sometimes. Later, when the chipmunk bit me instead of the food I offered it, I didn't feel so different from the Chippewas.

I noticed, too, that when my aunt and mother were frying frog legs, and the legs hopped around in the pan like they do, the Chippewa boys doubled up laughing. Even though they never ate any, I suspect they thought it wasn't so bad after all.

⊰[Keeping Track]⊱

At home, by the lake and farm, we were familiar with such tracks as rabbit and game birds. There we could even pretty well tell whose horse had been down a dusty road by the shape of the shoe marks.

Up north the animal life was more abundant and quite different. The Chippewa boys showed us tracks and other signs of animals around us in the forest. At the time of year we were there, the woods were full of hazelnuts and blueberries. These lured bears in close to our camp, and if we wanted to harvest any of the berries, we needed to be ahead of the bears. We also needed to know if we were near any bears, so we quickly learned to look for little snatches of fur caught on bushes and to identify the tracks and scats. There was certainly enough food for all. We just needed to be careful.

Each morning, on the sandy beach below our campsite, we discovered tracks showing who had come for drinks of water during the night. We learned the difference between bucks, does, fawns; between foxes and raccoons. At other sandy places we found smooth trails like miniature toboggan runs, and we learned to keep a lookout for otters playing and sliding down to the water. Tracks can tell a whole lot but you do have to learn to *see*. Each species had its own track, and each individual within the species has its own track. Tracks can be collected by making casts or drawings. These can help you to memorize which tracks belong to which animal. If you keep a careful record for long enough and state when and where each cast or drawing was made, you can learn to judge how heavy the animal was, if it was old or young, or male or female. Animals go to chosen areas for eating, for raising their young, for mating, and their trails stay fairly consistent.

Animals are tuned to many important things which people no longer pay attention to. One of these is water, and animal trails very often either lead to water or follow underground waterways. When you are tracking, sometimes you come to a place where the tracks of several different animals show up. Perhaps there is a reason more than one animal came to that place. Many animals eat the same food, but some have "rights" to help themselves first. You can try to discover who came first.

One time we tried and tried to find out who was stealing chicken eggs from us. At night we put an egg out on a wooden surface which had been sprinkled with flour. Sure enough

The otters were playing and sliding down to the water.

{How to Make and Use Lichen Dye}

Materials needed: lichen (wolf moss), a 3-gallon enamel container, water, a cook stove.

Wolf moss is a common lichen in many parts of our country. It may be gathered at any time of the year and used fresh or dry. Place a goodly amount of lichen in an enamel container free from nicks or cracks, and cover it with water.

① LICHEN
ENAMEL POT
COVER WITH WATER

Put the pot on the stove and bring the water to a boil. Just at the boiling point, lower to a simmer and cook it for about an hour. Turn off the heat and let the lichen steep in the water overnight. The next day remove the lichen. The remaining liquid, called a *dye vat,* is now ready for use.

② BRING WATER TO A BOIL

③ SIMMER FOR 1 HOUR

④ TURN OFF HEAT. LET LICHEN STEEP OVERNIGHT.

⑤ NEXT DAY REMOVE LICHEN.

DYE VAT IS READY

To dye wool, moisten 1 pound of washed wool in water that is the same temperature as the water in the dye vat. Place the wool in the vat with a ratio of 1 pound of wool to 3 gallons of liquid. Simmer for an hour or more.

⑥ MOISTEN WOOL; SIMMER 1 HOUR

Simmering the lichen and the wool gives off a strong, pungent smell. Some people object to the smell and prefer to dye out-of-doors. When the wool has taken up a yellow green color, remove the pot from the heat and let it cool thoroughly. Then rinse the wool in clean water until the water runs clear and free of color. Keep the temperatures constant and squeeze —don't wring — the wool. Hang it up to dry in the shade.

⑦ COOL. (WOOL STILL IN POT)

⑧ REMOVE WOOL. RINSE

RINSE UNTIL WATER IS COLOR-FREE.

⑨ HANG IN SHADE TO DRY.

Lichen contains its own mordant. *Mordant* is a Greek word meaning "to bite." A mordant causes the color to bite or fix into the fiber, so it won't wash out or run. But lichen can be made to last in its sunny brightness for many more years by using wool mordanted with alum. To do this, add 1 pound of washed wool to a mixture of 4 ounces of potassium alum (buy at a drugstore) and 3 gallons of water. Simmer for one hour, cool, and rinse.

104

there were tracks each morning, but for some reason they were always blurred. Finally one day, there were clear, distinct mouse tracks. Since mice don't eat eggs, they must have come for a sample of the flour! The next night I left the egg, but I put white chalk dust under and around it. In the morning perfect fox prints were there in the dust.

Foxes love eggs. Some people even call them egg-suckers. They puncture a small hole in an egg with their teeth and draw the contents out by sucking it. If you have ever tried to empty an egg by blowing it so that you can keep the shell, you can imagine what a neat trick this is for a fox.

Colors from Plants

Lichen is one of the foods many animals of the forest eat. It is one of the all-purpose plants of the forest. In fact, lichen and its close relative, moss, are found just about everywhere. They are both used for food and as nesting material by animals. People use them for a variety of things, too. Most lichens appear to be dull and unattractive, but when they are wet by rain, they can become brilliant and catch sunlight in strange, glowing colors. They look fragile, but they are tough. Often they are a clue to woodland activity. You can tell when deer have been rubbing their antlers by looking at the moss and lichen on trees. When the plants deer usually brouse on are scarce, you will see the lichen cropped off quite high where the deer have reached up to eat it.

There is an old saying that one can tell the direction of north in the woods by which side of a tree the moss grows on. The idea is that moss grows best on the shady side of a tree which is usually the side away from the sun. That is most often the north side.

Mosses and lichens are some of the most beautiful and intricate forms in nature. Some grow so slowly that it should

105

be considered a crime to even touch them, but others reproduce rapidly. Some live on rocks, some on trees, and some in water — like sphagnum moss. Long ago these plants were cultivated and prized as a source of color. Until we invented artificial food coloring, lichens were one of the few sources of color that was safe to use in food.

Colors made from plants or chemicals are called dyes. Natural dyes are made only from things in nature; chemical dyes are man-made. Chemical dyes are usually very brilliant and colorfast, that is, they don't fade or run. Natural dyes are rich and subtle. Probably the most appealing characteristic of natural dyes is the way they blend together harmoniously.

The Indians in America knew of certain plants and other natural color sources; one of them is lichen. Because lichen also contains the one thing needed to make its color stay fixed, it is one of the easiest to use.

One time when I was doing some studies on natural dyes, an Indian lady told me about a cousin of hers who, she said, "knew color." She promised to arrange a meeting between us. Many months later the telephone rang and it was the lady. She said, "You can come now." I knew that her father had died that week, so I didn't ask any questions, thinking she needed some kind of help.

When I arrived at her home there were large numbers of sad, solemn-faced people gathered about. I was ushered through the house to a remote corner where I waited by myself. After a time a young man came in and shyly introduced himself as her cousin. He said he had recognized me by my sweater made of handmade wool, colored with natural dyes. He also told me many interesting things about color plants. He was a professor of Indian culture, and I found out from him that Indians traditionally protect certain areas where plants for producing colors grow especially well.

In our hurry to build more highways and houses, we have covered over almost all of those places. When I met my

{How to Make a Pine Needle Basket}

Materials needed: pine needles, number 18 or 20 tapestry needle, heavy cotton or linen thread, scissors, knife.

The "eye" or the beginning of the bottom will strongly determine the firmness of a basket. Other factors such as the quality of the pine needles; the binding cord, grass, or thread will affect the basket too. But the Indians say that the eye of the ninth basket reveals the soul of the maker!

Essentially the basket is a series of pine needles coiled and sewn together. Select long, dry needles. The best gathering time is in the spring. They should not be old and brittle or have begun to show spots of decay. Moisten the approximate amount you need to use at one time in warm water. When thoroughly dampened, put them on an old towel to be kept moist while you work.

① DAMPEN PINE NEEDLES

(OLD TOWEL)

A large handful will be enough for practicing eyes. It is said never to start a basket until three eyes have been made. To make a perfect eye may take many tries.

Thread a strong, large-eyed, blunt-nosed, short tapestry needle, preferably number 18 or 20. Use heavy-duty cotton or linen thread. Cut 3 yards, thread it, fold it in half, and knot the end.

Take three *shanks* of pine needles (nine needles) and lay them over the palm of your left hand with the stubs lined up across your index finger. Lay the thread alongside of the pine needles with the knot hanging an inch longer than the pine needle stubs, away from you, along the left side of the pine needles.

Loop the thread around your palm and the back of your hand, bringing it across below the knot. Hold all in place with your left thumb. The thread is then whipped on (tightly wrapped around) the pine needles. This pulls the needles together.

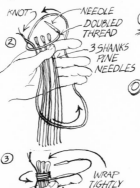

KNOT — NEEDLE DOUBLED THREAD — 3 SHANKS PINE NEEDLES

② ③ WRAP TIGHTLY 3 TIMES

Take your fingers out of the loop after the first few winds have secured the pine needles. Drop your needle and thread down through the loop. Pull the

knot end at the top until the loop disappears. Snip off the knot end close to the stubs. Whip around the pine needles for about an inch.

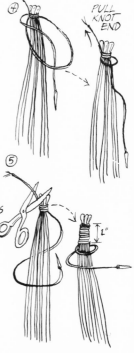

④ PULL KNOT END

⑤ 1"

The wound part is now bent around to become a flat circle shape. The stub end of the shanks cross the end of the wound pine needles where the needle and thread are dangling. Take the needles and wind the thread around the place where the shanks and the stubs cross to hold the circle shape firm. Do this three times making it tight but not too tight.

107

⑥

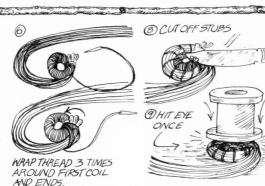

WRAP THREAD 3 TIMES AROUND FIRST COIL AND ENDS.

The pine needles are then coiled again around the wound coil and are fastened to it by placing the threaded needle under three of the wound threads, pulling needle and thread through, and then around the pine needle coil, then under and through three more wound threads and around the coil again. This is continued until the second coil is bound to the first.

⑦ **THREAD NEEDLE UNDER 3 WOUND THREADS**

THEN AROUND SECOND COIL

REPEAT FOR ALL OF COIL.

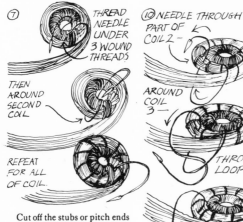

Cut off the stubs or pitch ends with a sharp knife. Now, place the eye on the floor and with a walnut or thread spool hit it soundly — once. This completes the eye.

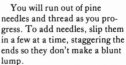

⑨ **HIT EYE ONCE**

The third coil is added by bending the needles around the second coil and sewing them on. The needle is poked in between a couple of pine needles in the second coil close to and behind a stitch in the second coil. (Take care not to pierce a pine needle.) Then wrap the needle and thread around the third coil and drop the needle through the thread loop formed and pull tight. This is a basket or blanket stitch and is used from now on.

⑩ **NEEDLE THROUGH PART OF COIL 2 —**

AROUND COIL 3 —

THROUGH LOOP —

PULL TIGHT.

— REPEAT

You will run out of pine needles and thread as you progress. To add needles, slip them in a few at a time, staggering the ends so they don't make a blunt lump.

When new thread is needed, the new knot is buried in the coil and the needle pulled through and forward to the position of the next stitch. The basket is continued in a flat disk until the size is reached that you want for a bottom. To start up the sides, gradually work the coils to a position of being one on top of the other rather than side by side; the stitching is the same. The coils should appear smooth on all surfaces.

⑪

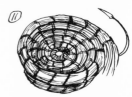

As you work your stitches, they will seem to make a spiral pattern as you progress outward from the eye — if you work evenly. Usually the widest separation between the rows of stitches is no more than 1 inch.

A simple finish for the top edge is a basket stitch around the top coil. The pine needle ends on the top coil are cut in a staggered way so that the coil ends smoothly and without a blunt end. The basket is moist, and as it dries, it will loosen so it is important to work snugly.

⑫

friend's cousin, he was working hard with the government to safeguard those that were left. He said that Indians only take plants after giving a prayer of thanks and asking for renewal. He tried to persuade me not to print my dye recipes for fear that printing them would encourage people who have no tradition of caring and love to take too many plants.

This conversation made me think about more than color. My brother, cousins, and I had grown up turning to the woods, streams, meadows, and lakes as places to learn, to enjoy, and as sources of materials for our needs. I feel that learning to intelligently use the natural materials found in the woods and fields is important, not only in how to see them better and to appreciate them, but to make the things we need or want and to make them well.

As people came across our country "clearing the woods," they learned to make many everyday tools and necessities out of that wood. They made such things as rakes, shovels, hinges, latches, locks, nails, and wheelbarrows. They made boxes, bins, plates, spoons, baskets, handles, and furniture of all descriptions. People learned how to use the seeds, pods, fruits, and leaves of plants and trees — and preserving them — enjoying them for their beauty, as well.

At Mill Lake we made small pillows stuffed with pine needles. The pillows always smelled fresh and clean. We thought acorns, pine cones, and seeds were endlessly fascinating and sometimes, especially on rainy days, we made things from them.

⌡[The No-Peace Pipe]⌠

One time we cousins decided to make some peace pipes. We carefully hollowed out the biggest acorns we could find, made a hole in the side of each one, and put a length of straw into that. Since no one in any of our families smoked, we had

109

no firsthand knowledge of what a real pipe should be like, but you could blow air in and out of these and that seemed just right. We always had a working theory that somebody had invented everything that was made, so that we could become inventors too, even if we didn't have a plan.

When we got the acorns dry and clean, we ground up the acorn filling and stuffed it back into the acorn. Then we were ready to smoke the peace pipes. We all piled into one big hammock, facing in the direction away from the cottage, and solemnly lit our pipes. We drew deep drafts of air through the filling to get it lit and, by concentrating carefully, got them puffing in great style. It wasn't long before the gleeful swinging of the hammock slowed down. Soon it was sagging and limp arms and legs could be seen hanging over the sides. After that, one by one, four little boys and one girl spilled out and rolled in agony on the ground. It wasn't just that we had all made ourselves sick and had to take medicine and be put in bed; we had also rolled into a patch of poison ivy. Our peace pipes brought no peace at all — only stomachaches and weeks of itching and scratching. Acorns aren't bad, however. They make a beautiful brown dye color, and their meal can be used for making bread.

Our native forests were mostly hardwood trees so we didn't have the variety of pine cones that are to be found in other parts of the country. Lodgepole pine and spruce furnished our cones, and we used them in combination with all kinds of seeds and pods. My favorite project was to make wreaths and swags for Christmas decorations, but we made many other things as well.

In wintertime we thought about Christmas toys and ornaments and about the birds which would come back in the spring. There was a lady in our town who came from Poland when she was a young girl, and she showed us how to hollow out eggs and decorate them with feathers and paint. There were still many people living in our town directly from the

110

{How to Make Christmas Wreaths}

Materials needed: pine cones, pods, leaves, wood or chicken wire, glue, hand drill, wire.

My favorite project for all my cones and pretty pods is to make wreaths. There is no end to the combinations of things that can be put together, and there is no end to the way they can be put together, either. Since wreaths are round and are usually hung up against a wall or door, there is a top and a backside.

A good idea is to make a plan for arranging your collected materials on the backing. It's very disappointing to have all your construction on one part and find that you don't have enough of just the right pieces to do more.

A piece of thin plywood or masonite cut to the correct size and then drilled with many fine holes all over makes a good base or backing for such a wreath.

Florists wire can be strung through those holes and around or through pods and cones — even through leaves. An arrangement for hanging the wreath should be made after drilling the holes. Usually a sturdy wire wound through the holes at the top, but not showing over it, works out well.

Other bases that can be used besides plywood are chicken wire, wire and moss, boughs twisted and tied together, and even cloth stuffed like a circular pillow. If wire is not used for mounting, glue will work, and sometimes both are used together. If using glue, a flat-surface base is important.

Work from large pieces to small pieces when mounting and from flat to lumpy for the best results. Flat glossy leaves laid overlapping and covering the base can be sewn through with the wire and are an especially pretty base covering. Pine cones sawed off like bread slices make flat, flower disks, which other, smaller things can be added to.

The prettiest wreaths result from careful planning and some trial and error. Combining round and long, rough and smooth, shiny and coarse objects is a challenge, and the results are fun to see and more fun to give.

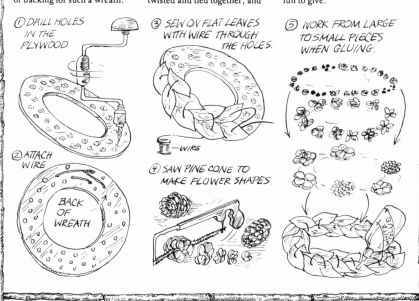

① DRILL HOLES IN THE PLYWOOD

② ATTACH WIRE

BACK OF WREATH

③ SEW ON FLAT LEAVES WITH WIRE THROUGH THE HOLES.

—WIRE

④ SAW PINE CONE TO MAKE FLOWER SHAPES.

⑤ WORK FROM LARGE TO SMALL PIECES WHEN GLUING.

{How to Make a Christmas Bird}

Materials needed: jackknife, wood, paint, glue, clothespin or string, and drill.

To make little birds for Christmas ornaments, we first used willow sticks and later graduated to hardwood. Pine and balsa are also easy woods for beginners to use.

Choose a stick about an inch in diameter and long enough to be held in a good grip. The bird head will be at the tip of the stick and carved first; the body will be blocked next.

Hold the stick with the left hand, pointed downward and braced against the floor. It is almost always best to move a knife with the grain of the wood and away from you, even if it's tempting not to.

Gently carve away a curve under the neck and head and another curve behind the head above the back and in front of the tail.

Carve the body of the bird to a rounded shape. When you can recognize the general shape of the bird, free it from the stick by a few cuts into the stick above the bird shape. Take the blocked-out bird into your hand.

③

REFINE SHAPE WITH SANDPAPER

It should be about an inch thick and 2 inches long. More carving may be necessary to get a sharp outline of a beak and thin tail, but you may be able to do these just with sandpaper on such a small bird.

BIRD IS ABOUT 2" LONG

Now carve another curve behind the stomach and under the tail. Your first carving will look very crude, like three ½-inch nicks in your piece of wood. Leave the body and carve the head and tail ends narrower.

CUT
CUT
CUT

① CUT OUT VERY ROUGH SHAPE.

② ROUND OUT BIRD SHAPE AND CUT OFF STICK

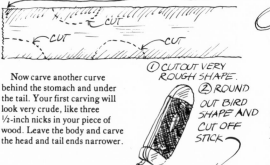

④ PAINT

GLUE ON A CLOTHESPIN OR DRILL A HOLE FOR STRING OR THREAD.

When your bird is the shape you want, you are ready to paint it any fanciful color pattern you wish for your Christmas tree. The bird can be glued to a clothespin or you can drill a small hole through his middle, bottom to top, to attach a string for hanging.

"old country." There was a Norwegian settlement where we went to church suppers, and they served the most wonderful food. There were Swiss dairy farmers and Swedish people who farmed or worked as lumberjacks. One silver-haired Swedish man taught us how to carve with a jackknife and how to make ornaments for Christmas trees out of wood shavings. He loved to carve little birds and to paint them in all their bright colors. He taught us to really look at the piece of wood we were carving and to think carefully about the bird. I think he loved the birds and forests as much as his own home and family.

{ Part Four }

SKY ABOVE

Wind, Clouds, Stars, and Sun

EATHER is one of the great dramas of the world, and in my corner of Wisconsin, it was always a concern of everyone. We paid attention to each chance change in the daily patterns. At the lake, learning to recognize changes in the weather was as important as knowing how to swim was for us to grow up safely. Summer, when we were there, was the wet season, and the storms were necessary for growing tall Wisconsin corn. But to me those summer storms were more. I loved them — in fact, I looked forward to them and relished them. Rainy days were cozy with fireplace fires, marshmallow roasts, card games, and time for the piano, mandolin, ukulele, and banjos.

Full-blown electrical storms were much more than just rain. They meant no electricity. They meant no telephone. They meant running and racing to secure boats so they wouldn't be battered, to turn the canoe upside down in the grass, to bring in the porch pillows, and to close windows. The great screened porches upstairs and down had huge canvas shades that could be lowered as protection from storms, and it was always an exercise in speedy coordination to get them lowered and secured ahead of the hardest wind

We watched the lightning dance around the lake.

and rain. One time when I was still too small, I was assigned one whole canvas by myself. It was huge, and the wind blew so hard that I went sailing almost to the ceiling as I tried to control it.

If the storm was at night, it meant going to bed by candlelight. How scary it was to get to the first landing of the stairs. The great stuffed deer head there seemed even more huge. As the candle flickered, his shadow moved and his glass eyes seemed real. If there was a clap of thunder at that minute, it was a real temptation to become a sissy then and there! There were no ceilings upstairs so the storm's lashings were all the more resounding on the roof.

We cousins would watch wide-eyed as the lightning danced around the lake, sometimes splitting a tree, sometimes striking a boat, but mostly tearing monumental clouds in two with its zigzag of flame lighting the whole sky. We knew what it could do. We had a horse whose hindquarters had been cleaved by lightning and an aunt whose heel was burned off by it. I have stood in the kitchen and seen it dance in a complete circle around the room while I was watching from the center of the floor. It is so mysterious, so powerful, so free that more than fear I was, and still am, inspired to awe.

Our weather in Wisconsin was dramatic in other ways too. The summer my cousin came from Texas was the first year I knew about tornadoes. Until then they were only something I had read about in school books. But patterns change and that summer produced a real tornado. None of us felt just right that day, and our uneasiness grew as the sky became yellow and the birds stopped singing. It became so quiet that when my aunt said we should fix the canvas, the sound of her voice was earsplitting. It also seemed unthinkable. There was no wind — no leaf or grass stirred. Why prepare for a storm? Suddenly things happened! Just as we turned to shut the windows against the beating from possible wind and rain, one by one the panes of glass tumbled out and onto the grass

119

outside. The air pressure inside the house had become greater than that out-of-doors! Wind began to rage, but we weren't allowed to go batten down the boats. Trees were yanked out of the ground as if by a huge, invisible hand, and many things were destroyed. We discovered after it passed that it had come in a path leaving behind a ravaged and destroyed countryside. Fortunately we had been on the very outside edge of the tornado.

⌡{Danger on the Ice}⌠

Nothing was ever insignificant about the weather. From my earliest memory, I knew we were all its puppets, especially out-of-doors. As we cousins grew, our grownups carefully taught us, and we learned from experience. Life on the lake had its own rules and the weather ruled over most of them. Our round-bottomed rowboat and canoe were as dangerous as hot-blooded horses. Being out too far on a windy day had temptations, though. It was hard to manage rowing and paddling in the deep troughs of water crested with white caps. But it was also exciting, and imagination soared with each triumph. We learned daily and grew to scorn the weekender who stayed out too long on a windy day and didn't know how to get to shore safely. We saw my mother swim to save a drowning weekend boater on two occasions, and we saw others who could not save themselves or be saved.

The winter weather was just as tyrannical as that of summer. When we went to Mill Lake during the winter, we brought little sails, ice hockey sticks, plenty of hot thermos bottles, and firewood for toasty bonfires in the snow. It was glorious to catch the wind in your sail, let it pull you on ice skates all the way across the lake and then to tack back using all your skill. My skates were figure skates, but the boys had "hard toes" for hockey, and the hockey games and skating

120

races went on for hours. When we were old enough, we learned to sail my uncle's iceboat. Iceboats are very fast and dangerous. Sometimes the sailing speed was so great, they hardly touched the ice, leaving the driver with little control, but lots of excitement.

Iceboating was even more exciting in our neighboring lake, Lake Geneva. In summer inland races, called regattas, were held on Lake Geneva. In winter as soon as the ice was thick enough, courses were marked out and the iceboat races began. As the lake ice expanded, fissures (cracks) sometimes opened up in the middle like huge rips in the ice sheath covering the lake. Naturally, these were very dangerous to skaters and boaters.

When I first learned to sail an iceboat by myself, the boat I used was a single seater and made for speed. I thought it was wonderful. I climbed in and the minute I was seated, its big sail filled with wind and away we went, boat and me, skimming on its trim runners and barely touching the ice under us. My uncle clocked the speed at better than 50 miles per hour as I sped past him. Suddenly I approached open water. How had I come across so much lake so fast! I stretched for more control of the halyards, and as I did, my hood blew off, my coat unbuttoned, and my scarf blew right across my face. I couldn't see a thing with the scarf plastered across my eyes. All I could do was feel! Somehow managing to keep the sail full of wind, I hauled and hauled until the racer was up on one runner but coming around and pointed toward home in a sharp tack. Whew!

The woolly scarf was snatched away to the winds, and I gradually maneuvered back to my uncles and cousins who were waiting turns. It was ten degrees below zero, but I was so excited I felt no cold. That night was the last I remembered for a long time. I woke up coughing and miserable, and my blankets and pajamas were wringing wet. I was sure my head was breaking into a million pieces at least. Mother gave me

121

hot lemonade and tried to comfort me, but when I was next aware of her, it was many days later. She told me I had pneumonia and was not to try to get up. How could I get up with the whole weight of the world on my chest? To this day I still cough all the way down to my boots when winter comes. I don't complain though, because I can still see that open water in my mind's eye, and I know exactly how lucky I am.

Iceboating and skating weren't the only things going on at the lake. Fishing for ciscos was one of the special features of winter. It required planning and a good knowledge of the lake too. Little shacks were built and hauled out to spots where fishermen thought there might be fish under the ice. Inside the floorless shack, a couple of holes were punched through the ice, and chairs and stools were installed for fishermen to perch on. Sometimes small pails containing coal fires or kerosene burners were added on especially cold days. Ciscos are meaty white fish much like a trout. They like pure cold water and are hard to catch in summer because they stay down too deep. Naturally, it's always a game between fish and fisherman to find which lure will make the catch.

One time when I was still too young to go ice fishing, my uncle came to our house. He was out of breath and his errand seemed urgent. It seemed that cisco fish were biting, and he had no yellow beads which were the successful lure of the day. My mother rummaged through her button box and sewing supplies to see if she had any to give him. Then she remembered that I had a pretty bracelet made of, wouldn't you know, yellow beads. And they were just the right size to string above a fishhook. Without a backward look, my uncle took them, flung himself out the door, and clatter-trapped down the road to the lake in his old fishing car. Of course promises were made about returning the beads, but promises sometimes have a way of being forgotten. In all my growing-up days, I can't remember wanting to have or even to wear *any* bracelet, much less a gaudy yellow one. Just the

Suddenly I approached open water.

same, it was mine and those old fish should have chosen some other color — red for instance.

For me the ice was like lightning; it had power and mystery. It roared and clapped like thunder. It, too, was dangerous and fascinating. The birds and animals seemed to know the exact moment when the ice on the lake would first freeze, and they were almost never trapped and frozen into it. Once in a while we would rescue a duck or goose that had lingered too long, but at our end of the lake there often remained an open place in the ice before the final freeze. Ducks and geese would gather there during their late fall visits to nearby grain fields, and it was a magnificent sight to see the leaders signal "time to go." Sometimes it took a whole day for them to get organized and such a noise they made! The birds would circle until the last group had taken off and usually the lake froze that very same night.

As winter progressed and the ice expanded, it pushed and pushed against the breakwaters, and by spring the pileup of ice became gigantic. In shallower lakes, very thick ice threatens the fish; but mostly fish seem to know — just as birds do — what's coming and what to do. In spring and fall the water in lakes "turns over." The top and bottom water changes place when the top water becomes cold and heavy. For a while when it's turning, the waters mix up completely, and that is some of the best fishing time in deep lakes. There is a saying:

> *When the wind is from the north,*
> *fisherman don't set forth;*
> *Wind from the east, fish bite the least;*
> *Wind from the west, fish bite best;*
> *But wind from the south* blows *the bait*
> *in fishes' mouths!*

Since rainstorms and winds in our hemisphere tend to come from the southeast, it seems that fish know that the low

124

pressures that accompany stormy weather are good times for feeding! It has always been surprising to me to find that people know so much less than fish and birds do!

⸱[Riding the Wind]⸱

The winds can tell us many stories, but we need to *see* them and hear them. We have a family of red-tailed hawks that live in the woods nearby. Each year one of the great pleasures of spring is to see the squawking, squeaking, screeching baby hawks as they learn to fly. First we see them being led from their nest to perch on a nearby snag and then back to their nest. Next, they sail. Their nest tree is on a little ridge, and their mother leads them flying toward the creek. It's all downward gliding, so it's pretty easy. Once they get to the creek, mother redtail shows them a place where the air is always moving upward. When their glide down is accurate, they can catch the updraft and gain enough altitude to sail back to their nest. Nearly always one of the baby birds misses the return flight while its brothers and sisters sail safely, if clumsily, back to their landing.

It's a noisy, wearing day for mother redtail, but each year it's the same. How does she know that wind is there? We can only guess. Looking at the situation, I can only add up three possible factors. Can you guess what they are?

The first is that there is always movement of air between masses of land and water. Second, the nest is on a ridge, so air would be moving up or down or around it. Finally woods would heat the air around them to different temperatures than rocks and water so that would cause air to move too. If all of these movements came together, maybe they go up, and mother redtail has discovered that they do!

The sound of the wind is another important storyteller. Sometimes it makes hollow noises and sometimes just secret,

125

{ Kinds of Clouds }

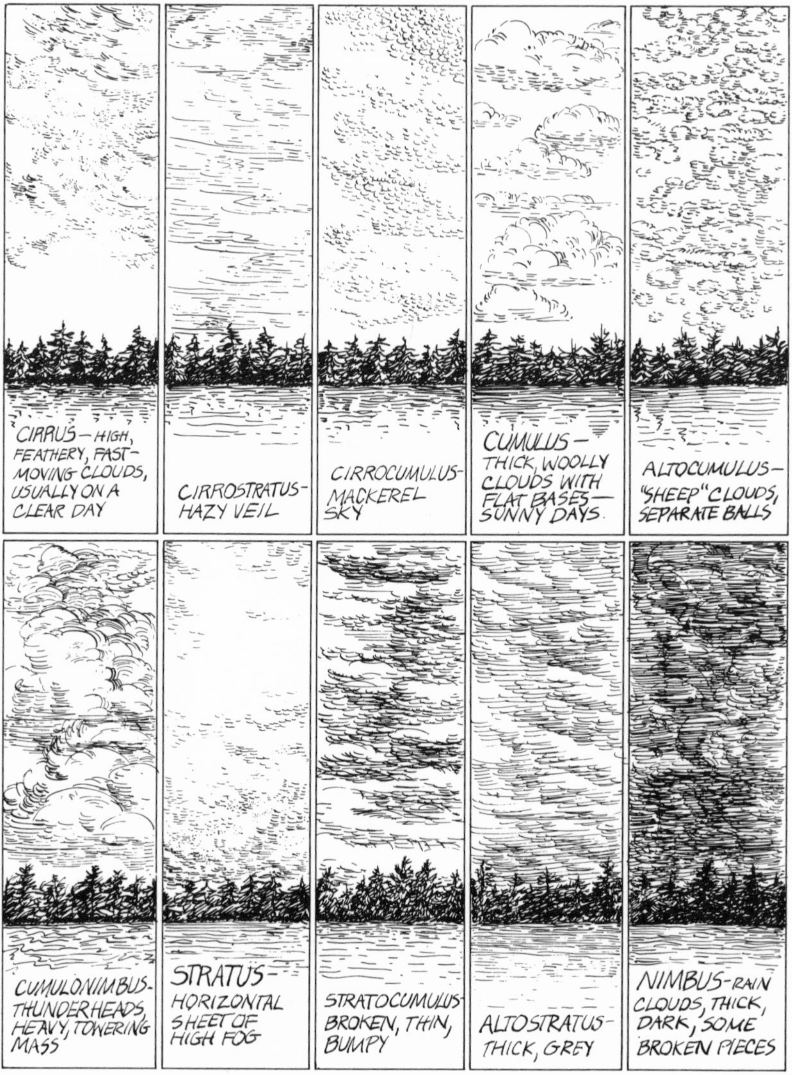

CIRRUS — HIGH, FEATHERY, FAST-MOVING CLOUDS, USUALLY ON A CLEAR DAY

CIRROSTRATUS — HAZY VEIL

CIRROCUMULUS — MACKEREL SKY

CUMULUS — THICK, WOOLLY CLOUDS WITH FLAT BASES — SUNNY DAYS.

ALTOCUMULUS — "SHEEP" CLOUDS, SEPARATE BALLS

CUMULONIMBUS — THUNDERHEADS, HEAVY, TOWERING MASS

STRATUS — HORIZONTAL SHEET OF HIGH FOG

STRATOCUMULUS — BROKEN, THIN, BUMPY

ALTOSTRATUS — THICK, GREY

NIMBUS — RAIN CLOUDS, THICK, DARK, SOME BROKEN PIECES

rustling noises. We all pay attention if it howls and rages, but the sounds we hear every day differ, too, according to the air and how it's moving. Usually if a train whistle or horn sounds hollow, it is a sign of possible rain, and the air *is* hollow with little pressure. On those days you may notice that everything sounds close and loud: traffic near your house, voices a distance away, especially over water. On noisy days people become cross and nervous. The air is low and it's quite likely to storm on those days. The nervous rustling of leaves, the riffles across the lake surface, the switching of breezes from north to east to south and back again to southeast, all of these whispers and changes tell. A door bangs suddenly, a curtain billows into the room, a porch lamp creaks on its hinges. It's the wind, telling.

Did you know you could even look at the wind? Pick out a chimney that smokes and watch it every day. One day the smoke goes straight up. That means there is no wind, but maybe one day the smoke goes straight out at the side of the chimney. Wind — but what wind? The smoke goes along with the wind, so it's easy to discover by looking what wind it is. What if the smoke is all broken up and not going in any direction at all? That's probably a good day to look at the clouds, too. Putting the information from both of them together, you can find out what the weather story is.

Clouds can give you almost as much information as wind. Clouds are the storm signals of the sky. There are four kinds and each one has a job to do. If all goes right, the cloud you see can deliver either a storm or rain or snow or fog or bright sunshiny days. Their names are cirrus, cumulus, nimbus, and stratus. Each of them has a family and since they are important, I'll tell you their names too. Before weather was a science, people invented names for some of the clouds they knew. Some of them stayed well known, like *mare's tail* for wispy cirrus, and *mackerel* after a popular fish for the cirrocumulus. To me mackerel clouds look more like a sky full

127

of wool that hasn't been washed. It isn't hard to imagine how people began to give names to clouds.

I suppose everyone knows that people used to have weather gods that they prayed to. There is a story about a mission teacher who was trying to get his converts to stop praying to so many gods. He told them only to pray for rain when the wind was from the south! He did that to get them to believe in his own god because he knew storms always came from the south. People have prayed to sun gods all through the ages, and when you think about it, it's really hard to separate the sun from everything that has to do with us on the earth. Until we knew more about the vastness of space and the sun's place in it, the sun certainly must have seemed like a god.

One of my teachers once had us do an experiment you might like to try. It will help you to understand our delicate relationship to the sun. Our earth is like a ball and is moving through space very fast. Take a ball about the size of your fist and tie a string around it securely. Now standing in one place, start to swing that ball at the end of the string around and around your head. You will feel the ball pull harder and harder against the string end you are holding. You are like the sun in relation to that ball which represents the earth. If the string broke or something caused it to move unevenly, the ball would fall or spin out of control. That's what would happen to us, if that miracle of pull from the sun changed. So you can see why people began to think of power even beyond the power of the sun itself.

⊰Sun Time, Sun Signals⊱

People use the power of the sun in many ways. They always have. Before the ancient scientist Archimedes invented the gears that made clocks possible, there were all sorts of other methods for telling time. The sundial is one,

{How to Make an Equatorial Sundial}

Materials needed: board for the dial surface about 12 inches by 12 inches, pencil and string or drawing compass, broom handle or spike, protractor, road maps, level.

While sundials are not the very best method for telling time, they can teach us many things — not only about time, but also about how people can use their own ability to observe and see their world. For example, in order to make a sundial, the direction of north has to be found.

Can you imagine how early man found north in the daytime without a compass? One way to do this is to measure the shadows cast by the sun. Use a level surface and draw three circles on it, one inside the other, all having the same midpoint.

At the center mount a perfectly vertical upright, such as a tall spike or a cut-off broom handle. The shadows that the vertical makes can be used to measure both noon and north.

Early on a sunny morning, mark the place where the shadow of the upright stick crosses the biggest circle. Later, on the same day, watch and mark where the shadow falls across the circle in the late afternoon. Make a straight line connecting these two points.

Repeat the same process for the next two days on the two inner circles. Do this at the same times each day. Mark the center on each of the three connecting lines and draw a line along those three center points. They will line up perfectly if the vertical is true. This line should point to north and mark noon solar time.

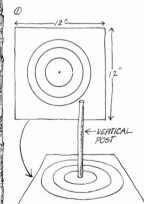

①

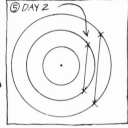

② EARLY, DAY 1

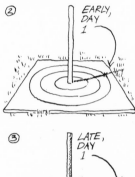

③ LATE, DAY 1

④ CONNECT THE TWO MARKS ON THE LARGEST CIRCLE WITH A LINE.

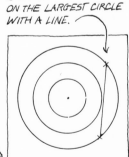

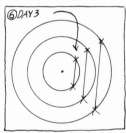

⑤ DAY 2

⑥ DAY 3

⑦ THIS LINE POINTS NORTH AND TO NOON, SOLAR TIME

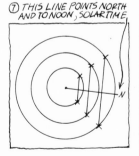

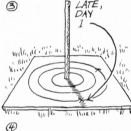

With the help of a watch, you can mark similar shadow points every 15 minutes. Or you may complete your sundial by using the degrees of latitude for your location and a protractor to measure them on your dial.

The latitude is important for measuring by the sun because our earth tips a little.

The *vertical* of your dial represents the tipping angle of the earth or *axis*. The level surface the dial is on represents the *plane* of the earth's surface. As such a plane moves away from the North or South poles toward the equator that plane changes its angle in relation to the equator from parallel at the poles to perpindicular at the equator itself.

If you are somewhere between the north pole and the equator, like I am, you must find out where! And that is called your angle of latitude. If you get out a road map of your area, you will find degrees (of angles) of latitude on the side edges of it, so check to see where your location is on the map, and run your finger across to the side margin and find the place that your degree of latitude is written. Subtract that degree from 90 degrees (the vertical degree the equator represents to the axis). Now, keeping the shadow of the broom handle pointing north, tilt the dial surface to that angle (or that many degrees) from horizontal and your dial will be accurate for your location.

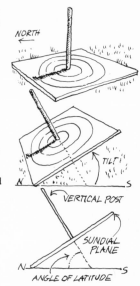

Your finished dial face will look like this:

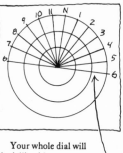

Your whole dial will look like this:

Of course there are many other ways to make sundials and through the years when they were used, they became mathematical feats. The same is true of hourglasses and water clocks. The basic principles were fairly obvious to any person who could observe, but the superb and really intricate refinements people made in time pieces, especially for royalty, were amazing.

A little pocket sundial, called a journey ring, was built and can still be purchased for use today. It can only have come about because people paid attention to the sun all year, and many people made many corrections. Like the spinning wheel, the real reason we gave up the old style ways was for speed and convenience, not because the old way was not good.

Where I live in the mountains, when someone asks how many miles it is to a distant place, we are apt to answer in hours instead of miles because that is really what matters here. Sometimes, no matter how convenient our new tools are, it is good to be in touch with nature's place in our plans: in this case, range after range of mountains.

An equatorial sundial can demonstrate well how our tipping earth is in very special relation and balance with our sun. Perhaps as you learn about that relationship, you will help us all to learn how we can find even more help from the sun in the future.

and when I was little, nearly everyone's garden had a sundial to indicate time. Sundials only work on sunny days and during daylight, so you can see why people looked for other methods to keep track of the time. Ancient people were accustomed to the natural world around them and turned to it first for their answers. The sun's shadows, the night sky, and dripping water were all used as indicators of time for thousands of years before we turned to mechanical devices.

Besides telling time, the sun can tell you what time of year it is by its position above the horizon. As I raced to dress by the warm-air register on dark winter mornings, I used to wonder if people in China were taking sun baths in my sun. After all, that's where it went. Then I learned to watch a certain nearby roof and the position of the sun in relation to its peak and chimney. When day-by-day the sun appeared lower and lower in the sky, I started counting the days until Christmas. When the sun moved back up, higher and higher in the sky, I counted the days left of school. Soon we would move to the lake.

We learned the trick of sending signals with sunlight too. We had great times learning the Morse code. I made certain grownups pretty irritated with my tap-taps. The most important code signal was the universal one for distress, the letters SOS, which originally meant "save our ship." When you go hiking or camping, there is always the chance of becoming separated from your friends or lost and sometimes injured too. We had a certain tune we whistled when we couldn't see each other. But if you're ever really lost, it's a good idea to know how to flash an SOS.

If you have lost direction, the sun can help again. Just as it's helpful to know about the moss growing more on the north side of trees, it's also helpful to know that in the Northern Hemisphere, or anywhere in this country or Canada, the sun makes its journey through the southern part of the sky. In the morning, it starts rising in the east and in the evening it sets

131

How to Make an SOS Signal and a Heliograph

Materials needed: wood for stand and frame mount, frames, mirror, string, cardboard, scissors.

SOS (. . . — — — . . .) may be sent by a simple heliograph (sun helio) made by using something shiny. The idea is to cause sunlight to be reflected in a flash. The flash can even be the world famous SOS; three shorts, three longs, three shorts, if you really need help. The flash is directed toward an area where help may be attracted — even at an airplane! Other distress signals are three shots fired or three smoke fires in a row.

The heliograph has more uses. It is a way people use the sun to save their own time and energy. By constucting a simple revolving stand and mounting three frames at equal intervals, you can flash messages over great distances.

PLYWOOD SCREWED TO POST SO HELIOGRAPH CAN REVOLVE

A mirror is mounted in the first frame, and the frame is hung so that it can swing to catch the light. The second frame is bisected by string fastened at each corner which makes a cross in the middle. Then a mat with a 3-by-3-inch-square hole cut from it is also mounted in this frame. The third frame has a 2-by-2-inch hole. The three frames are mounted in a row as shown.

FRAME 1

MIRROR; MOUNTED TO TILT AND CATCH THE SUN.

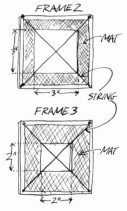

FRAME 2

MAT

STRING

FRAME 3

MAT

A tiny bit of the backing is scraped off from the center of the mirror. Look through that hole and line up the place where the strings cross with the object set to receive your flash. The mirror should be tilted to capture the sunlight, which should be reflected directly toward the object.

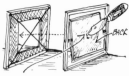

SCRATCH TINY HOLE IN CENTER OF MIRROR BACK

If the sun is not at the best angle to be reflected from the mirror, another mirror can be used to reflect onto the first mirror. Signals can be sent by blocking the light with a piece of cardboard in front of the third frame. You block it to make short and long flashes of light.

TO MAKE FLASHES—

PASS A BOARD IN FRONT OF PIN-HOLE IN MIRROR

To mount the heliograph, we used a fallen, straight branch with a scrap of plywood screwed to the top. The branch was about as tall as my shoulder.

We could flash messages to cousins in boats on the lake. Heliographs are a great help to surveyors when they are measuring land.

132

in the west. In winter it's stingy and doesn't go so high east and west, but in the summer the sun stretches the days and travels in a big swing. Even so, at noon it's almost always just about south; so if you're heading north, turn your back on it, and keep your shadow in front of you.

Finding their way has always been a concern of people everywhere for as long as anyone can remember. Can you imagine yourself setting out in a little sailboat across an unknown ocean with only the sun and stars to guide you? Ancient people knew how to use the stars and the sun as guides, and we can too. The stars, like the sun, have always been there and are a part of our natural world.

At the lake we cousins used to go out at night to a nearby golf course and gather night crawlers (big worms) from the smooth, damp greens to use for fishing the next day. Because it was summer, the sky was very special and exciting. We would make bets on who would be the first to see the northern lights (aurora borealis) that year, and we would wish and wish on the many falling stars we saw.

Later one of my cousins worked summers at Yerkes Observatory near home, taking pictures of stars, and he taught me about a whole new and unbelievable world from nebulae to black holes! The myths and magic that have grown up about the night sky can't begin to compare with the reality, which is the most mysterious of all. We cousins used to have arguments about how big is big, and I'm sure the Milky Way was usually the inspiration. Who can comprehend how big the Milky Way is and then another and another? Seven hundred years ago, a man named Teng Mu said, "How unreasonable it would be to suppose that, besides the heavens and earth which we can see, there are no other heavens and no other earths." Do you agree?

Sometimes I used to lie on my back on the pier or in a boat or in the meadow on a summer night. These places were ideal for speculating about stars and for learning them. Of course,

133

the sky changes every month, but its changes are orderly and predictable. Though the whole skyful of stars wheeled and changed, the tiny North Star always stayed put. It was very pleasant to be able to look up and find it just where I expected to find it — in line with the Big Dipper pointers. From May through June we watched and loved the evening star, Venus, at Mill Lake. It set with a quiet beauty and grace, almost like a Madonna. Sometimes it was reflected in the water with its own silver path. Cold Jupiter always seemed reliably brilliant and red Mars — my star, I thought — could be easily located and distinguished from all the others. My brother assured me that there were important differences between stars and planets, but at that time it didn't matter to me. They were all assuring, stable, friendly, and part of why I liked the night.

As I continued to learn, it became even more comforting to me to realize that what could be seen is such a tiny bit of all that is out there. If the powers that were so great and important could keep everything here *and* there *and* beyond there in working order, then our job seemed to become pretty simple by comparison. Probably this gets down to figuring out how we fit in, how well we learn the laws of nature; and, at least at night, it's somehow possible to believe we can get pretty good at being a part of it all.

⟨Flying by Flashlight⟩

People have always used stars to guide them at night. Of course, finding your way has first of all to do with using good sense and all your knowledge of how things work out-of-doors; but, at night, if you can see stars, you can always find direction if you know one thing. That one bit of knowledge is how to find the small, faint, all-important North Star, Polaris. People have invented stories all through the ages about how to find this star and what it means.

134

Sometimes I used to lie on my back in a boat on a summer night.

The seven-star figure known to most of us today as the Big Dipper is also known as the Bear, The Great Bear, or Ursa Major; and the Little Dipper is known as Ursa Minor. These two figures travel all year long in a circle around the North Star, going all the way from right side up to upside down, always with the Big Dipper pointing to the tip of the Little Dipper's handle, which is the North Star. In our hemisphere, the North Star can be seen from any location, all the way down to the equator where it will disappear behind the earth's curve. It appears in the sky as many degrees above the horizon as you are from the equator.

When I was still a young woman in school, I learned to fly an airplane. Soon, it came time for me to learn to fly at night. The lightweight planes we flew in those early days were often ill-equipped by today's standards, and sometimes they were not maintained very well. The plane that was available to me for night flight was an old Taylor Craft. The only reason for using it was because the lights in its tail and wings actually did light up for other people to see. Most of the other planes around had no such luxuries. In order to see the instrument panel, it was necessary to carry a flashlight because there were no lights inside of the plane. The first few times I began to fly at night, I had reason to be forever grateful for all the many nights I had spent in other years memorizing the stars and being comfortable about the night. Those first few flights were on moonless, totally black nights.

For a pilot to fly without any instruments or any visible horizon is very difficult. At first I saw strange constellations and weird "falling stars." Finally by flying with my left hand and holding the flashlight with my right hand to see the instruments, I made a 360-degree circle until I could sort out the North Star, old Polaris. Knowing what time of year it was, I had a fair idea of how high Polaris was above the horizon. From that I figured out that the strange constellations below Polaris *must* be the bright lights of

136

towns and highways. Now when I'm in the air at night, it's a wonder to me how I could not have known they were the lights of towns because it seems so obvious. But then it was the very first time I had ever been *in* the night sky, and it was a different experience than being on the earth and looking out at it. I was just one more of the millions of people who have discovered what that star can mean for safe navigation.

The constancy of that little star has ever amazed people. Great leaders have sought to identify themselves with its character. One story about an Indian chief is worth telling because it says so well what people of all time have felt. The chief, Smohalla, was describing his own beautiful and colorful flag. He explained, "This is my flag and it represents the world. God told me to look after my people. All are my people. There are four ways in the world, North, South, East, and West. I have been all those ways. This is the center. I live here. The red spot (in the flag) is my heart. Everyone can see it. The yellow grass grows everywhere around this place (yellow on flag). Green mountains are far away all around the world. There is only water beyond, salt water. The blue (a strip on the flag) is the sky, and the star is the North Star. That star never changes; it is always in the same place. I keep my heart on that star. I never change."

{How to Spin Raw Wool}

Materials needed: spindle, wool yarn, raw wool.

It is thought that the idea for spinning first came from people noticing how some animals and plants made fluffy balls of waste which stuck together. Some early man may have rolled a bit of this downy stuff on his thigh with the palm of his hand. Doing a lot of it made a pile, so he wrapped it on a stick.

When the stick became troublesome, a weight was added to the bottom of it. This eventually became what was known for thousands of years as a drop spindle. In many parts of the world, it is still the only spinning method used. Actually a spinning wheel is another version of this ancient technique.

You can make a drop spindle for yourself using a slender straight stick, such as a dowel, 12 inches long, and adding a weight to the bottom. A potato makes a good weight, though not very permanent. People have spun everything from gold to dog hair on drop spindles, but wool is the best for learning.

To spin wool, the dowel is strung as shown in the drawing with a piece of fuzzy yarn for the string. A hank of combed wool is held in your left hand about shoulder high and palm up.

Your fuzzy yarn end is laid on top of this wool and your thumb closes over it, holding the two together. The right hand takes the top of the dowel and gives it a twist like a top. The fuzzy yarn hangs, full length, straight down from the left hand to the dowel top.

Once the spindle is set turning, let go and with your right hand reach to the raw wool and draw some down around the string. Keep the end of the fuzzy yarn in place gently with the wool to be pulled through about 5 inches.

Then with your right hand, spin the dowel again and tighten your left thumb on the wool and yarn to control the spinning. This pulling down is called the draft. The spinning motion of the dowel will twist up the fuzzy yarn which should be catching the wool as you pull the wool out from your hand.

When you close your thumb, you are preventing the spin from going into all the wool at once. Repeat: spin dowel, loosen clasp of left hand, pull wool, close left thumb, repeat, keeping spindle going until all your wool is spun out of your hand. It can be wound up on the dowel and your own spun yarn can be the starting fuzzy yarn for the next bit of combed wool.

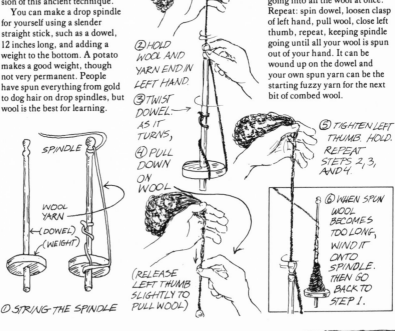

RAW WOOL — WOOL YARN END

② HOLD WOOL AND YARN END IN LEFT HAND.

③ TWIST DOWEL: AS IT TURNS,

④ PULL DOWN ON WOOL

(RELEASE LEFT THUMB SLIGHTLY TO PULL WOOL)

SPINDLE

WOOL YARN

(DOWEL) (WEIGHT)

① STRING THE SPINDLE

⑤ TIGHTEN LEFT THUMB. HOLD. REPEAT STEPS 2, 3, AND 4.

⑥ WHEN SPUN WOOL BECOMES TOO LONG, WIND IT ONTO SPINDLE. THEN GO BACK TO STEP 1.

138

{Lore and More}

THE SAYING "How can we know where we are going, if we don't know where we have been" applies to many parts of our lives. Most surely it applies to the knowledge of making useful things. Several of the projects mentioned in earlier chapters have to do with basic crafts; that is crafts that have their origins and roots in ancient times, crafts that have served mankind continuously and well with very little change.

Early people, even if they lived in large towns, were aware of the out-of-doors and their dependency on nature. In this century we are still dependent on the ways of nature, but we have also found clever ways of hiding that fact from ourselves. As we increasingly ignore nature, we begin to do something else. We behave as though nothing has ever happened before *now,* the present. Our ability to *see* our world has become so changed that we invent and reinvent things people have already and always done.

Perhaps what was a necessity at one time may now be crafted only for beauty or pleasure, and this can give a wonderful new freedom. This new freedom makes it all the more important to understand our place in the long tradition and to value what has gone before us. Understanding of old techniques can give insight. Traditional ways can also add richness and challenge to our efforts. For example, years ago I taught myself to spin wool into yarn. I taught myself because I could find no one to teach me, even though I could remember seeing Indians patiently sitting and spinning on simple stick-and-whorl spinners. At the time I wanted to learn, spinning was an art already given over to machines. It was intriguing to me to learn about the ancient Egyptians.

139

They achieved unbelievable cloth. Some of the pieces found in tombs cannot be imitated by our best machines. I was also surprised to find out that the early American settlers could spin as well as any machine. One girl in the South was recorded to have spun one pound of cotton into a thread 115 miles long. The fineness of her achievement was not considered unusual!

The reason hand spinning was given up was not because of quality. It was given up because the flying shuttle was invented, and power looms made it possible to use great quantities of yarn and so make more cloth. The days when your own sheep gave you enough wool to spin into yarn for the family clothing and blankets were over as soon as the shuttle was invented. The man who brought his loom around from one household to another throughout the year stopped coming, and wool and cotton were sent directly to the big mills.

The earliest peoples figured out how to spin and weave, to make baskets and then pottery, to use hides and preserve them as leather. They learned to hunt, first with crude clubs and rocks, and then with bows and arrows. Today we still use woven cloth, baskets, pots, and leather; and everywhere in the world the bow and arrow are used for sport, if not for hunting, and are still enjoyed. These basic crafts are as old as man. They use natural materials and require our keenest senses. These crafts can continue to give us a fresh understanding of our world and how it came to be, as well as unending pleasure in mastering them.

The directions for making grandmother's rush mat were for a simple article woven by hand. They included the two parts of everything that is woven. These two parts are called the *warp* and the *weft*. That is why some people call basket-making *weaving,* for baskets contain the structured fiber, or warp, and the filler, or weft. However, when you become interested in weaving, you soon find that today we refer to

(*Text continued on page 144.*)

How to Make a Simple Loom

Materials needed: Popsicle sticks, wood strips, hand drill, glue, dowel or branch, thread or yarn to weave with. Optional: shuttle.

A simple beginning loom may be made for weaving such things as belts or table mats. First you must construct heddles. In this case, they will be anchored in their frame and will be rigid. A rigid heddle made of wood or plastic can be purchased, but satisfactory ones can be constructed out of narrow pieces of wood, such as Popsicle sticks.

Pierce each piece with a hole like a paper punch makes. Put the hole in exactly the same spot on each piece of wood. Make a lightweight frame of 1-by-1/8-inch (or 1-by-3/16-inch) strips of wood. Cut four pieces the width desired for the weaving you plan plus 2 inches. For example, frame pieces for a 12 inch wide weaving will be 14 inches wide. Now you are ready to glue the hole sticks to the frame. Place the two frame strips parallel and flat separated from each other by the same distance as the length of the hole sticks. Lay the sticks on top of the frame pieces, leaving a space between each Popsicle stick about the same size as the holes you cut. Make sure the tops and bottoms line up smoothly along the edges of the frame pieces and that the holes are all in a row. Glue the sticks to the frame pieces. Now glue the top frame pieces to cover the hole sticks exactly matching the position of the underneath frame so that the finished heddle frame appears the same on both sides.

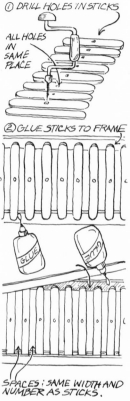

① DRILL HOLES IN STICKS

ALL HOLES IN SAME PLACE

② GLUE STICKS TO FRAME

SPACES: SAME WIDTH AND NUMBER AS STICKS.

Next measure and count the warp material. The warp runs the length of the weaving and is the base of the woven material. To measure the warp, decide how long you want your material to be and then add ½ yard to that measure. Then count the number of heddles and heddle spaces. A loom built to weave material that is 12 inches wide can have about 48 holes and spaces.

If your material is going to be a yard long, add ½ yard, giving you a length measure of 1½ yards times the 48 holes and spaces you counted earlier. *But* don't do any cutting, yet.

What you want now is to have one big loop of yarn that measures 3 yards around or 1½ yards if pulled tight. The loop will be made up of 24 circlings of 3 yards each in one continuous loop. Tie a string tightly around one end of this loop of warp material.

③ MAKE THE WARP.
ADD ½ YD. TO EACH LENGTH OF STRING BEYOND DESIRED MATERIAL LENGTH

TIE

CUT UNTIED END.

Carefully cut the end of the loop that is opposite the string tie, so that you now have 48 equal lengths of yarn tied together. This is your warp. Put each warp thread through either a heddle hole or a heddle space, one after the other. It is important to fan the warp threads out and start at one side of your loom and of the warp threads and work, one-by-one, to the other side. This way your warp threads will not crisscross.

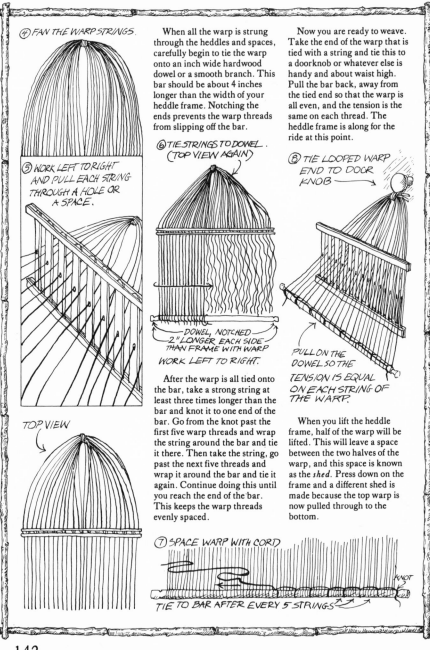

④ FAN THE WARP STRINGS.

⑤ WORK LEFT TO RIGHT
AND PULL EACH STRING
THROUGH A HOLE OR
A SPACE.

TOP VIEW

When all the warp is strung through the heddles and spaces, carefully begin to tie the warp onto an inch wide hardwood dowel or a smooth branch. This bar should be about 4 inches longer than the width of your heddle frame. Notching the ends prevents the warp threads from slipping off the bar.

⑥ TIE STRINGS TO DOWEL.
(TOP VIEW AGAIN)

— DOWEL, NOTCHED
2" LONGER EACH SIDE
THAN FRAME WITH WARP
WORK LEFT TO RIGHT.

After the warp is all tied onto the bar, take a strong string at least three times longer than the bar and knot it to one end of the bar. Go from the knot past the first five warp threads and wrap the string around the bar and tie it there. Then take the string, go past the next five threads and wrap it around the bar and tie it again. Continue doing this until you reach the end of the bar. This keeps the warp threads evenly spaced.

Now you are ready to weave. Take the end of the warp that is tied with a string and tie this to a doorknob or whatever else is handy and about waist high. Pull the bar back, away from the tied end so that the warp is all even, and the tension is the same on each thread. The heddle frame is along for the ride at this point.

⑧ TIE LOOPED WARP
END TO DOOR
KNOB →

PULL ON THE
DOWEL SO THE
TENSION IS EQUAL
ON EACH STRING OF
THE WARP.

When you lift the heddle frame, half of the warp will be lifted. This will leave a space between the two halves of the warp, and this space is known as the *shed*. Press down on the frame and a different shed is made because the top warp is now pulled through to the bottom.

⑦ SPACE WARP WITH CORD

KNOT

TIE TO BAR AFTER EVERY 5 STRINGS

142

A length of *weft* material, which is the filler or what you use to weave with, is moved through these sheds, and this is how cloth is made. Start with the frame pulled up, and put the weft in through the shed from left to right. Leave a tail of weft thread hanging down on the left side of the warp. Next press the heddle frame down creating the other shed and put the weft material through this shed from right to left.

After each up or each down move, the heddle frame is pulled gently but firmly forward forming an even line before the weft thread is put in through the next shed.

The weft thread can be wound into a small ball or onto a shuttle. This way the weft can be unwound as it is needed. Another little trick that makes this loom easier to use is to tie a sash around one end of the bar, bring it around behind your waist, and tie it onto the other end of the bar. This makes it possible to keep a good tension on the warp as you weave.

KEEP WEFT IN A BALL OR MAKE A SIMPLE CARDBOARD SHUTTLE.

DEVELOPED WEAVING

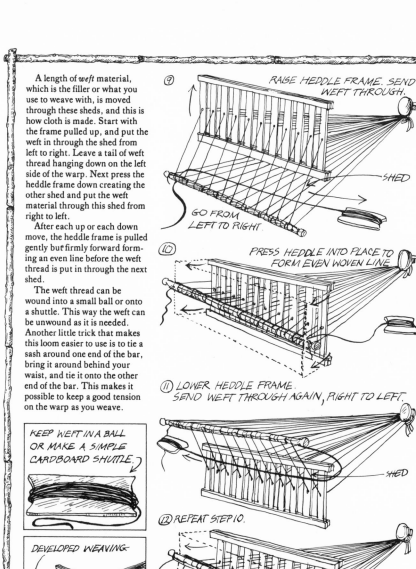

⑨ RAISE HEDDLE FRAME. SEND WEFT THROUGH.

SHED

GO FROM LEFT TO RIGHT.

⑩ PRESS HEDDLE INTO PLACE TO FORM EVEN WOVEN LINE

⑪ LOWER HEDDLE FRAME. SEND WEFT THROUGH AGAIN, RIGHT TO LEFT.

SHED

⑫ REPEAT STEP 10.

NOW BACK TO STEP 9.

143

two kinds of weaving: on-loom and off-loom. The differences have to do with the devices that the warp is built on and how the weft is worked through it. People have been weaving for thousands of years so you can imagine that there are many, many, many ways to go about weaving something.

There are a great number of things in the outdoors to weave with. Once you start, you may never stop. Sedge grass, pine needles, strips of cedar bark, willow stocks, cattail leaves, flax leaves: the list is endless. The warp is important in providing strength for your projects. Most five-and-ten stores supply cotton-rug warp string, but any stout, strong material will do — even wire. One time I unwound a copper dish-scrubbing mitt and added it here and there in a weaving for a special effect. Your own imagination is the only limitation when you begin to weave.

Weavings of Grass, Coils of Clay

About the time primitive people were finding out that hair and fur made fuzzy streamers which could be twisted, made strong, and even spun to extend the length and twist, they were also starting to use sticks and grass to construct containers. These containers or baskets were made to use in gathering and storing food. Early people wove rushes and sticks to make coverings for floors. It can be argued that basketmaking was the mother craft of both weaving and pottery. One thing that cannot be argued is the fact that baskets have never been made successfully by machine. As Osma Tod points out in her book, *Earth Basketry,* "it still takes a good eye and nimble fingers" to construct a basket.

My feeling about basketmaking is that it combines the best pleasures of both weaving and pottery, and it is less restrictive than either one. In each basket there is the opportunity for an almost unlimited exploration of natural materials and their

{How to Make Rush and Willow Baskets}

Materials needed: willow, rushes, knife or scissors.

Use willow which you have gathered in the spring, peeled, and allowed to dry, and now have soaked until pliable. Select pieces of the same diameter 3/16 inch to 1/4 inch. Take eight of these about 16 inches long and one a little over half that long (about 10 inches). Divide the eight into two groups of four, placing them side by side with ends even. Place one group over the other at right angles, holding both in your left hand between index finger and thumb.

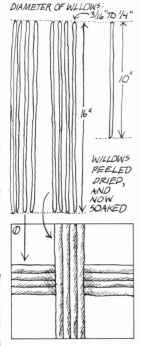

DIAMETER OF WLLOWS:
3/16" TO 1/4"

10"

16"

WILLOWS PEELED DRIED, AND NOW SOAKED

Now take a weaver which may be of smaller diameter but is cut as long as possible for you to work with; also keep the weaver the same size diameter throughout. Weave it under the four to the right and over the four on the bottom, under the four at the left, over, under, over, under, making two complete rounds.

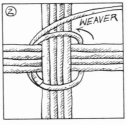

WEAVER

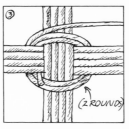

(2 ROUNDS)

Then begin to separate the spokes, weaving over and under each individual spoke instead of a group of four. Be very careful and work as evenly as possible. When you have woven one row of individual spokes, you will find that using an even number of spokes makes the weaver come out the same way each time instead of alternating. This is true of all circle weaving. To alter this requires uneven warp

numbers; so insert the half spoke into your weaving, across the center and into the other side enough to secure it.

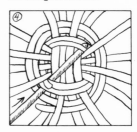

Continue to weave until the bottom is the size you want it. To make the basket turn up start pulling the weaver tighter which will bring the spokes upright. If the willow dries, dampen it with a sponge as you work.

FOR SIDES: PULL WEAVER TIGHTER

145

When you have woven it to the desired height, a border may be made. The simplest border is to bend the willow spokes back down into the weavers. If the willow bends leaving a loop, you may weave more willow sticks through these loops making a good stout edge.

⑦ AT TOP — BEND WILLOWS BACK INTO WEAVING —

OLD WEAVER
NEW WEAVER
(INSIDE OF BASKET)

SPLIT RUSHES — SAVE WHOLE, CLEAN ONE FOR TOP OF BASKET

Rush is constructed much the same but the preparation is different and the edges are usually wrapped. Rush stalks are gathered early in their season and split open and scraped clean of the pith inside. Rush may be split many times until quite fine or used whole for sturdy spokes, but cleaned of pith.

RUSHES

SCRAPE CLEAN. DRY IN SHADE.

⑧ WEAVER TO REINFORCE TOP ROW

WRAP RAFFIA AROUND TOP RUSH AND DOWN BELOW A STITCH.

If your weaver needs to be added to, it can be spliced by paring the ends back a couple of inches and inserting the new pared end over the old one. The spliced ends and the inserted half spoke should be facing the inside of the basket so they don't show.

If you are weaving in the same manner as described for willow, save a whole, cleaned piece of rush to use around the top edge. This can then be wound and bound using the finer splits as raffia. Wrap the "raffia" around the top piece several times and then a couple of wraps should be extended down to become a stitch through a weaver below those being covered at the top. This is for added strength but can also create an interesting rhythm and pattern.

Rushes have always been used for baskets. One of the earliest known uses occurs in the story of the baby Moses being hidden by his mother in the bulrushes (cattails). His waterproof basket was made of rush and lined with the traditional filler of clay and pitch. I have heard and read that there are no basketmaking rushes in the country. It is true that we do not have some of the ancient varieties, Juncaceae, but cattails along abound everywhere and are usable in all their parts. Other rushes are to be found, and their leaves, hollow stalks, and root bark are often fine basket material.

character. I have loved using natural dyes for many years, loved learning plants and the dye substances that come from them. Most of these can be used in making baskets. The Smithsonian Institute, according to Mrs. Tod, lists 103 different basket materials used by the Indians in our country. That means that just about everywhere there is some natural material suitable to use for making or coloring a basket.

Baskets have been used for more than containing and storing things. The Indians used them for many purposes, from backpacks for carrying babies to the storing of evil spirits.

One time a friend of mine who has a remarkable collection of Indian baskets was asked to the home of one of the last true and respected medicine men. The great man had just died, and his friends knew of the Indian medicine tradition of storing the evil spirits which has sickened his patients in baskets. The baskets were hidden in very old and hollow oak trees. The Indians didn't want anything to do with the spirits themselves, but they felt my friend would be safe and might like to find the baskets. This he did after some search. One huge hollow tree yielded up basket after basket, all tiny little gems, each with its own cover, and some no larger than a thimble — but all containing evil spirits! Some were so fine they looked like glass! My friend told me that one of the saddest traditions, for anyone who loves Indian baskets, is that of burning the baskets along with other worldly possessions on the funeral fires at the time a persons dies. This may be one reason that some baskets are learned about only in tales.

It's obvious how baskets and weaving are related because you can see the warp and weft construction in both. However, it isn't so clear how baskets and pottery are related. Of course, many pots and many baskets have similar shapes and similar uses too, but actually, the construction was similar to start with. Look at the coils of pine needles in a pine needle basket. Early people made the first pots by using

147

coils too, but made of clay. They built the coils inside of baskets, sometimes using only shallow baskets for support around the pot bottom and sometimes baskets for the whole pot. It is thought that a pot was first fired when a clay-lined basket was put in a fire to cook food, and the basket — easily replaced — was burned away!

Besides coiled baskets, which are sewn together and sometimes completely wrapped to hold the coil firm, there are baskets which are woven, and some are twined. As in cloth weaving, the warp material is usually stronger. In any case, it must be strong enough to support the basket. The weaver, or weft, may be the same material as the warp or entirely different. Two materials which seem to appear almost everywhere in our country are rush and willow. A basket made from either material can be as individual as you are.

{Arrowhead Art and Leathercraft}

Bows and arrows are one of the most ancient and interesting crafts. Making them can lead you into all kinds of activities from searching for the perfect materials for each set of arrows and matching performance bows, to learning how to use the finest skills in constructing them, and finally to the thrill of actually putting your work to the test with a target. Besides finding out if you have made them well, you can discover how strong you are and how keen an eye you have when you score a bull's-eye.

The lore that goes along with archery is as old as man himself, for as people evolved from using clubs, they began making crude bows. Archeologists have found evidence that clubs and bows were both used at the same period of time. In our country, we think of the use of the bow and arrow in connection with American Indians, but it was when people migrated from Asia that the bow came to North America.

148

{How to Tool and Lace Leather}

Materials needed: cowhide, knife or scissors, sponge, pencil or stylus, jackknife, swivel cutter.

Western leather designs are handed down from the days when the Spaniards lived in California and decorated their elaborate saddles with designs taken from the plant life around them. Beautiful as those designs are, there is no reason to feel that they are any better than those you might make using your own ideas. That's what the Spaniards did when they came to this country. Before that, leather designs had been mostly geometric designs. This was because people thought that if you made a picture of the exact plant, you would bring evil days to the plant!

After making a plan for a project, select your leather, usually cowhide, and carefully arrange the pattern pieces for the best use of the size and shape leather you have. A simple rectangle cut to use as a bookmark makes an ideal beginning project, but you may want to go beyond that.

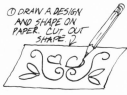

① DRAW A DESIGN AND SHAPE ON PAPER. CUT OUT SHAPE.

At any rate, make a design for tooling and for your pattern pieces on paper. You may cut your leather pieces either with a knife or scissors depending on the thickness. Trace around the edges of the pattern pieces laid out on the flesh side. Make sure

that when you turn them over to use with the grain, they will not be backwards. Cut the piece out.

② TRACE SHAPE ONTO FLESH SIDE OF LEATHER

③ CUT OUT PIECE

Now sponge from the flesh side of the first piece you wish to tool. Make sure not to wet the leather too much, making damp spots show through to the other side, but make it wet enough to thoroughly soften the piece. You should not be able to squeeze any water out of it. If you do get it too wet, let it dry completely before working again.

④ DAMPEN LEATHER WITH WET SPONGE

FLESH SIDE

After dampening the leather, place the matching design piece of paper onto the grain side and draw firmly over the design lines, not the texture part, if

any. You can use a pencil, or a tool available for that purpose (a stylus), or a sturdy knitting needle. If you use a pencil, hold it at an angle and be careful not to mark the leather with the lead. A line will appear in the softened leather that is actually a dent in the surface.

PAPER PATTERN

LEATHER — GRAIN SIDE UP.
⑤ PRESS IN DESIGN WITH PENCIL OR STYLUS.

(DESIGN IS DENTED INTO SURFACE)

Never go back over your tracing. Leave your lines clear. Now you are ready to carve, if your design calls for it. You will need a special tool for this called a swivel cutter. I suppose your jackknife could be used but, if possible, learn to use the swivel cutter. This is used to follow the design you have traced in your leather and carve it out. It cuts a fine line into the leather. Cut with strokes moving toward you! With the flat edge of a jackknife or a spoon handle, press the leather along one side of this cut line to make a beveled look. It's a good idea to practice all three of these things — wetting, tracing, cutting — before working on your project, if you have an extra scrap of leather.

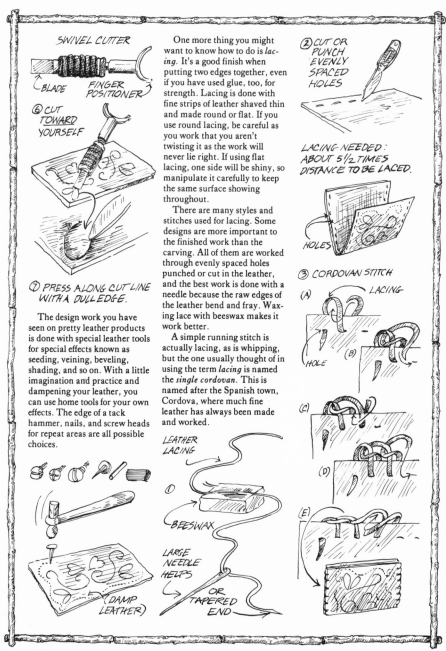

SWIVEL CUTTER

BLADE   FINGER POSITIONER

⑥ CUT TOWARD YOURSELF

⑦ PRESS ALONG CUT LINE WITH A DULL EDGE.

The design work you have seen on pretty leather products is done with special leather tools for special effects known as seeding, veining, beveling, shading, and so on. With a little imagination and practice and dampening your leather, you can use home tools for your own effects. The edge of a tack hammer, nails, and screw heads for repeat areas are all possible choices.

(DAMP LEATHER)

One more thing you might want to know how to do is *lacing*. It's a good finish when putting two edges together, even if you have used glue, too, for strength. Lacing is done with fine strips of leather shaved thin and made round or flat. If you use round lacing, be careful as you work that you aren't twisting it as the work will never lie right. If using flat lacing, one side will be shiny, so manipulate it carefully to keep the same surface showing throughout.

There are many styles and stitches used for lacing. Some designs are more important to the finished work than the carving. All of them are worked through evenly spaced holes punched or cut in the leather, and the best work is done with a needle because the raw edges of the leather bend and fray. Waxing lace with beeswax makes it work better.

A simple running stitch is actually lacing, as is whipping, but the one usually thought of in using the term *lacing* is named the *single cordovan*. This is named after the Spanish town, Cordova, where much fine leather has always been made and worked.

LEATHER LACING

① BEESWAX

LARGE NEEDLE HELPS

OR TAPERED END

② CUT OR PUNCH EVENLY SPACED HOLES

LACING NEEDED: ABOUT 5½ TIMES DISTANCE TO BE LACED.

HOLES

③ CORDOVAN STITCH

(A)   LACING

HOLE   (B)

(C)

(D)

(E)

The account of Ishi, a Yahi Indian, provides a clue to that migration — a clue that was living up until his death in 1916. There are three different traditional positions for firing a bow. One of these is the Mongolian, and when the lone Indian, Ishi, was found, it was discovered that the position he used for firing his bow was almost exactly that used by the ancient Mongolian people. All other tribes had long since modified and adapted to the requirements necessary for firing from horseback or canoes.

In Europe, archery was refined and even became the sport of kings, but gradually people here chose not to use the long bow of England and Europe, and the one known now as the flat bow became the choice. Indians and Eskimos didn't always have perfect wood to use, and so ingenious bows were made out of the materials at hand. Bows have been found made out of pieces of whalebone, horn, and driftwood. One of the most famous was made by the Plains Indians out of strips of mountain-sheep horn glued together and bound with sinew. Glue for bow making was made from various things, even boiled salmon skins! Early North American bows were so valued for their strength that an Indian would trade as many as two good horses for one bow.

Arrows and arrowheads are just as interesting as bows because the best wood and rock were often hard to find and were treasured and traded. One of the best rocks for making arrowheads is obsidian, and all through history we can find old trade routes where obsidian was one of the sought-after materials. It looks like black glass and is extremely hard. The art of making arrows and arrowheads become so developed that individual men could be identified from the arrowheads alone, by the way the materials were handles and the individual techniques used.

Another of the very old crafts which was developed first for protection and shelter and then for pleasure and making useful articles is leathercraft. Remains of old civilizations all

151

over the world show that as people evolved, they gradually learned how to use hides and to preserve them. American Indians had their own ideas about leather; people in the Middle Ages had theirs; Egyptians, too, had a method for leather preservation. If a hide is not tanned, it will rot. This is because it is organic. The nitrogen content in the animal cells will cause a hide to decompose. Gradually all different people and tribes figured out how to stop that. And one of the common old ingredients used again and again all over is the animal itself; that is, the brains and liver. These were made into a paste or solution. Even today they are used in some of our big commercial tanneries instead of chemicals.

In the recipe for tanning a hide at home, the fur is left on. In leathermaking the hair side is usually removed. For tooling and making articles of leather, that is the kind of leather you choose. The Indians where I live remove that hair by a long soak in saltwater or sometimes by rolling up the hide with the hair covered in wood ashes and a little water. This, I suppose, is like what is done commercially in the lime vats. After a couple of days, the hide is unrolled and the hair is scraped off.

Hide for leather tooling and making belts, purses, and saddles, has two layers. The side which the hair was scraped from is called the *grain* side. This also holds the glue material you try to remove when you tan the skin. The underskin, or *flesh* side, is the tough, rough side. Tooling and finishing is done on the *grain* side.

◀[Better Than We Found It]▶

All of these basic crafts are close to nature and the out-of-doors. Seeing and being ready to use and appreciate all the abundance provided by gardens and yards and woods and fields and animal friends can occupy an entire lifetime. Then

｛How to Tan a Prime Hide｝

Materials needed: animal hide (rabbit, squirrel, goat, sheep, deer), alum, saltpeter, salt, newspapers, scraper or dull knife, detergent, borax, neat's-foot oil, sandpaper.

A prime hide is in top condition with no blemishes and full maturity of coat and skin. Perhaps you would like to know just a little about what happens to a skin that changes it from a stiff, hard piece into a nice, soft and usable leather. It is really called *tawing,* but most people use the words *taw* and *tan* to mean the same thing now. The word *tan* comes from the tannic acid which is found in lots of plants in nature, but especially in live oak trees. Tannic acid is important in tanning and tawing.

The important thing is to replace the matter that is in the skin cells. This matter is almost a glue — very stiff, and it must be removed before the skin can become soft. In this recipe, the borax and detergent make this glue into a kind of gelatin so that the underskin can be peeled, and the cells can be broken down and softened by the rubbing. The more rubbing, the softer your finished skin! The alum and salt mixture pulls the liquid out of the skin so that the cells don't hold any more glue or gelatin. Then more rubbing and scraping makes it even softer than before.

A hide can be either fresh or frozen. If frozen, thaw in lukewarm water.

Step 1: Wash: this can be done in a washing machine. Use 1 cup borax, 1 cup detergent, and cold water. Agitate for 15 minutes for small skins, 30 minutes for goats and larger. Rinse twice in cold water.

① WASH HIDE.

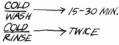
COLD WASH → 15-30 MIN.
COLD RINSE → TWICE

Step 2: Towel dry the skin and lay it hair side down, on an old rug or towel. Rub hard, especially at the edges, to loosen underskin and fat. Now try to peel the loose underskin and scrape off any excess fat with a blunt knife. The skin *must* be free of *any* fat and meat.

TOWEL DRY HIDE
②
HAIR SIDE DOWN
OLD RUG OR TOWEL

③ RUB HARD TO LOOSEN FAT.

④ USE BLUNT KNIFE TO PEEL AND SCRAPE OFF LOOSE SKIN AND FAT.

Step 3: Hang the skin up with skin sides together to dry the hair. Don't leave it up more than a few hours because odor develops.

⑤
← HIDE, HANGING WITH SKIN SIDES TOGETHER

Step 4: Place the hide, hair side down, on a layer of six to eight newspapers. Cover the skin side with a mixture made up of 1 cup powdered alum, 1 cup saltpeter, and 1 cup plain table salt. You can get the alum and saltpeter at a drugstore. Rub the mixture in. Cover the skin with more layers of newspaper and roll it up tightly. Don't allow the salt mixture to get on the hair. Store the hide in a cool place.

153

⑥

ALUM 1 CUP

SALT PETER 1 CUP

TABLE SALT 1 CUP

NEWSPAPER

HIDE, HAIR SIDE DOWN. MIXTURE MUST NOT TOUCH HAIR.
RUB MIXTURE INTO SKIN
⑦

COVER WITH MORE NEWSPAPERS

ROLL UP
⑧

STORE IN A COOL PLACE.

Step 5: Two days later check the mixture on the hide. Shiny spots must be covered with more mixture. Roll up and store again. Goat skins take about ten days to cure, rabbits less.

⑨ DAY 1 DAY 2

MIXTURE

OPEN. RUB MIXTURE INTO ANY SHINY PLACES.
ROLL UP AGAIN.

Step 6: Curing is finished when the skin is *white* when scraped with a blunt knife. Unroll the skin and place it on a rounded surface, if possible; then start scraping with a blunt knife. Finish the whole surface this way. It will be snowy white and not very stiff. A final finish can be done with an electric sander or by rubbing with sandpaper. Doing the sanding gives a suede finish. Oil, such as neat's-foot oil, is sometimes rubbed in too.

No tanning is easy, but the results of a lot of rubbing and scraping are worth it and give you something that nobody else

⑩ SCRAPE WITH DULL KNIFE

RUB WITH SANDPAPER (ON BLOCK)
OR USE ELECTRIC SANDER

can imitate. Each hide is different, and they are all useful. If you goof on your first efforts to tan, cut the skin into strips and use it for rawhide. Rawhide is useful for many, many projects.

In the early years of our country the fur trading industry was one of the things that lured men to the western territories. They trapped and skinned their catches and canoed the waterways back to towns where bundles of furs were traded for huge amounts of money. It was a dangerous business, and the men who lived that way had to be tough and clever. They learned a great deal from the Indians who had used hides for everything from houses to babies' blankets.

When we cousins camped *up north* each summer, we were always presented with a gift to take home. Each one was made of buckskin and usually was decorated with beads. Gloves, moccasins, and vests were some of these treasures.

The buckskin was the softest thing imaginable. I wish I knew how it was made, though of course I never will! When I asked, my friend just smiled! Buckskin is made from deerhide and has no hair on it. It is lovely, soft, and either white or tan, depending on what it is used for.

Some recipes are known and can be found in books written especially about tanning or Indian crafts. Just the same, I am sure each tribe had its own special secret, because buckskin is not the same everywhere. Also, the more people I have met who tan, the more different ways to tan I have found. The one I have written here doesn't use dangerous or hard-to-find chemicals so I, personally, have found it a good old favorite to use at home.

154

instead of wasting, we learn to treasure, nurture, and to cherish. People of other times come to life in our minds and become sources of wonder.

One of the most surprising and interesting classes I ever took was at the University of Wisconsin and taught by a wonderful lady named Helen Allen. It was, of all things, the history of embroidery. Imagine! But think! Where did the color and thread come from? Why did people do it? How did they first learn?

In my imagination I found myself slogging across the world with Marco Polo and reporting to the king's court about those delicate Oriental decorations. Wars were fought and civilizations flourished because of their command of color! *Color!* How could people have cared that much! I think part of it was that they could see and were aware of what nature gave in treasured portions to those who knew her secrets. Like people of old, we learn to know how the world can help us to live and enjoy ourselves, and like people of old we have the choice, still, to use it all up or to leave the world better than we found it because we were here. That's hard. Can you do it?

{More Books to Read}

Amsden, Charles. *Navaho Weaving: Its Technique and Its History.* Fine Arts Press, Santa Ana, Ca., 1969. The standard work on this subject.

Birrell, Verla. *Textile Arts.* Shocken Books, New York, 1973. A big section on all kinds of weaving techniques; a great resource.

Boy Scouts of America. *Revised Handbook for Boys.* New Brunswick, N. J., 1940. Still a great all-around handbook.

Brooklyn Botanical Garden Record. *Plants and Gardens, Vol. 20, No. 3: A Handbook.* 1968. This has standard dye references; for ages eight and up. Botanical Gardens address: 1000 Washington Ave., Brooklyn, N. Y. 11225.

Burgess, Thornton W. *Burgess Book of Nature Lore.* Bonanza Books, New York, 1975. Burgess will always be interesting and beautiful for all ages.

Candy, Robert. *Nature Notebook.* Riverside Press, Houghton Mifflin Co., Cambridge, Mass., 1953. An actual notebook by Robert Candy and his boy.

Condon, Geneal. *The Art of Flower Preservation.* Sunset Books, Lane Book Co., Menlo Park, Ca., 1962. Thorough and inexpensive.

Davenport, Elsie. *Your Handspinning.* Craft and Hobby Book Service, Pacific Grove, Ca., 1964. Pictures and good information. Address: P. O. Box 626, Pacific Grove, Ca. 95950.

Fat Cabin Press. *Tanning.* Fat Cabin Press, Arcata, Ca. A short easy pamphlet — good.

Garriott, Edward. *Weather Folklore.* U. S. Govt. Printing Office Report, Grand Rivers Books, Detroit, Mich. Interesting and fun.

Hammett, Catherine. *Your Own Book of Campcraft.* Pocket Books, Inc., New York, 1960. Easy to use and helpful.

Hart, Carol and Dan. *Natural Basketry.* Watson Guptil Publications, New York, 1976. Complete, easy to use, good pictures.

Hunt, Ben. *Ben Hunt's Big Indiancraft Book.* Bruce Publishing Co., Milwaukee, Wisc., 1942. Ben Hunt's books are all a treat to use and read — a creative resource.

Leach, Bernard. *A Potter's Book.* Trans-Atlantic Arts, Inc., Hollywood, Fla., 1962. Every serious potter owns this book.

157

Lesch, Alma. *Vegetable Dyeing*. Watson Guptil Publications, New York, 1970. Excellent and easy.

Nauman, Rose and Hull, Raymond. *Off-Loom Weaving Book*. Charles Scribner's Sons, New York, 1973. Easy to use and inspiring, good pictures.

Phillips, Mary Walker. *Macrame: Step-by-Step*. Golden Press, Western Publishing Co., Inc., Racine, Wisconsin, 1970. Pictures and easy projects.

Pringle, L., ed. *Discovering the Outdoors*. Natural History Press, Garden City, N. Y., 1969.

Ress, Etta Schneider. *Community of Living Things in Field and Meadow, Vol. 1.* Nat'l Audubon Society Creative Educational Society, Inc., Mankato, Minn., 1956. Pictures and identifications.

Seton, Julia. *American Indian Arts*. Ronald Press, 1962. Julia and Ernest Thompson Seton books are all fun and interesting — outdoor and Indian works.

Tod, Osma Gallinger. *Earth Basketry*. Bonanza Books, New York, 1972. One of the best basket books, out of print, but easy to find in libraries.

Tod, Osma Gallinger and Benson, Oscar H. *Weaving with Reeds and Fibers*. Dover Publications, Inc., New York, 1975.

Wigginton, Eliot, ed. *Foxfire Books*. Anchor Books, Doubleday and Co., Inc., Garden City, New York, 1972.

Znamierowski, Nell. *Weaving: Step-by-Step*. Golden Press, Western Publishing Co., Inc., Racine, Wisc., 1967. Easy with simple projects.

158

{Index of Crafts}

159

A Handbook of Reflective and Experiential Learning

This handbook acts as an essential guide to understanding and using reflective and experiential learning – whether it be for personal or professional development, or as a tool for learning.

It takes a fresh look at experiential and reflective learning, locating them within an overall theoretical framework for learning and exploring the relationships between the different approaches.

As well as the theory, the book provides practical ideas for applying the models of learning, with tools, activities and photocopiable resources which can be incorporated directly into classroom practice.

This book is essential reading to guide any teacher, lecturer or trainer wanting to improve teaching and learning.

Dr Jennifer A. Moon works in educational development at the University of Exeter. She is an experienced teacher and course leader in education and professional training. A leading expert on reflective learning techniques, she has worked in all stages of education, professional development and counselling. Her previous books include *Learning Journals: A Handbook for Academics, Students and Professional Development*; *Short Courses and Workshops*; *Reflection in Learning and Professional Development*; and *The Module and Programme Development Handbook* (all RoutledgeFalmer).

A Handbook of Reflective and Experiential Learning

Theory and Practice

Jennifer A. Moon

RoutledgeFalmer
Taylor & Francis Group

LONDON AND NEW YORK

First published 2004 by RoutledgeFalmer
11 New Fetter Lane, London EC4P 4EE

Simultaneously published in the USA and Canada
by RoutledgeFalmer
29 West 35th Street, New York, NY 10001

RoutledgeFalmer is an imprint of the Taylor & Francis Group

Typeset in Garamond and Gill by BC Typesetting Ltd
Printed and bound in Great Britain by
MPG Books Ltd, Bodmin, Cornwall

British Library Cataloguing in Publication Data
A catalogue record for this book is available from the British Library

Library of Congress Cataloging in Publication Data
Moon, Jennifer A.
  A handbook of reflective and experiential learning: theory and
practice/Jennifer Moon.
     p.   cm.
Includes bibliographical references and index.
  1. Active learning–Handbooks, manuals, etc. 2. Experiential
learning–Handbooks, manuals, etc. 3. Learning–Handbooks, manuals,
etc. I. Title.
  LB1027.23.M66   2004
  370.15'23–dc22   2003021645

ISBN 0–415–33515–9 (hbk)
ISBN 0–415–33516–7 (pbk)

Contents

Preface

A practical and theoretical approach

This handbook is concerned with two topics that have normally been seen as separate, with their own literatures and their own experts who were not necessarily experts in learning as a general topic. There have been experts in reflective learning, experiential learning and student learning, with relatively little meeting of minds or ideas about practical issues. With changes in educational practice and, in particular, the developing emphasis on reflective learning in higher education, these experts need to work together. Experiential learning is, for example, very often assessed through written work that is, in essence, reflective. The use of learning journals is an example. As there is more interest in the theoretical perspectives of reflective and experiential learning, we see the literatures beginning to overlap. Now it is timely to do the theoretical exploration work in order to sort out the nature of the overlap – how reflective and experiential learning are the same and how they differ. In order to do this, we have started with the basic questions about the process of learning itself. We have related both reflective and experiential learning to a basic model of learning, and then considered how they relate to each other.

Handbooks are both theoretical and practical. With the increase in the use of reflective and experiential learning in higher education and professional development, teachers might be asked to be involved with these kinds of learning and there is a need for supportive literature, which is both theoretical and practical. People who would not consider themselves to be reflective are being asked to encourage their students to reflect, when they know that some of their students may be more reflective than they themselves are. On the practical side, this handbook covers topics such as how to introduce reflective activities and then to improve the quality of the reflection. It covers assessment issues, considers work experience as a form of experiential learning and provides many further activities that may be used in different contexts to facilitate different forms of learning.

The book is divided into a number of parts that move from a broad view of learning in general, to reflective and experiential learning, and how they relate to this general view of learning and to each other. It then goes on to more practical issues, ending with practical activities. There are several points in the book where material is summarized, so 'beginning to end' reading of this book is not essential. Some readers may be more interested in the general material on learning in the first four chapters; some might want to start with the summary of the generic view of learning in Chapter 5 and move through the theoretical material on reflective and experiential learning. Some may be interested in the chapters that concern the implementation of reflective learning, and some may want to pick from the practical activities only in Chapters 10, 12 and the Resources section.

Acknowledgements

The other reason for these initial words is to say some thanks for forbearance. The glimmerings of ideas for this book were first made explicit over three years ago in an excited telephone call to a friend in which I recall saying, 'You know I said I would write no more books – well . . . I have changed my mind. . . .' There are many thanks due to family and close friends whose contacts with me have been touched in various ways by that change of mind. I should thank also those who have unwittingly been the guinea pigs for the ideas and practical activities that are included in the book – many workshops have been based on the ideas discussed in the book. I would also like to thank the publishers for their support and their tolerance of the changing form of this book as it has been written (or do I say 'it has written itself'?).

Introduction

A book often directs its writer. I should have known that when I started writing – even with a set of planned chapters in front of me. Now, as I come to this introductory chapter, late on in the process of writing, I notice how the book differs from the original plan. However, as an alternative introduction, I could also say that this book is a research project in itself and research is generally about discovery and not of knowing the answers before one starts. So this is what the book is – it is both a book that wrote its own way around and about material on reflective and experiential learning, and a research project that has been written according to the findings as they emerged.

Boundaries

I start by looking at some of the boundaries of this book. It is largely focused on sophisticated learning, though there are many ideas introduced that could be directed towards the earlier developmental stages of the process of learning. The text is mainly concerned with learning in relatively formal situations but there are also implications for non-formal and everyday learning. I have not been able to develop all these areas of reading as much as I would like in this book. In particular, I wanted to think further about everyday learning situations but space limitations create their own boundaries. When terms are applied in formal situations and caught up in theory that primarily relates to the formal situations, we tend to forget their relevance to the activities of everyday life and so it is with these words – 'reflection' and 'experiential learning'. I take the position in the book that we all reflect and that all learning is based on experience. All learning is therefore 'experiential learning' in one sense. Learning from a lecture is still a matter of experiencing the lecturer's words, and many other things about being in the lecture theatre. Learning is learning from experience – but for the sake of clarity, we move towards more specific uses of the terms from the middle part of the book. The book is essentially about conscious learning. One form of learning that is largely excluded from consideration here is the learning of physical skills, though it is acknowledged that there is a link between reflective processes and actual skill.

The aim of the book is to develop greater understanding and more practical use of reflective and experiential learning as forms of more sophisticated learning. Both forms are well reviewed in relation to their own literature – they are reviewed in the context of reflective and experiential learning respectively but there is relatively little in the literature that links them with the new literature on what we term here 'generic' learning. They are somehow seen as being apart from other forms of learning and are treated in a different manner – there are whole programmes based on 'experiential learning', for example – as if it is learning that is different. From reading and previous writing, however, it is evident that these forms of learning are intimately related – and sometimes, but not always, they coincide.

There is also a practical aim to this book which becomes particularly important towards the end where there are chapters on practical ways of introducing and exploiting reflective and experiential learning in educational and other situations.

Routes into and roots of . . .

There have been many roots to this book and many routes into it. There are some obvious roots in other topics of my previous books which had their own roots described in their early pages. They also had their 'short-comings' – areas to which I wished to return in more detail. For example, in the first book, on reflection and learning (Moon, 1999a), the idea of learning journals intrigued me and led directly and quickly into the second book on learning journals (Moon, 1999b). Issues that arose briefly in both these books were assessment and the notion that there might be a 'depth dimension' to reflection. There were also issues relatively unexplored about how learners could be helped to develop reflection. This latter issue became evident as reflection was introduced more and more into curricula. The learning journal book left me with a sense of excitement and curiosity about learning in the everyday sense from experience – what role does reflection play? Although I did address how we learn from learning journals, I felt that there was more to do on this topic.

The next book about effectiveness in running short courses and workshops might seem to be a different track but it led to more thought about the relationship between learning and teaching or facilitation and again to the role of reflection and learning from experience (Moon, 2001a). It also led me, in a large way, back to David Kolb's work (Kolb, 1984) and the manner in which it is exploited as a quick explanation of 'how we learn from experience' in so many texts. *The Module and Programme Development Handbook* (Moon, 2002a) did, perhaps, have less in common with the other three texts – but it is about precision in understanding what is going on in learning. It contrasts with much that has been written about reflection and experiential learning where assumptions are made so often without question and where imprecision may be a stimulus to curiosity.

A further academic route into the writing of this book has been my (latter) involvement with the very successful work experience modules developed in a partnership between Exeter and Plymouth Universities (Watton and Collings, 2002). Seeing the students going into work situations in order to learn about work and to learn about learning raised intriguing questions. What did the students learn; how did they learn from the experiences in work and what did they mean to them? Were they assessed on what they were learning? How were we able to guide them in their learning in this 'teacher-less' and 'curriculum-less' environment? There were interesting marketing issues with the module too – trying to 'sell' it to the schools in the universities so that they would support their students in pursuing the module. I thought about how the learning in the module could support the learning of students within their disciplines (Moon, 2002b) and that brought me back to reflective and experiential learning.

A major learning point for me, which arose from the learning journal book, was the value of maintaining a learning journal alongside any major life event, in particular those that involve ongoing thought. Three years ago when I began to consider the writing of this book, I started such a journal. It is a source of comments, observations, inspirations, questions, 'excitements' about sources of ideas (notes from literature are separate), and so on. It has allowed a range of questions to be kept alive over time. There are now over a hundred written (A5) sheets of it and it has been helpful in shaping this book at a deep level as well as in more superficial ways. In particular, the pages of the journal remind me of some of the high points of my own learning in the context of this book. Among them are the following:

- Early on in the writing project, I went on holiday with a new friend, camping together and kayaking on Cornish rivers. I had camped before and kayak locally – but the circumstances were new and there was much to learn! I recognized that there might be something in common here with the kind of learning in work experience where generally known skills are used in new circumstances. I decided to write about what I had learnt. This process is described in more detail in Chapter 12. It was a source of much learning both about the activities and also about learning from reflection and experience.

- Not much later I decided to treat an emotionally disturbing incident as a source of learning from experience in a similar way. Again I learnt a great deal – and, in particular, I became acutely aware of the labile nature of emotion and how my accounts written in subsequent days varied – I could say 'slid around'. This is an important issue in reflective writing and led to considerations about depth in reflective writing: the concept of the 'slipperiness' of reflection and knowing features in the text.

- Another important high point in the progress of my learning was when I was asked to run a session for potential members of the Institute for Learning and Teaching in Higher Education (ILTHE). The day before the workshop I was still wondering how I could help the participants to understand the nature of reflective writing. I began to write a story about an incident in a park. I then wrote it again in a more reflective mode, and again in a mode of deeper reflection (as I understand reflection to be). I used the exercise the next day, and it seemed to be helpful and generated much discussion. I have since used it with many staff and students who have to use or understand reflective writing. 'The Park' is reproduced in Resource 5. I have since developed several such exercises (Resources 6 and 10) and a framework that accompanies them (Resource 9).

- 'The Park' was the first use of fiction in the exercises designed for staff and educational development purposes. Since then I have seen great potential for the use of fiction in the development of reflective and experiential learning. After all, on a constructivist view of learning (Chapter 1), experience is all fiction – of our own or others' making. I have become very interested in the role of story telling in education as a means of enhancing learning in a wide variety of fields. Meeting and working with Maxine Alterio (McDrury and Alterio, 2002) was a great inspiration and there is more work to be done in this field. It seems to connect with the current considerations of how to bring more creativity and imagination into higher education learning.

- The 'high points' so far might suggest that this book is based entirely on personal experience and while, of course, it is in a sense, there has been a great deal of academic reading. Much of the reading is simply a matter of sitting down and reading, and writing notes. But then, every so often, there is real inspiration – the learning journal is out, the pen flies, not on notes for future reference, but on new ideas, questions, pro-activity that is engendered by the material. Margaret Donaldson's (1992) book, *Human Minds* was one such high point of inspiration. It is an extremely interesting book and encouraged me to think a great deal about the link between emotion and learning and my own prior experiences in counselling and personal development.

Another such book was Marton and Booth (1997). I read this several times and took detailed notes. It is a book that seems to bring together much of what has been written about the student learning experience and provided a substantial foundation for Chapter 1 on generic views of learning. Writing a learning journal seems often to bed particular experiences in their location. I read this book on a sun-drenched window seat in late afternoons in an old holiday cottage, thinking about what it was saying about reflective and experiential learning.

There is a third set of authors who have remained an inspiration for some years. They researched and wrote about the development of learners' conceptions of knowledge. I consider that this is important material and note how it is not often cited more than in passing. I have mentioned Perry (1970) and King and Kitchener (1994) in earlier writing. In some ways, their ideas are quite difficult to get across but more recently I came across Baxter Magolda (1992) whose findings are similar to those mentioned above, but whose work is much more accessible. She uses quotations extensively to illustrate the ways in which learners in college conceive of knowledge.

I have mentioned the work on academic literature that has gone into this book. It is a feature of the book that the literature comes from a range of disciplinary sources. The topic of learning, after all, belongs to everybody and it cannot avoid appearing in every sub-discipline in the fields of education and professional development. I have drawn on the following areas of literature: adult education; professional development; student learning; staff and educational development; developmental psychology; cognitive psychology; journal writings; personal development; work-related learning; experiential learning in training and development; everyday learning and the development of scientific thought.

Some notes on the style and use of words

As usual, I have considerations about gender. I am not masculine and nor is half the population, so I do not want to use 'he' all the time and I dislike the grammatically incorrect 'they'. I am female and to use 'she' is 100 per cent right 50 per cent of the time. I therefore use the female gender wherever I am referring to a person. I have also tended to avoid the word 'student' since not all learners are students and I refer mostly to 'learners'.

There are a number of technical words that emerge particularly in Chapter 1 and then appear again somewhat later in the book. I have had to look up the definitions sometimes for these words and I imagine that this might be an issue for the reader. I have therefore compiled a Glossary of the more difficult terms that appears before the Bibliography. One term that needs to be introduced immediately is 'generic views of learning'. I found the need to coin this term in order to distinguish between the generic views of learning largely described in Chapter 1 and the specific material on reflective and experiential learning that appears later in order to consider the links and not to perpetuate division.

This book is about probably most of the learning that anyone does (with the exception of physical skills). It is called reflective and experiential learning because these are the terms that people are using widely and which, I consider, require further elucidation. In fact, reflection probably plays a part in most good quality learning and all learning is experiential in one sense. The book is written to fulfil the following aims and as an exploration of:

- how experiential and reflective learning relate to what I call generic views of learning;
- how they relate to each other;
- their role and value in formal education;
- practical issues in their implementation in formal education.

The book also provides practical methods of using experiential and reflective learning.

Overview of the book

A handbook is a general text that combines theory and practical information. The theory in this book is in the first half and the general aim of this is to consider reflective and experiential learning as forms of generic learning. This approach is, as far as I know, new. In the literature of reflective and experiential learning, both forms of learning are discussed in relation to their own literature rather than in relation to more generalized views of learning. Reflective learning is reviewed against other literature on reflection, reflective practice and so on – and the same is true of experiential learning. It is timely to relate them to the processes of learning in general and to question their somewhat 'specialized' status.

Having laid a basis for a generic view of learning in Chapter 1, the next three chapters elaborate on aspects of the generic view that have particular relevance to reflective and experiential learning. These three aspects are described as manners of framing learning. They cover the development of conceptions of knowledge (Chapter 2), the role of emotion in learning (Chapter 3) and the approach adopted to learning by a learner (Chapter 4).

Chapter 5 follows the development of the view of generic learning but taking stock, looking back over the generic view of learning and forward to deal with one defining issue for both reflective and experiential learning – that they do not rely on a formal taught curriculum. In this context, we explore the idea of mediation in learning, providing some critical views of the often simplistic manner in which the notion of mediation is interpreted. The following chapters are concerned with the elucidation of reflective and experiential learning as forms of learning in themselves and then in relation to the generic view of learning (Chapter 6), then to each other. Reflective learning is often involved in experiential learning, but they do not coincide completely. The view of reflective learning in this book is a development of that in my earlier books and materials. Chapter 7 is a further stage of development of this material in relation to the 'depth' dimension of reflection. The view of experiential learning is developed in a brief literature review in Chapter 8 while Chapter 9 draws together the material on reflective and experiential learning.

Chapters 10, 11 and 12 present the more practical part of the book. The subject matter of these chapters has been developed in response to issues that have arisen in formal educational circumstances as tutors have instituted reflective and experiential learning within curricula. Chapter 10 deals with the difficulties that are often faced when reflective learning is introduced either on its own or as an element in experiential learning. It refers to a range of resources and exercises that can be used to facilitate reflective learning, some of which are in the Resources section at the end of the book. Chapter 11 also discusses an issue in reflective and experiential learning, it concerns assesssment. The final chapter provides additional ideas, resources, techniques and exercises that are designed to exploit reflective and experiential learning, usually in formal educational situations (Chapter 12). Chapters 10 and 12 include some substantial exercises. Some of the materials are included in the Resources section that follows. Since the Resources section includes material that may need to be directly copied for use with students, copyright is waived in this section and the materials may be photocopied freely.

Finally, a Glossary of the terms that have emerged in the early chapters in this book is provided, followed by an extensive Bibliography.

Part I

A generic view of learning

Chapter 1

The process of learning
The development of a generic view of learning

Introduction

In the Introduction, we indicated that Chapter 1 is the first of a set of four chapters that build a generic view of learning prior to considering how reflective and experiential learning relate to this. The first section looks at the issue of terminology that is used concerning the idea of learning and suggests that misuse and lack of vocabulary may skew our view of learning. New words and concepts are added to facilitate a clearer view of what learning might be. The second section of the chapter presents two ways of looking at learning – the 'building bricks' view and the 'network' view. The latter is pursued and developed throughout the remainder of the chapter particularly in relation to 'meaning' in learning, on which basis the two views particularly differ. The discussion also considers the social or individual connotations of 'meaning'. The next section illustrates some of the points made about 'meaning' and we introduce and explore the idea that all learning is based on experience. In the course of this discussion the terms 'external' and 'internal' experience are introduced.

There is constant emphasis in the chapter on the manner in which learning is a process with many events influencing and modifying each other simultaneously. A process in constant flux is difficult to describe in a linear manner. That learning is a process of constant mutually occurring modifications is one general principle that underpins this book and another is the centrality of the process of identifying figure from ground. This is elucidated by Marton and Booth (1997) and it is the important description of learning in Marton and Booth that this chapter generally follows in its middle and later sections, though other ideas are introduced.

In this chapter, new words are used in specific ways. Such vocabulary is listed in the Glossary at the back of the book.

Some basic ideas about learning

To deal properly with a topic requires focus and boundaries or the discussion will be woolly. We look again at some boundaries of the topic of learning as well as boundaries that are imposed for the purposes of this book. Boundaries are sometimes about words to be used. There are many confusions in the terminology of learning and there is a lack of vocabulary that probably confuses us even more. It is not always easy to see ideas are missing if the words are not present. We rely on words and ideas as tools of investigation and if we do not have them, the investigation process is distorted.

The confusion between learning and teaching or instruction words

The action of helping another to learn (as in teaching or instructing) is different from the action taken by the learner in learning. This may seem very obvious but words for instruction and words for learning are frequently confused in the manner in which they are used. Often the meanings elide and this occurs particularly with the words 'learn' and 'teach'. Young children tend to confuse the processes of teaching and learning. A child might say 'I'll learn you to climb that tree' meaning 'I'll teach you'. Some languages do not distinguish between teaching and learning, having the same word for both (e.g., Russian). Adults, even those involved in teaching or instruction, are apt to use the words in a manner in which they overlap. In a recent document concerning quality assurance issues in education, a statement suggested that teachers should have particular 'learning intentions' for their students. A teacher can only hope that a student learns – she cannot do the learning for her. Learning and teaching are separate operations and while learning can be carried out in a separate place from teaching (distance learning), and learning can occur without teaching, teaching or instructing without a learner as object of the activity does not make sense. In this book, a variety of words will be used to describe the process of aiding or mediating learning in order to help the learner to learn more effectively. Words and phrases such as 'teach', 'instruct', 'facilitate learning' will be used according to the context.

The confusion between teaching and learning is illustrated in another way when words are applied to learning when they are more to do with the instruction process. For example, Harrison (1991) talks of 'learning events' which encompass 'structured training . . . [and] . . . other approaches through which people can acquire knowledge'. Similarly, it is not unusual for activities on courses such as brainstorming, syndicate work, or games and simulations to be described as learning methods when they are really methods of facilitating learning. In academic education, a lecture or tutorial might often be called a method of learning when it is primarily a method by which a teacher instructs or manages the learning of others. The instructor does not know the effect of her instruction on the learner's learning other than by direct questioning or observation. It is not possible to assume that, when confronted with any particular method of instruction, all learners react by learning in the same manner.

The literature is full of other examples in which there are assumptions that what is taught is learnt or that the subject matter of training is learnt without modification by the learner other than as erosion or distortion of memory. The teacher can only have intentions based on experience and laced (usually) with hope and faith, and a set of skills of presentation of ideas, of influence and means of facilitation of that learning. The significance of the confusion of teaching and learning is that it leads us to make unwarranted assumptions about the processes and intentions of the learner and therefore it misguides the teacher in her activities. This is an important issue that extends to all learning situations where another is involved in the influencing or management of the learning.

Even models of learning may also confuse learning and teaching. The Kolb cycle of experiential learning (Kolb, 1984) is widely used as a means of describing learning, particularly in training situations. In fact, it is more often used as a model of the management and facilitation of learning – a teaching rather than a learning model (Moon, 1999a). The model is based on the notion that the best learning is achieved though involvement of reflection and action and it puts action into a management of learning model. The implications of this are discussed later (Chapters 8, 9).

Setting up a vocabulary for learning and teaching

In a previous book, it was noted that that some of the difficulties with understanding the processes of learning and teaching may be due to missing words in the language. Lack of vocabulary may explain some of the confusion as well. There is, for example, no word that describes the material that a learner is learning – what she might seem to be 'taking in' (in colloquial terms). Correspondingly, since there is also no word for what it is that a teacher conveys, we are not easily able to articulate that the material that is learned by the learner is not the same as the material that is produced by the teacher. This lack of vocabulary sometimes leads to the elision of words for teaching and learning as described above. For this book we use the words 'material of learning' for what is learnt by the learner and correspondingly 'material of teaching' for the subject matter of teaching (what the teacher teaches).

Some more terms that are useful in the description of learning and teaching processes are 'learning challenge' and 'teaching challenge'. By these are meant the challenge that a learning task effects for the learner and correspondingly, the challenge for the teacher in conveying the material clearly and appropriately to a learner (Biggs, 1999, uses the latter term). The same material of teaching may pose more or less of a learning challenge to different learners, depending on a variety of factors such as prior knowledge and conceptions of the task, as well as how the learner is feeling that day.

Another gap in vocabulary is in the distinction between the act of learning something and the act of expressing that learning. For the moment, we continue with the simplistic view of learning being the 'taking in' of ideas – then the expression or *representation* of that learning is the manner in which the quality or quantity of the learning is evidenced (Moon, 1999a). Most assessment procedures assess both the ability to learn the material and the ability to express that learning in a written response, in action, in an examination, or in fulfilling whatever the task that is set. In many cases, the inclusion of both processes does not matter. However, it should be noted that unless learners can express their learning effectively, what they know will not be recognized. This is a particularly important matter for a dyslexic person who may have successfully learnt the material of learning, but is unable to represent it effectively in some modes.

Not only is it important to note the distinction between learning and the representation of learning but, for the process of reflection, it is important to recognize that the representation of learning is a further source of learning (Eisner, 1982, 1991). As a learner puts ideas down on paper, she is sorting out her understanding of those ideas and is learning more since the organization and clarification of ideas are a process of learning. Some forms of representation of learning are more orientated towards further learning than others. For example, a learner who is explaining to another some material that has been covered in a lecture, is likely to be learning considerably. The same learner writing a response on the same material in an examination may well be learning less. Another who draws a diagrammatic representation of the material may be learning as much or less that the first – but the learning will be of a different type. Different forms of the representation of learning give rise to more or less learning opportunity and to learning of differing qualities – depending on the type of representation. This may not matter in formal education since it is assumed that we have to assess learners anyway, though it calls for greater thought to be given to the purposes of setting tasks such as essays. It has been argued that, since that much of the representation of learning in higher education is in the form of assessment tasks, a broader range of tasks would have a secondary effect of enhancing learning in a broader manner (Eisner, 1982).

Setting another boundary: skills and pre-conscious thought

To learn something can mean to come to know or to have knowledge or it can mean that a person is able to do something. Sometimes this is clarified as 'knowing that' and 'knowing how'. Going back to the content of the previous sections, skill is a form of the representation of learning and it is the ability to do something that has been learnt. Few writers seem to address the apparent difference between skills and knowledge even when they have noted the distinction and the confusion continues (e.g., Carter, 1985). One reason for this is the broad use of the term 'skill'. For example, all the following may be called 'skills':

- the ability to analyse a piece of literature ('cognitive' skill);
- the ability to give a good presentation in terms of content and delivery ('presentation' skill);
- the ability to handle a saw and make a clean straight cut in a piece of wood (physical/practical skill);
- the ability to write an essay ('study' skills);
- the ability to use a computer keyboard to type (physical/practical skill);
- the ability to score a bull on a dartboard (physical/practical skill).

In those tasks listed above is a range from fairly pure physical activities to those that involve deep interaction with the meaning of the task, in other words, they involve some 'knowing how' and some 'knowing that'. Most of the tasks involve several apparently quite different activities. It is likely that the blanket application of a theory of learning to this breadth of activity is not appropriate. It is difficult, for example, to equate the activity involved in learning to hit a target with a dart with the ability to learn how to work with meaning in order to analyse a piece of literature. The evident range of meaning of 'skill' does not facilitate clear thinking in the current 'skills agenda' in education. A new more focused vocabulary might help.

In terms of the boundaries of learning as it is described in this book, like Jarvis (1992), we would make it clear that we are not including the learning of pure physical skills such as typing or sawing wood or the physical acts of movement. Sometimes such physical skills are deployed in the process of learning knowledge – such as in the process of writing or in moving the eyes across a page in the process of reading. The book does not directly concern what has been called 'incidental' learning (Marsick and Watkins, 1990; Coffield, 1998; Eraut 1999) or everyday learning (Heller, 1984; Henze, 1992; Steiner, 1998), with pre- or unconscious thought such as in intuition (Claxton, 2000; Atkinson and Claxton, 2002). However, much that is written is relevant to these concepts.

The adoption of a general stance on learning: two views

In this section we begin to map the learning process. The introduction of the two views here serves to clarify the features of the model we adopt. In general terms, there is no obvious manner to consider the material that contributes to making sense of learning. It is complex and it seems that every concept relates to and modifies every other concept. This interactivity of the system is one of the several themes that will appear again and again.

We start with a situation in mind that involves instruction. It can be convenient to talk about learning being 'taken in', though we said that this use of terminology would be reviewed. In the first model of learning, the assumption is maintained that material of teaching is somehow 'taken in' or 'absorbed' by the learner, and retained in the same form as it is encountered (bar some modification because of memory). It is assumed that appropriate or effective learning would have happened if the learner has reasonably efficiently absorbed the material of teaching. The learner would then, at a later stage, be able to represent it reasonably closely to the form in which it was presented by the teacher. This accords with the 'building a brick wall' view of learning in which the teacher provides for the learner the 'bricks of knowledge'. It is assumed that teacher knows how these will fit the pattern of the wall. The wall – knowledge – is thus built up. Incorrect 'bricks' of knowledge are noticed in the representations of that learning, for example, in the way a learner speaks, in an essay or assessment task, or in the learner recognizing the incompatibility of some ideas. These incorrect ideas are then replaced by correct ones.

We have rejected the 'brick wall' view of learning elsewhere (Moon, 1999a). This model of learning makes it difficult to see learning apart from instruction, and does not deal helpfully with the vast majority of human learning situations – which is everyday learning with no act of active teaching involved. The constructivist view of learning, which we apply below, focuses on the activities of the learner in making sense of her world.

On a constructivist view of learning, a more useful metaphor for the development of learning than the brick wall is a vast but flexible network of ideas and feelings with groups of more tightly associated linked ideas/feelings. In the network some groups are far apart and some are near to each other and there are some relatively isolated ideas that have very few links to the network while others are well interconnected. Entwistle and Walker (2002) draw evidence from phenomenography (citing the work of Marton, e.g., 1994), neural science (citing Edelman, 1992), computer science and biology (citing Wilson, 1998) for this view of meaning where it is represented by a 'linkage among neural networks' (Wilson, 1998). Entwistle and Walker see understanding as being 'actively constituted' by the 'assembling and ordering . . . of . . . recollected sense impressions and knowledge' (2002,

p. 20). They emphasize the involvement of emotion (see Chapter 3 of this book) but do not expand on the nature of its role. The term 'cognitive structure' has been used as a convenience to describe the network of knowledge and understanding and associated feeling or emotion – 'what is known' by the learner at a particular time (Ausubel and Robinson, 1969; West and Pines, 1985; McAlpine and Weston, 2002).

In this view of learning, new ideas are linked into the network, but in being linked, they may be modified in the process. This is described as assimilation in learning (Piaget, 1971). The distinctive feature of this view of learning is the further process of accommodation (ibid.). Unlike the situation in the 'brick wall' metaphor, the material of learning does not just accumulate as knowledge, but the new material of learning itself can influence change in what is already known or understood – or it can change itself under the influence of what is already known. This is the more complex process of accommodation (Carey, 1988; Wilkes, 1997).

In the constructivist view of learning, there are two important developments beyond the notion of an 'accumulation'. First, there is the notion that the cognitive structure is flexible with the potential always to change, sometimes without the addition of new material of learning from outside the person. Second, the state of the cognitive structure at a given time facilitates the selection and assimilation of new material of learning. In other words, it guides what we choose to pay attention to, what we choose to learn and how we make meanings of the material of learning or how we modify what we know or feel already. The process of learning is not, therefore, about the accumulation of material of learning, but about the process of changing conceptions (Bowden and Marton, 1998). Given that learning usually implies that a person becomes progressively wiser and better at learning and understanding, a better phrase might be 'transforming conceptions'. This term seems to accord with the material on the development of the conceptions of knowledge (see Chapter 2).

Following on from the line of thinking above, there are implications for the idea of making meaning of something. If the cognitive structure is conceived in the manner suggested, then that something that is meaningful is a judgement made by the learner by relating the new material of learning to her current cognitive structure (Pardoe, 2000). This implies that a judgement of 'meaningfulness' cannot technically be made in the abstract or by another person. It brings the discussion to the stance taken by Kelly (1955) who suggested that man continuously constructs and reconstructs a view of the world on the basis of making sense of perceptions. Zuber-Skerritt puts it thus:

> people understand themselves and their environment and anticipate future events, by constructing tentative models or personal theories of themselves and their environment, and by evaluating these theories against personal

criteria as to whether the prediction and control of events (based on the models) have been successful or not. All theories are hypotheses created by people.

(1992, p. 57)

Kelly considered humankind to act as scientists perpetually developing ways of understanding events, testing those theories and rejecting, modifying or accepting them for the time being. He recognized that groups of people could share common views of the world (constructions of their experience) so they might have the same theories. In other words, they might share the same meaning of an object. He also believed that there is considerable variation in people's willingness to modify their theories in response to change (Bannister and Fransella, 1974).

The development of a concept of 'meaningfulness'

We have suggested that meaningfulness is a judgement to be made by the learner in the context of the sense of her cognitive structure (at that time). This is unintentionally illustrated by Ausubel and Robinson (1969) in making their alternative case that meaningfulness is a quality of the material of learning itself. These (American) writers try to argue that the three letters 'lud' will not be perceived by a learner as meaningful because the learner will not have associations for the term in her cognitive structure. They conclude, therefore, that meaningfulness is a quality of the material of learning and that the cognitive structure is simply an accumulation of knowledge. In fact, anyone aware of British culture is likely to have meaningful associations for 'lud' in the colloquial response to a judge ('me lud').

For the moment, we retain the idea that 'meaningfulness' is an individual judgement. The nature of meaningfulness in the constructivist approach is crucial for the relationships between the processes of learning and instruction and for the attempt to tease out the nature of experiential learning. If meaningfulness were a judgement that could be made objectively of the material of learning, a much closer relationship between the material of teaching and the material of learning would be implied. The teacher would know exactly what is going to be meaningful to the learner. However, if, as we are suggesting, meaningfulness is a judgement to be made by the learner, then the automatic relationship between teaching and learning is confirmed. If 'learners can create any number of meanings, intended or otherwise, out of the same learning experience' (Winitzky and Kauchak, 1997), judging what is meaningful to a learner becomes basically a matter of informed guesswork because the teacher does not have access to the brain of the learner. However, the accuracy of the guesswork can be enormously increased through experience and careful consideration of the cues provided by the learner as to her state of understanding of the material of learning. In accordance with these ideas, Angelo and Cross (1990) suggest the use of frequent and simple tests that provide feedback about the state of the learner's understanding for the teacher. Such ideas also lie behind notions of 'constructive alignment' in the curriculum (Biggs, 1999; Moon, 2002) in which there is deliberate alignment between the curriculum intentions, the learner's understandings and the forms of assessment that indicate the state of the learner's understanding.

The degree to which accommodation of the learner's existing cognitive structure occurs in the process of learning something new will vary. The process will be controlled by the learner's effort to balance the relationship between the new material of learning and the existing cognitive structure, however, external factors, including the influence of any teacher, can influence this process. A highly motivated learner on a short course that is interesting to her, where she trusts the teacher and knows that the new material of learning can improve the way she operates in the workplace, is likely to allow considerable accommodation in her cognitive structure. Another learner, who may not really want to be on the course or may have little confidence in the instructor, at the same time may not allow her cognitive structure to accommodate. She may not pay attention, or she may use other areas of cognitive structure to justify the rejection of the course material by developing arguments against its content.

The content of most material of learning that we encounter as learners is relatively as we expect it to be (Dart, 1997). In this context, 'expecting' something means that it is relatively in accordance with our cognitive structure as it is at that time and with changes that can be anticipated. The processes of assimilation and accommodation probably do not, therefore, involve great change. Sometimes, because of the state of the learner at the time (e.g., emotional state), or because of the dramatic nature of the material of learning itself or because of the difference between the learner's state and the material of learning, new material of learning provides a considerable challenge. An example is where new material of learning powerfully challenges personal beliefs or self-concepts that have become embedded in a personal orientation to the world. Accommodation, then, may lead to considerable change in attitude and behaviour. Initially the demands may be too great and the learner might amass arguments against the new material and justifications for the status quo. Even if extensive accommodation eventually occurs with regard to the subject matter, it may take some time for other areas of cognitive structure to become consistent. For example, a fundamental change in political belief may imply the development of different understandings of why people are poor and thence the adoption of different attitudes to poverty. This, in turn, may suggest that various areas of personal behaviour should change in order to maintain consistency of attitude and behaviour. For the individual, this might imply involvement with a different social group, and so on. With each change may come new learning that, in turn, will have an impact on the state of the cognitive structure, perhaps challenging again the initial major change. The term 'cognitive dissonance' has been used to describe the – often uncomfortable situations – in which new material of learning is in conflict with the learner's cognitive structure (Festinger,

1957). There may be a period during which a learner partly recognizes the conflict and variously tests the credibility of the new material of learning and the reliability of her current cognitive structure. Learners with a more sophisticated conception of the structure of knowledge become more able to recognize and find ways of working with inconsistencies (see Chapter 2).

Meaning in the social context

To maintain reasonable simplicity in the discussion of learning, cognitive structure and meaning above, we took an individual line, suggesting that meaning in learning is a matter for the individual. This idea does not need to be changed, but expanded. That a learner interprets (learns) new material of learning in her own manner and does or does not make sense of it for herself, not only implies adoption of an individual psychology of learning. The process of actually accommodating to new information must be individual, but the practices and the tools that a learner uses for this process have usually been developed as a social process. Humans do not learn everything from scratch. Knowledge is accumulated in ways that have been largely agreed through social means (Wilkes, 1997). Even the means of agreement are learned and socially agreed. On this basis, the notion of meaning resides between the locus of social agreement and the individual's efforts to understand, for herself, on a personal level. Having understood something, the individual then contributes to the pool of social meanings by adding her perspective when she represents her learning in some form (e.g., orally). There have been attempts to reconcile the views of learning that emphasize either the social or the individual orientation to learning and a useful line seems to be that taken by Marton and Booth (1997). Marton and Booth suggest that both have their place and that the most promising view of learning is that of an interaction between the social and the individual. The person and the world cannot be seen as separate but as existing in a dynamic relationship.

The use of language is a particularly important way in which our development of personal meaning is influenced socially. Language is a fundamental tool of learning, and ideas presented in the earlier pages of this chapter show how meaning is shaped through agreed language. In the first part of the chapter, it was observed that the manner in which we have been socialized to think about learning is affected by the socially agreed vocabulary of learning – some people do not distinguish between teaching and learning partly because their language does not have separate words for teaching and learning. In addition, it was suggested that exploration of the idea of learning may be constrained by the absence of vocabulary. The very tools that we have available for making meaning are socially constructed.

We do not, therefore, build meanings alone, but in conjunction with the collected experiences of others who may be teachers or scholars, or peers, past or present and all embedded in a culture of learning that is also socially agreed (Lave and Wenger, 1991). The following list summarizes some of the ways in which learning is affected by its social context:

- the manner in which understandings have been constructed in past social situations;
- the tools used in order to develop those understandings (e.g., language);
- the conventions associated with the knowledge (e.g., the notions of the disciplines and their methods of working with knowledge);
- the manner in which learning is expressed (e.g., in speech/written conventions/in action etc. – there are social conventions governing these);
- therefore the manner in which there is learning from the representation of learning (see earlier in this chapter).

We can make a major generalization that as humans, the more there is similarity in our life experiences, the more likely it is that we will share or at least comprehend each other's constructs. There are other factors in learning (covered in the following three chapters) to which the social paradigm is relevant. One is developmental and concerns the individual's conception of knowledge (Chapter 2). If an individual believes that some or all of her knowledge or ideas are fundamentally right or wrong, then logically she can only accept one version. If her social milieu contains alternative views about certain issues (e.g., different moralities about sexual behaviour), then she will not be able to comprehend views outside of her own. One mechanism for dealing with this is to decide that the holder of an alternative view 'is not like me', i.e., to create a social division to explain the difference in views, rather than accepting that views can differ. Other factors in an individual that influence learning are emotion or feelings (Chapter 3) and the approach that learners take to a learning task (Chapter 4). While these various factors modify learning or the approach that an individual takes to learning, a generalization can be made that encompasses all of these influences. A learner learns from experience. In other words, the material of learning is an element of experience that may be relatively discrete (we learn that apples and strawberries are in the rosacae family of plants) or more diffuse (we learn how it is to be in a new work environment). In addition, experience is likely to be thoroughly mediated by social influences and modified by other factors within the individual.

Learning, experience and meaning: an illustration

We build meanings by working with experience. We learn (something) *in relationship* to our present and prior experience since the prior experience (i.e., the state of the cognitive structure) guides how we respond to a present experience (Jarvis, 1992). The nature of experience is individual in the sense that it is an individual who experiences it, but it is also social, in that all experience is mediated by the social surroundings. An example from geology illustrates some of the issues in the consideration of experience as the basis for learning and emphasizes both the constructed nature of knowledge and the relationship between individual and social influences on learning.

There is a type of limestone quarried at Beer in Devon, that has long been valued because it is easy to quarry and to saw to shape, and then in the atmosphere it hardens to form an excellent building stone. It has been used for construction of many major buildings. A learner, Alice, in an adult and continuing education programme, sees on curricular details, that she will be going on a field trip to Beer to visit the underground quarries and to learn about the geology of the site. She has not heard of Beer or of Beer stone at first. Beer is a word and a place. The word might initially trigger associations with the drink, but this link will probably fade away as the meaningfulness of Beer, as a place, gains ascendancy. The notion of Beer stone might be meaningless at present – but is likely, having been listed in the curriculum, to be potentially meaningful to the learner when she relates it to other types of stone. A male colleague, Georgio, another learner, made a trip to Beer while on holiday and saw the quarries. As a result he has a cognitive structure that enables the concept (of stone) to be meaningful. The meaning might be associated with seeing the material but also with the stories told of the history of the quarrymen on a guided trip round the quarries. His meaning for 'Beer' will, in some measure, be directly shaped by social means in the form of the story-telling by the guide.

Before the trip the Alice asks Georgio about Beer and Georgio expresses his learning in the form of a story about the stone – its appearance and texture but also the memories that he has of the signatures of the seventeenth-century quarrymen that he saw on the walls of the quarries, etc. The story is socially constructed and triggers prior experiences in the mind of Alice (e.g., of once trying to inscribe her name on a slab of limestone). Eventually there is a lecture on the course that includes reference to the chemistry and geological origins of this limestone that gives rise to its qualities. The study of limestone could be part of biology – in that it is developed from biological material (shells), or maritime studies (since it was formed under the sea) – and so on. The fact that the ideas are being covered in geology means that any investigation in a practical sense will be geological, and any reports written will have used geological terminology. Geology, like other disciplines, is a human construction in itself.

Eventually Alice and Georgio and the other learners go on the field trip and see, touch and in other ways experience Beer stone. Alice can accommodate her prior knowledge gained from her conversations with Georgio to the new and personal experiences of the stone. The concept of Beer stone might then said to be more meaningful to her.

The paragraph above illustrates the social nature of learning and knowledge and how the learning process itself is socially mediated. Before the lecture on Beer stone from her conversation with Georgio, Alice had a number of experiences that created a 'slot' for the meaning of Beer stone in her cognitive structure which was represented by a set of expectations (Entwistle *et al.*, 2002). These prior experiences are likely to have influenced the manner in which she received the new information. For example, if she was told in the lecture that a feature of the stone is that it is so hard that it cannot be scratched, she would have material to re-evaluate (e.g., was Georgio credible when he told her about the quarrymen's signatures? Was he talking about some other stone? Is the lecturer credible? – etc.). There might be cognitive dissonance which would be disturbing.

External and internal experience

The paragraphs above begin to indicate the role of experience in learning. We have moved far now from the notion that learning is 'built up' or accumulated. We talk about the material of learning being an element of external prior experience but what we have inside our heads is also the representation of relevant experience. Before her visit to Beer and sight of the stone, Alice built up an internal mental experience which was to do with scratchability, chemical and geological qualities as well as the story of quarrying processes and so on. When she saw the rock, the learning process involved the interaction or flux between these forms of experience. It is useful to introduce the terminology 'external' and 'internal' experience to make a distinction here (Marton and Booth, 1997). External experience is the material of learning when we are learning about something outside of ourselves. It is the object, idea, the concept, the image – whatever it is that the learner wants to assimilate. In contrast, the internal experience is the experience that the learner brings to the learning situation from her current cognitive structure. It is the sum of prior experiences of the object. It is what she sees as related ideas with the effects of her understanding of the nature of knowledge (Chapter 2), relevant emotional influence (Chapter 3) and the influence of how she sees the learning task (Chapter 4). For example, if she feels that she only needs to memorize a few facts, she will have no need to draw on deep internal experience (Zsambok and Klein, 1997).

An important phenomenon that relates the external and internal forms of experience is appresentation (Marton and Booth, 1997). Appresentation is the manner in which a part of something that is perceived as an external experience can stimulate a much more complete or richer internal experience of the 'whole' of that thing to be conjured up. For example, seeing a familiar face triggers an internal experience of the whole person. The face depicted on a video-conference screen triggers an internal experience of a whole person and it is the whole person, with associated other perceptions, with whom communication is made. We do not relate our behaviour only to the part that we see. Internal experience can therefore be much richer than external experience and when we have information about an object, we will tend to respond to it on the basis of the appresentation of the object in internal experience instead of the thinner information 'of that moment' from the external experience of it. Of course, it is possible that the internal experience triggered is not appropriate, for example, the face on the video screen could stimulate an internal experience of a different person that does not match the face.

We briefly return to the idea of 'meaning'. On the basis of the paragraphs above what is the 'meaning' of something? Meaning changes with experience of a particular object, but it may change with alterations in the experience of other objects that are related to the first object. Going back to the example of Alice above, later in her programme, after her visit to Beer, Alice might learn more about the chemistry involved in the fossilization process. Beer stone, itself, might not have been mentioned in the lecture on fossilization, but her broader knowledge about stone and fossilization will invest more and possibly different meanings in the concept of Beer stone. We mentioned how thinking about Beer stone in buildings led to an enriched concept too. There might be, however, different qualities of meaning: on the field trip, someone jokes that Beer stone is, of course, hardened by painting beer on it. This too can become part of the 'meaning' of Beer stone – a meaning that might be exploited again in humour, or myth or in writing a story. Meaning is not present or absent but something that is invested in the internal experience of an object. When interpreting or representing meaning, the learner will pull out the meaning relevant to the context. A poem relating to the East Devon coast might pull out very different meanings of Beer stone to those meanings with which the learner works in an examination question about the geology of limestone – but they are all meanings of Beer stone.

Figure and ground in learning

In order to clarify the nature of reflective and experiential learning, we need to clarify the nature of learning itself. The distinction of the figure from the ground in a situation is a fundamental concept in learning that relates to many different aspects of the learning process (Marton and Booth, 1997). To illustrate the idea of figure and ground in learning, we return to the example of the learners on a field trip. It is the next year and another group is going to Beer. The field trip is arranged and the students go to Beer presumably, from the context of the programme, to see the stone, touch it, learn about its commercial properties, see it in its geological context, and maybe to consider its significance in architecture. This year, however, nobody has actually briefed them on how they should focus their attention.

They are level 1 (i.e. first stage of a higher education programme) learners without much background in geology. They just have a general knowledge that the trip is something to do with the course. At Beer, one learner is fascinated by the social history of quarrying and listens attentively to stories about the lives of those involved, imagining them walking along the miles of funnels with their candles in an environment of fantastic noise and dust. Another is intrigued by the structure of the caves, and how they reflect the different periods of their development in the form of the quarrying. Another learner is conscious that there is likely to be an examination question related to Beer stone, and focuses her attention on what she can learn of the physical and commercial qualities of the stone. Another learner enrolled on this programme because she likes the social circumstances of field trips and the visit to see Beer stone is a means to a social end. The students have different intentions for the trip and, without a briefing, may feel uncertain how to focus their awareness. They will have 'pulled' different figures forward for their learning, from broadly what is the same ground. As a result, they will have developed different constructs. This may or may not matter. If they are to be assessed on their knowledge of Beer stone, then it will be unfortunate if their knowledge is largely of the social history of the quarrymen. If the trip is to give them a general feeling for the history of the quarrying industry, then their learning may be 'good enough'.

Frames of reference

On the same trip, there can be many different forms of learning. Learners may have different focuses of concern and they focus their awareness on different things accordingly. In other words, they have different frames of reference in any situation. Briefing or initial guidance for the trip would have suggested a frame of reference that they could use in order to guide their learning on the programme. Within the chosen frame of reference, the distinction of figure from ground is made. So far, in this example, the difference between the frame of reference and the figure/ground system may seem straightforward but in reality, there will be a fluid situation in which the frame of reference is constantly influenced and re-influenced by the distinction of figure from ground. To complicate matters further, there are many frames of reference operational at the same time in any learning situation (see below).

Going back to the example of the field trip, we suggested that the learners' frames of reference could be influenced by knowledge of curriculum requirements, a briefing from a teacher, interest or social matters. The teacher could not be seen as *providing* the frame of reference, because the frame of reference is constructed by the learner. Factors that influence the learner's frame of reference might be her perception of the briefing in relation to her motivation on the programme, her own intentions related to anticipations of the learning situation and prior knowledge. Two other important influences on how learning tasks are framed are the learner's understanding of what it is to learn, how learning relates to the structure of knowledge, and any relevant emotional influences. These other important influences on the framing or learning are considered in Chapters 2, 3 and 4.

We have suggested above that a learner's prior experience influences the frames of reference used and that prior experience is part of the internal experience. The constructed frame of reference could be said not only to direct the attention outwards towards aspects of the material of learning, but also to influence the manner in which the internal experience is 'assembled'. So if a learner's frame of reference concerns the physical nature of the Beer stone, the ideas relevant to this are brought to the fore in internal experience to facilitate appropriate learning. The frame of reference could be said to be a guide and to act as a driver of the system of internal and external experiences in learning so that we learn what it is that we want to learn in an appropriate manner. It enables the learner to focus on *relevant* aspects of the external experience (Marton and Booth, 1997).

The paragraph above, of course, simplifies the situation. Learning in a field situation is immensely complex with many influences occurring all the time. There may be constant framing and reframing of reference and constant distinctions being made between figure and ground, all functioning at different levels simultaneously. This is an important issue when it comes to the development of situations in which students are expected to learn the complexities of real life from experience (Chapter 12).

We focus largely on learning in formal situations because some of the points to be made in this chapter are clearer in this kind of 'laboratory' situation. In such a situation, for example, a learner's frames of reference for learning are deliberately influenced. Cues are given to help learners to develop appropriate frames of reference and within that to focus on the relevant factors. While the curriculum may be important as one cue to learning, in many situations now, learners are provided with a list of learning outcomes that indicate to them what they should achieve at the end of a period of learning (such as a module) (Moon, 2002a). These indicate to the learner the quality of knowledge and/or skill that will need to be demonstrated in order to 'pass', with detail provided in assessment criteria. More guidance to enable learners to frame their learning effectively will come directly from the teaching process and from material such as handouts, and reading lists.

Variation

We return to the mechanics of learning to introduce another concept that almost inevitably follows from the notion of figure and ground. In a given situation there may or may not be features to be perceived as figures against the ground that enable the learner to learn. Either the figures do not match the learner's intentions, or they may not differ from those already learnt, in other words, there is no variation in the external experience from the relevant internal experience within the cognitive structure of the learner.

Going back to the example of the Beer stone, the actual experience of seeing and touching the rock and other experiences of the field day are likely to lead to learning. However, if the learner was to pay a second visit to Beer very soon after the first, then, oversimplifying the example, there may be no more learning to do about the rock. A manner of interpreting this is that there are no differences between internal and external experience and therefore no need for new learning activity. In order that there is to be new learning, there needs to be variation in the experience. Learning, on this basis, is a process of experiencing variation and choosing to accommodate to that variation – which will, in effect, change the experience (Marton and Booth, 1997). It is easiest to see that the variation in the external experience is that which leads to learning, in other words, there is new material of learning. However, on the model we are using of internal and external experience, learning can also result when there are changes in the internal experience, while the external experience remains the same. Let us take a new example.

The example is of a learner, who is learning how to change a wheel by watching a video of the procedure. On the basis that variation is essential for learning, we could say that a learner wanting to learn how to change a car wheel by watching the same video of the procedure twenty times, will probably have ceased to learn after the first few viewings. But the chances are that the learning is continually enhanced for further viewings because the learner creates her own variation by changing the aspects of figure and ground to which she attends. In other words subtly she changes her frame of reference, seeing new aspects of the process. She is working with variation in her external experience through the guidance of her internal experience. She could actively interact with the process by identifying questions to herself while she is viewing. The questions create variation by changing the frame of reference. So variation may not only be in a change of a learning object, but through the learner changing the frames of reference adopted, which is an active form of learning.

We have suggested that learning occurs in response to variation in the external experience as well as through changes in frame of reference that enable the learner to see something differently in the same situation. There seem to be at least two other ways in a learning situation in which variation can occur and thus lead to more learning. Both of these involve active change of the internal experience by the learner in a process of reflection. The learner may only watch the video once or twice, but then reflect on the content of the video, relating it to other knowledge and understandings and bringing that knowledge to bear on this situation and thereby varying aspects of her internal experience. There is no contact with the actual material of learning in external experience, but the learner is using the ideas that she can summon from her cognitive structure to enhance the learning process. Moon (1999a) introduces the term 'cognitive housekeeping' for this operation of the process of reflection (Chapter 6).

The other important manner of creating variation without change in the learning situation is through the representation of the learning. The learner may have seen the video once, and she may now be asked to put the learning into practice by changing a wheel in the manner demonstrated. For the moment, we will assume that she has not changed a wheel before. As stated earlier, learners can learn through the representation of their learning. As the learner goes through the process of changing a wheel, she will be working with the learning from the video and with the practical considerations that feed back to her from the practice of wheel changing. There will be variation between her 'educated' internal experience and the new learning from the representation of the learning. Her learning about changing a wheel will have come from the video and from practice and will be enriched as a result. This works on the assumption that there are no negative factors that come to bear on the process, for example, it is possible that difficulties or failure in the practice of changing the wheel might block her learning by bringing emotional influence to bear on the process of learning. In contrast, emotional encouragement can make learning easier (Chapter 3). Both of these two forms of learning to change a wheel can be seen as forms of reflective learning.

We can summarize the concept of variation: learners learn from variation in learning situations. There are at least four forms of variation. They are when the following happens:

- there is change in the external experience in the material of learning;
- with the same material of learning, the learner changes her frame of reference and perceives different details, thereby changing her external experience;
- the learner works with her internal experience and relates it to other prior experience and learns more as a result (cognitive housekeeping);
- the learner represents her learning and learns from comparison of the variation of the external experience between practices.

We shall expand on these ideas in later chapters, in particular, Chapter 6.

Fazey and Marton (2002) describe the result of work in which there was application of the concept of variation to a number of teaching and learning situations. These included learning in music, motor skills and familiar academic work and unfamiliar topics. Situations were presented that encouraged learners to vary their approach to learning to a particular task or topic and sometimes there was a control group (experiencing little deliberate variation). A simple example working with motor co-ordination was throwing up a shuttlecock in different ways (with variation) and the same way, with little or no variation. Those experiencing variation learned better. In some of the situations, learners who practised with non-varying material of learning had learnt better than those experiencing variation immediately after the learning session, but those experiencing variation retained the material better. Fazey and Marton not only illustrate the significance of variation in learning, but also they demonstrate its importance as a principle for pedagogy.

Variation is therefore central to learning. We have said that learning is different from teaching. But because pedagogical situations are characterized by the management of variation for learners, we briefly focus on teaching. In effect, we have said above that the efficient learner is one who manages her own relationship to the variations in order to learn according to her intentions. Both for learners whose learning is facilitated by a teacher and for learners working alone, central to the process of management of variation is an awareness of the state of flux between internal and external experience. Marton and Booth (1997) use the term 'architecture of variation' for situations of instruction to suggest that the teacher of a group of individuals needs to take into account the range of ways in which her material of teaching might be perceived by the individuals. The examples that are given to illustrate this point are mainly situations where the learners are being instructed to learn a specific concept, which needs to be grasped 'correctly'. In this case, management of the architecture of variation is a matter first of all of the teacher managing what she perceives to be the external experience of learners. It is also a matter of anticipation of potential variations to be perceived by the learners and influencing them towards the comprehension of the concept. The idea of 'advance organizers', advocated in the 1970s ties in with these ideas (Ausubel, 1960). Advance organizers are intended to help the learner to orientate and organize her internal experience of an object of learning so that the learning process can be guided by internal experience as effectively as possible.

In effect, there are many less formal ways of influencing the internal experience at the beginning of a learning situation than the advance organizer. The kind of management of potential variation will differ according to the level of learning and the discipline. For example, in the humanities or with more mature students, it may not be the intention of the teacher that all the learners learn exactly the same but that they can pursue their own perceptions of the material of teaching and interpret it for themselves. In this case the 'architecture of variation' will require a different kind of management by the teacher – a form of teaching that is more 'inspirational' rather than specific. Herein we meet some of the apparent differences between adult and child learning – pedagogy and andragogy (Knowles, 1980). An adult's needs are likely to be to make sense of previous understandings – that may form potential variations for a new learning situation. In a child's learning, variation is likely to be characterized by 'gaps' in understanding or misconception, due to lack of prior knowledge.

Learning knowledge and learning to learn

We can summarize the process of learning as described in this chapter. We learn through the assimilation of the material of learning. When there is information external to the person, the material of learning is conceived as an external experience. We learn through the comparison of external experience with the current internal experiences that we bring to bear on the material of learning. Internal experience is the relevant prior knowledge and experience. This guides the means of assimilation by guiding our frames of reference in relation to external experience, enabling us to focus on the relevant variations in the current external experience and taking account of the variations between current internal and external experience. In the process of assimilating new material of learning, the cognitive structure accommodates. We talk of conceptions being changed or transformed in the process of learning. In learning, these processes operate in at least two ways. Our examples, in this chapter, have largely related to the content of learning, learning about something, but we can apply the same processes to learning how to learn. As a learner progresses, in other words, becomes a more efficient learner, she learns more content, but also learns more about learning. The subject matter of the next three chapters concerns the process of learning to learn and as such, they are particularly relevant to reflective and experiential learning.

Introduction to Chapters 2, 3, 4 on the framing of learning

Particular types of frames of reference are the topics of the next three chapters. These chapters explore frames of reference which seem to have a particular bearing on the manner in which reflective and experiential learning become more sophisticated processes variously following maturation, personal development and education. A basic assumption with the frames of reference that are the subject of these chapters is that framing material of learning in one way is more effective for learning than framing it in another way. The chapters cover:

- conceptions of the structure of knowledge (Chapter 2);
- emotion and learning (Chapter 3);
- approaches to learning (Chapter 4).

Mostly it would seem that the process of learning to learn is not conscious and intentional, but is led by the challenges that are inherent in the material to ensure that this progression occurs. For example, learners who have been given clear and easy-to-follow lecture notes on handouts may have to learn to learn from their own notes as they progress in a programme or move from one teacher to another. Learning to learn can be characterized as the improving ability of the learner to manage the framing of her learning in order to fulfil more sophisticated purposes or to cope effectively with more complex material of learning. In different ways, the topics of these next three chapters all address different aspects and there are also many ways in which they are also interdependent. We bring the three types of framing together at the end of Chapter 4.

Chapter 2

The framing of learning
The conception of the structure of knowledge

Introduction

This chapter concerns the developing conceptions of the structure of knowledge (often shortened to development of conceptions of knowledge). This is a frame of reference that has much to do with the process of learning to learn (see Chapter 1). Most humans in a reasonably stimulating environment seem to progress to a certain point in their understanding of the nature of knowledge. This is evident in the manner in which they represent their learning. An example is in the way in which they might use knowledge to justify judgements that they make and it is particularly evident in the judgement of moral issues (King and Kitchener, 1994). A growing sophistication in understanding of knowledge seems to be assumed in most processes of formal education, but it is not a quality that has often been made explicit. If knowledge grows and changes, then it should not be viewed as a 'commodity' (as in the current jargon), but as a process (Polyani, 1969).

This chapter is concerned mainly with the outcomes of four projects in which the development of the conceptions of the structure of knowledge has been studied. These have been, mainly, but not only, in student populations. These studies are broadly summarized and the inter-relationship with other observations of student learning is described (for example, level descriptors and student assessment).

Development of conceptions of the structure of knowledge

Studies of conceptions of knowledge

We have looked at the body of research and thinking on the development of conceptions of knowledge in previous writing in different contexts of learning and reflection and the previous writing is brought together in this book with no contradictions. For example, in Moon (1999a), the work was used to support the notion that there is a developmental progression in the capacity for reflection. In Moon (1999b and 2002a), it was used in a pedagogical sense to support the idea that materials designed for learners should not be too 'tidied up' and simplified. Learners need to be challenged with their material of learning in order to make progress in their ability to manage increasingly complex situations of learning. Since the first book was written, the conviction has increased that the learner's conception of the role of the structure of knowledge is highly significant in the effectiveness of learning and its interaction with the teaching process, particularly at higher levels. Reference to these ideas, however, is not widespread, though there are exceptions in some recent publications on learning (e.g., Morgan, 1995; Beaty *et al.*, 1997; Savin-Baden, 2000; Entwistle and Walker, 2002). William Perry's work was once well known and featured as a topic in most programmes of educational psychology (Perry, 1970; O'Reilly, 1989).

We cover this material on the learner's understanding of the structure of knowledge through reference to four studies that could be said to have built on and complemented each other's work (Perry, 1970; King and Kitchener, 1994; Belenky *et al.*, 1986; Baxter Magolda, 1992). A useful area of literature that seems closely related to the discussions in this chapter is the development of the understanding of science (e.g., Songer and Linn, 1991; Reif and Larkin, 1991). Since it is likely that there are cultural influences on the conception of knowledge, it is important to be aware that the research in the four studies is based on work with western subjects largely with personal histories of white western education systems.

Perry's work on learners' conceptions of knowledge

Perry worked in the 1960s and the 1970s. He considered that he was exploring the students' intellectual and ethical development and his work was based on extensive and relatively unstructured interviews with students at Harvard and later Radcliffe in the USA. He describes how the students' conceptions of knowledge and the way they saw themselves as 'knowers' changed over their years at college. He worked mostly with male students though in the early stages he included a few female students, who seemed to perform in a similar manner to the males. Perry describes the students' progression through a sequence of what he termed 'positions' in relation to their epistemological understandings. He suggested that a student's epistemological position provides a frame of reference for the manner in which the student interprets meaning – in this case, in his college experience. In the initial position, which Perry described as 'basic dualism', students view knowledge in terms of polarities – 'right and wrong', 'black and white', 'them and us', and so on. He saw the learners in this position as passive, accepting the knowledge of 'truth' from authorities (e.g., their teachers) without question. As the students progressed, in the interviews he observed them moving towards the recognition that it is possible for experts to hold opposing opinions, and that there can be multiple perspectives on an issue. He described this as the position of multiplicity. It is a time when the students come to recognize an initial difference between opinion and 'fact'. At this stage they were gaining confidence in holding opinions with the sense that they 'had a right to their opinion' (Belenky *et al.*, 1986). In the final position of 'relativism', he saw students coming to understand the need to base their opinion on evidence. They saw knowledge as relative to the context in which it was situated, recognizing that that is constructed. In other words, they understood and could work with the idea that the nature of knowledge is relative to the frame of reference that is applied to it by the learner in the prevailing circumstances.

A significant feature of Perry's approach to the development of understanding is what he called 'commitment'. He suggested that students who had reached the position of relativism in their conception of knowledge, made difficult decisions (e.g., about personal issues) by reliance on 'personal commitment'. They decided to commit themselves to one side or the other of the dilemma. 'Commitment' could either be interpreted as a special element of this stage, or a strong statement of the recognition of ultimate personal responsibility for decision. However, King and Kitchener (1994) did not see 'commitment' as the final stage of development and suggested that there is development beyond this that Perry either did not see in his samples, or did not recognize.

Belenky, Clinchy, Goldberger and Tarule (1986)

In contrast to that of Perry, the work of Belenky, Clinchy, Goldberger and Tarule (1986) was exclusively with women. These researchers considered that although female students appeared to function similarly to males in the Perry study, the interviews may have been biased. Belenky *et al.*'s study was also conducted by long semi-structured interviews, but they included a series of embedded questions that were designed to match the women to a position on Perry's scheme. There were ninety college students or alumni and forty-five women from family agencies. The transcripts of the interviews were coded blind and the writers felt that that five 'epistemological perspectives' were evident in the transcripts. The first perspective was described as 'silence'. These 'silent' women saw themselves as incapable of having a voice of their own, and they felt themselves to be at the whim of authority. The second perspective was 'received knowledge'. The group of women with this perspective felt that they could receive and reproduce ideas, but they were not able to create their own knowledge. The third perspective of 'subjective knowledge' was characterized by women feeling that truth and knowledge are 'personal and private, subjectively known or intuited' (ibid., p. 15). The next perspective was 'procedural knowledge'. Women in this group sensed that they had knowledge, and could 'apply objective procedures for obtaining and communicating' it (ibid.). Those with the perspective of 'constructed knowledge' viewed knowledge as related to its context. They saw themselves as 'creators of knowledge' and valued 'both subjective and objective strategies for knowing' (ibid.).

The epistemological categories identified by Belenky *et al.* were recognized to be abstracted from reality and not necessarily universal (Ryan, 2001). The writers did not feel that their subjects were totally consistent in their viewing of knowledge and nor did they feel that they had evidence to suggest a developmental progression. Their identification of perspectives clearly had a strong resemblance to Perry's positions and the writers indicated from this that it is likely that men would have similar categories to their thinking.

King and Kitchener (1994)

King and Kitchener (1994) worked on what they called 'reflective judgement'. They adopted a broader remit that that of the other two projects described above, studying both genders and a range of ages in empirical studies that lasted over fifteen years. They used subjects' capacity to work on what the project team called 'ill-structured' problems as an indicator of how they considered knowledge and how they used it in solving problems for which there was no definite answer. Ill-structured problems have no 'right or wrong' answer, but require reasoning and personal judgement. Ethical issues provide a good example. The term is adopted in this book with the same definition. Significantly, the writers noted that many of the tools used to judge 'critical thinking' and other forms of intellectual development rely on 'structured' problems where there is an actual solution to be sort, usually in a standard manner. They saw the intellectual requirements for such functioning as at a lower stage of intellectual development. Subjects were given a series of these specially designed problems. Probe questions attempt to investigate the kind of thinking that underlaid the response that was given. In other words, rather than observing the ways in which subjects indicated their view of knowledge in discussion in an interview, they were required to represent their view of knowledge in set tasks. The tasks tested subjects' conception of knowledge and their processes of justification for responses that they produced in problem-solving situations. Such issues in reasoning are particularly tested in the cognitive skills of the manipulation of knowledge in the higher levels of formal education, such as analysis, evaluation and argument. It is at this level in higher education that learners would be expected to be able to deal with issues where there is uncertainty and unpredictability.

King and Kitchener identified seven stages of development towards reflective judgement and saw reflective judgement as existing only at the most advanced two stages. The writers describe the stages as 'qualitatively different networks of concepts that affect ill-structured problem solving' (1994, p. 47). The characteristics are summarized below:

> In the Pre-Reflective Stages (1, 2 and 3), people do not acknowledge that there is the possibility that knowledge can be uncertain and because of this, they cannot understand that there can exist problems that do not have a correct solution. This means that they do not need to seek reasons or evidence for the solution to a problem. There is an assumption that authorities carry 'the truth', and all they have to do is to learn this truth. These stages would be characteristic mainly of young children who start to move beyond when the complexity of such issues as religion confront them – or when they recognize that those that they consider as authorities pose differing views.
>
> In the Quasi Reflective Thinking Stages (4 and 5), there is an acknowledgement that some problems are ill-structured and that there may be situations of uncertain knowledge. While those do provide evidence for their reasoning, they do not know how to use it appropriately. In the earlier stage, while everyone is seen as having a right to her own opinion, the reasoning of others who disagree with them must be wrong. Later there is recognition that different frames of reference rely on different forms of evidence. However, there is lack of understanding that evidence and consequently chosen frames of reference need to be compared and contrasted.
>
> There are two Stages of Reflective Judgement (6 and 7). In these stages people understand that knowledge is not given but constructed and that claims of knowledge are related to the context in which they are generated. This implies further that a response to an ill-structured problem in one time might be different at another time. In the earlier stage of reflective judgement, there is a tendency to develop judgements on the basis of internal considerations. In the most sophisticated stage, intelligence is reflected as a skilled and sensitive ability to work with the complexities of a situation, with imagination that is used in the proposition of new possibilities and hypotheses. There is a willingness to learn from experience. Particularly characteristic of these highest stages of functioning, is the recognition by the subject that her processes of reasoning influence the response that she makes. Such meta-cognitive processes are particularly important for later discussions of reflective activities.

There is obviously a similarity between these stages identified by King and Kitchener, the epistemological perspectives of Belenky *et al.*, and the positions of Perry, though King and Kitchener did not agree with the notion of 'commitment' in Perry's work. 'Commitment' seemed to contradict the concept that all knowledge is provisional and may be re-evaluated at any time and they considered that the most advanced stages of reflective judgement may represent stages of greater development than was evidenced in Perry's work. Again in disagreement with Perry, they considered that the earliest stages of development are more characteristic of children than of college students. Like Belenky *et al.*, King and Kitchener felt that their subjects tended to progress in their levels of intellectual functioning when they were in educational situations.

Another interesting issue with regard to the development of conceptions of knowledge in formal education is whether different disciplines enable learners to progress more or less quickly through stages such as those described by King and Kitchener. Perry's students were from a liberal arts background and, if discipline is relevant to the development of particular conceptions of knowledge, then this sample demonstrates bias in this direction. Different disciplines provide different qualities of 'learning to learn experiences' for learners. For example, those who study the humanities are likely to confront the use of a variety of frames of reference (e.g., critical studies of art and literature) much earlier than students studying maths and sciences. There is anecdotal evidence that students who learn about the theory of knowledge, as a subject, find the ideas helpful as a support for their future studies (Moon, 2002a). Earlier they will have a broader understanding that knowledge is not simply a commodity to be acquired, but is constructed, and structured differently in different contexts.

Baxter Magolda (1992, 1994, 1996)

Baxter Magolda's main work on 'knowing and reasoning in college' (Baxter Magolda, 1992) was published a little before that of King and Kitchener. It is positioned at the end of the description of the studies of conceptions of knowledge because it provides quotations that usefully illustrate all four studies. Baxter Magolda studied just over a hundred college students over a five-year period, still retaining seventy of the students in the fifth year. Her interest was on conceptions of knowledge in terms of hypothesized gender differences. She did not strongly substantiate her gender difference hypothesis, but did provide useful confirmation of the stages of conceptions of knowledge that had first been identified in Perry's 'positions'. She used semi-structured interviewing as her research method and identified four 'domains' of knowing and reasoning which broadly match the sequences of the other workers described above. She was particularly interested in the emergence of the student's own 'voice' – an idea that emerged in Belenky *et al.*'s work and that has importance in the study of reflective learning later in this book.

'Absolute knowing' is the least developed stage in Baxter Magolda's scheme, wherein knowledge is seen as certain or absolute and formal learning is a matter of absorption of the knowledge of the experts (e.g., teachers). She describes a second stage as 'transitional knowing', in which there are doubts about the certainty of knowledge – a sense that there is both partial certainty and partial uncertainty. The third domain is represented by 'independent knowing' – when learners recognize the uncertainty of knowledge, and feel that everyone has her own opinion or beliefs. This seems to be an embryonic form of the most sophisticated domain, that of 'contextual knowing' in which knowledge is seen as constructed, and is understood in relation to the deployment of evidence that best fits a given context.

Baxter Magolda's system of four domains seem usefully to summarize the findings of the various investigations of the development of conceptions of knowledge which have more stages described while using apparently the same general ideas in the progression. The multiple stages of the other studies could be seen as providing the detail of the transitions between the stages. It is interesting to note Baxter Magolda's observation that students shifted between domains and might work on different conceptions for different topics at the same time. This supports the adoption of the simpler four-stage system that she used.

We can summarize this section, in which studies have been reviewed, with quotations from Baxter Magolda's book. These are quotations from students within different domains of their conception of knowledge, talking about their understandings of learning:

Absolutist – knowledge is certain or absolute.
For example, Eileen – I have to see what I'm learning, and I have to know why. I have a good memory and it's very easy for me to memorise facts. The advantage is that it's kind of cut and dried. The information is there – all you have to do is to soak it up in your brain.

(Baxter Magolda, 1992, p. 77)

Transitional stage – there is partial certainty and partial uncertainty.
For example, Bob – I took a different teacher in the sophomore level of the subject, and I learned to interpret things differently. When you have someone else give you a different interpretation of the same subject, you're forced to go back and do comparisons. And I thought, well, why would this person teach this subject this way and be successful and at the same time there's a person teaching it in a different way but still being successful? It begins to change you a bit.

(ibid., p. 103)

Independent knowing – learning is uncertain – everyone has her own beliefs.
For example, Sandra – I guess I take everything in and then I go home at night and kind of sort out what I want and what I don't want. Some things, I guess – maybe because of my morals and values – will sit better with me and will seem like fact for me. And other things, I'm just like 'I don't really think so'. And I throw them out.

(ibid., p. 141)

Contextual knowing – knowledge is constructed and any judgement must be made on the basis of the evidence in that context.

For example, Gwen – As you hear other people's opinions, you piece together what you really think. Who has the valid point? Whose point is not valid in your opinion? And [you] come to some other new understanding. Even if it's the same basic belief, maybe [you will be] able to look at it from a more (multi)dimensional perspective.

(ibid., p. 173)

Subsequently Baxter Magolda worked with many of the students in their various destinations after they left college (Baxter Magolda, 1994, 1996). She found that her subjects often progressed quickly to the stage of contextual knowing especially if they were required to make significant independent decisions.

Conceptions of knowledge for learning: some other studies

We have described the studies on the conceptions of knowledge at some length because they are not widely discussed elsewhere and are very relevant to this book. In this section first we review three ways in which the models of different conceptions of knowledge have been recognized implicitly in other work on learning. This provides useful supporting evidence for the studies above. Then we take a more general view of how differences in the conception of knowledge might affect the manner in which a learner learns from her experiences.

The first case comes from a study of an agreed and well-used set of level descriptors in UK higher education e.g., SEEC (2003), (Moon, 2002a). Level descriptors are descriptions of the kind of learning that is expected from learners at given stages (levels) in education. These descriptors had been developed and agreed by representatives from many disciplines. There was no deliberate involvement of educational theory at their inception, but in the words used to describe student learning there is considerable evidence of the changing views of the conception of learning discussed above. There were references, for example, to learners being increasingly able to handle unpredictable or ill-structured material, to their ability to make judgements on the basis of analysis of evidence, to their understanding of the constructed nature of knowledge and of their increasing independence from 'authority'. As a learner develops her understanding of the structure of knowledge, she can frame her learning more effectively and with greater flexibility because she will have an appreciation of how her areas of knowledge inter-relate.

While the idea of level implies that all learners at a particular level in education might be functioning in the same way, the reality is probably different. Perry noticed that subects who differed in the manner in which they viewed the structure of knowledge often co-existed at the same educational stage and this might be evident in their ability to use evidence to support an argument. One of Perry's articles captured the significance of this in a title: 'Different Worlds in the Same Classroom' (Perry, 1970). He gives the example of a (male) lecturer lecturing on three possible theoretical explanations for a phenomenon. One student, assuming that there are correct and non-correct answers to everything, waits for the lecturer to tell him which is the correct theory so that he can then learn it. Another has a fairly similar orientation, though recognizes that the matter is not quite so straightforward. He understands that the lecturer may be presenting the material in a way that will force students to work on their thinking but still expects there to be a correct outcome. The third student recognizes that the appropriate theory is appropriate because, after an examination of the underlying assumptions, it is best supported in that context. The assumptions that the lecturer makes about the way in which the students are thinking will determine how he structures the material of teaching and, correspondingly, how well the students will learn from the session.

In terms of education in the UK, a time when the point made above may seem particularly pertinent is in Master's degree programmes. Learners who have not been in formal education for a long time often work alongside new graduates and overseas students who may have different views of teaching and learning. In a short time, they are all expected to be using the sophisticated concepts of knowledge in essays and research processes that are characteristic of the descriptions of Master's level.

The second case in this section is a study of assessment by Miller and Parlett (1974). Miller and Parlett studied the assessment process of thirty students who were being assessed in their final examinations. They found that students fell into three categories that were reliably recognized by independent judges. There were 'cue-seekers', who actively sort information about their examinations, the interests of the examiner, and asked for hints. The second group was labelled the 'cue-conscious'. They talked about the need to be aware of the information and hints, and the value of making a good impression on the examiner, but were not active in these pursuits. The third group was labelled the 'cue-deaf' and seemed to think that working as hard as possible would bring success.

In the study, there were statistically significant differences in the performances of the students in their examinations. The 'cue-seekers' were most likely to get firsts, the 'cue-conscious' were more likely to get upper seconds and the 'cue-deaf' were most likely to get lower seconds. In considering what might lie behind these different approaches to assessment, Miller and Parlett looked at the positions of Perry. They felt that the 'cue-seekers' seemed to characterize relativistic attitudes to knowledge and assessment. They understood the role of assessment in the system, and what they needed to do to achieve success. Like the cue-seekers, the cue-conscious understood 'that there was a technique involved' and that 'authority could be affected by spurious things such as personal likes and dislikes; and marking might not be perfect' (1974, p. 63) but they were not committed actively to do anything about it. The cue-deaf seemed to believe that examinations were about learning the 'right' body of knowledge as decreed by an authority who was a teacher who was seen as knowing what was best for the students. Another way of interpreting the work of Miller and Parlett is to suggest that the cue-conscious students, whose functioning was equated with more sophisticated conceptions of knowledge, were more able to detect the appropriate relevance in learning situations (see Chapter 1). In this respect, this work also relates to the work on approaches to learning that is described in Chapter 4.

The last case study relates conception of knowledge to reflection and as such is directly related to material later in this book (Chapter 7). There are a number of schemes in the literature that describe qualities of reflective writing arranged in different depths of reflection (e.g., Van Manen, 1977; Hatton and Smith, 1995). A new framework is presented in this book which draws on the literature on reflection and the experiences of practitioners (p. 214). The several levels of reflective writing relate to work on conceptions of knowledge. The initial level in the framework is the description of an event without further processing. The second level is reflection in which only one point of view is used and in the later stages there is more sophisticated reflection in which the learner is aware of there being potentially different views of the same event. She also recognizes the role of her own processing in influencing the form of her reflection, and this will include an awareness of her emotional state on any conclusions that she might reach.

Conceptions of knowledge and learning processes

The examples above begin to relate the theoretical approaches to the conception of knowledge to 'real-life' events in education. How do the different conceptions of knowledge relate to the theoretical ideas about learning that were introduced in the previous chapter? This chapter was introduced as relating to the process of learning to learn, in contrast to much of the last chapter that was about the process of learning content and we suggested that the same principles apply to it as were applied to the learning of content. Thus, we can say that the development of the conception of knowledge is a matter of learners modifying their view of knowledge in progressively more sophisticated manners according to the schemes described above. It is more useful to say, however, that they frame the manner in which they work with knowledge in progressively more sophisticated manners. This enables them to deal with more complex learning or representation of learning tasks. The conscious or unconscious decision about how to frame knowledge means that the learner is working with her internal experience as opposed to the material of learning (her external experience). She is bringing a way of thinking about her learning process to the process of accommodating new material of learning. In the previous chapter, we described this as a flux between internal and external experience.

As a learner becomes more sophisticated in the manner in which she conceives of knowledge, we can say that she becomes more flexible in the manner in which she works with knowledge – and more flexible in the way in which she sees knowledge is used by others. Most of what we do with knowledge relies on knowledge that has been generated by others. On the basis of King and Kitchener's work, learners who use true reflective judgement understand that learning is constructed and are also able to understand the ways in which others (who have less advanced conceptions of knowledge) view learning. In an assessment of evidence to justify a position in an argument, a sophisticated learner is more able to see that it is possible to view the same matter from a number of different frames of reference, and to work with different figures and grounds in the same situation. An example of this arises in Miller and Parlett's work on assessment. The 'cue-seeking' learners were able to see assessment within a broader frame of reference – as a feature of a system (i.e., higher education) – in which they choose to succeed. They had more choice of frames of reference.

Furthermore, in the progression towards understanding of the constructed nature of knowledge, learners become more metacognitive, understanding that their own processes as learners affect the manner in which they construe knowledge. This does not mean that they are always in control of the manner in which they learn; the next section on personal management of learning suggests that there may be many more variables at work here. However, if a learner understands her own processes of learning, her awareness gives her more tools available to improve or change an approach to learning or behaviour in a given situation. For example, if a learner knows that a certain aspect of work triggers feelings of discomfort, she is more able to work to alleviate it.

Entwistle (Entwistle and Walker, 2002), referring to studies of the conceptions of knowledge, talks of the development of a 'nested hierarchy' of conceptions. This implies that the sophisticated learner can have a more flexible approach to learning through her 'expanded awareness' of the nature of knowledge and how it is constructed. He relates Perry's work to the outcomes of interviews with adults of varying levels of educational attainments (cited from Saljo, 1979). Saljo found that the subjects displayed different conceptions of learning – from learning as 'acquiring information' to learning as 'making sense of ideas and the real world' and later as 'developing as a person' (ibid., p. 18). While these are conceptions of learning, Entwistle sees them as relating to the epistemological sophistication of the individual. In other words, if knowledge is seen as absolute (lowest epistemological stages), then learning is a matter of being able to memorize and reproduce it. If knowledge is recognized to be constructed, then the assimilation and accommodation processes are a part of the person, and in learning the material of learning, the person is transformed.

Holding a conception of knowledge as constructed does not make life easier but, in fact, complicates it because it means that everything is potentially questionable and, as a result, there are more areas of uncomfortable cognitive dissonance to be managed. In a sense, this may reinforce Perry's notion of commitment as an unsophisticated response to an initial recognition of the complexity implied by the view of knowledge as constructed. The learner copes by saying: 'In this chaos of constructed knowledge, I have to make up my own mind and hold on tight to my view.'

Barnett (1997) puts the developing sophistication of knowledge into a broader context of how we might wish higher education students to function. While he rejects some elements of Perry's work as 'a psychological theory of cognitive development', it is difficult to see how the attainment of the levels of critical thinking that he describes, is not underpinned by a developmental sequence of the kind suggested in this chapter. This is particularly the case when the sequence is illustrated in the words of the students (as in Baxter Magolda's work).

Chapter 3

The framing of learning
Emotion and learning

Introduction

This second chapter of the three that consider the framing of learning, focuses on emotion and feeling in learning. Current thought about the role of emotion in learning has been stimulated by Goleman's concept of emotional intelligence (Goleman, 1995, 1998). Without appropriate self-management, a learner will not have the capacity to cope with maximum efficiency in learning tasks or to progress in her understanding of the structure of knowledge. However, this is not all there is to the relationship of emotion to learning. A brief review of the literature suggests that there are a number of different kinds of relationships between emotion and learning.

The first section of this chapter takes a broad view, considering some beliefs about emotion and learning and then clarifying terms. We then consider the different forms of relationships that are suggested in the literature, starting off with 'emotional intelligence'. The categorization in the literature seems to neglect a number of situations in which an emotional experience leads to change in orientation and often change of behaviour. In the apparent absence of other terms, 'emotional insight' is adopted. This seems to be a useful concept in relation to the process of reflection and the learning that can emerge from it. In the following section, we review the nature of emotional insight and a particular approach to it (Donaldson, 1992). The final sections of the chapter look at the manner in which the relationship between emotion and learning relates to conceptions of the structure of knowledge (Chapter 2) and to more general issues about learning in Chapter 1.

This chapter does not attempt to be a comprehensive review of the literature, but is concerned with plotting the manner in which the literature on learning attempts to deal with the influence of emotion. There are many overlaps. Ideas relating to all the other relationships between learning and emotion, for example, are included in the (very) broad sweep of material on emotional intelligence.

An interpretation of the relationship between emotion, feelings and learning

We use both terms 'feeling' and 'emotion' in this chapter because it is difficult in the literature to make a clear distinction between the uses of the terms. Feelings can be emotions (e.g., anger, excitement, etc.). However, feeling can imply a more generic behaviour – we can 'feel' in control of a situation (e.g., a learning situation) or confused, and in a particular feeling state that affects the manner in which we learn which could not be said to be 'emotional'. All of these meanings are relevant to this section. They are a linked set of ideas, which do not always accord with each other, but accord in their different ways with important aspects of learning. They could be seen as different 'angles' on the same topic. A major problem in trying to tease out the relationship of emotion to learning is how to make sense of the different 'angles' in the literature. For one writer, feelings and emotion represent one link to learning. For another, using the same terminology, the relationship will be different. For example, one will be talking about the actual experience of feeling something (e.g., excited, upset) while another will be talking about a person's knowledge about managing emotion or feeling in others. A particular example here is the literature on emotional intelligence (Goleman, 1995, 1998). The literature may also be a mix of advice and information that tends to simplify issues (e.g., in the training literature). In some writing, emotion is seen more as a negative influence on learning that needs to be controlled (e.g. in parts, Wilkes, 1997) or causes distortions in subsequent learning (Postle, 2000).

We should note, at this stage, that some writers actually characterize the process of reflection by the automatic inclusion within it of feelings or emotion (e.g., Boyd and Fales, 1983). That is not the position taken in this book. We would say that emotion is probably involved in all learning not only in reflection (Jarvis, 1987; Marsick and Watkins, 1990). We return to this issue in Chapter 6.

If emotion is involved in all learning, there is the question of whether that relationship is of one type of emotion, or many. Lewis (1990) suggested that they are inter-related like a fugue and virtually impossible to separate. We would disagree, and suggest that there are a number of different ways in which emotion and learning affect each other and that some greater definition is possible. We attempt here to make initial sense of observations and the literature on emotion and learning. The following groupings seem, at this stage, to be appropriate and they are discussed in more detail and their categorization is revised below:

- emotional intelligence;
- feelings as the subject matter of learning (part of our external experience): we can learn about how our feelings impinge upon our lives and those of others (e.g., counselling and self-development literature);
- feelings and their involvement in the learning process.

Emotional intelligence

To many, the term 'emotional intelligence' might seem to be sufficient as a means of explaining the relationship between feelings and learning. Much has been written about it in the past few years. The idea of describing, in one term, the ability to manage personal emotions and the emotions of another emerged from a number of sources. One, in particular, was Gardener's notion that the quality of human 'intelligent' functioning is determined by much more than is encompassed in 'IQ', and that it involves a number of facets – including elements of inter- and intrapersonal abilities (Gardner, 1983). Goleman (1995, 1998) expanded and developed the idea. For Goleman, 'emotional intelligence' includes self-awareness, impulse control, persistence, zeal and motivation, empathy and social deftness. It 'guides our moment-to-moment decisions . . . enabling or disabling through itself' (1995: 28). This is a broad view of emotion that has been helpful in considerations about learning and teaching (Mortiboys, 2002) and it extends beyond the notions of emotion as something 'to be controlled' or as 'baggage' to be managed in a new situation (Beard and Wilson, 2002). Its emphasis is on management of emotion and it is clear that feelings sometimes do need to be managed in order that a particular form of learning can take place. For example, a student in a lecture on philosophy might have difficulty in concentrating on the learning if she is highly excited about a new relationship. Another way of interpreting this is not of feelings 'getting in the way', but of intellectual material in the way of another entirely life-enhancing and worthy pursuit – that of potential romance! We should remember that the 'guidance' role of emotion in a learning situation may not coincide with the goals of the intellect in a social situation.

There is value, therefore, in the identification of something that can be called 'emotional intelligence'. It has been important in reframing our view of what it means to be 'good' at learning and managing learning. It recognizes the importance of many other factors in contributing to effectiveness that go beyond the traditional notions of pure cognitive ability (IQ). However, a powerful approach engendered by the adoption of a term such as 'emotional intelligence' at the same time might have the effect of narrowing and too easily summarizing what seems to be a very complex array of functions. In addition, such simplification seems also to make emotional control easy to manipulate and 'improve'. Goleman makes many suggestions about solving human problems by working with the concept of emotional intelligence (for example, dealing with melancholy (1995: 69); lifting moods (ibid., p. 72); dealing with difficulties in marriages (ibid., p. 129) and trauma (ibid., p. 210), and acquiring self-mastery (1998: 47)). Similarly, Brockbank and McGill (1998) say emotional intelligence means judging when to deal with and when to 'park' emotion (1998: 193–4) in order to deal with another matter. Emotional intelligence can make the management of emotions sound easy.

However, there are important ideas in the writings of those who promote the concept of emotional intelligence that do not require the adoption of the concept as a whole with all of its summarizing and simplifying connotations (Salmon, 1995). For the purposes of this text, we distinguish 'self-management as a learner and management of personal learning situations' from the management of the feelings and emotions of others, both of which are incorporated in the notion of 'emotional intelligence'. An excellent counsellor who displays empathy and understanding may not be a person who is an excellent manager of her own learning. As a concept, 'emotional intelligence' has served an important purpose of awareness raising, but we need to recognize that its broad definition serves also to blur understandings of the relationships between emotion and learning.

Feelings as the subject matter of learning

Feelings are involved in the process of learning but also are the subject matter of learning. In other words, they can be part of external experience. It is possible to learn about the emotions without actually experiencing them, for example, learning how they affect people and their management in counselling, therapy and relationships (e.g., Heron, 1989; Postle, 2000; and other references in Moon, 1999a). The relationship between the processes of learning about emotion and working with one's actual emotions can tend to become confused. At times it will be completely 'dispassionate' with no emotional involvement other than that associated with the learning situation. At other times the learning about emotion will be associated with actual emotional experiences (i.e., involving the internal experience). For example, people who live together learn that a particular look from their partner is associated with forms of behaviour that may have consequences for the manner in which they relate to each other at the time. A 'grumpy' look may have emotional consequences for the observer – and the consequences may then consciously or unconsciously guide her subsequent behaviour. In other words, the grumpy look in the partner may cause the observer, in an emotional reaction, to reframe the determinants of her 'relating' behaviour for the duration of the grumpiness in the other. She may, for example, treat the other 'gently' until there is a change in expression. The observer may feel emotion, but has also learnt about emotion in this example and knowledge and experience have become interlinked.

Feelings and their involvement in the learning process

Following the constructivist model of learning, we can identify several ways in which feeling can be involved in the learning process. First, feelings influence what we actually know about something. If it is the cognitive structure that is the basis of 'knowing', emotion is a part of the cognitive structure. What we know becomes associated with feeling, though the associations do not need to be permanent. Thinking about war for one person may generate a feeling of discomfort and fear. For another person, the idea of war may bring about a sense of excitement. Thinking about a particular person is likely to generate feelings that are associated with that person – love, sexual desire, dislike, and so on. It is interesting to speculate as to whether anything that we know is separated from associated feelings. When we try to recall something that has been forgotten, it is often the experience of the associated feelings that occurs before the name or nature of the object 'comes to mind'. Thus, awareness of feeling may be a system that operates more quickly than awareness of the knowledge object.

The association between feeling and knowing may be another area in which vocabulary is deficient. Above, the word 'sense' was used to describe a word concerned with emotional experience ('excitement'), whereas we would normally associate 'sense' with seeing, hearing, smelling, and so on – which is not the intended meaning in this case. In a similar way, the word 'war' may often be said to generate 'dark' feelings. Again, we have used a 'sensory' word to arrive at a meaning that is probably more to do with feeling (of threat, fear, unease, etc.). Poetry exploits words and word combinations that generate feeling (see p. 173, 230).

If we are saying that what we know is associated with feelings, then feelings are part of the internal experience that guides new learning and are, in this way, associated with the process of learning. This second way in which feelings influence learning is in the process of learning itself, within the action of accommodation in which internal experience is related to any current external experience. So new learning about war is matched against existing knowledge and feelings already present. Third, however, new feelings may be generated in the process of learning. New emotion or feeling seems to arise as a result of the flux between internal and external experience. Thus, the idea of war, having been a source of negative feelings, might become associated with excitement in the context of the new information. The possibility of being involved in action might appeal to the learner. In another example, Donaldson (1992) observes the delight that there can be in the process of new learning.

The fourth manner in which emotion tends to be associated with learning is commonly alluded to in the literature. It is where feeling or emotion creates a condition conducive or not conducive to learning – it is seen as a potential facilitator or as a block to the learning process. Above, we have described feeling as being related to knowledge about grumpy behaviour in another, and both then acting as a guide for adapting behaviour (treating the partner gently). In that situation, the feeling is directly associated with the material of learning. However, emotion that is not directly associated with current feeling can also affect learning. This situation is most noticeable when learning is facilitated or blocked but these may be extremes on a continuum (Mulligan, 1992). The simplest example here is when internal experiences of non-associated feelings interfere with a learning process. For example, the new relationship might get in the way of learning in a philosophy lecture. A state of high emotional arousal (negative or positive), or very low arousal can make learning difficult.

Other situations in which emotions that are not associated with the learning affect learning are where the source of the 'emotion' may seem to be generated externally to the learner. For example, we talk of there being an 'atmosphere' of fear or threat that inhibits learning. The learner is disrupted by her perceptions.

There is also a considerable literature on the manner in which certain atmospheres seem to make learning 'easier'. Material pertaining to this idea arises in various cultures of the study of learning though it seems unlikely that we are talking of different situations. One example is 'accelerated learning'. Over the years there have been many publications on accelerated learning, arising initially in the training and development culture (e.g., Rose, 1985; Lawlor and Handley, 1996) and there are now reinterpretations of the idea within teacher education. Accelerated learning, in its original form, was the generation of an external atmosphere designed to enable the learner to reach a relaxed state which is considered to facilitate learning. This often involved the use of baroque music to encourage an appropriate brain state.

Another approach to facilitative atmospheres for learning is represented in a body of literature that describes the generation of 'flow' of feeling states (Csikszentmihalyi, 1990). Flow occurs when a person is absorbed by a task, when she loses track of time, and when she seems to be achieving the objective without effort. Claxton (2000), in particular, applies these ideas, describing the state in which learners might study for hours, deeply focused on their subject matter. A personal experience of flow is evident after deep involvement in writing, when it seems to be an effort to 're-enter' the world beyond the writing. Some link the processes of flow and 'accelerated learning'; Beard and Wilson, for example, talk about 'Flow learning through relaxed alertness' (2002, p. 132). Whether flow or accelerated learning are or are not describing similar states is an important area to explore.

Another way in which emotion may facilitate or inhibit learning comes from the person-centred learning literature and this relates the manner in which a person feels about herself to her success in learning (e.g., Rogers, 1969; Heron, 1989). Rogers talked about the conditions that facilitate learning (e.g., positive self-regard). On the other hand, learning is a neutral process. We have a tendency to regard learning as 'happening' only when the learning is in a direction that is approved or desired. Learning occurs also in very unsupportive situations – but the learning may not be the learning that is expected – it may be about how best to avoid the unpleasant situation.

We can summarize the points made in this section so far. We have moved beyond the initial three groupings of relationships between emotion and learning (p. 46). The new schema involves concepts of 'relevant' and 'non-relevant' emotion to distinguish between situations in which the feelings and emotion are related to the material of learning involved and where they appear not to be directly related. In summary, so far, emotion influences the learning process in the following ways:

- where relevant emotion is an influence on the structure of our knowledge, i.e., what we know;
- where relevant emotion has an influence on the process of learning: as part of our internal experience it influences the manner in which we process new material of learning;
- where relevant emotion arises from the process of learning (i.e., it arises not within the external experience, nor directly in the internal experience that we bring to learning but within the process of flux between the internal and external experience which results in accommodation);
- where emotion that is not directly relevant to the learning situation affects learning (e.g., in accelerated learning, 'flow' states and person-centred learning).

Do these, however, represent the full range of forms of relationship between emotion and learning?

The possibility of another form of emotional learning

Writing this chapter on emotion and learning has been a learning process. While there is much general material on the relationship of cognitive processes to emotional learning, as we have suggested above, it seems to treat the topic from a variety of angles with little in the way of systematic approaches. Initially it appeared that the topic of emotion and learning was largely covered in the sections above, but it then became apparent that there is an area of literature and experience that is not covered by the headings already written. For the moment we use the term 'emotional insight' for this. This new area would certainly overlap with some of the concepts of 'emotional intelligence', but the latter concept does not clarify the matter.

The form of emotional insight has become evident through examples. We therefore start with examples and move towards the definition of the term later. In the literature on which this section was based were several texts that seemed to be about feelings and learning, but would not directly match any of the headings above. Boal's work on theatre and therapy (Boal, 1995) is one example (see also p. 174) as are many of the states described in Storr's study of solitude (Storr, 1988) and the use of story-telling in the context of professional development (e.g., Winter *et al.*, 1999; Bolton, 1994; McDrury and Alterio, 2002) (see p. 174). It was noticeable also that learning about how to conduct counselling (i.e., learning about emotional behaviour) is covered above but we did not cover some of the learning that occurs as client behaviour changes. Also there are the experiences of encounter or sensitivity training (Rogers, 1969; Heron, 1989) and many alternative therapies, even the practice of hypnotherapy (e.g., Hartland, 1982). In addition, work on dreams may bring about a change of orientation (Progoff, 1975; Reed, 1985; Shohet, 1985). In all these examples, after an intervention, something seems to happen to the orientation of the learner in the way she perceives her world and, as a result, she may behave differently. She may try to describe this in terms of 'knowing something different', but often the change is apparently more profound than the description. The initiation of the change may be cathartic or it may be more subtle. Sometimes these kinds of change occur after an event such as a rite of passage or a meeting that has 'stirred the emotions' in some way. The source of learning or the nature of learning that has resulted in the changes may not be at all obvious if we seek it within the traditional frames of reference of cognitive learning.

The particular relevance of this form of learning in this book is in its role in reflective work in which learners might be engaged. In a previous publication on the use of learning journals (Moon, 1999b), we queried the form of learning that might emerge from the use of learning journals. Some learning in reflective learning journals clearly is related to consolidation of knowledge and the greater development of understanding. In the book, the chapter on learning from learning journals (1999b, Chapter 2) explored this but there has always seemed to be something missing. There can be learning that results in a behaviour change that seems to be more profound than simply knowing something.

What we are describing as 'emotional insight' is difficult to describe because the term 'emotional' is 'slippery' with many different concepts attached to it. It is helpful to use the notion of learning as 'change' here, but it is not quite change of conception (as in Marton *et al.*, 1997), rather, it might be change of something else for which we may not have a word, there may be lack of vocabulary here. The idea of change of orientation seems to be a reasonable description of it at present. It is not far from the ideas expressed by many writers. For example, Mulligan distinguishes feeling from reasoning (cognitive processes) as 'one of the two major ways in which we make judgements about the world. It underlies our preferences and our values and emphasizes what is subjectively important to us' (2000: 56). The use of the word 'judgement' tends to imply the operation of emotional insight through the agency of reasoning, rather than a process that has a complete form in itself. McDrury and Alterio talk of the way that emotional insight reveals likes and dislikes, 'our values and preferences in contrast to thought being based on theories, frameworks and concepts . . . [and] . . . more objective' (2002, p. 41).

While, therefore, there seem to be many who have seen emotional insight as a form of learning, the nature of this learning is not so obviously explored and, correspondingly, nor is its relationship to other learning explored. We imply that the emotional nature of a person might itself 'learn' but such learning may be different from the manner of knowledge learning (Epstein, 1993). We note Carlson's observations again that 'integrating theories of emotion and theories of cognition is a longstanding challenge' (1997: 112). How might this 'learning' process relate to the traditional view of learning? One model of mind that can encompass the observations made in this section is that of Donaldson (1992), though to summarize the richness of this work in a few lines is to do it some disservice. Donaldson has worked primarily on child development, and her ideas have a basis in well-researched material, particularly in this age group. She suggests that mind has a structure that is subject to processes of development with characteristic changes in the operation that signal the emergence into the next phase. The main characteristic that identifies the different 'modes' of mind is what Donaldson calls the 'locus of concern'. The idea of locus of concern is applied to both emotional ('value-sensing') and thought ('intellectual') processes. The locus of concern of a baby is 'here and now'. Later there is development of an ability to have concern for things in the past or the future. In the third locus there is a greater generalization and an ability to deal with the nature of things rather than specific events/objects. The fourth and most sophisticated locus is concerned with abstract relationships, such as mathematics and complex reasoning. Donaldson's work seems to relate to the material of those working on the conception of knowledge (see Chapter 2) in the progression that she describes.

The loci of concern, described by Donaldson, follow a developmental sequence but in a sense become 'available for use' only by the developed adult. Emotion and thought are seen by Donaldson as separate, but acting together in different ways to produce different forms of mental activity. This is similar to the views expressed in the sections above. Most commonly, they work together in the third locus of generalization. A person becomes more skilled in deploying emotion and thought to achieve her goals. Most significantly for the arguments in this chapter, Donaldson suggests that the greatest form of development of emotion and intellectual thought is in the fourth locus of abstract relationships, where there are more pure forms of functioning of these components. While it is easy to observe academic or deep thinking work as intellectual with little involvement of emotion, Donaldson proposes that there is an equivalent state for an emotional or value-sensing state. She roots her reasoning in cultural and historical tendencies for particular ways of functioning, suggesting that the more pure emotional states are most clearly represented in Buddhism and Zen, in states of ecstasy (Laski, 1961) or spirituality. However, the way in which people clearly 'learn from' or change as a result of experience suggests that such functioning may be much more common. This brings us back to the series of examples with which we began this section that are not intellectual processes but relate to Donaldson's view of emotional development (therapy, learning from story, etc.). We therefore suggest that emotional insight is a common activity that becomes evident when we acknowledge and label it as relatively distinct.

Emotion and learning: drawing the ideas together

We have suggested, therefore, that emotion and learning have a number of different relationships and we can reconsider the headings that were employed. 'Emotional intelligence' as a term is important in applied situations where it emphasizes that good functioning (management, teaching, teamwork, and so on) involves emotion. However, as we have noted above, the term seems to be somewhat 'all-encompassing'. We chose to see it largely in terms of self-management.

We then looked at feelings as the subject matter of learning. At times there may be a very close relationship between learning about feelings as subject matter, and emotional learning as described in the last section. The section on feelings and their involvement in or as an influence on the learning process indicated a number of different ways in which emotion is involved in learning. It is linked to knowledge which, as the cognitive structure, guides new learning. It is part of the process of learning itself; feelings emerge as a result of learning and, whether or not related to the topic of the learning, emotional states can block or facilitate learning. Finally, we came to understand the possibility that there is something beyond all of the above that is apparent when people work with their emotions and in some way, change their orientation. We called this emotional insight.

Donaldson's work on the nature of mind promotes the idea that emotion is involved in all learning, sometimes with cognitive or intellectual processes, and sometimes, in a more pure form. This is a helpful model to support the exploration of reflective and experiential learning in later chapters. In suggesting that there is not one, but a number of different relationships between learning and emotion, including one form that is emotional insight, it might be reasonable to talk of *emotional processes* and learning, rather than the more simplified notion of emotion and learning.

We can suggest that emotion relates to learning in the following ways:

- Emotion influences the structure of knowledge.
- It influences the process of learning.
- It may arise in the process of learning.
- Emotions that are not directly relevant to the learning facilitate or block learning.
- There is emotional insight where the emotional orientation of the person changes.

Emotional processes and learning: an example

While it has been important for the development of this section to view all these relationships between emotion and learning as separate, it is likely that, as processes, they are often all active, interweaving with cognitive processes metaphorically 'without seams'. There are times, however, when the identity of the processes become clearer, for example, when feelings are overwhelming and block learning, or when they need to be controlled or in the purer forms of emotional learning such as learning from mediation. We illustrate the varied relationships between feelings and learning by reference to a situation reported by Marsick and Watkins (1990). In the context of a study of informal and incidental learning in the workplace, Marsick and Watkins viewed the learning of a group of self-identified adult children of alcoholics who met to explore their experiences in relation to problems in their functioning in the workplace. There was an assumption that there would be factors in common in their feelings and behaviour because of their early experiences. For the group, the intention was to move beyond the stage of therapy to an understanding of the emotional situations that they had experienced. We consider the different relationships between emotion processes and learning under the headings identified above:

- *Emotional intelligence* is illustrated in the statements about development of self-management (in this case, in terms of the group and the work of the facilitator). It was evident in the concern to maintain the group as a group focused on the development of competence rather than as a therapeutic situation. The tensions between these ways of working needed constant adjustment.
- With regard to *feelings as the subject matter for learning*, the group talked about their feelings in objective terms. Examples were the exploration of family dynamics, or expressions of what they wanted from the group, e.g., a request from a member of the group for 'an alternative to working with men who intimidate me' (1990, p. 138).

- *The links between emotional processes and learning* were evident in the following ways:
- Emotion that had an influence on the structure of knowledge: one of the participants commented to another that he reminded her of her alcoholic father because both were tall. She said that this resulted in 'a kind of feeling freeze' (ibid., p. 139).
- Emotion that had an influence on the process of learning: the very basis of the group illustrated this. Feelings engendered by the alcoholic parents had influenced the learnt behaviour of the participants and hence their involvement in the group.
- Emotion that arose in the process of learning: the concept 'double hit' is introduced (ibid., p. 141) in which the work on one case 'triggered learning in a second person of a similar or greater intensity' (ibid.).
- Where emotions not directly relevant to the learning situation affected the learning: the value expressed for the 'double hit' was that in direct work with a participant there might often be 'a natural tendency to distance ourselves psychically from new, painful learning.' In contrast, 'In observing others . . . learning, the process can be less threatening or, conversely deeper, since our defenses are down' (ibid., p. 150). In addition to this example, much in the chapter concerns the process of creating a helpful emotional climate that would facilitate learning.
- *Emotional insight* was illustrated in the following way: the processes in this group described by Marsick and Watkins were both cognitive and emotional and the value of both was the major consideration in the design of the intervention. Initially, a more therapeutic stance was taken. For example, there is reference to the exploration of family-of-origin dynamics being 'highly emotional and cathartic' (emotional insight). Later frameworks were introduced to enable the participants to recognize and understand the situations they had been in and to enable them critically to review and adapt their views of themselves and behave differently in future situations.

Emotional processes and the generic view of learning

Chapter 1 introduced concepts of frames of reference, the distinction of figure from ground and the importance of variation in order that learning can take place. Where emotion is the subject matter of learning, it is material of learning in external experience like any other material of learning. When it is involved in the learning process, it is part of the internal experience of an object and therefore will influence the learning by guiding the frame of reference and the determination of the figure from ground. However, while cognitive processes might often be accessible if not actually conscious, some of the influences of emotion on learning seem to be less accessible, sometimes because we do not have appropriate vocabulary. Thus, going back to the example of adult children of alcoholics in the last section, the woman who experienced a specific reaction to a male participant because he was tall and reminded her of her father would probably, under previous circumstances, just have 'irrationally' disliked or feared the man. Under the conditions of therapy, she became aware of the emotional influences on her behaviour.

Emotional insight seems to be different from other emotional involvement in learning. Therapists and counsellors and others who work directly with people learn about the kinds of intervention that can bring about emotional insight. Schools of therapy might adopt particular metaphors through which to work (e.g., Freud) or areas of function and activities (such as the use of dreams, hypnosis, art, drama, etc.) but there does not seem to be an agreed theory that covers all these forms of emotional change or insight. The search for a unified theory would seem to be blocked in several ways. First, the relationship between learning and emotional processes appears to be varied, second, those who work with the more pure forms of emotional insight tend to be experts in their field, often with cultural boundaries to their vision and they do not necessarily have an overview of the whole picture. Third, there are cultural issues. As Donaldson suggests (see above), work on emotional insight is not well developed in the West at the current time. In terms of the generic view of learning, emotional insight would seem to be characterized by the change of a particularly significant frame of reference that results in a considerable reorientation of many frames of reference that affect significant areas of life.

Emotional processes and conceptions of the structure of knowledge

The previous chapter considered research into the development of conceptions of knowledge (Perry, 1970; King and Kitchener, 1994). How does this material relate to emotion and feelings? We touch on this topic here by making some observations that need to be developed.

We first reiterate what may be an incidental point that arose in the discussion of Donaldson's model of mind. The loci of concern in the model move from 'here and now', to past/future to anywhere/anytime to the capacity for abstract relational thinking. King and Kitchener's 'stages' of reflective thinking assume an underpinning of the loci of concern. The level of conception of the structure of knowledge that is implied in the higher stages of reflective thinking requires a capacity to think in the abstract. However, this point may only relate to emotion and learning in the need to understand the role of emotion in order to make more sophisticated judgements (see below).

King and Kitchener address the issue of the emotional development of the college students with whom they worked, in two pages (1994, pp. 246–7). In these pages they consider a number of different ways in which emotion relates to learning with emphasis on the development of facilitative and supportive situations for learning. There is relatively little concern for the way in which sophisticated processing such as reflective judgement requires some understanding of the relationship of emotional aspects of the self, to the learning.

It is clear that to function in the more sophisticated stages of development, a certain level of general self-management as a learner is required ('emotional intelligence'). Because reasoning at that level is a controlled process, and may involve systematic examination of evidence, there is a need for some level of personal recognition and control of the way in which emotions might steer judgements by influencing the frames of reference that are adopted. However, we have said that emotion is part of what we know as feelings are associated with knowledge. To work with uncertainty and weigh up alternative solutions to a problem (King and Kitchener, 1994) may require deep recognition of the relationships of personal emotional influences on knowledge as well as a metacognitive understanding of how emotion shapes frames of reference. To suggest that we can ever 'know perfectly' how our (personal) emotions influence our processes does not seem possible at present.

Chapter 4

The framing of learning
Approaches to learning

Introduction

The third chapter in this set of three on the framing of learning focuses on the learner's approach to learning. The material on the approaches to learning is based on a well-known body of literature, which concerns the manner in which a learner tackles a learning task. As in the previous two chapters, this chapter is about an aspect of framing that concerns learning to learn. The approach that a learner adopts will be influenced both by her conceptions of knowledge and her personal ability to manage her learning. These were the subject matter of the previous chapters. Some of the factors that contribute to the approach that a learner adopts are related to the local context of the learning in contrast to the conception of knowledge that would appear to be a more general trait.

The first fairly long section of this chapter explores the concept of the approach to learning with reference to the literature. The second and third sections bring in the subject matter of the previous chapters: the conception of knowledge and the role of emotion in framing learning and we consider the relationship of approach to both of these. The last section suggests that the approach that is adopted to learning by a learner is likely to be a culmination of a variety of influences that include the conception of knowledge and emotional state. In other words, the learner's conception of knowledge and emotional state may sometimes influence learning by affecting the approach to learning adopted by the learner. There is discussion on the possible inter-relationships of these influences on the framing of learning. The chapter concludes with a short section that anticipates subsequent chapters on reflective and experiential learning.

Deep and surface approaches to learning

The significance of the approach that learners take to learning tasks for the results of the learning process has been a key development in research on learning. These ideas were summarized in an earlier book (Moon, 1999a) and accounts that are particularly helpful are found in Candy (1991), Wilkes (1997), Marton and Booth (1997), Marton et al. (1997), Trigwell and Prosser (1999), Biggs (1999), and Entwistle et al. (2002). We describe these briefly below.

Research in the late 1970s in Sweden began to suggest that a major variable in learning, particularly in formal education, is learners' understanding of the nature of the learning process and their conception of any learning task itself. This influences the approach that they might tend to adopt towards that task. The research culminated in the descriptions of approaches to learning as 'surface' or 'deep'. In a typical surface approach, the general intention of the learner is to 'absorb' (in her terms) as much of the content as it is necessary for the task at hand. The learner might do this by memorizing material in a routine manner without reflecting on it or the underpinning purposes or structure of it or without relating it to previous learning or knowledge. A consequence of this approach may be a superficial 'learning', but the learner might have difficulty in reiterating it in forms other than the manner in which it was initially learnt. She is unlikely to be very interested in the material because interest would tend to drive her towards making sense of it (and taking a deep approach). A surface approach is not necessarily associated with low intelligence. It may also be a consequence of the learner's belief that this is the 'proper way' to learn or it can be a consequence of a state of anxiety or pressure, for example, in learning for assessment situations. Vicious circles can be set up with a surface approach proving inadequate for tasks at hand, and the learner consequently becoming anxious and perpetuating her inadequate approach.

In contrast to the surface approach, a deep approach to material of learning is characterized by an intention in the learner to understand the material of learning, seeking the meaning and understanding the ideas in it. The learner who takes a deep approach seeks the underpinning principles and endeavours to relate the material to previous knowledge and understandings. She may question the logic and argument. A learner who is interested in a topic is likely to take a deep approach and it appears to be harder for learners to sustain this approach when they are anxious or under pressure (Entwistle, 1996).

Entwistle (1988) illustrates the approaches to learning from studies of students reading an article. Those who adopted a surface approach had the intention to 'memorize those parts of the article that they considered important in view of the questions they anticipated afterwards. Their focus of attention was thus limited to the specific facts or pieces of disconnected information that was rote learned'. In contrast, those who took a deep approach to learning:

started with the intention of understanding the meaning of the article, [they] questioned the author's arguments, and related them both to previous knowledge and to personal experience, and tried to determine the extent to which the author's conclusions seemed to be justified by the evidence presented.

A particular significance of this work on approaches to learning is the manner in which it is conducted. Earlier studies of learning had often confused the teaching and learning processes in formal educational situations, exploring learning through the activities of teaching and instruction or within the learner's environment. In studies of approach to learning, the learner and her process of learning became central with a recognition that what is important is not how others, even relevant teachers see or design a learning task, but how the learner sees it and how she responds to it. This phenomenographical approach involves discovering the learner's perceptions of the task at hand and thus it becomes possible to recognize these considerable differences in approach to learning and the consequences in the effectiveness of performance.

There are many examples of how this work on approaches to learning has been applied. Most of the work, in particular in the early days, was based on student work on texts. However, it has subsequently been related to many other areas of student learning and as this has occurred, the ideas have been expanded and refined. For example, Hounsell (1997) looked at the approaches that students take to writing essays and how the approach adopted relates to the quality of the essay produced.

Hounsell's findings are supported by work using the SOLO taxonomy ('structure of learning outcomes', Biggs and Collis, 1982). SOLO is a model that is most easily applied to student writing, though has been applied much more widely. It is a hierarchy of five levels of complexity in the structure of represented learning. Written work that characterizes the simplest stages takes few aspects of a topic and simply lists them. At the stage of greatest complexity ('extended abstract'), learners write coherently within a structured whole and they are able to generalize principles from their work to other situations. In a crucial piece of research, Van Rossum and Schenk (1984) demonstrated that the taking of a deep approach to learning was necessary for learners to reach the more complex structures implied by SOLO, and that the learning achieved in those taking a surface approach was not adequate for this. Moon (1999a) used the ideas from SOLO and approaches to learning to link the process of learning with the form of representation of learning. She used the term 'best possible representation' to suggest that the choice of approach to a task acted as a kind of limiting factor (Odum, 1968) on any representation of the learning. Moon's model made a distinction between the approach adopted to learning and the representation of learning in a structured form and we return to it in Chapter 6.

In later work by Biggs in Australia and at Lancaster University, inventories were developed to standardize the questions that were asked of students about their study (Entwistle and Ramsden, 1983; Biggs, 1993). The sequence of questions was shown to be a reliable means of determining how students view their study and how they intend to approach a task. In the course of this work another apparent approach to learning was identified and labelled the 'strategic' approach (see also Miller and Parlett, 1974). The strategic approach differs qualitatively from deep and surface approaches. While the latter two are more closely identified with reference to the quality of the learning, the strategic approach concerns the way in which a learner chooses to tackle a task. The aim of a strategic learner is to succeed, particularly in assessment tasks. She will take a deep approach if she perceives that this is the method of success but if she can 'get by' with the use of memorization, she will learn in that way. Her commitment is to success on the programme, not necessarily to interest or the nature of the learning. The 'strategic' approach seems not to be the same as deep and surface approaches, but is a quality that steers the choice of deep and surface approaches within formal settings – a superordinate frame of reference. There seems to be plenty of evidence that modern learners in higher education need to be strategic. Passion about their own interests in a discipline will not enable them to progress successfully through a modular programme in which there is frequent assessment (Svensson, 1997).

The distinctions between deep and surface approaches to learning are, of course, stereotyped in order to display the distinction between them. This has become evident in the application of these ideas to Asian students in academic education. Marton and Booth (1997) indicate that memorization can be involved in a deep approach to learning where the intention of the learner is to use it to understand the meaning of the material. While memorizing is associated with surface approaches to learning in Western education, repeatedly memorizing the same ideas to study was associated in research with the reviewing of different facets and different ways of seeing the same idea in the Asian students (Kember, 1996). In this way the Asian students attained understanding as it was 'built up stage by stage' (Marton and Booth, 1997: p. 44). The students saw their methods as enabling them to apply the ideas to other situations. What we cannot know is how much students are relating other prior knowledge to that which they are memorizing. However, the important ideas that emerge from this work are that forms of memorization can be a means to understanding when used in accordance with the intention to understand.

The deep approach, used in a reasonably strategic manner, not only tends to produce higher quality learning in assessment tasks but enables the recall of content in a more effective manner after a period of time (Marton and Saljo, 1984; Prosser and Miller, 1989). It could be said that the material of learning is stored more efficiently by those taking a deep approach because it has had the effect of changing conceptions, rather than being assimilated as relatively isolated ideas that might be 'filed' inappropriately (Harvey and Knight, 1996). Students taking a deep approach to their learning and who are reasonably strategic tend to achieve higher classes of degree in formal education

(Ramsden, 1992). However, it has been observed that taking a predominantly deep approach to learning does not lead as reliably to good results as the taking of a surface approach relates to attainment of poor results (ibid.).

The literature on approaches to learning has never suggested that learners consistently adopt one approach. Ramsden opens a chapter on approaches to learning with six quotations about deep and surface approaches to work in different subjects in higher education. The reader is invited to guess how many students made the comments. They were, in fact, made by three students, each illustrating a deep and a surface approach with their approach depending largely on their perception of programme requirements. We should probably be able to assume that most students who have reached higher education are capable of taking a deep approach. However, they often manage reasonably well with a surface approach for much of their study.

The nature of the encouragement for learners to work in one way or another is an important matter. We have already mentioned that the learner's conception of the process of learning is important. However, there are other factors. Since we are taking a phenomenographical stance and the learner's perception is all-important in determining the approach, we could say that the encouragement is part of the learning environment. This could include any teachers, their teaching or assessment processes, and the physical, sociological and psychological surroundings of the learning. The learning environment is anything that the learner herself perceives as influencing the manner in which she learns. Generalizations about the environment of learning are therefore difficult to make. For one learner the noise of a busy road outside can be distracting enough to mean that she adopts a surface approach to a task when she knows she needs to understand it well. Meanwhile her friend in the same room on the same task adopts a surface approach because she thinks that this is adequate. Marton and Booth (1997) discuss aspects of the learner's perception in greater detail.

Emotion and approaches to learning

Chapter 3 list different ways in which emotion relates to learning. We suggest that emotion can affect learning partly through its more direct effect on the approach adopted by learners. A study by Entwistle and Entwistle (1997) illustrates aspects of this. A group of students was interviewed during the revision period for their examinations. Students who adopted a deep approach indicated that their learning gave them a sense of satisfaction. Sometimes it was an 'aha' response as 'confusion on a particular topic was replaced by insight'. Sometimes it was a sense of achievement – of now being able to understand something that had previously not been clear. There was a sense of 'provisonal wholeness' in their learning, a sense that something was 'clicking into place or locking into a pattern', though there was potential for more learning at a later stage. Students who adopted a deep approach were able to talk about their learning with a sense of confidence that they could explain it and apply it elsewhere. The idea that there is a particular quality of learning that must have taken place in order that the subject can explain her learning in a coherent manner is important for the later development of these ideas about learning. In contrast to the deep approach group in the same study, the surface approach group did not feel confident enough to explain their learning and in emotional terms, they were apt to feel panicky and anxious about the prospect of the forthcoming assessment. They might have thought that they 'knew' the material, but either their sense of 'knowing' itself, or their judgement as to the kind of 'knowing' required was defective. They probably did 'know' isolated bits of information, but not in a manner that they could relate them to whole ideas, or apply them. In this way, emotion seems to be generated as a result of the appropriateness or inappropriateness of the approach adopted.

A second form of relationship between emotion and approach is illustrated above in the tendency of students under the effects of stress to adopt a surface approach to their learning. It is frequently an experience in formal education that students will start new work with the intention to learn in a meaningful manner, taking a deep approach, but as the pressures build for assessment tasks, examinations, and so on, they 'surface' and increasingly struggle to get by using memorizing. For a student who intends to take a deep approach, or who is interested in the subject matter, this is a disturbing process that, in itself, brings more distress and initiates the vicious circles described earlier.

The work of Entwistle and Entwistle (1997) seems also to illustrate what we have termed emotional insight (p. 50) in relation to the approach adopted. The students used metaphors such as learning 'clicking into place' when they used a deep approach.

Approaches to learning and conceptions of the structure of knowledge

There is anecdotal evidence of a relationship between conception of knowledge (see Chapter 2) and the approach adopted to learning, particularly where quotations from learners are included in the literature on the development of conceptions of knowledge. As illustrated earlier, Baxter Magolda's (1992) work uses many quotations. For example, at entry to college, Gwen was at the stage of Absolute learning (p. 38) and she provides a good example of a surface approach to learning. She describes how she learns in relation to her note-taking:

> I try to keep ideas real separate . . . when I'm taking my notes . . . so I can visually see a breakage between ideas and subtopics of a main idea. I think

that when you read over your notes so many times, you remember what they look like – so sometimes you almost find yourself looking in your mind as to what the page looked like and how your notes were arranged.

(Baxter Magolda, 1992, p. 31)

Barry, who was at the 'Independent' stage (p. 38) in his conception of knowledge and further on in his college career, says of seminar situations that provide a good illustration of a deep approach to learning:

I want to be challenged. I am in a gender theory course that has a lot of women's studies students in it. I feel challenged. My own politics are closely like theirs but I don't have the background . . . that they do. When I speak up, I really have to concentrate on what I think, communicate it effectively and then, if there is a discrepancy between what I and what someone else thinks, then I feel I can grow.

(ibid., p. 53)

More links between the approach to learning and conceptions of knowledge become apparent when learners' ideas of the nature of learning are considered. The stage of conception of knowledge is likely to affect the way in which learners perceive the process of learning. There rarely is more than a passing reference to this (for example, Beaty *et al.*, 1997 and Morgan, 1995). Mostly the reference is to Perry's work only and not to that of the other writers on conceptions of knowledge who have both confirmed and expanded Perry's model (see Chapter 2). Entwistle and Walker (2002) make more detailed reference than most others. They talk of the development of a 'nested hierarchy' of conceptions of the nature of learning. This implies that the sophisticated learner can have a more flexible approach to learning through her 'expanded awareness' of the nature of knowledge and how it is constructed. They relate Perry's work to the outcomes of interviews with adults of varying levels of educational attainments (cited in Saljo, 1979). Saljo considered that the subjects displayed different conceptions of learning – from learning as 'acquiring information' to learning as 'making sense of ideas and the real world' and later as 'developing as a person' (ibid., p. 18). While these are conceptions of learning, Entwistle and Walker see them as relating to the epistemological sophistication of the individual. In other words, if knowledge is seen as absolute (lowest epistemological stages), then learning is a matter of being able to memorize and reproduce it and this characterizes a surface approach. If knowledge is recognized to be constructed, then it is a part of the person, and in learning the material of learning and the existing knowledge can become transformed. This corresponds to a deep approach.

Meyers (1986) makes a different link between the work on conceptions of knowledge (refering to Perry's work) and approaches to learning in his recognition that the ability to think critically is limited by the epistemological stage of the learner. More sophisticated thinking ability would be associated with a meaningful understanding of subject matter (a deep approach). Meyers considers that 'the real value of Perry's work is the insight it offers into the reasons why most students do not think critically' (ibid., p. 97). Helpfully he suggests that students can be more able to think critically in one area of study than another. He gives the example of a student who was very able to think critically in an accountancy programme, but was not critical in his religious belief system. This inequality of progress in different areas of learning invites further investigation.

There is also an inter-relationship between the learner's conception of knowledge and the repertoire of choices of behaviour that are present for her. If she understands knowledge to be 'right' or 'wrong' and she sees the teacher as a purveyor the 'right', then the task of learning is to learn what the teacher says and, at best, simply to use it to modify previous knowledge. On the other hand, learners who see knowledge to be constructed have a greater repertoire. They can question the material of teaching. New material of learning can either be 'added' to what they know in an unquestioning (surface) manner or they relate it to what they know already and can think it through, perhaps changing how they construe broader knowledge areas in a deep approach. The approach that they adopt will need to take context and purpose into account, and strategic skills are needed to support this judgement in formal contexts where what is learnt is tested by specific methods.

The framing of learning and the approach adopted: an overview

This chapter on approaches to learning as a form of framing learning has suggested many factors that can influence the manner in which a learner approaches her studies in a formal setting. In some senses they could all be summarized as 'the environment of learning' in that anything could be perceived by the learner as an incentive to adopt a particular approach to her learning. However, this generalization is not always helpful, and in the formal learning situation there are some very obvious elements that consistently influence a learner's approach. We draw the following from the text above as factors that may influence the approach that a learner adopts to a task. Some factors that may influence the approach to a task are:

- the learner's conception of the learning process;
- influences of any teaching or assessment requirements;
- perceptions of the demands of this learning task;
- personal aims and outcomes associated with the task;
- personal prior knowledge of the subject or subject matter;
- the learner's emotional orientation in terms of self-management;

- her experience of the current physical or psychological environment;
- relevant learning habits;
- the learner's conception of the structure of knowledge;
- the learner's emotional orientation in relation to the task.

Clearly, whether a learner seeks to engage with the meaning of a task, or simply tries to retain the surface characteristics of it can be very significant in determining what is learnt, how well it is learnt and what can be done with the knowledge. Any one of these factors that influence approach alone could persuade the learner to adopt one approach or the other towards a particular learning task. In a situation of formal assessment, for example, the nature of the assessment task is likely to be influential. If the learner is very stressed at the time, stress may be the prime influence. So, in relating the approach that a learner adopts to the framing of a learning task, we could say that one 'route' of influence is:

Factors that may influence the approach → do influence the approach to learning adopted

↓

determine the framing of the learning process for the specific learning task.

However, this is simplistic and denies any separate influence of what we have listed as the 'factors that influence approach' in the learning situation. For example, we have already suggested that factors such as the learner's conception of the structure of knowledge and emotional orientation can influence the way in which a learner frames her learning independently of the approach adopted. Additionally, we have suggested that the whole theoretical background of the material on the approaches to learning is based on formal educational situations (Bowden and Marton, 1998). In formal situations, expectations of the quality of learning are overt through teaching processes and assessment tasks and there is encouragement for deeper engagement with subject matter. In other words, 'approach' is a concept largely tied to formal learning. To broaden our context to all learning suggests that it would not be appropriate to consider that these factors only influence the framing of learning through the approach that a learner adopts, though sometimes, this may be the case. We can redraw the map to suggest that the approach to learning takes the role of an intermediary variable, using the factors discussed above:

Factors that may influence the approach or the framing of a learning task

- influences of any teaching or assessment requirements;
- perceptions of the demands of this learning task;
- personal aims and outcomes associated with the task;
- personal prior knowledge of the subject or subject matter;
- the learner's emotional orientation in terms of self-management;
- the learner's emotional orientation in relation to the task;
- her experience of the current physical or psychological environment;
- relevant learning habits;
- the learner's conception of the learning process;
- the learner's conception of the structure of knowledge.

determine the framing of the learning process for the learning task

In this revised map, the variables listed above (e.g., the learner's emotional orientation to the task) may influence the approach that the learner takes to the learning task but independently may also influence the engagement with the task (e.g., through bringing about increased confidence or uncertainty).

As with the variables that affect the framing of learning, the approach adopted by the learner relates not to the content of what the learner learns, but to the way in which she perceives and then enacts the learning process which is the external experience of this learning. The variables listed influence her internal experience of the learning task and the cues in the task determine to which of those she pays attention. They will be those which are relevant to her internal experience. Any variation in the external experience in comparison with the internal experience may mean that she learns to tackle the task in a different manner.

The framing of learning in relation to learning, reflective and experiential learning

We now return to the 'bigger picture' and the notion that it is the experience of a learner that determines ultimately what she learns and the approach that she adopts to the learning. We cannot influence a learner other than through what she experiences, and we cannot make her experience something in a particular way though these processes can be 'engineered' with an intention that they will influence the experience of a learner. Such 'engineering' could be said to extend from brainwashing, to training, to classroom teaching, to counselling, to the presentation of documentary programmes in the media. These are all attempts to influence the experience of a learner such that she learns in a particular manner. What may vary most here is the nature and level of the intention of the agent who attempts to influence and the differences in technique may reside largely in the different frames of reference within which the material of teaching is presented. The next chapter explores in more detail the nature of interaction between these external influences on the learner and the process of learning (mediation of learning). This is in recognition of the fact that one of the perceived characteristics of reflective and experiential learning is that they are 'untaught'.

Part II

Exploring reflective and experiential learning

Chapter 5

Reflective and experiential learning
Taking stock

Introduction

This chapter performs a number of functions. It could be said to have a 'pivotal' role in the book. The first section is a summary of the generic view of learning that has been developed in the earlier chapters of this book. This includes vocabulary that will be used later in discussions of reflective and experiential learning. The second section is an overview of the exploration of reflective and experiential learning in the chapters ahead. The third section is concerned with one feature that reflective and experiential learning both have in common – that both occur relatively independently of a teaching (mediation) process.

A summary of the generic view of learning

Important vocabulary in this section is emphasized in italics. We have indicated that the focus of this book is on the relatively conscious learning of ideas and largely not the learning of physical skills. We could say that a person learns when she retains an idea in such a manner that she can use it to guide new learning. Our interest has been on the nature of good quality learning that contributes to a person's knowledge.

We describe learning in relation to a simple example. The learner is learning about the leaf of a tree that she thinks that she has not seen before. The process of learning involves the bringing to bear of relevant prior knowledge and experience of tree leaves on the current *external experience* of the leaf and its context – the tree. This is the process of *assimilation*. In trying to identify the new leaf, the learner focuses her attention on different aspects of the leaf and its nature in a process that is guided by her *internal experience*. This will be a matter of contrasting them with other generalities –in a process of distinction of many *figures from many grounds* that is driven in a relatively controlled manner by the invocation of different *frames of reference*. Initially, for example, the learner might be seeing this leaf in relation to other leaves on other trees. She might look at the leaf in terms of its physical structure, in terms of how it seems similar to or different from other leaves that she knows and her knowledge of taxonomy. She might look at the leaf and tree in the context of its apparent ecology.

The learner is noticing, in this process of shifting figures and grounds, the *variations* between the content and relationships of characteristics that she has in her internal experience, and what she observes to be new or different in this leaf. Her previous (internal) experience will enable her to use her frames of reference in order to focus on relevant features, with relevance guided by her purpose for the learning. For example, if she has reasonable prior experience of leaves, she will focus not only on the leaf colour because the colour may not indicate the species. If the leaf is yellow, it might be autumn, or the leaf might be diseased, or yellow because it is yellow by nature. These are all frames to be examined. *Appresentation* will mean that if she can only see some aspects of the tree and leaf (e.g., if she is looking at a picture of the unidentified leaf and tree in a book), she will 'fill in' more details than those to which she has current and direct access. When the learner develops knowledge of the leaf, she changes the structure of her concepts, thus changing her *cognitive structure*. As a result of assimilation of the ideas about the leaf, the cognitive structure may be modified in order to adapt to the new material of learning in the process of *accommodation*. The learner's general view of the nature of leaves will be expanded or modified in relation to its prior status.

Also affecting the framing of learning will be factors of a more general nature such as *emotion*. For example, there may be a sense of excitement (the tree is very unusual) or the learner might be under pressure of time and therefore frames the whole process of learning with an attitude of expediency.

The discussion of learning as a general topic has been presented in this book with its focus on experiential and reflective learning for two main reasons. First, experiential and reflective learning are forms of learning. As such, we can only understand them by referring to learning in more general terms. They are figures in the ground of learning and trying to understand them without reference to the broader frame in which they reside can only lead to a partial picture. As we have mentioned previously, there are some well-known attempts to identify the nature of experiential learning as a cycle of processes (cycle of experiential learning, see Kolb, 1984) with many wider implications drawn. Out of the context of other learning, the model and therefore its implications are not well founded.

The second reason concerns, in particular, the three chapters that explore the framing of learning because, in different ways, they have specific relevance to later discussions on reflective and experiential forms of learning.

An overview of reflective and experiential learning (Chapters 5–9)

To start the process of teasing out the meaning of reflective and experiential learning, we return to the rationale for considering these two areas of learning in one book. We said in the Introduction that they are both topical, and indeed, increasingly topical as aspects or representatives of what are called 'employability skills' in higher education (Moon, 2003). In addition, neither is clearly defined. Two people, even if they are working with the same learners, may have different concepts for the terms and their role in learning. Confused students may be the first to notice. The concepts for these forms of learning need to be better defined. We need to consider if the terms represent single or multiple activities and while the meanings are clearly inter-linked, their actual relationship is not obvious. In considering both, we need to clarify how reflective learning is involved in experiential learning and whether it is essential or only sometimes involved. All the time, we are relating these specific forms of learning to the generic view that has been developed in the earlier chapters.

This part of the book consists of five chapters that focus on reflective and experiential learning. In the current chapter we explore a feature in common between reflective and experiential learning: that they are both conducted without the direct mediation of a teaching process.

Chapter 6 focuses on reflective learning, forming a basis for it in the previous work of the author and then extending both the literature review and relationship of reflective learning to the generic view of learning. Reflective learning is interpreted as a function of what has been described earlier as internal experience. Chapter 7 covers a new perspective on reflective learning – the depth of reflection. It provides a framework to describe and form a basis for assessment of depth of reflection. Depth is related to the framing of learning that was described in Chapters 2, 3 and 4. In Chapter 8 we focus on experiential learning, first of all reviewing the literature and then considering it as a form of generic learning (Chapter 9). Finally, in this group of chapters, we explore the relationships between experiential and reflective learning – how much they overlap and to what degree they are separate and have a distinct identity.

The Resources section continues the exploration of reflective and experiential learning in a more practical manner.

Reflective and experiential learning and the mediation of learning

One main factor that brings reflective and experiential learning together in a significant way for the management of education is that both are forms of learning that are relatively independent of mediation. In this way, this learning extends beyond formal education and becomes very important in self-managed continuing professional development. These forms of learning also characterize much of the extensively ignored learning that happens in life beyond the formal systems of education – what we call everyday learning in this book. If reflective and experiential learning are relatively independent of teaching, we need to question the implications of that fact.

Instruction or teaching is essentially a means of providing, for the learner, material that has been processed either in order that the learner will be more easily able to assimilate it or in order to challenge the learner to learn more about learning itself. Laurillard (1993) used the term 'mediated learning' for situations in which learning is aided directly by another person or through the use of a medium that simplifies the material of teaching. Thus, there may be a teacher or an instructor present, or a computer program or a textbook (that has been created by a teacher) may be used. The idea of 'mediation' is useful because it focuses on the material of teaching rather than on the activities of the teacher. The characteristics of mediation in the learner's process of learning are made clearer when they are related to unmediated situations. In an unmediated situation, the learner is responsible for choosing what to learn about something. We explore this in relation to an example, in this case a learner is attempting to learn about an insect that she has come across, an insect that looks like a bee.

The learner looks at the insect. She might be seeing shape, colour and movement, hearing sound and movement, recognizing different patterns of behaviour, and so on. For a reasonably observant learner, gaining knowledge about the insect will entail initial effort in recognizing it as distinct from other insects such as bees, wasps and flies (figure against ground). It might involve noticing that there are several species of the insect and that they can look quite different. In most learning situations, the learner will have a purpose for learning and this will play a part in framing her attention to relevant aspects of the object of learning and it may affect and be affected by the approach that the learner takes to the learning. In addition, we have suggested that factors to do with emotions and the learner's conception of knowledge may also influence the manner in which the learner goes about the task. She may tackle the learning in a manner that accords with her disciplinary background, for example, a scientist might tackle the process in a more scientifically systematic manner than a colleague from the humanities. In essence, in an unmediated situation, the learner herself will decide how to direct her attention through engagement of frames of reference that she decides to use either in informed or less informed ways. They will organize her learning process and the manner in which she accommodates to the new ideas. As part of this process, if it is to be effective, she will be evaluating the amount of the learning and its reliability in relation to her purposes or intents. These do not necessarily stay the same. Over the duration of learning, she might be getting cold or hungry, finding the activity less appealing than earlier and hence modifying her intentions.

There are many different ways in which mediation can operate but all the time it will be an attempt to modify the experience of the learner (Marton and Booth, 1997). It is not the material of learning, itself, that is mediated. This suggests a revision of the term 'mediated learning' to 'mediated (learning) experience'. We can still say that the process of learning is mediated and that teaching is one means by which the learner's process of learning is mediated. As we said in Chapter 1, teaching is a separate activity from the act of learning and its intention is to guide and facilitate learning.

The teacher's role in mediating learner experience can take many different forms, all with different roles in the simplification and guiding process. Mediation may be a face-to-face situation such as teaching or lecturing or advising. It may be a distance learning programme, which can direct the learner to a range of different learning activities. It may be in the form of printed material – textbooks, books or television. Mediation may also occur in the provision of assessment criteria only, with little direction before the learners begin to learn. The assessment criteria then have the function of guiding the learning required. This is the process used in National Vocational Qualifications (NVQs).

To take a step further in looking at the role of mediation in relation to learning, we use the example of a lecture on the insect discussed above. The lecture can perform some of the following mediating activities with regard to the learner's processes – all the time, guiding her towards appropriate frames of reference and guiding her in how to manage the framing of her learning about the insect. The lecturer can do the following:

- take into account what she perceives to be the content of the learner's internal experience of the insect so that the level of complexity of the material of teaching is appropriate;
- simplify and provide structure or classification in the material of teaching;
- highlight variation between what she perceives to be the learner's internal experience, bearing in mind what she perceives to be the current external experiences;
- act as a resource for clarification so that the learner can work to achieve coherence in her cognitive structure;
- signal to the learner what she believes to be the appropriate conceptions of the knowledge; the emotional connotations and the approach the learner should adopt for the learning process;

- enable the learner to know to what standard the learning should be performed (often with reference to a task in which the learning is to be represented by the learner).

Essentially what we are calling 'mediation of learning experience' is any act in which the material of teaching is modified with the intention of affecting the learning situation of a learner. This could involve simplification or it may mean that the material is made more challenging in order that the learner's processes of learning are challenged. Alternatively, it may involve suggestion to the learner of how to use her learning processes differently.

Some would say that there is a clear division between the learner having direct ('raw') experience of something (e.g., the bee-like insect described above) and the mediation of the learning experience (e.g., Laurillard, 1993). This is the point at which we can start to look at what we mean by 'experience' in terms that are relevant to learning in order to lay a base for consideration of 'experiential learning' later in the chapter.

Mediation and experiential learning

The idea that there is a dividing line that can be drawn between situations of direct and mediated experience is attractive and tends to underpin many assumptions made about what is called 'experiential' learning. The idea follows on from the assumption that there is a different process in experiential learning from other forms of learning, which is then described separately in the literature. However, the notion of a strict dividing line becomes more problematic in examples such as the following, which is drawn from a discussion of this issue in Moon (1999a). The example considers different ways of learning about ancient texts, such as the following:

1 An interested adult visits a museum to view, handle and read from an ancient text.
2 An interested adult visits a museum to view, handle and read from a facsimile of an ancient text.
3 A theology student handles and examines an ancient text in its original form.
4 The student listens to a taped version of the ancient text and writes notes as she listens.
5 The student examines and reads an edited copy of the ancient text.
6 The student attends a class in which there is a presentation about the text with a teacher quoting from an ancient copy of it.
7 The student attends a tutorial class in which there is a presentation about the text by another student, with the student quoting from an ancient copy of it.

8   Students are given some specific assessment criteria that relate to their learning or knowledge of a text.

Which of the above are experiential and which are mediated? We could say that 1 is experiential. We might say that 2 is experiential but it is not quite the same. We might say that 3 is experiential but then in the context of her programme of study, the student might have been given very clear directions as to what to read and how to experience the reading of the text and then it might not be experiential learning. Number 4 is mediated if the intended learning is focused on the nature of the actual text as an object, but not if the intended experience is about the learner making sense from the language and words of the text. Number 5 is mediated if the task is about the ancient text but it is not mediated if the task is about making sense of the ideas presented and, perhaps relating them to those in another text. We could probably say that 6 is mediated, but then what of 7? Is 7 mediated for the students who listen and not mediated for the student who presents the material? What, also of 8 which might seem to involve both mediated and experiential learning?

Whether these situations exemplify mediated learning or learning from direct experience depends to some extent on the purpose of the learning. Any number of examples could be given, but in the end we could provide plausible rationales for many of them to exemplify mediated experiences of learning or direct experience. We suggest, therefore, that there is a continuum between the process of learning from direct experience with no help or support given to the learner and the processes of learning from mediated material but the nature of the continuum is likely to vary with the purpose for the learning. An additional complication is that 'purpose' can apply to the intentions of the teacher and to the intentions of the learner though the teacher could put huge effort into mediating a learner's learning experience with the learner being completely unaffected.

We take this a step further: it could be said that learners mediate their own experience through the processes of bringing prior experience into the present, and bringing them to bear on the new material of learning. It is perhaps salutary to remember that once we have engaged in the process of learning, the encoding of the experience in the language of the brain is a multiple pattern of nerve impulses and chemical reactions in the brain. It is in the same form whether we are learning about volcanoes by sitting beside an erupting volcano or learning about one from being taught in a classroom, or watching television. It is worth remembering this when encountering the plentiful literature that states that 'learning by from direct experience is best'. The same reasoning applies to learning through different media, for example, 'e-learning' or the lecture. Without exception, the most important medium is the nerve impulse. It might be reasonable to assume that the learning from sitting by a volcano will be richer, with many more connections and connotations and probably the role of emotion in learning would be much stronger than would be the case in a lecture about earthquakes. Some teachers are better than others at evoking emotion in their mediating actions and for some learners, the involvement of emotion will be more relevant than for others.

On the basis of the reasoning above, we can consider what some characteristics of good mediation of learning are likely to be:

- clarity about the purpose of the learning and the kind of understanding that the teacher hopes the learner will achieve (i.e., the result of the learning);
- the mediation process anticipates the nature of relevant prior experience of the learners, in other words, the internal experience that they are likely to bring to bear on a new situation, and guides them to bringing this into the current learning situation;
- the anticipation of the manner in which learners perceive the process of learning so that mediation processes can guide them to take an appropriate approach to learning (see Chapter 4).

Mediation of the experiences of learning, reflective and experiential learning

This is not the whole story about learning in formal situations, or about the mediation of learning but it serves to question many beliefs about the relationship between learners, experience and reflective and experiential learning.

In the section above we have described the processes of mediation in the experience of learning. The logic of this is that a defining characteristic of reflective and experiential learning in formal learning situations is that there is relatively little direct mediation. It is not possible to say that there is no mediation because there is usually some level of stated purpose to activities in which people learn in formal education and this is a form of mediation because it guides learning. Largely, therefore, reflective and experiential learning are forms of learning that are recognized to take place with little mediation of the learning. There are relatively few directions given by a teacher or other agent about the details of the learning – though a general purpose may be set.

Chapter 6

The nature of reflective learning

Introduction

Reflective learning is the topic of this chapter and the aim of the chapter is to relate reflective learning to the picture built of generic learning in the earlier chapters in the book. The first section of the chapter is concerned with clarifying the terminology such as reflection, reflective learning, reflective writing and reflective practice. The focus is on reflection and reflective learning. The second section is a review of new literature on these areas. In the third section the different forms of reflection suggested by the literature and common observation are defined in relation to previous work conducted by the author. This forms a basis for a consideration of the relationship of reflection and learning (fourth section). In the fifth section we deal with some common beliefs about reflection.

With the development of a clearer picture of reflective learning, it is possible to move on to a consideration of how it relates to the generic view of learning developed in the earlier chapters of this book. Against this material we can consider if learning can either be 'reflective' or 'non-reflective'. The next section explores the role of frames of reference in different forms of reflection and it explains how learning from reflection is problematic – particularly when formalized in educational situations. The final section of the chapter provides a link to the subject matter of Chapter 7, which, in essence, follows on the exploration of the nature of reflective learning through consideration of another dimension of reflection – the depth of reflection.

A discussion of terminology

The concept of reflection is represented by a number of different words that are in current parlance. We talk of 'reflection' itself, 'reflective learning', 'reflective writing' and 'reflective practice'. 'Reflection', as a process, seems to lie somewhere around the notion of learning and thinking. We reflect in order to learn something, or we learn as a result of reflecting – so 'reflective learning' as a term, simply emphasizes the intention to learn as a result of reflection. The content of 'reflective writing' is not a direct mirror of what happens in the head, but it is a representation of the process within a chosen medium – in this case, writing. The representation of reflection in the form of writing is likely to differ from that represented in other ways such as speech or in a drawing. In making a representation of personal reflection, we shape and model the content of our reflection in different ways and learn also from the process itself. In other words, there is secondary learning.

'Reflective practice' is a relatively new phrase that came into use particularly as a result of the work of Donald Schön (1983, 1987). Schön's first book was actually called *The Reflective Practitioner*. 'Reflective practice' emphasizes the use of reflection in professional or other complex activities as a means of coping with situations that are ill-structured and/or unpredictable. The idea of reflective practice was developed initially in nursing and teacher education and is increasingly being applied across the professions. It is, in essence, a professionalized form of 'reflective learning', but any kind of definition has remained problematic (Lyons, 1999).

On the basis of the reasoning above, we will be using the terms 'reflection' and 'reflective learning' interchangeably as the main terminology, recognizing that 'reflective writing' and 'reflective practice' represent expansions of the ideas in different directions and these terms will be used appropriately.

The literature of reflection and reflective learning

A major summary of the literature on reflection is contained in Moon (1999a). It was further developed in Moon (1999b), which focused on an application of reflection and reflective writing in learning journals. This latter book reviewed issues such as the nature of learning from reflective writing, reflection in journals in different disciplines and areas of work (e.g., professional development) and how to help learners to start reflecting.

Since the end of the 1990s not only have ideas about reflection continued to spread across professions in their professional development agendas (e.g., Burns and Bulman, 2000; Taylor and White, 2000; McAlpine and Weston, 2002) but they have also crossed many disciplines in undergraduate studies (e.g., Stewart 2002; Lowy, 2002). Now there is a great deal of literature available on how to introduce reflection into disciplines (e.g., Jones, 2002; Race, 2002), or how to embed it in programmes (e.g., Knowles *et al.*, 2001). In addition, there is a wealth of material about reflection in the context of personal development planning (PDP) which is being introduced across whole institutions at present (Moon, 2001b). Reflection also plays an important part in employability skills and student work experience (Moon, 2003). Hinnett (2003) has recently provided a general review of the applied uses of reflection in two linked papers.

There has been some concern to continue to relate reflection to learning and to understand the relationship between reflection and effective behaviour (Ferry and Ross-Gordon, 1998; McAlpine and Weston, 2002). Related to this is an increasing awareness of a 'depth dimension' of reflection (see Chapter 7) and the recognition that superficial reflection may not be effective as a means of learning (Mezirow, 1998; Kember *et al.*, 1999, 2000; Kim, 1999). These ideas are developed in this chapter and in Chapter 7. In a very different area, there is also increasing acceptance of the value of reflection in qualitative research methods (e.g., various topics in Denzin and Lincoln, 2000). What is still substantially missing from the literature, however, is good empirical evidence that the development of reflection in academic contexts has long-term and definite benefit to the majority of learners (Mackintosh, 1998).

There is still relatively little literature that directly and explicitly links and explores reflection and learning from experience. However, the work of McAlpine and Weston (2002) is a valuable example. It is small-scale, but detailed and, on an empirical basis, predicts much of the theory presented in this chapter. McAlpine and Weston were primarily interested in the reflective processes of exemplary teachers and how they used their prior experiences to reflect on and to maintain the quality of their teaching in an ongoing manner. Central to the activities of these teachers were processes of monitoring and decision-making in relation to their goals. They used a range of areas of knowledge in order to maintain these processes. For example, they used knowledge of the learners, of pedagogy and of the content of their teaching. In this process they were observing and learning about the principles of their action, which further guided more teaching. McAlpine and Weston say:

> Transforming experiential and tacit knowledge into principled explicit knowledge [in this case] about teaching requires . . . intentional reflection for the purpose of making sense of and learning from experience for the purpose of improvement . . . Reflection requires linking existing knowledge to an analysis of the relationship between current experience and future action . . . They go on to say that reflection aids in the reflective processes themselves, thereby building or expanding knowledge.
>
> (2002, p. 69)

Some definitions of reflection and reflective learning

Moon (1999a) set out to clarify the nature of reflection, having observed the extraordinary complexity of the literature in this area. Some of the literature seems to suggest that reflection is no more than a form of thinking (the 'common-sense view of reflection', see below). However, that does not accord with the manner in which reflection is often operationalized in formal education (the academic view of reflection, see below). Enormously complicating the situation, too, is the literature from various disciplines, including education, professional development and psychology, that appears to use the idea of reflection in many different ways. The definitions have been refined and developed.

The common-sense view of reflection

The common-sense view of reflection is developed by examination of how we use the word 'reflection' in everyday language. We have said that reflection is akin to thinking but there is more to be added to this. We reflect usually in order to achieve an outcome, or for some purpose. We may, however, simply 'be reflective', and an outcome might then be unexpected. Reflection is an activity that we apply to more complex issues. We do not reflect on the route to the bus-stop, or on how to do a simple arithmetical sum where there is an obvious solution. We think it through or plan it. However, we might reflect on whether or not to complain about something when the complaint may generate difficult consequences. In addition, the content of reflection is largely what we know already. It is often a process of re-organizing knowledge and emotional orientations in order to achieve further insights.

On the basis of the reasoning above, a common-sense view of reflection can be stated as follows:

> Reflection is a form of mental processing – like a form of thinking – that we may use to fulfil a purpose or to achieve some anticipated outcome or we may simply 'be reflective' and then an outcome can be unexpected. Reflection is applied to relatively complicated, ill-structured ideas for which there is not an obvious solution and is largely based on the further processing of knowledge and understanding that we already possess.
>
> (based on, but extending the definition in Moon 1999a)

Reflection applied in academic contexts: a development of the common-sense view

Since the late 1990s, the theory and practice of reflection have attained a much more significant role in educational contexts. Unless there is clarity about the strictures that tend to be imposed upon reflection in these specific contexts, there is the danger that we will make an everyday activity technical. Reflection that is a requirement of a curriculum is likely to have some characteristics that are specified in advance. On this basis, it is useful to recognize a second view of reflection in order to encompass its application in the academic context. It would not be appropriate in academia, for example, to say that professional development is enhanced when a person goes for a sunny walk in a reflective mood. We would require something more tangible and directed – or the reflection might be expected to occur within a given structure. An element of the structure is likely to be a description of an incident. Furthermore, the outcome of reflection, which is most likely to be reflective writing, is usually seen by a tutor, and is often assessed. This can lead to some students writing the 'reflective' material that they think will be viewed favourably by their tutor (Salisbury, 1994). In addition, evidence of learning or change of behaviour may be expected to result from the process of reflection. These factors are also likely to influence the nature of reflective learning (Boud and Walker, 1998).

On the basis of the paragraph above, we can add to the common-sense definition of reflection as follows:

> Reflection/reflective learning or reflective writing in the academic context, is also likely to involve a conscious and stated purpose for the reflection, with an outcome specified in terms of learning, action or clarification. It may be preceded by a description of the purpose and/or the subject matter of the reflection. The process and outcome of reflective work are most likely to be in a represented (e.g., written) form, to be seen by others and to be assessed. All of these factors can influence its nature and quality.

In practice, the way in which reflection is used in educational situations is often quite narrowly defined. For example, it may be defined in terms of learning from recognized error or ineffectiveness in practice (Mackintosh, 1998; Hinnett, 2003) and it is often subject to some of the beliefs that are discussed later in this chapter. An example of such a belief is that reflection is always about the self.

Views of reflection that are focused on the outcomes of the process

As indicated above, much of the book *Reflection in Learning and Professional Development* (Moon, 1999a) was devoted to an exploration of how apparently different accounts of reflection in the literature could be describing the same basic process. It was observed that while accounts seemed to assume the common-sense view of reflection, their focus was on the ways in which reflection can be applied and how they produce a particular outcome rather than the mechanics of the process. This different focus seems to explain the diversity of the literature on reflection and the manner in which it has become complicated. From evidence of the literature, Moon suggests that the following outcomes can result from reflective processes:

- learning, knowledge and understanding;
- some form of action;
- a process of critical review;
- personal and continuing professional development;
- reflection on the process of learning or personal functioning (meta-cognition);
- the building of theory from observations in practice situations;
- the making of decisions/resolution of uncertainty, the solving of problems; empowerment and emancipation;
- unexpected outcomes (e.g., images, ideas that could be solutions to dilemmas or seen as creative activity);
- emotion (that can be an outcome or can be part of the process, see Chapter 3);
- clarification and the recognition that there is a need for further reflection.

(developed from Moon, 1999a, 1999b)

Although 'learning' (as above) is deemed to be an outcome of reflection in its own right, we could say that all the outcomes in the list are concerned with how we use understanding and knowledge to achieve other purposes. In other words, these factors link reflection with the process of learning.

A basis for discussion of reflection and learning

Reflection and its roles in learning

If the process of learning is implied in all the outcomes of reflection that are identified in the previous section, does that mean that we can say that reflection seems to be involved in all forms of learning and, in that case, is simply a part of the learning process? The consideration of reflection in learning in Moon (1999a) suggests that reflection is involved in some forms of learning, but probably not all. We return here to the work on the approach to learning adopted by a learner (see Chapter 4) that suggests that a deep approach is where the learner seeks to understand the meaning of material in relation to previous knowledge. A surface approach is characterized by the attempt to memorize the facts. Moon (1999a) linked the idea of approach to reflection in the proposition of a continuum from surface to deep approaches to learning. In this model, learning is conceived as a sequence of stages from superficial 'noticing' (perceiving, superficial observation), 'making sense', to 'making meaning', 'working with meaning' and finally 'transformative learning' which indicates the deep approach end of the continuum. In the latter stage, the learner is willing extensively to modify her cognitive structure and is able to evaluate the sources of her knowledge and her process of learning. The representation of the learning from these progressively more sophisticated stages relates closely to the increasing complexity described in the SOLO taxonomy (structure of learning outcomes) of Biggs and Collis (1982) (see Chapter 4).

We use the SOLO model as an initial indicator of the relationship between reflection and learning but can develop the ideas of this relationship beyond the model itself. We can identify here four ways in which reflection is involved in learning. First, reflection is involved in the process of meaningful learning when a learner takes a deep approach. In terms of the stages of learning described above, this would imply that reflection is increasingly involved from the stage of 'making meaning', through 'working with meaning' to 'transformative learning'. Second, reflection is involved when meaningful learning is represented meaningfully (e.g., in writing, orally, etc.) because we have to modify ideas in order to represent them (see Chapter 1). The process of modification involves taking into account the purpose and format of the representation as well as reformulating the current understandings to meet it. Often there is greater understanding of ideas once they have been represented. The act of teaching is an example of the representation of meaningful knowledge. There is a common adage that understanding is bettered only when it has been taught to another. There is a secondary matter to learning from the representation of learning – we learn from the process of representation and from the material that is generated as a result of representation.

The next two ways in which reflection is related to learning are poles of another continuum. The third manner in which reflection is involved in learning is in the 'upgrading of learning' (Moon, 1999a). Here there is no immediate new material of learning, but ideas learnt in a relatively non-meaningful way are reconsidered in the light of more or different prior experience (i.e., are reviewed with different frames of reference). In this way, less meaningful learning is made more meaningful ('deepened'). For example, childhood history learning tends to remain in corners of the brain as stereotypes – King Richard the Lionheart was 'good', King John was 'bad'. In upgrading this knowledge, we might reconsider the reign of King Richard (or King John) in the light of a more sophisticated knowledge of history or politics. In more substantial terms 'upgrading' could be said often to be the process of traditional adult education. Typically prior learning, that is characterized by a collection of relatively factual and non-theory-bound ideas, is reviewed and recontextualized in the light of a more coherent and theoretical approach and through the processes of discussion and critique.

In the fourth way in which reflection is related to learning, we generate apparently new and meaningful ideas (knowledge and understandings) that are not immediately related to specific existing knowledge though clearly they are based on what we 'know'. This is the form of learning that is most obviously called 'reflective'. An example is a learner who needs to evaluate her study skills over the past semester. She needs to recall difficulties and achievements and to relate them to the study ability that seems to be demanded by her level of work. It is not a straightforward process, but one of moving around in different ideas (framing and reframing). This learner has a purpose for generating understanding but we should not ignore the common occurrence of day-dreaming – the reflection under the cherry tree on a sunny day – when there is no particular intention to learn or to seek new meaning, and yet inspiration is suddenly there. We say 'the penny dropped' or 'I saw the light'. Some would call this intuition (Atkinson and Claxton, 2002).

In addition to being part of process of learning something that is identifiable as described above, reflective processes also play a part in the enhancement of other learning. In these situations reflection could be said to enhance conditions that favour learning. Some examples are the following:

- Reflection slows the pace of learning. A helpful idea that expresses this is the provision of 'intellectual space' (Barnett, 1997).
- Carl Rogers wrote much about the importance in learning of the development of a sense of ownership of learning by the learner (Rogers, 1969). To reflect on something is to bring it into ownership. This may be related to the suggestion by Elbow (1973) that reflective or personally expressive writing facilitates learning, and Selfe and Arbabi (1986) that students who write reflectively about their process of problem-solving become more able at solving that type of problem.
- Reflection also encourages metacognition that supports learning. Learners who achieve well are more often those who are aware of, and able to reflect on, their own learning processes, their weaknesses and strengths (Kuhn et al., 1988; Ertmer and Newby, 1996; Hadwin and Winne, 1996; Dart et al., 1998).

So we are suggesting that reflection not only plays a part in the process of good quality learning, but it is also important in the development of appropriate learning behaviour. However, the stucture of the material of learning needs to be brought into the picture and this develops the picture further.

The interplay between the structure of the material of learning and intentions to understand

There is another important issue to consider in the relationship between reflection and learning. In the common-sense view of reflection, it seemed entirely plausible to suggest that reflection occurs when the material of learning is relatively complex or is relatively ill-structured. As yet that idea has not been linked into the section above about how reflection is related to learning. We come back to constructivism. The structure of the material of learning is related by implication to the intention of the learner to achieve meaningful learning. It is the learner who judges the structure of material of learning in relation to her current level of understanding and her intentions. Material of learning that is challenging and apparently ill-structured to one person may be well-structured and a small learning challenge to another. In terms of the learner's intentions, the same material of learning may be both challenging and not challenging to the same learner. An arithmetical theorum can be used as a simple rule to follow or the learner may be asked to explain the intricacies of its proof – which may be a complex task. When we bring these learning challenge issues into the considerations of the relationship between reflection and learning, some new forms of relationship emerge.

We can pull together the ideas from the sections above, taking into account now the material of learning and the learner's intentions.

Reflection and learning: a summary

In terms of the material of learning, we have said that reflection or reflective learning occurs:

- when learning is relatively ill-structured or is challenging to a learner;
- when the learner is intent on meaningful learning/wants to understand the material for herself.

In assimilating new material of learning, reflective learning occurs:

- when the new material of learning is challenging either in relation to internal experience or to the intention of the learner and the learner wants to understand the material in a manner that is meaningful to her (takes a deep approach).

In learning from the representation of learning, reflection occurs:

- when representation is challenging to the learner because of the task of representing the material or in presenting the ideas;
- when there is new (secondary) learning that occurs as a result of representing the initial learning and that represents a new learning challenge.

When there is no new material of learning and the learner is attempting to develop her understanding on the basis of what she knows already, reflection occurs:

- in situations of 'upgrading' of existing ideas where meaning is made from prior experiences that were not necessarily meaningful to the learner;
- in situations in which there is reconsideration of existing ideas that may be meaningful in order to seek additional or deeper meaning;

- where there is general reflection without a specific intention to make meaning – but meaningful ideas occur.

Reflection also appears to enhance the conditions for learning in a number of ways, which we can summarize as 'reflection facilitates good learning behaviour'.

Some beliefs about reflection

There are some particular views of what reflection is which could obstruct further understanding (Moon, 2003). We discuss the following:

- Emotion is central to reflective processes.
- Reflection is about 'my own' processes (i.e., always in the first person).
- Some people cannot reflect.

We have discussed the various *roles of emotion in learning*. To some, reflection is seen to be characterized by its emotional components. Others note significant roles for emotion in reflection. They suggest, for example, that reflection and feeling act in an interdependent relationship with emotion (Taylor, 1997); that emotion is represented sometimes as tacit knowledge (McAlpine and Weston, 2002). They also suggest that past emotional experience 'highlights' issues to be dealt with (Mezirow, 1998; Boud and Walker, 1998); or there is recognition that reflective learning may demand 'emotional stamina' (Mezirow, 1998). In Chapter 3 we made an assumption that emotion was intimately involved in all learning – not just reflection. A number of different relationships between emotion and learning were identified and we suggest that any of these can be operative in reflection. It is possible that the nature of reflective activity leads to greater awareness of emotion and greater account being taken of the role of emotion but we would not say that emotional involvement characterizes reflection. Some possibilities are that:

- Emotion may be the subject matter of reflection – feelings are labile and become involved in or complicate issues that are the subject matter of reflection.
- There may be a more permissive attitude towards the involvement of emotion in reflective activity than in other areas of formal education.
- Reflection involves the 'slowing of the pace of learning', it is more possible to recognize the role of emotion in the process of learning when it is slowed down.
- Chapter 3 suggested the existence of a form of learning that has particular emotional content – emotional insight. From the examples of emotional

insight it might be possible to say that reflective processes are sometimes an important medium for emotional insight.

- We have suggested above that one outcome of reflection is metacognition. Metacognition involves the consideration of personal emotional functioning along with other modes.

There is further discussion of emotion and reflection later in this chapter.

Another belief about reflection is that *it always concerns the self* – in other words, it is always about the role of the 'first person' (I). There is no reason why this should be the case, although the self does tend to be central in many of the ways in which reflection is applied in formal educational contexts, for example, in learning journals, in professional development and in personal appraisal. It is possible to reflect, for example, on morality issues in a personal relationship whether it is one's own relationship, or that of others. In deep forms of reflection (see Chapter 7), the first person is involved because awareness of the role and processes of the learner herself is drawn into reflection.

Finally, there is often a belief that *some people cannot reflect*. Much of the latter part of this book is based on the observation that when asked to reflect in formal educational situations, many learners have difficulty in understanding what they should do or they resist reflection (Boud and Walker, 1998; Jasper, 1998; Tomlinson, 1999; Lucas, 2001). In contrast, other learners will have no difficulty and will not understand the problems encountered by their colleagues. There are also cultural norms that may resist 'navel-gazing'. Since reflection is suggested to be an element in good quality forms of learning, we clearly take the position that everyone can reflect, though this may not always be a conscious activity and may not be done willingly when required. The acceptability of overt reflective processes may be related to different practices in disciplines. Assuming that everyone *can* reflect does not assume that everyone uses reflection effectively to improve performance. Ferry and Ross-Gordon (1998) and McAlpine and Weston (2002) present evidence that professionals vary in the effectiveness with which they use reflection and that this is not just a function of their level of experience.

Reflective learning in relation to a generic view of learning

In the remaining sections of this chapter we relate the view of reflective learning developed in the first part of this chapter to the generic view of learning developed earlier. Learning is presented in this book as a process of the accommodation of the current cognitive structure of the learner to new material of learning (usually represented as the external experience), under the guidance of internal experience, which will take account of the intentions of the learner. New material of learning has, so far, been seen as a variation between the internal experience and external experience of the object. In a given situation there will be many simultaneous variations and to manage relevance is to use appropriate frames of reference to distinguish the significant figure material from the non-significant ground material.

We have conceptualized internal experience as the sum of intention and prior knowledge and experience of the object and have suggested that it guides the process of meaningful learning, in this case, new material of learning. What we are describing as 'internal experience' would seem to accord with some aspects of the role of reflection in learning, for example, in the case of reflection within a process of meaningful learning of new material of learning. We now need to explore the role of reflection in internal experience in relation to the presence or absence of new material of learning. Above we categorized reflective learning in the following ways (in a different order now):

- there is new material of learning;
- there is no new material of learning;
- when there is learning from the representation of learning.

In the case of reflection where there is *new material of learning* that is relatively complex or ill-structured and/or where the learner intends to understand meaningfully, reflection seems to accord with the functions of the internal experience in the process of guiding learning and accommodation. Reflective learning is simply part of the operation of internal experience in meaningful learning of relatively complex material.

What happens, however, when there is *no new material of learning?* The new material of learning has, up to now, been broadly equated with external experience. We used examples of learning about the geological nature of Beer stone to illustrate this. We have said that reflection may not involve any new material of learning. In this case the learner is dealing with material that is already part of the cognitive structure and the outcome is a reorganization of cognitive structure with accommodation to newly developed ideas (Ward, 1999). The concepts of variation and relevance are as valid in this form of reflective learning as they would be in situations where there is the processing of external experience. We have used the term 'cognitive housekeeping' to describe the re-ordering of thought where there is no new material of learning (Moon, 1999a).

A further issue now is how we conceive of this process in terms of internal and external experience when there is no new material of learning. Since we are dealing with a model, the reconceptualization is a matter of seeking the best explanation. It is probably easiest to conceive of reflection of this sort mainly as a process of internal experience. This fits with some observations, for example, we may find reflection easier when we find ways of externalizing it and thereby engaging external experience processes. This is illustrated in the next chapter on depth in reflection which introduces phrases such as 'standing back from the event' (p. 95). In addition, the role of representation of reflection in learning journals (p. 159) or through work with critical friends (p. 147) is a process of engaging external experience in what would otherwise be an internal process.

The process of '*upgrading*' learning also fits the pattern of learning when there is no (immediate) new material of learning and we conceive of a similar process of reordering cognitive structure through the processes of internal experience.

Learning from the meaningful representation of learning is more complex because there is a secondary process of learning that is involved in which there is learning from the representation of the initial learning. First, there is the transformation of the initial knowledge into the format required for the representation. This usually will mean a reformulation of what was initially learnt so that it meets the demands of the task – an example would be the marshalling of ideas within the development of an argument. The ideas may be known, but are not directly associated with this particular context and need to be applied. The process of organizing internal experience towards the appropriately marshalled argument may often involve reflective learning. Second, there is the opportunity to learn more from the represented form, in this case the argument, which has now become an object of external experience (i.e., is now potentially new material of learning). Depending on the form of representation, there are greater or less opportunities to learn from the representation of learning. In the case of written examinations, there may not be much learning in the second part of the process because there is often little opportunity to read through scripts. On the other hand, the initial drafting and then the redrafting of written material can be the source of much learning. The process of reflective writing relies on learning that results from the process of writing.

We describe learning from the representation of learning here as if it is a two-stage process of representing initial learning (e.g., in writing) and then (later) learning from the representation (learning from the written material). The process is often likely to be integrated so that adjustments to the ongoing representation process can be made by learning from what has already been represented. In terms of learning processes, this would be a delicate and rapid interplay between internal and external experience using tightly controlled frames of reference. We might call this self-evaluation or self-feedback. Sometimes the learning from the representation of the learning will involve taking into account the simultaneous reactions of others (e.g., when representation is performance) as well as from personal processes.

'Reflective' and 'non-reflective' learning

Viewing reflection now in the context of internal experiencing, it becomes evident that we should again take note of constructivist principles and check some assumptions. We have essentially defined non-reflective learning as the kind of learning that is relatively unchallenging to the learner and that does not involve much restructuring of the cognitive structure, and in which processes of internal experience are fairly inactive. But is it as simple as this – is this distinction of learning into reflective or non-reflective categories appropriate or are we talking here of a matter of degree of 'reflectiveness'? We can look at this issue through some examples. The task of memorization of a list may not seem to be very reflective and may not seem to involve much processing of internal experience (except when seen in the context of Kember's work (1996)). Another example, say, the consideration of the rights or wrongs about a friend's casual love affair, may seem to be very reflective. But is this the whole story? The rights and wrongs of a love affair could be processed by some in a non-reflective manner because those people view moral issues categorically as 'right' or 'wrong'. This may come from pre-existing religious conviction or it may be because their conception of the nature of knowledge is at the absolutist stage (Baxter Magolda, 1992, see Chapter 2) or these two explanations may coincide. There is nothing to reflect on and there is little need for a process of internal experience.

The point made here is that it is not possible to say that a task is reflective or not reflective because we cannot determine how the internal experience of another operates or the nature of the other's prior experience or her intentions. It is only possible to say that a task is designed to stimulate reflective or non-reflective learning – to stimulate the activities of internal experience – or not. We cannot even say that a list for memorizing is a non-reflective task because the whole list or some items can stimulate reflection in some subjects. Items in the list might remind a subject of a prior experience, which leads her into reflection on personal issues that have been triggered.

Frames of reference in reflection

We use the example of the 'rights' and 'wrongs' of a love affair to move on to a consideration of the application of frames of reference in reflective learning, and in particular to the notion that there can be different frames of reference for the same event.

The framing of learning is discussed in Chapters 1 to 4 in relation to situations in which there is new material of learning. Different frames of reference are used in the processing of new material of learning. The framing is guided by the learner's internal experience. Observation of the theory and practice of reflective learning in this chapter would suggest that these ideas apply equally well to the processes of internal experience when there is no new material of learning involved. Thus, the conception of knowledge, the approach to the learning and emotional factors can be seen to be involved in framing the processes in reflection.

There are some interesting points that differentiate the experience of learning about an object in external experience and when processing is purely internal. When there is an external object, there is a reference point, which probably has some permanence. The workings of internal experience progress in relation to the object that is to be learned. In a process of reflection, there may be no external reference points. For example, when reflection is on the self, there is no one particular way in which to understand ourselves and there is no stable means of assessing what we know about ourselves. No-one else can see the world in the exact manner of another. Reflective learning, when there is no external experience, is very 'slippery' and subject to the influence of an even more slippery entity, emotion. Here more issues arise. Since reflection is an internal process, current reality is likely to coincide with the emotional influence on any reflective activity. We may only be aware of the influence of a mood or emotion on internal reflective processes when we are in a different mood a few days later. For example, if I am feeling angry when I reflect on something, the anger may influence the process of reflection. Because the feeling of anger is congruent with the outcome of my reflective processes, I may not notice the influence of the anger until I consider again the same issue on a day when I do not feel angry. The influence of emotional state on reflective work is more obvious when the reflection is represented (e.g., in writing), and can be reconsidered.

We can give another example of the manner in which emotional frames of reference change. It is a common observation that, when asked to engage in reflection, most women may initially be more comfortable with the idea than most men. Workshops on reflection in academic contexts may include 20 per cent of men – not often more (from personal experience). Perhaps women are more able to be reflective or are more open to the idea of reflection because the menstrual cycle gives many women the actual experience of seeing an issue in different emotional states on successive days. An implicit understanding that the same object/issue can seem different on different days may be 'good practice' for managing personal reflection on complex issues.

We mentioned the role of variation and relevance in the context of learning (see Chapter 1). Where there is new material of learning, learning is the experiencing of variation between the new material of learning and the internal experience and the choice then to accommodate to that variation because it is in accordance with the learner's intentions. However, where there is no new material of learning, we have to conceive of variation as being within the internal experience. In this way, an important aspect of reflective learning is the bringing of different frames of reference to bear on the same material of learning in order that new variation can be developed to which to accommodate. The judgement of the relevance of any variation elicited is also to be made within internal experience and is also likely to be subject to the current frames of reference. We have said above that there is no source of objectivity in reflection and it is easy to go round in circles without being able to shift into new frames of reference that would allow the development of new variation and hence new learning. We can use an example. A teacher on a Master's programme is asked to write a reflective account of an incident that she has experienced in her school as part of an assignment. The situation chosen is in a dance lesson in a primary school classroom (Resource 10, p. 217). The teacher reflects on her behaviour and her ability to cope when there was an incident concerning the management of a statemented child. In reflecting on the incident, what is it that is relevant to the 'story' that the teacher will 'tell' in her assignment? What are the aspects of the situation that lead her to learn from it – indeed, what did she learn from it? How can she manage objectivity when the incident happened yesterday and she was very disturbed by it? The management of variation and relevance in learning is a much more complex situation in reflective learning than learning about new material of learning that is relatively much more stable and where there is an external reference point.

Another dimension of reflection: depth

Another factor is raised by the example of the teacher in the dance class (see above). The example in Resource 10 provides three written accounts of the same incident. The teacher in question might have written any one of the accounts, but if she is new to this kind of writing, it is most likely that she will have written the first account which is descriptive and demonstrates relatively little of the quality we might expect from reflective writing. The accounts differ in what we term 'depth'. Any resultant learning for the writer of this material will be a situation of learning from the representation of learning. On this basis, there are two potential sources of learning – learning from the process of writing and learning from the process of reading back what is on the page and reflecting on the implications of that. Chapter 7 will consider what is meant by depth in reflection and how depth of reflection is related to the resultant learning.

At the end of Chapter 7 there is a general summary of the material on reflection and reflective learning as forms of learning.

Chapter 7

The depth quality of reflective learning

Introduction

The last chapter introduced a new dimension to reflection – that of depth. It is part of the common experience of reflection that is demonstrated in statements such as 'she was in deep reflection', but the idea of depth has become more important as reflective activities have been increasingly applied in formal education and professional development. There is a frequent observation that while an initial struggle of getting learners to reflect can be overcome, it can be difficult to persuade them to reflect in other than a superficial manner – which might be little different from descriptive writing (Lyons, 1999). This chapter explores what we mean by 'depth', how it might relate to the learning process and the difference in outcome between deeper and more superficial reflection.

The treatment of depth in this chapter is in two sections. The first introduces the concept of depth, relates it to the literature and describes framework for reflective writing that are structured in terms of depth. The second section of the chapter explores the nature of depth in reflection in relation to the generic view of learning described in the earlier chapters of this book.

The final section of this chapter is a summary of the content of the two chapters on reflective learning – this chapter and Chapter 6. In discussing depth in reflection below, we mainly refer to reflective writing both because it is in the context of written reflective work that the issues of depth mainly arise and because written work is tangible. It is important to recognize that reflective writing involves learning from the representation of learning (see Chapter 6).

Depth of reflection and its measurement

We use the terminology 'levels of reflection' to imply a hierarchical model of reflective activity that demonstrates progression from what is little different to description to a profound form of reflection. Most models that incorporate the notion of depth of reflection do not imply that the levels are qualitatively different, though they may use specific terms for the different levels (e.g., Van Manen, 1977). Examples of reflective writing at different levels are provided in Resources 5, 6 and 10.

Frameworks that incorporate the idea of depth of reflection have often been developed as a result of practical work with learners. Some examples are Hettich (1976, 1990), Van Manen (1977), Mezirow (1981), Wedman and Martin (1986), Ross (1989), Sparkes-Langer *et al.* (1990), Sparkes-Langer and Colton (1991), Hatton and Smith (1995), Barnett (1997), Kember *et al.* (1999) and Kember *et al.* (2000). Generally this material seems to be consistent, attributing similar qualities to the deeper levels of reflection and generally viewing superficial reflection as descriptive. However, much of the work seems to be lacking substance in its approach and had not been put into general use. This may be because it has not been sufficiently developed with appropriate support materials. There are exceptions that are described below.

In the frameworks described in the references above, deep reflection is generally characterized by perspective transformation (Mezirow, 1991, 1998), transformatory critique (Barnett, 1997), or transformative learning (Moon, 1999a). These terms refer to the ability to revise the 'meaning structures' (Taylor, 1997) which are the bases of judgements. In other words, we are talking here about a review of the manner of the function of internal experience and what frames of reference are used and how. In turn, this implies a functional understanding of the constructed nature of knowledge and a meta-cognitive stance. Another quality of deep reflection is its critical orientation to one's own and others' understandings. A number of writers have commented on the inadequacy of much activity performed in the name of reflection because it is non-critical and non-reflective (or non-reflexive) (Kim, 1999). Taylor and White (2000) provide a well-illustrated argument of the inadequacy of the reflective practice model and the importance of criticality in professional situations:

> The primary focus of reflection is on process issues . . . Its focus on knowledge is primarily confined to the application of 'theory to practice' . . . Reflexivity takes things further. Specifically, it problematizes issues that reflection takes for granted . . . For example, it assumes that through reflection the worker can become more adept at applying child development and attachment theories more effectively. Reflexivity suggests that we interrogate these previously taken-for-granted assumptions.
>
> (2000, p. 198)

All those who discern levels of reflection seem to agree with the statement above, but use different terminologies so 'reflexivity', like 'critical reflection' or perspective transformation would be seen as the deepest level of reflection. In addition, among the theorists there is an implied agreement that deeper reflection yields better quality outcomes in terms of learning.

Kember *et al.* (1999) provide a well-developed and substantiated levels framework for written reflection. They developed the early work of Mezirow (1981) with seven levels of reflection described from 'non-reflective action' to 'premise reflection' (which matches other descriptions of deep reflection). They tested the hierarchy of levels and it appeared to be generally reliable. In a later paper (Kember *et al.*, 2000), a questionaire was developed to test the ability of students to engage in reflective thinking. The four levels in this construct were still substantially based on Mezirow's work, with 'habitual action' at the least reflective level and 'critical reflection' at the deepest level. This framework was shown to be a reliable indication of reflective thinking in learners.

The work of Hatton and Smith (1995) is probably the best-known frame-work of levels of reflection. This was developed in experimental work on the reflective writing of teacher education students. It was then formulated into a tool for wider use. A brief description of the levels follows (using some of Hatton and Smith's own words):

- Descriptive writing – writing that is not considered to show evidence of reflection. It is a description with no discussion beyond description.
- Descriptive reflection – there is description of events. The possibility of alternative viewpoints is accepted but most reflection is from one perspective.
- Dialogic reflection – the work demonstrates a 'stepping back' from events and actions leading to a different level of mulling about discourse with self and exploring the discourse of events and actions. There is a recognition that different qualities of judgement and alternative explanations may exist for the same material. The reflection is analytical or integrative, though may reveal inconsistency.
- Critical reflection – 'demonstrates an awareness that actions and events are not only located within and explicable by multiple perspectives, but are located in and influenced by multiple historical and socio-political contexts'.

Hatton and Smith's work was used with several cohorts of higher education work experience placement learners. For assessment purposes, these students were required to produce a reflective account. Initially the accounts had been disappointing since they were so superficial. The tool, therefore, had a purpose both for guiding the work of the learners, as well as providing a rationale for assessment purposes (i.e., by providing assessment criteria). An interesting point that became evident in the process of this work is that we should take care not to reject all descriptive writing. Some description is necessary in a reflective account that is used in an educational situation to provide the background for the reflection. However, this 'statement of how things are' has a different role in the writing from the role of reflection and should not be confused with the latter.

Despite the use of Hatton and Smith's framework, it was still difficult to help learners to properly understand the nature of deeper reflection. They seemed to need actual examples of reflective work in order to understand what was required. A further stage was then to develop the exercises to which reference was made earlier (Resources 5, 6 and 10) where different levels of reflection are based on one initial descriptive account of a particular situation. The use of these exercises is described in Chapter 10. In association with two of the accounts (Resources 5 and 6) but, separate from them, a rationale was constructed which identified ways in which reflective activity characterized the different levels so that a progression from superficial descriptive to deep reflection was demonstrated. These exercises have proved helpful for many learners who have to write reflectively, and for the staff either in managing the reflective work of students, or for their own professional development.

A further stage of the work above involved the development of a generic framework of reflective writing. This drew on the rationales associated with the practical exercises and on observations of the use of the exercises and the comments made by staff and students working on them. It is intended to be generic and can be used in association with any of the reflective exercises. It describes four levels in a notional continuum from superficial and descriptive to deep levels of reflective writing. It is important to note that it does not relate by terminology or number to specific accounts in the exercises. The Generic Framework for Reflective Writing is reproduced in Resource 9.

We could say, in the terminology of Fazey and Marton (2002), that increasing depth in reflection relies on an increasing awareness, use of and sophistication in the use of variation in the internal experience (i.e., in cognitive housekeeping processes). These ideas are developed below.

Logically, there is no 'end-point' of deep reflection – it can go on and on examining issues in a wider and wider context and at different points of time from the event (see below) to infinity. However, in most situations in which reflection is applied, there will be logistical reasons for limiting the account, for example, word limits in the academic context. An element of strategy is, therefore, to be able to write appropriately within given constraints. It has become evident both in the development of the exercises on levels of reflection and from working with learners, that deeper reflection often requires more word length than superficial reflection, especially if, within the word length there is to be a short description of the event/issue. It is not unusual to ask for 'reflective pieces' in, for example, 200 or 500 words in educational situations and short word limits may inhibit deeper reflection. Extending the word limit in these situations has been observed to encourage deeper reflection.

Theoretical bases for the concept depth of reflection

There is relevant underlying theory to this list of characteristics of deepening reflection. We suggested in the previous chapter that reflective learning is, essentially, a purposeful framing and reframing of material in internal experience with the intention of learning. There is not necessarily an input of new material of learning. Increasing the depth of reflective learning implies a development in the ability to use different frames of reference with associated flexibility, openness and awareness of the range of relevant issues. Frames of reference as described in Chapters 2, 3 and 4 are particularly relevant. These forms of framing are the developments of the conception of the structure of knowledge; the role of emotion in learning; the learner's approach to learning.

Conceptions of knowledge and depth in reflection

The ideas that characterize the more sophisticated conceptions of knowledge also underpin deeper levels of reflection. For example, the stages of reflective judgement (King and Kitchener, 1994) and that of 'contextual knowing' (Baxter Magolda, 1992) include the idea that knowledge is constructed and that it is supported by evidence that is related to a particular context. There is use of multiple frames of reference (flexibility) and there is the suggestion that reasoning, at this level, implies a consideration of the processes of reasoning themselves (metacognition).

At the other extreme of the continua of conceptions of knowledge, there is an assumption that knowledge is 'right or wrong' and is 'given'. This understanding of knowledge really cannot provide any basis for reflective activity at all as we have described reflection as occurring in situations where there is not an obvious solution or where knowledge is ill-structured. Reflection is not about the seeking of 'right or wrong' answers. It may be that the attainment of the slightly more developed conceptions of knowledge coincides with the beginning of the ability to be reflective.

Emotion and reflection

Chapter 3 explored aspects of the relationship between emotion and learning. It concluded that there are many relationships between emotion and learning (p. 44). Deeper and more sophisticated levels of reflection must rely on some understanding of how emotion affects the process of reflection and, in practice, the reflection must demonstrate a practical ability to manage personal emotional processes in relation to the subject matter of the reflection. This is implied in the process of metacognition and further, in the judgements that are made of the quality of personal reasoning. It is manifested in the awareness of the 'slipperiness' of reflection (Fraser, 1995; Fenwick, 2000).

The approach to learning and reflection

Since meaningful processes of learning involve reflection, one way of looking at the relationship between approach and reflection is simply to say that where there is reflection, there is a deep approach to learning and vice versa. However, there is another angle. When learners are given tasks that involve reflection, in the same manner as in other areas of study, their approach can be to produce writing that looks generally reflective, but that does not yield personally valuable learning. This strategic approach may be the starting point for many learners who do not entirely understand why they are being asked to reflect, or what is expected of them. However, there is a complex variety of factors that characterize the deeper levels of reflection, and guidance on what we might call 'techniques of deeper reflection' is rarely available. It is likely, therefore, to be mainly those who adopt a deep approach to the task of learning from reflection with the intention to pursue meaning, who find their ways into deeper levels of reflective activity. Perhaps there are a few who, in taking a relatively strategic approach to reflective tasks, stumble across useful understandings of the subject matter which encourage them subsequently to adopt a deeper approach.

Characterizing depth in reflection: a summary

We have said that depth in reflection is characterized by increasing ability to frame and reframe internal and external experience with openness and flexibility. It is related to the increase of the range of variation that is taken into account in the reflective process and to the ability to recognize and manage relevance. It also requires sophistication in a number of areas of development, in particular, the learner's conception of the structure of knowledge and the notion of knowledge as constructed which appears to underpin most deep reflection. In deep reflection, the learner requires the ability to manage emotion, and where appropriate to work with it, understanding also the manner in which it is related to the context of the reflective and learning process. In addition, the learner will need to be able to frame her approach to learning in accordance with her (and given) intentions for the task.

Reflection and reflective learning as forms of learning: a summary of Chapters 6 and 7

- There are several words in the vocabulary of reflection that may be used in different ways. These include reflection, reflective learning, reflective writing. Reflection and reflective learning are used interchangeably in this book, but reflective writing is a form of representation of learning and there are secondary learning processes involved.
- The term 'reflective practice' seems to relate to the work of Schön (1983, 1987). It emphasizes the use of reflection in professional or other complex activities as a means of coping with situations that are unstructured and/or unpredictable.
- Three views of reflection are provided:
  - a common-sense view;
  - a view of reflection when it is applied in academic contexts;
  - theoretical views that are focused on the outcomes of reflection.
- Earlier books by the author have reviewed the relationship between reflection and learning. This material and later considerations suggest that the role of reflection in learning where the intention is to do the following:
  - understand the meaning of new material of learning;
  - learn from the process of representing (meaningful) learning;
  - learn in situations where there is processing of existing ideas (i.e., where there is no new material of learning).
- In addition, some specific situations in which the process of reflection enhances the conditions for learning have been identified.
- Reflection is seen as having a role, therefore, in the process of good quality learning, and in the development of appropriate learning behaviour.
- Some views of reflection that might tend to create a source of confusion in the literature are recognized and discussed:
  - that emotion is central to reflective processes;
  - that reflection is always about 'my own' processes (i.e., always in the first person);
  - that some people cannot reflect.
- In terms of its relationship to a generic view of learning, reflection is seen more or less to coincide with the process of 'internal experience' (Marton and Booth, 1997) which guides meaningful learning when there is new material of learning. Where there is no new material of learning, reflection involves a reordering of internal experience in order that new ideas are developed from existing experience. We described this as the engagement of different but appropriate frames of reference in internal experience important in reflection. In this way, variation is produced and new learning can occur.

- In relation to learning, reflection is the purposeful framing and reframing of material in external or internal experience (depending on whether there is new material of learning) with an intention in the learner of learning from the process.
- In both cases, reflection and reflective learning occur when the intention is for meaningful learning and/or when the material of learning is relatively ill-structured, complex or unpredictable. We do not appear to reflect on straightforward or simple material unless there are several simple ideas that need to be combined. However, on the basis of a constructivist view of learning, it is the learner's intention and her regard of meaningfulness and the learner's view of the complexity/ill-structuredness that are relevant.
- Another dimension of reflection is evident particularly when reflective learning is used in academic practice – that is termed 'depth', and depth of reflection is represented in a hierarchy of 'levels' of reflection.
- It is commonly observed that when asked to engage in reflective writing, learners will often not manage much more than a descriptive level of reflection. To support their ability to reflect at a deeper level and to facilitate assessment processes of reflection, frameworks for reflective writing that incorporate the notion of depth have been developed.
- Depth of reflection seems particularly to be characterized by increased flexibility and ability to manage the framing process in an open and flexible manner. Depth is demonstrated in the following:

  - the learner's intentions for the learning;
  - the increase of the range of variation that is taken into account in the reflective process;
  - the ability to recognize and manage relevance;
  - the sophistication of the learner's conception of knowledge;
  - her ability effectively to frame emotional factors;
  - her understanding of the effect of emotion on learning;
  - her framing of the approach to learning that she adopts.

Chapter 8

Exploring experiential learning

The literature

Introduction

Chapters 6 and 7 have attempted to tease out the meaning of reflective learning in order to provide a basis for the more practical approach in later chapters. A similar process will be applied to experiential learning. As with reflective learning, one concern of this book is to consider its relationship to the literature of learning as well as to its own literature (i.e., on experiential learning). A further stage is to consider to what degree reflective and experiential learning refer to the same or similar processes and to what degree they are distinctive. This is complicated by the fact – as will become evident in this chapter – that experiential learning is seen in a number of different ways with different processes therefore being involved. Often it is the allocation of a common term – 'experiential learning' or 'learning from experience' that often seems to be the factor in common between these diverse behaviours. Terminology is discussed below.

As has been mentioned earlier, while the literature on reflection and reflective learning has been well explored in previous books of the author, apart from one chapter in Moon (1999a), the literature on experiential learning has not been treated in the same way. It therefore needs to be treated here in more detail.

The first section of this chapter provides a broad context for the terms 'experiential learning' and 'learning from experience'. The former term tends to focus on the formal learning situations that are the main topic of this book. The next section returns to discussions in earlier chapters on the meaning of experience but now experience is taken in the context of discussions of experiential learning. We then look at the matter of defining experiential learning. There is no one appropriate definition because there are many different ways in which the term is used. In some, there seems little concern about the process of learning but the focus is on the purpose for the learning (e.g., for consciousness-raising). These latter definitions do not help in the effort to find distinctive features of this learning process. The section concludes with a description of the 'boundaries of meaning' of experiential learning. We then discuss some of the concepts of experiential learning in which the sequence of stages of the process are captured in 'experiential learning cycles' (for example, as in Kolb, 1984). The next section identifies some of the issues on experiential learning that remain unclear and the final section draws together key points.

Experiential learning and learning from experience

The earlier chapters of this book show that all learning is, in effect, learning from experience. Among others who explicitly express this are Dewey (1938), Chickering (1977), Boud *et al.* (2000), Jarvis (1987), Laurillard (1993) and Michelson (1996). On this view, what is signficant about this learning that makes it worthy of exploration as a topic in itself?

To start this consideration, the distinctions drawn in various places between the 'learning from experience' and 'experiential learning' seem to be particularly helpful. Usher and Soloman (1999), for example, see 'learning from experience' as 'taking place in the lifeworld of everyday contexts'. In contrast, they see 'experiential learning' as 'a key element of a discourse which constructs experience in a particular way, as something from which knowledge can be derived through abstraction and by use of methodological approaches such as observation and reflection' (ibid., p. 161). A similar view is expressed by Brah and Hoy (1989). The review of the literature that follows would support this distinction. While this book has taken a generic view of learning as its basis, the discussion of experiential learning in this chapter is directed towards the more specialized sense of it made by Usher and Soloman – usually in the context of formal education. It is still, however, a term 'with a spectrum of meanings, practices and ideologies' (Warner Weil and McGill, 1989a, p. 3). One particular use of the term that is somewhat narrower than most (and not used here) is where 'experiential learning' is interpreted as situations in which prior learning is accredited and thereby incorporated into programmes of formal learning (Evans, 1992).

On the basis of the above, we do not seek a unified 'experiential learning theory' (Saunders, undated). However, we can still inquire into the range of meanings, how the term is generally understood and how elements of experiential learning relate to the generic description of learning and to reflective learning.

There is a vast literature on experiential learning in a variety of fields. There are examples from training and development, adult education, school science education, work experience and work-based learning, nursing, outdoor education and other forms of professional development, management and, more specifically, decision-making (e.g., Zsambok and Klein, 1997), political and social activism (e.g., Friere, 1970). There is also much literature dedicated more directly to experiential learning itself (e.g., Warner Weil and McGill, 1989b; Boud and Miller, 1996; Greenaway, 2003). We seek the meaning, first, with reference to the word 'experiential'.

Experiential learning and experience

In the context of experiential learning, even the notion of experience is treated in many different ways with different aspects of the idea emphasized. The approach that is adopted hinges to some extent on how writers view the relationship of learning to experience (see above). For some, the experience in the process of experiential learning is special (Beard and Wilson, 2002) and far from the more generalized meaning of experience used earlier. But maybe it is special because it is deliberately associated with a deliberate act of learning. Winter (1989) helpfully points out that having an experience and learning from experience are different: 'Experience' is not quite the same thing as '*learning* from experience'. We have heard the witticism directed at a colleague who is supposed to have had 'ten years' experience'; 'No,' comes the reply, 'They've had one year's experience repeated ten times over' (Winter, 1989, p. 8).

Many writers are relatively clear that the experience in experiential learning is generally not mediated experience (see Chapter 5). However, some see the experience as specific and as a formal element of a curriculum which is usually active in some way, or more active than other elements of the curriculum (Beard and Wilson, 2002). Examples are field courses, games and simulations, work experience placements, aspects of outdoor education, years abroad within programmes, and so on (Boydell, 1976; Chickering, 1977; Green, 1995, 2003). Also looking at experiential learning within the context of education, Newman (1999) distinguishes between those approaches to experience that concern the life events of the students, and those in which the experience is constructed through such techniques as role play and simulation. In the former situation he suggests using methods such as visualization and writing to elicit the material; in the latter, he suggests further activities that would normally be used to encourage reflection on the resulting material (see Chapter 10).

These educationally orientated experiences are often 'engineered' by a facilitator and tend to include what we could regard as the more objective views of what experience might be. Sometimes they appear to suggest that all there is to experiential learning is to have an experience and then to follow through a sequence of activities such as is depicted in the Kolb cycle (Kolb, 1984). There is an assumption that the learning that can result from the experience, if the activities are manifested 'properly', is a commodity called 'knowledge'. This tends to be the view of the training and development literature (Moon, 2001a). The recognition of the 'slipperiness' of experience brings greater conceptual complexity to the view of experiential learning and greater realism. As Eraut says, 'Tidy images of learning are usually deceptive' (2000, p. 28).

Marion Milner illustrates very well the difficulty of learning from experience in her various studies of her own behaviour from journal writing and psycho-analytic techniques (Field, 1952; Milner, 1957, 1987). She found that different interpretations of the same event would occur from one day to the next. Fraser picks up the same point: 'We internalise our knowledge of the world in a manner which is consistent with our world view. If that manner is jaundiced and fragile, then how do we know that we are "seeing" anything other than a reflection of our own fragility?' (1995, p. 59). Such comments relate to the material on emotion and learning (see Chapter 3) and to the idea that one aspect of deepening reflection is the understanding that learning is influenced by current states of mind and perspectives of understanding (see Chapter 7). Other good examples of learning from experience are provided in Lennon and Whitford (1994), and in particular, Seller (1994).

Another writer who recognizes the constructed nature of experience in his approach to research on learning from experience is William Torbert (1972). Torbert adopted both phenomenological and empirical methods in his study but, like Milner, started with his own behaviour. While his book is not easy to follow, he raises many issues about the nature of experience that are still current and unresolved.

It is those who see the experience in experiential learning as constructed who can begin to recognize the wider issues involved in the process (Sutherland, 1997). Newman (1999) provides a well-reasoned demonstration of the subjective nature of experience when he discusses his experiences of a visit to South Africa. He describes the potential distortions in the experiences of the visit. First, with reference to experiences recalled from the visit, he describes walking down some stairs into a basement and seeing a mural on a wall. He used this as the basis for the potential of short stories (i.e., reconstruction of material as a creative writer rather than a rapporteur). Second, he looks at the reconstruction of experience in terms of experiences forgotten – the ability to 'forget' the details of a death. Third, he talks of the manner in which immediate experience is endowed with different sets of meaning according to (for example) the listener. Finally, he points out that many human experiences are vicarious. For example, he describes the ways in which he learnt about experiences of different people who had been victimized in their communities through the stories they told. He recognizes that stories construct and distort to purvey the most poignant or important aspects of a story to others for information or entertainment. He goes on to demonstrate how it is the construction and reconstruction of experience that lead to and support conflict. This latter principle and its reverse underpin many of the more political uses of experiential learning. To summarize these and other points, Newman says 'Experience is complex . . . We construct and reconstruct our experience, falsify it, break it up into episodes, allocate to each episode particular truths of our own (1999, p. 19). Cell provides another dimension to this in his suggestion that 'We tend to experience what we believe we will experience' (1984, p. 178).

Despite the evidence for the constructed nature of experience, the naïve view persists that experience represents the 'authentic' representation and voice of the individual (Usher and Edwards, 1994; Fraser, 1995; Usher, 2000a, 2000b). On a reasoned basis, it is hard to deny the significance of the role that socially developed culture and norms play in the construction of individual experience and its interpretation. An experience itself has no meaning until it is endowed with meaning by the individual who mainly draws on socially constructed meaning (Jarvis, 1987).

It is useful to round off this section on experience in experiential learning with an important point made by Dewey, whose work on exploring the idea of experience was highly influential in the development of the field of experiential learning. Experiential learning tends to have an aura of 'good' around it (see later). Some of this comes from the enthusiastic but often simplistic writings on the topic. Clearly what is learnt from experience cannot be either 'good' nor positive to the learner. Dewey (1938) makes this point through his distinction between education and experience: 'some experiences are mis-educative. Any experience is mis-educative that has the effect of arresting or distorting the growth of further experience' (ibid., p. 25). He goes on to talk of other ways in which experience may stunt development, before making the main point of his book that traditional education 'offers a plethora of examples of experiences of the kind mentioned' (ibid., p. 26). Many would suggest that the alternative progressive education is equally capable of providing a source of 'mis-educative' experiences (Peters, 1966).

The problem of defining experiential learning

With a variety of views of experience, it is hardly surprising that the matter of definition of experiential learning is complicated. In various articles and books, Boud has defined and redefined experiential learning in a manner that would be difficult to challenge or improve and a review of his position concludes this section. However, since experiential learning is, itself, at least in part, a constructed term (Usher and Edwards, 1994), one set of meanings of it is the meanings of all of those who have contributed to the literature, and therefore we include a sample of other definitions.

It is worth noting at this point that the development of the meaning of experiential learning has a historical dimension. Houle (1976), Boydell, (1976), Cunningham (1983) and Boud (2001) provide interesting historical perspectives.

Some definitions

We begin with a general comment from Fenwick (2000) who also works at defining experiential learning. She summarizes the breadth of views of experiential learning in the educational context:

> the notion of experiential learning has been appropriated to designate everything from kinaesthetic-directed instructional activities in the classroom to special work-place projects interspersed with critical dialogue led by a facilitator, to learning generated through social action movements, and even to team-building adventures in the wilderness. Definitional problems continue when one tries to disentangle the notion of experiential learning from experiences commonly associated with formal education such as class discussions, reading and analysis and reflection.

We now provide a general flavour of definitions of experiential learning:

> The insight gained through the conscious or unconscious internalization of our own or observed experiences which build upon our past experiences or knowledge.
>
> (Beard and Wilson, 2002, p. 16)

> The contrast between non-experiential and experiential learning is one between more and less abstract and more and less linguistic sets of symbols that are employed in the transactions in which learning takes place.
>
> (Tumin, 1976, p. 41)

> experiential learning means that learning that occurs when changes in judgements, feelings or skills result for a particular person from living through an event or events.
>
> (Chickering, 1977, p. 63)

> experiential learning . . . is synonymous with 'meaningful-discovery' learning . . . which involves the learner in sorting things out for himself by restructuring his perceptions of what is happening.
>
> (Boydell, 1976, pp. 19, 20)

> experiential learning is learning that is rooted in our doing and our experience. It is learning which illuminates that experience and provides direction for the making of judgements as a guide to choice and action.
>
> (Hutton, 1989, p. 51)

The . . . term 'experiential learning' insists that there can be no fundamental distinction between what is personally understood and what is personally, intimately experienced through living . . . We cannot come to know any aspect of the world without taking up a particular kind of stance towards it.

(Salmon, 1989, pp. 131, 133)

Experiential learning concepts offer a way of structuring and sequencing learning that leads to the increased effectiveness of the experience.

(Green, 1995)

Experiential learning is the strategic use of challenging outdoor and indoor experiences to stimulate insight and improvement. Its most basic purpose is to assist individuals, teams and whole organizations in increasing their business successes.

(Rumsey, 1996, cited in Saunders, undated)

[In experiential learning] the fact that the learner, not the educator, must be able to apply the knowledge gained from the teachings is the bottom line.

(Saunders, undated)

Experiential learning is a process in which an experience is reflected upon and then translated into concepts which in turn become guidelines for new experiences.

(Saddington, 1992, p. 44)

The received professional ideology of experiential learning is that it empowers individuals to gain control over learning and hence their lives and to take responsibility for themselves. [It is] widely regarded as empowering learners perhaps in ways that non-experiential learning does not.

(Griffin, 1992, pp. 32, 31)

Sometimes the definition of a topic is presented indirectly instead of directly. In a recent workshop, experiential learning was presented as differing from formal learning in that it is largely unstructured; begins with the experience, not principles and concepts; is more personal or individualized; may be 'unconsciously acquired' and is 'usually more permanent' (Noble, 2002).

Another indirect, but rather important source of views about experiential learning is teachers and learners involved in programmes that overtly use experiential learning. Burnard (1991) sought such information from nurse tutors and their students. He summarized the main responses as learning by doing and personal learning and learning that involved reflection. It was seen as active rather than passive and, in this situation, was contrasted with 'lecturing' or 'being taught'. He says, 'The idea seems to be that in experiential learning, we learn by taking part and learn something that is personal to us, whereas in the lecture approach, we are more passive; we adopt knowledge [from the public domain]' (ibid., p. 217).

A significant view of experiential learning is evident in the design of one Master's programme in 'experiential education' (Saunders, undated). Students on the programme are from widely differing backgrounds. There are two bases for the programme design – the first is that students are required to 'leave the classroom and develop meaningful learning experiences for themselves'. The second is that 'raw, direct experience is complemented with careful thought and reason. In this light, core seminars are orientated towards the analysis and questioning about the fundamental theory of experiential education' (Saunders, undated). One of the most useful definitions that takes a wide range of interpretations into account (see below) is that of McGill and Warner Weil (1989). They see experiential learning as:

> the process whereby people individually and in association with others, engage in direct encounter, then *purposefully* reflect upon, validate, transform, give personal meaning to and seek to integrate their different ways of knowing. Experiential *learning* therefore enables the discovery of possibilities that may not be evident from direct experience alone.
>
> (ibid., p. 248)

As we have said, the views of experiential learning differ widely. Seeking unanimity from this range of views is not possible.

Typologies of experiential learning

Another way of working with this array of definitions is to produce a typology. We ended on the definition of McGill and Warner Weil, who also produced a typology as a means of ordering presentations in the First International Conference on Experiential Learning in 1987. Their typology describes four 'villages'. Their 'villages' represent clusters of inter-related ideas and concerns and the significance of the ideological aspects of experiential learning is evident in their choice of categories. The first village is concerned with 'assessing and accrediting learning from life and work experience as the basis for creating new routes into higher education' and other opportunities. The term often applied here is APEL (accreditation of prior experiential learning). The second 'village' 'focuses on experiential learning as the basis for bringing about change in the structures, purposes and curricula of post-school education. This includes work on simulation, role play and learning from work experience in higher education. In terms of theory, it tends to lean towards the managed sequences of experiential learning such as the Kolb cycle (Kolb, 1984). The third 'village' is concerned with 'consciousness raising, community action and social change'. Examples here are the work of Friere (1970) and Hart (1990) and the fourth is concerned with 'personal growth and development' and examples are Progoff (1980) and Rowland (2000).

Another typology that is very different is that of Davies (2001) who suggests three approaches to experiential learning. The first approach includes
those who have developed sequences for the process of experiential learning.
This is epitomized by the work of Kolb (1984) and Boud and Walker (2000).
The second approach is represented by those for whom the significance of
experiential learning in relation to the learner's views or behaviour is the
main consideration. A third approach is concerned with comment on the
processes of experiential learning. Mulligan's view of the internal processes of experiential learning would seem to exemplify this approach
(Mulligan, 2000).

The definitions of Boud and associates

While it is tempting to pick out issues raised in the list of definitions of
experiential learning above, it is a selected list, it is very wide-ranging but
does not cover the field. In a number of publications, Boud and his colleagues
have noted the general features and significant boundaries of the literature
of experiential learning and beyond adding a few points, we accept this as
an appropriate characterization of this complicated literature. In effect, they
progressively identify the boundaries of experiential learning. In 2000, Boud,
Cohen and Walker developed five 'propositions' about experiential learning.
They are:

- Experience is the foundation of, and the stimulus for all learning.
- Learners actively construct their own experience.
- Learning is a holistic process.
- Learning is socially and culturally constructed.
- Learning is influenced by the socioemotional context in which it occurs.

(ibid., pp. 8–14)

These are statements that are completely in accord with the content of the
generic view of learning in Chapters 1, 2, 3, 4 of this book. Andresen *et al.*
(2000), now using the term 'experience-based learning', restate the propositions as assumptions (ibid., pp. 225, 226) and add other 'features that
characterise and distinguish it from other approaches' (ibid., p. 226). These
are taken from Kolb (1984, p. 38):

- involvement of the whole person – intellect, feelings and senses;
- recognition and active use of all the learner's relevant life experiences and
  learning experiences;
- continued reflection upon earlier experiences in order to add to and trans-
  form them into deeper understanding.

It will be noted that these statements also coincide completely with the earlier
material in this book, though in 1984, it is likely that the statements would

have been seen as quite distinct from the then current views of learning. One incidental characteristic of experiential learning, therefore, is that it is based on theoretical principles that have often been ahead of their time.

Andresen *et al*. go on to mention three further factors that may characterize the practice of experience-based learning:

- intentionality of design' – meaning that learning 'events' may be 'structured' (2000, p. 226);
- 'facilitation' – experiential learning situations tend to be managed by 'facilitators' rather than 'teachers' (ibid.). The former are normally seen as having equal status as the learners and aid the learning rather than providing material of learning.
- 'assessment of learning outcomes' – there tend to be processes of assessment of learning or practices that are particularly characteristic of experiential learning. Andresen *et al*. mention learning journals, negotiated learning contracts, peer assessment and self-assessment (ibid., p. 227).

Finally, they mention what they deem to be 'essential criteria' of experiential learning. These are:

- that the learning that results is personally significant or meaningful to the learner;
- that it is important that the learner is personally engaged with the learning;
- that there is a reflective process involved;
- that there is acknowledgement that there is involvement of the whole person in all her capacities and relationships with the present and related past experiences;
- that there is recognition of the prior experience of learners;
- that there is an ethical stance of concern and respect for the learner, validation, trust and openness toward the learner which value and support the 'self-directive potential of the learner'.

(ibid., pp. 227, 228)

There are a number of more general statements that we can add as a result of the current perusal of the literature. They provide mostly what might be called 'outside boundaries' and are fairly obvious but are important. The first is that experiential learning takes effort. It will not just occur automatically when a person has an experience. Mason (2000, p. 115) says: 'intentional learning through experience requires more than just trusting in haphazardly metonymic triggering of randomly stored memories'. In the same book, Criticos (2000) cites the Chinese proverb, 'I hear and I forget, I see and I can remember, I do and I understand' (ibid., p. 161). He comments: 'If experience in itself was so valuable, then humans who are enmeshed in experience ought to be more knowledgeable than they are. Sadly the only conclusion that can be reached is that we do not learn from experience' (ibid.). He suggests that experience must be processed in order that knowledge can result from it. It is likely that this is one of the most important statements in this chapter.

The second 'outside boundary' of experiential learning follows on. It is that it is not just any experience that can result in learning but specific experiences, often at the 'right time' and in the 'right place'. While Davies and Easterby-Smith (1984) agree that experience is the 'key to the development' of the managers whom they studied, it is not just a matter of 'any experience', but 'that some kinds of experience provide more effective development than others'. They identified the 'best' experiences for learning to come from situations in which their managers confronted novel situations and problems where their existing behaviours were inadequate (which, in terms used previously, were therefore ill-structured or challenging). Managers with steady and unchanging work experiences did not seem to develop as much.

The third boundary is that 'unlearning' can be a more important gain from experiential learning than 'learning'. In a sense, this statement contradicts the notion of learning as change, but it does emphasize that change, and changing back to the pre-change state – in other words, flexibility and openness to the possibility of mistake or error – can be important in learning. Brew (2000) provides a detailed account of such learning.

Finally, we return to the topic of the subjectivity of experience. Boud and Andresen and their colleagues do recognize this in several statements above, but do not emphasize it. Unless we recognize the 'slipperiness' of our processing of experience, we are looking at learning and, indeed, teaching, in a naïve and non-progressive manner. Experiential learning should explicitly recognize the subjective nature of experience.

We can summarize the four 'outside boundaries' of experiential learning that we have added to those of Andresen *et al.* above:

- Experiential learning takes effort.
- Learning can occur from some experiences more effectively than from others.
- 'Unlearning' from experience can be more important than learning more.
- Experiential learning should explicitly recognize the subjective nature of experience.

It is interesting to note that the social and ideologically orientiated 'four villages' approach of Warner Weil and McGill (1989a) overlaps with the material above approach in some places, but mainly could be said to build on the basis of these various sets of statements.

The sequential approaches to experiential learning

This section is concerned with approaches to experiential learning that involve the detailing of sequences of the activities involved in the process of learning experientially (see Davies' typology, above). Probably the most common understanding of experiential learning is that based on the work of Kolb (1984) with his cycle of experiential learning which was developed from the work of Piaget, Lewin and others. Arguably it is because of the 'recipe' type of approach that is demonstrated in Kolb's work (Rowland, 2000) that 'experiential learning' has become so much a topic of discussion and use in educational and training circles. Basically Kolb's work and others that are based on it (e.g., Gibbs, 1988; Dennison and Kirk, 1990) make learning seem easy, though one might say that no approach would gain so much popularity if it did not work or have some value. One of the tasks of this section is to question why the Kolb cycle might 'work' and in what respects it may be deficient.

In its simplest form, the Kolb cycle has four elements drawn in a cycle, with elements linked. Notionally the entry point is 'concrete experience'. According to Kolb and Fry (1975), immediate concrete experience is the basis for observation and reflection. These observations are assimilated into a 'theory' ('Formation of abstract conceptions') from which new implications for action can be deduced ('Testing implications of concepts in new situations'). These implications or hypotheses then serve as guides interacting to create new experiences (ibid., p. 1). The 'new experiences' are, then, in effect, new concrete experiences for further processing in the cycle. The usual interpretation of the cycle appears to be somewhat static, but Kolb not only suggested that learners might 'recycle' many times, but also that they start their learning at any stage in the sequence (Kolb, 1984). He also observed that people functioned more and less effectively in the stages of the cycle, for example, they might be more keen on the theorizing aspects of the task than the active testing phase. The implied differences in 'learning styles' have been widely applied (e.g., Honey and Mumford, 1992; Sadler-Smith, 1997; Rider and Rayner, 1998).

There are many criticisms of the Kolb cycle, some because it is simplistic (Jarvis, 1987; Rowland, 2000; Moon, 2001a) or 'formulaic' (Marsick and Watkins, 1990); some because it does not go far enough in considering factors such as the transfer of learning (Wallace, 1996). Some note that it is too much based on the notion of experience as a phenomenon of the individual, or that the notion of experience is simplified – tending to be small scale (Newman, 1999) or does not take account tacit knowledge (Eraut, 2000). Newman captures many of these sentiments in saying of the Kolb cycle:

I find it too ordered, too regular, too predictable. It seems to imply an impera-tive: that we must move through the cycle, that we must move on to the next stage, rather than letting experiences enter into our souls to rest there, develop, change and influence us in some more disordered, unexpected and 'natural' way.

(1999, p. 84)

As is not unusual in academic writing, one of the main problems about the cycle lies not with Kolb's work, but with the ways in which his work has been reinterpreted. It is another feature of the Kolb cycle that there are many sets of wording for the various phases of it (e.g., Boydell, 1976). Some-times these are helpful (e.g., Gibbs, 1988). Sometimes the words used to depict the stages are hard to relate to the original, particularly with regard to the stage of abstract conceptualization and in many reinterpretations, the stage of testing is stated as 'action' or the sense of 'doing something' (Dennison and Kirk, 1990). For the sake of later interpretations, it is a shame that Kolb did not say more about the nature of the observation and reflection stages (Moon, 1999a).

There are, however, some fruitful interpretations of the Kolb cycle. Moon (1999a) analysed the stages in experiential learning that she could identify from four theorists writing before 1993 (Steinaker and Bell, 1979; Boyd and Fales, 1983; Boud *et al.*, 1985; Atkins and Murphy, 1993). Between them the following phases were identified (it is interesting to note the tendency to avoid the language of reflection in these earlier accounts):

- the 'having of' the experience;
- recognition of a need to resolve something;
- clarification of the issue;
- reviewing and recollecting;
- reviewing feelings/the emotional state;
- processing of knowledge and ideas;
- eventual resolution, possible transformation and action;
- possible action.

(taken from Moon, 1999a)

A more recent example of a sequential approach to experiential learning is Cowan (1998) who redrew the Kolb cycle 'rather like an over-stretched spring' (ibid., p. 37) in order to incorporate more detail of reflective processes based on Schön (1983, 1987). He suggests that a sequence of activities for learning could begin with a period of anticipation in which the goals of a task were considered in relation to prior experiences. The next stage is a deeper exploration of the task. Part of the way through the task there is period of 'reflection-in-action' – a review of progress. There is then a period of consolidation of the learning, followed by reflection on the whole process.

Cowan considers that the process incorporates a number of cycles round the original form of the Kolb cycle.

Another considerable development of the ideas of Kolb is presented in Boud *et al.* (1985) and in a more refined form in Boud and Walker (2000). Again this depiction of learning from experience focuses more on the role of the processes of reflection, recognizing several phases of it in the preparation for experience, the experiencing itself and the processes following the experiencing, during which learning might be consolidated. In both Cowan's and Boud and Walker's models of experiential learning, there are added considerations that avoid some of the more mechanistic qualities of the basic Kolb diagram. Both, for example, acknowledge the role of prior experience. Boud and Walker also incorporate some of what Mulligan calls the 'internal processors of experiential learning' (Mulligan, 1992) which seem to be rather important and to coincide with the 'outside boundaries of experiential learning' mentioned above. One, for example, is 'intent'. Mulligan uses the term 'willing'. We use the term 'effort' as an outside boundary. One could say that we are not likely to learn from experience unless there is some intention or will to learn – on the other hand, work on incidental learning suggests that we do 'pick up' material of learning relatively unconsciously – but it depends at what level we define 'consciousness'. In formal learning situations, it would seem reasonable to say that intent that is 'unclear or unfocused' is a barrier to learning (Boud and Walker, 2000). Both sources also refer to the important role of emotion or feelings in learning from experience – an issue to which we return in Chapter 9. Mulligan adds a number of other 'internal processors' – memory, thought, sensation, intuition and imagination – but perhaps the list could be infinite depending on the breadth of conceptions of learning and experience.

It is interesting to note the way in which the Kolb cycle (and similar depictions) are used – particularly in the field of training and development. Often the cycle is used more to underpin a process of the management of learning, than necessarily as a description of the learning process itself (Moon, 2001a). The cycles provide a sequence of activities to support learning. The Cowan model, for example, represents blocks of activity in which students are told how to behave with respect to the material of the task. In this context, it is relevant to note a point to which we will return in relating experiential to reflective learning. In the Kolb diagram, the stage of reflection precedes the stage of abstract conceptualization (which is often labelled as 'learning'). In the earlier discussions about the place of reflection in learning, we have suggested (p. 82), even in the definition of reflection, that it is seen as a process that works with the material that has already been learnt. In other words, reflection follows initial learning. This observation both justifies the approaches of Cowan and Boud and Walker that identify reflection as functioning at several phases of learning from experience.

Some general issues in experiential learning

Two of the issues described in this section focus on the later stages of the cycle of experiential learning and one relates to the early stage of a task. The first described concerns the ability to progress in the learning after having 'an experience' and the second concerns the transfer of learning from the episode of experiential learning to another context. Both of these issues are relevant to a large part of the literature on experiential learning, but the first is most obvious in relation to the closed nature of the cycle of experiential learning as depicted in the Kolb cycle. The third issue described in this section does not tend to feature much in the literature as a specific topic and it is how learners learn to learn from experience in a formal context.

Progression in experiential learning: the role of evaluation

When something is depicted as a circle, a reasonable question is: 'where does progression occur?' Kolb and others to some extent deal with this issue in talking of spirals or 'spring' formations where the testing phase of learning yields a new and different concrete experience, which then is 're-cycled', but this still does not entirely move out of the cycle. It is possible, for example, that the test phase is inept and indicates to the learner that the abstract conceptualization is appropriate when, perhaps it is not. For example, a teacher sees a colleague using a new way of explaining to young children why a penny at the bottom of a glass of water looks larger. She works out how to explain it and the next day, runs the session. The children are quiet and do not ask questions. She assumes that they have 'understood' to the desired degree and uses the same explanation again in another class. The children in the first class had not 'understood' in the manner intended and the teacher did not recognize this because her testing did not include the appropriate evaluation – her 'evaluation' was based on the silence of the children. The teacher 'learnt' from her experience but did not learn 'correctly'. Because she had no external feedback and evaluated the 'wrong' characteristic of the learners, she perpetuated her learnt (erroneous) behaviour. There was no incentive to modify it. The brief but helpful statement of Cell (1984) that we tend to experience what we believe we will experience, is important here. The involvement of a more critical stance of the action by the teacher herself might have avoided this self-perpetuating situation. The involvement of a deeper form of reflection (see Chapter 7) at several stages in the process is a means of becoming more critical. This might involve some imagination (Mulligan, 2000 – see above), so that the action of the teacher and the children's responses are seen in a broader context. Another method is to involve others. We have noted the somewhat individualistic orientation of much experiential learning. A formalized manner of involving others in experiential learning is through the use of action learning techniques (McGill and Beaty, 1992). In this way, proposed actions and their consequences are exposed to the constructively critical view of others.

Transfer

Transfer of experiential learning from an educational context to the situation of its main deployment – such as the work situation – is a major issue. There is a broad but rather depressing literature on the transfer of learning and though it is evident that humans are good at transferring ideas and skills learnt in one setting to another there are still somewhat contrary messages in much of the literature (Bennett *et al.*, 2000). Tennant says: 'The problematic nature of transfer seems to me quite amazing. This is because educational discourse is imbued with the language of transfer; the idea that what is learned has some generic application is a fundamental tenet of education' (1999, p. 166). Tennant reviews and assesses various approaches to this issue including that of the 'situated learning' theorists, for example, Lave and Wenger (1991) and Greeno (1997) whose views are sometimes interpreted as suggesting that learning is context-bound. He suggests that the issue is not a matter of whether or not transfer occurs but how best to facilitate and maximize the transfer, and when and why transfer does not occur as in the example from Wallace (1996).

Wallace (1996) describes a particularly graphic example of a situation in which learning from an experience did not transfer to a work situation in the manner intended and he analyses what would have improved the situation. Wallace was involved in an 'intensive outdoor management training course' in which there were physical tasks, theoretical lectures, and occasions for reflection on performance. The course yielded intense feelings and an ethos of self-improvement was engendered. He found that back in the work situation, he retained little of the learning and that experiences seemed irrelevant, despite the explicit assumptions about relevance and transfer that were made by the organizers of this course (and many others). He felt that his 'transfer problem' was 'rooted in the way that the team tasks and the setting were . . . far removed by design from . . . [his] . . . routine managerial work and its context' (ibid., p. 18). He suggests that, while there may have been effective learning on the course, the contexts were too different. He suggests that the more different the context of the experiential learning situation, 'the more additional learning is required for transfer into the context of use and the greater the need for learning support (ibid.).

Moon (1999a) observed similar problems in short course training situations and suggests a range of reflective activities that will enable the better integration of experiential learning into workplace practice. They are deliberate activities that follow the sequence below ('current' practice is that as practised prior to the course):

- the development of awareness of current workplace practice;
- the clarification of the new learning and how it relates to current understanding of current practice;
- the integration of new learning and current practice;
- the anticipation or imagination of the nature of improved practice (in other words – responding to the question 'how will the new learning make my practice different?').

Probably the most significant part of this sequence is the use of imagination. Tennant (see above) would add other factors to this list such as the importance of a community of discourse through which learning occurs and is communicated and, in particular, a supportive climate in the transfer context (the workplace) (1999, p. 177).

Learning to learn from experience in the formal context

The main concern here is with experiential learning in formal educational contexts. Often in an experiential learning situation, students who have been used to a teacher being present who tells them what they need to learn are suddenly responsible for learning apparently important ideas without a teacher. Teachers observe that students do not automatically know how to learn from experience in a formal context and that they do not automatically know how to help them (Boreham, 1987). Sometimes it is a matter of the methodology and sometimes it can be a problem that relates to the perceptions of the learning task of student and teacher being different (Burnard, 1991). Often it is a matter of lack of clarity about the task in design terms – a matter that is raised in subsequent chapters.

Experiential learning: drawing out the key points

The literature on experiential learning is diverse and there is no easy summary that can pull it all together. While it is possible to make some generalizations about reflective learning that suggest it to be a certain kind of mental activity, even that kind of generalization cannot be made of experiential learning as it is depicted in the literature. It is a term that tends to be developed to suit the contexts in which it is applied (Sutherland, 1997). As Usher and Edwards point out, it is not 'something found in nature . . . different groups give it their own particular meanings and construct it in their own ways' (1994, p. 201). This is inevitable when, as indicated several times in this book, all learning is based on experience.

However, the term 'experiential learning' does have particular connotations or otherwise it would be meaningless. In some respects we come back to the definitions mentioned above. Some of the connotations of experiential learning are that:

- It is not usually mediated or 'taught'.
- Following from this, the material of learning is usually direct experience.
- There is often a sense that experiential learning is a favoured manner of learning, is 'better' or is more meaningful or it is 'empowering'. The sense of 'empowerment' may come from the manner in which the experiential learning is used, rather than the form of learning itself.
- There is usually reflection either deliberately or non-deliberately involved in experiential learning.
- There is usually some active phase of the learning ('action', 'doing', 'experimentation', and so on).
- There is usually some mechanism of feedback present.
- There is usually formal intention to learn.

The intention to learn at a particular time or from a particular experience is what justifies the use of a specific term such as 'experiential learning' and provides a distinction from incidental and what we call 'everyday' learning. We pick up these connotations of experiential learning in the next chapter.

Moving on: an important note

In many cases of experiential learning, particularly those where the aim has been to empower or raise the consciousness of a group of people, the description of the process of learning is too imprecise to be analysed in relation to generic learning or compared with reflective learning. However, in contrast, in situations in which experiential learning is depicted as a sequence of events, there is something more tangible, particularly since 'reflection' is often seen as having a specific role in the process. It, therefore, has to be these forms of experiential learning in which the learning process itself is better described that we take forward into the next chapter.

Chapter 9

Experiential learning and reflective learning

Drawing it together

Introduction

In the last section of the previous chapter we summarized the nature of experiential learning. Following on from that, we return to the questions posed about experiential learning:

- What is experiential learning in relation to a generic view of learning?
- How is reflective learning involved in experiential learning and is it essential or only sometimes involved?
- Does reflective learning sometimes or always involve experiential learning?

The previous chapters (in particular, the list of connotations of experiential learning in the last chapter) have laid the groundwork for the response in this chapter to the questions above. Here we can draw the threads together and use the general picture to explore the relationship of experiential learning to the generic view of learning (see next section). Through this consideration, some of the connotations of experiential learning also begin to provide a better understanding of the processes of experiential learning. For example, the involvement of action in experiential learning means that a learner must represent her learning and this, in two ways, is likely to improve learning. The following section, in a similar manner, analyses the cycle of experiential learning as presented by Kolb (1984). The Kolb cycle seems to 'work' as a tool for learning by employing at least three helpful learning activities which all involve reflective learning.

The sections described above draw a picture of the process of experiential learning as a sequence of learning activities that may work alone, or may be grouped. We are then broadly able to summarize experiential learning. The summary leads into the last section of this chapter which concerns the relationship between reflective and experiential learning. This chapter concludes the theoretical examination of reflective and experiential learning and leads into the more practical concerns of the last three chapters.

Experiential learning and the generic view of learning

A list of connotations of experiential learning was an outcome of the last chapter. In this chapter we use these connotations of experiential learning as a starting point for exploring the nature of experiential learning in relation to the generic view of learning developed in the first four chapters. Since reflection is included in the connotations of experiential learning this implies that the discussion is immediately drawn on towards a consideration of how reflective learning interrelates with experiential learning.

The connotations of experiential learning (now abbreviated) are that:

- Experiential learning is not usually mediated.
- The material of learning is usually direct experience.
- There is often a sense that it is a specially good form of learning.
- Reflection is usually involved.
- There is usually an 'active' phase of the learning.
- There is usually some mechanism of feedback present.
- There is usually an intention to learn.

This list of somewhat variable characteristics represents both ways in which we define experiential learning and the outcomes of it. The points will be discussed in this chapter, sometimes in a grouped manner and not in the same order as the list.

There is usually an intention to learn

The 'intention to learn' is mainly what makes experiential learning worth considering as a specific form of learning, otherwise, it is little different from incidental and everyday learning. There are reasons for using the qualifying word 'mainly'. We can say that there is always an overt intention for engaging in a particular act of learning, but some of the learning process involved may be incidental learning and therefore unconscious and not fully intentional. For example, a student nurse is told how to put a bandage on a sprained ankle. She is asked to practise on her colleague. There is a conscious intention to learn from the whole experience, but there is likely to be much unconscious and incidental learning during the process. For example, she might find that getting her colleague to sit on a lower rather than higher stool makes the ankle more accessible – a useful insight that is not intentional in the learning process (Eraut, 2000).

Experiential learning is not usually mediated; the material of learning is usually direct experience and reflection is usually involved

These three connotations are linked through the notion of reflection. The chapters on reflective learning indicate that reflective learning takes place when the material of learning is not straightforward, or is relatively challenging to a learner who has the intention of attaining meaning (i.e., takes a deep approach). There are several possible situations described in which material of learning can be challenging to the learner, particularly when it is relatively ill-structured. Material of learning can be challenging when:

- it is complex in relation to the learner's prior experience;
- it is not complex itself but the learner's prior experiences do not or cannot guide the process of learning (e.g., the learner does not have the pre-requisite prior understanding);
- it is not complex itself, but when the learner wants to use a frame of reference in a manner that is challenging to her (to 'problematize it', p. 28);
- perhaps the context of the learning is difficult or challenging.

It was indicated in the previous chapter that the directness of experience is relative to the learner. For example, it is possible that the same experience (e.g., learning to make crème brulée), can be complex to one learner (e.g., to someone who has no confidence in her ability to cook anything) but not complex to another who enjoys cookery, understands the techniques and terms but who has still not cooked this dish before. In relation to experience, we have suggested that mediation is a secondary process in which the material of teaching is simplified or recodified usually to create an easier or more certain situation for the learner (Chapter 5). Mediation thus usually reduces the complexity of direct experience. Sometimes, though, mediation can involve manipulation of the situation in order to increase the challenge to the learner and guide her into useful learning about her learning processes.

There are few generalizations that can be made about the nature of the experience in experiential learning because it is more or less complex, not in relation to other experiences, but as external experience in relation to a learner's internal experience. However, because experiential learning is usually unmediated and because it is usually direct and involves challenge to the learner, reflective learning is involved. The close relationship between experiential learning and reflective learning is an important way in which we can relate experiential learning to the generic view of learning.

In the language of the generic view of learning, the paragraphs above suggest that the learner may have relatively little guidance in sorting out how to frame her learning, the figure/ground relationships, decisions about what is relevant for learning, in other words, how to manage her own architecture of variation (p. 29). However, she can learn to learn from experience. As mentioned earlier, Fazey and Marton (2002) showed that learners learn more effectively when they are confronted with situations that challenge them to cope with a range of variations in experience (p. 28). However, the difficulty in managing variation and sorting figure from ground in un-mediated learning from direct experience can dominate the learning situation and the learner may feel she flounders around, looking for tracks of meaning to follow. This brings us to another of the purposes of mediation. It is not only about a process of 'teaching' but it guides the learner in what it is that she should be learning. As an example: a learner is sent on a work experience placement with the expectation that she will learn from the experience. She is asked to write a learning journal but she is completely unsure what to reflect on or how to frame her learning. The more complex or ill-structured the experience in relation to the prior experience of the learner, the more need the learner will have for an indication of what it is that she has to learn to fulfil set requirements. This is an important principle that is often forgotten in the enthusiasm for experiential learning.

There is often a sense that experiential learning is a specially good form of learning

The word 'good' is used above intentionally. There is a sense of evangelism in some of the writings that relate to experiential learning. This may relate to a sense of contrast between 'tedious' classroom learning at which only a few might be seen to excel and learning from life, between the 'bookish' route and that at the 'coal face'. Dewey (1938) and many later educational writers propounded the values of learning by discovery in progressive education.

However, if we reinterpret 'good' as 'effective', is experiential learning any more effective than formal learning? The initial response is likely to be a series of further questions. Who is it who is learning? What is being learnt? How does the learner want to use the knowledge (i.e., what is the purpose of the learning)? How conveniently can the experience be experienced (i.e., has the learner got time to go and sit at the bottom of a volcano for direct experience)? All these factors have a bearing on the effectiveness of a given episode of experiential learning and at present suggest that 'effectiveness' might be relative to matters such as the context and purpose of the learning situation.

However, there are other factors about experiential learning and the connotations of 'goodness'. Boud *et al.* (1985) and Boud and Walker (2000) have pointed out that one feature that is often associated with experiential learning is also that it takes account of the functioning of the whole person, including her emotions. If experiential learning is exceptional in respect of its holistic nature, then it might warrant its reputation on that basis. Certainly, in the way in which experiential learning situations are developed, there may be greater account taken of the emotional aspects of learning. In Chapter 3 we argued that emotion is part of all learning. If this is the case, experiential learning might not be different *per se* but it is different in the aspects of learning that are noticed and assessed. The question then is whether taking specific account of emotional aspects of learning improves learning or not. Many would argue that taking account of the 'whole learner' does facilitate learning. In this respect, then, the perceived effectiveness of experiential learning is part of the construed notion of experiential learning. It is good because it is seen as being good or is managed in a good way with account taken of the emotion or feelings of the learners.

There are other reasons why experiential learning can be particularly effective. Boydell (1976) stressed the special intention to finding meaning. Moon (2002a) looked at the ways in which learning from work experience could enhance academic learning (see Chapter 12). More significantly, others have mentioned the role of action and feedback that are usually associated with it and this is the subject matter of the next section.

In experiential learning there is usually an active phase of the learning; there is usually some mechanism of feedback present

The role of 'action' in experiential learning may either be emphasized strongly or relatively ignored in the literature. Indeed, the behaviour that can constitute 'action' is also somewhat variable. It tends to be taken into account in a greater way in work that follows the Kolb cycle (e.g., Gibbs, 1988; Dennison and Kirk, 1990; Cowan, 1998) because on the cycle there is clearly an active phase implied (Kolb, 1984). The 'action' may be reinterpreted in different ways that subtly shift it away from any notion of physical action. Boydell (1976) suggests, for example, that experiential learning can occur in lectures if there is interactivity between students or with the lecturer. Cowan (1998) uses the notion of testing as action while others see the phase as one of planning.

We need to consider what it is that relates these different words for action and the notion of feedback and how are they linked to experiential learning. In effect, they are all words for the representation of learning. In Chapter 1 and in other places in the book, we have seen that the representation of learning is a source of further learning (Eisner, 1982). Conceptualizations of experiential learning that incorporate the representation of learning, as a matter of course, imply greater effectiveness. In addition, because learning is represented in some form or other there will be a source of feedback to the learner and this too can improve the learning if the learner takes account of it.

There is another point here: in order to represent learning in a manner in which it is meaningful, it is likely the learner will have adopted a deep approach to the learning (Chapter 4, and Moon, 1999a). A surface approach would probably not lead to the ability to represent learning in an effective manner and therefore to enable the following of the cycle of experiential learning.

In this way, when the notion of action or a form of representation of learning is implied in experiential learning, there are automatically ways in which the learning is likely to be more effective. This reinforces the connotation of 'good' learning that we have discussed above and brings to bear material in Chapter 6 about the role of reflective learning in learning from the representation of learning.

Another look at the cycle of experiential learning

Following the reasoning of the sections above, we return to reconsider the learning that results from the cycle of experiential learning (Kolb, 1984). We reproduce it following Kolb's terminology but using the sequence as suggested in Chapter 6, reversing 'abstract conceptualization' and 'reflection'. In the light of the discussion above, what is it that is going on in the cycle that makes it seem effective?

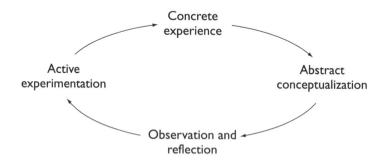

We suggest that the cycle seems to work on the basis of three components of the learning process that has been described in earlier chapters. It involves a reflective learning phase, a phase of learning from the representation of learning and a further phase of learning from feedback.

The reflective learning phase

In the first phase of reflective learning, the essence of a 'concrete experience' is that it is relatively ill-structured material of learning. This element of the Kolb cycle is therefore a process of reflective learning:

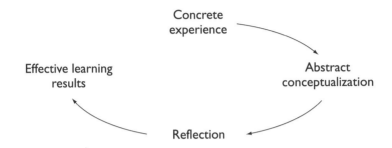

The process of reflective learning is a manner of learning that implies a deep approach to learning which is likely to be effective.

Learning from the representation of learning phase

However, the Kolb cycle does not stop at this point. In a separate operation of learning, the phase of learning from the representation of learning, learners are asked to represent their learning – which is another means of learning (see above). Learning is thus reinforced.

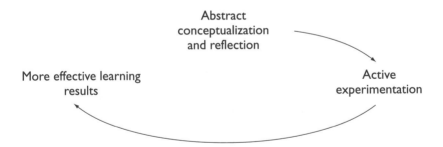

Learning from feedback

The third phase of learning from feedback somewhat overlaps with the second phase and implies that the cycle is seen (as Kolb suggested) as 'recycling' more than once. Learning from feedback in many ways is continuous with learning from the representation of learning but it implies also that we learn from situations in which things go wrong and then we have a chance to put the action 'right' in a further cycle.

Abstract
conceptualization
and reflection

Active
experimentation

Effective learning results
from the feedback

Feedback that is a modified
version of the initial
alternative concrete experience

In these ways, it would be appropriate to call the Kolb cycle a 'system'. As a system it includes several discrete ways of learning and of reinforcing learning. Alternatively it can be presented as a smooth flowing sequence that can be used by those who manage the process of learning. In other words, it can either be about a sequence of learning activities or it is about the facilitation of learning. When it works, it works because of the involvement of the different forms of learning which, combined with the powerful processes of reflection, tend to result in effective learning.

Summarizing experiential learning

The last two sections of this chapter represent the fulfilment of some of the aims of the book. In this section we can now summarize some of the ways in which experiential learning relates to what we have called the generic view of learning. In formal settings, experiential learning seems to be involved in:

- managed situations in which the learning is structured within a powerful system that tends to include an action phase;
- situations in which we learn from the representation of learning;
- relatively new situations to us in which we learn directly from experience with relatively little mediation;
- a range of situations that may not fit any of the above – a construct of the literature.

In addition, the term may be used to describe learning from everyday events in the course of everyday living. On the whole, the approach of this book is to categorize 'experiential learning' as a form of educational activity that is exploited in formal educational contexts.

Experiential and reflective learning

In the course of this chapter we have addressed the questions at the beginning of the chapter. We summarize the response to them here.

In Chapter 6, we indicated the situations in which reflective learning seems to occur, using the following headings to describe when reflective learning occurs:

- when there is new material of learning;
- when there is learning from the representation of learning;
- when there is no new material of learning and the learner is attempting to develop her understanding on the basis of what she already knows.

We have suggested that typical features of experiential learning situations tend to be:

- that the material of learning is ill-structured and challenging to a learner;
- in addition, the expectation is usually that learners will engage in meaningful learning;
- in some forms of experiential learning, representation of learning is required (e.g., when there is emphasis on action).

Learning journals and other reflective tools that require learners to reflect without new material of learning are often involved in experiential learning activities.

To a greater or lesser extent, therefore, all of the forms of reflective learning may have a role in experiential learning. The exception is where the experience is not ill-structured and represents no learning challenge to the learner. We use a simple example. A subject who regularly entertains and serves wine is asked to learn how to uncork a bottle and serve appropriate wine. The task of learning, we assume, represents no challenge to this learner. We have said that a task can be a challenge to one learner and not to another, so choosing a wine, uncorking and serving it could prove challenging to a non-wine drinker. However, we have also suggested that the same learner with the same learning task may be able to interpret and accomplish the task simply, as above, but may feel more challenged when, for example, uncorking and serving wine connoisseurs. The more challenging situation is likely to involve reflective learning; the simpler situation is not likely to involve reflection. Both, however, could be construed as situations of experiential learning.

The learning challenge may not come directly from the nature of the task, but the situation in relation to the learner. We have already pointed out that learners may be confronted with complex situations in which they are told to 'learn from the experience'. The learner might be on a work experience placement in a small business and told that her task is to learn from the experience of the placement. In this case, the challenge is, as we have shown above, in the appropriate framing of the learning and in the management of variations that will enable progress in learning. In such a situation much learning is likely to be incidental (Marsick and Watkins, 1990). The complexity is not in understanding what is learnt, but in the actions of drawing out and clarifying significant matters. In common parlance we might say it is in 'seeing the wood for the trees'. Reflective learning is involved. We are saying, therefore, that many situations of experiential learning involve applications of reflective learning.

So could we say that experiential learning is the same as reflective learning? We cannot say this because experiential learning is a construct that is accompanied by different meanings according to the context of its use. In addition, however, experiential learning, virtually by definition, will involve at some stage, an external experience of learning. This is not necessarily the case with reflective learning activities in which the learner may be working entirely with internal experience (cognitive housekeeping).

We have identified the processes of both reflective and experiential learning in relation to the generic view of learning in Chapters 1–4 and have discussed that:

- experiential learning usually involves reflective learning – except where the material of learning is unchallenging to the learner;
- reflective learning usually has an important role in experiential learning – however, it has an important separate meaning when there is no new material of learning and we reflect on what we 'know' already.

Part III

Working with reflective
and experiential learning

Chapter 10

Introducing reflective activities to learners

Introduction

This chapter is the beginning of the more practical part of the book. The next three chapters are practically based and are designed to support work in education or professional development to enable learners to learn by way of reflective or experiential learning. There are a number of references to resources that are in the Resources section at the end of the book. This chapter is primarily concerned with reflective learning. Reflective learning itself is significant in formal education but it plays an important role in most experiential learning. For this reason, the content of the chapter may be used to support either activity.

The first of these practically based chapters concerns the introduction of reflective activities to learners. This is presented as a two-stage process, which is explained in the first section. Both stages consist of a range of activities and exercises and resources that are intended to help learners to understand what they need to do to manage reflective writing or reflective learning.

The two-stage approach to introducing reflective activities: an explanation

The approach is based on two observations that have practical implications for the introduction of reflective writing activities to students – we have referred to both earlier. First, just presenting learners with a task of writing a learning journal, or reflecting on work experience or any task that involves reflection, is not always successful. Not all learners find reflection easy when it is introduced as a specific requirement. Some will simply 'take to it', recognizing its role in their learning and managing the process well. Some, who may be good students, will not understand what is meant by it and will ask 'what is it that you want me to do?' There are different views of what reflection is and the differences are just as likely to exist among staff as among students. It is worth remembering that staff who introduce reflective activities are likely to be those who understand reflection. They may not understand how other students or staff could fail to comprehend it. Differences in ability to reflect among staff has been demonstrated in difficulties that some experience in their own professional development requirements. It is therefore important when working with both staff and students, to consider carefully how reflection is introduced – both in order to enable students to function well, but also to ensure that staff are 'in tune' with the activities.

Sometimes there are inter-disciplinary issues in the understanding of reflection. The discourses of some subjects are, by nature, more likely to require reflective activity 'on paper'. In others, such as science subjects, the same activity is probably involved, but it occurs mentally and the written report may be the product but not the representation of reflection. We suggest that deliberately introduced reflective activity can play a role in supporting any discipline. It is of note that reflective journal activity is described in over thirty-two disciplines in the literature (Moon, 1999b).

There may also be cultural issues to consider in the introduction of reflective activity. Some languages do not have a word for reflection. Without a word to label a concept, there may be considerable difficulties in grasping the concept itself. We should be aware that misconceptions about the activity of reflection can occur very easily.

A second observation is that while most students do come to understand how to write reflectively, their reflection tends to be superficial and descriptive (Hatton and Smith, 1995). Relatively descriptive reflection can be what is required for a particular task. For example, it is unlikely that professional development bodies would want the profundities of personal reflection on the application for membership forms. However, where the objective of the reflection is to review personal understandings with a view to change through further learning, superficial reflection will often not be adequate. This suggests that an additional challenge to setting up reflective activities may often be of enabling learners to deepen, or make more profound, their level of reflection.

On the basis of the two observations above, a two-stage approach to the introduction of reflective activities has been developed. The first stage is termed 'presenting reflection'. This stage involves discussion and exercises and the provision of examples that introduce the idea of reflection and ensure that students come to a reasonable understanding of what is required in reflective writing. The task for students is to learn to be able to manage a basic form of reflective writing. This may still be fairly descriptive, but students should understand how it is different from pure description. Once students are reasonably accomplished in producing at least basic reflective writing (some will be able to produce deeper work from the start), then the second stage is introduced with more activities which focus on deepening the process of reflection ('deepening reflection'). The two-stage model can be seen in relation to the Generic Framework for Reflective Writing (Resource 9), which is described in Chapter 6. There is no suggestion of a direct relationship between the stages and the levels in the framework. Different learners will achieve different levels sometimes in accordance with different subject matter.

There is no one best approach to the presentation or to the deepening of reflection. At both stages, we suggest the use of multiple approaches, providing different ideas and activities around reflection rather than just verbal instruction. Topics for helpful discussion, activities and exercises are listed below as a set of ideas from which to pick and choose – or pick and adapt according to the local circumstances.

The suggestions are likely to have their greatest value at a teacher's first introduction of reflective activities as much will be learnt about learners' needs for guidance once one cohort of learners has passed through. It is very useful to capitalize on the experience of those students who have gone through the process of learning about reflective learning. They will know more than anyone else about the help that they needed. They will also have produced materials that, with permission, can be used as examples (see below). If it is possible to organize, an advice-giving session by the 'experienced' learners to the next group can be extremely helpful and enables them to recognize and consolidate their own learning.

Stage 1 Presenting reflection: helping learners to get started in reflective tasks

Approaches, suggestions and ideas are summarized in Figure 10.1.

Consider what reflection, reflective writing, reflective learning are

- *Academic and common-sense reflection.* When reflective activity is introduced into higher education, there are a number of assumptions that may be made where overt discussion may be helpful to students. First, reflection is not the sole possession of academia. We all reflect and this occurs whether or not reflection is introduced as a technique in higher education. However, when we ask students to reflect in their learning in the academic context, we are likely to be asking for an activity that is similar

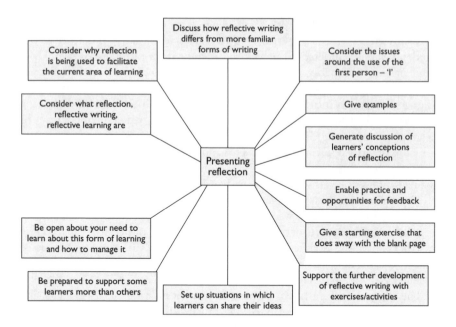

Figure 10.1 Presenting reflection

to, but not exactly the same as common-sense reflection (see below). Academic reflection will be more structured with an associated purpose. We may provide some structures in activities and exercises (see below). In addition, staff are likely to be viewing (if not assessing) the result of student reflection and in this way it will not be a private and personally motivated activity. If the outcome of reflective work is viewed, the object or context of the reflection will need to be described. In private reflections, we do not systematically describe what we are about to reflect on – we just do it. It is also likely to be assumed in an academic context, that learning will emerge from the process and the nature of the learning may need to be stated. Academic reflection is, therefore, more structured and more formal than what we will term 'informal' reflection. It is helpful if similarities between academic and common-sense reflection are clarified for students.

- *Some definitions.* In terms of definitions, a common-sense definition of reflection is presented on p. 82. In an academic context the definition is likely to be tighter because reflection is then a constructed and purposeful activity. The academic definition is on p. 83 (and represents an addition to the common-sense definition).
- *Helping students who do not understand what reflection is.* Students who indicate that they do not understand what they should do to reflect can be 'tricked' into being reflective for a moment. They can be asked to think

about what they have learnt from, for example, paid work situations in the past or how they felt about their learning in the previous semester, etc. It is likely that they will begin to reflect.

- *A model to support the development of reflective writing.* (Resource 1) It can be worth helping learners to think about what is involved in the process of reflective writing. A diagram (e.g., as in Resource 1) can provide a basis to discuss the kinds of content that may feed into the reflective process. The detail on the diagram could be simplified for this stage of presenting reflection.

- *Handout material to support the introduction of reflection.* (Resources 2 and 7) A handout on reflective writing ('Reflective writing: some initial guidance for students') is provided as Resource 2. The questions (Resource 7) can be added to the handout.

Consider why reflection is being used to facilitate the current area of learning

- *Clarifying the purposes of reflection.* It is important to be clear whether learners are being asked to use reflective writing as a means of generating knowledge (developing a 'product' of learning) or in order to learn the skill of being reflective (learning to use the process of reflection or reflective practice). In many cases, both process and product are important. The emphasis (process or product) of the learning will need to be represented in the criteria used for any form of assessment task.

- *Reflection as learning without a formal curriculum.* Another common reason why reflective writing is used is in order to learn from situations in which there is no formal curriculum to guide learning. These are usually ill-structured situations where reflection is used to generate knowledge (i.e., a product). Examples are situations of work experience, in placements, fieldwork in professional subjects, in the process of personal development planning (PDP) or other forms of experiential learning. Learners can be asked to discuss or write about their experiences of learning outside of the formal curriculum. What, for example, was their most significant moment of learning? How was the process of reflection involved?

Discuss how reflective writing differs from more familiar forms of writing

- *Charting the differences between reflective and essay/report writing.* (Resource 3) Resource 3 provides the basis of a chart that plots some of the differences between essay and report writing and reflective writing. This could be given to learners as a guide before they engage in reflective writing, or as a means of emphasizing the differences between these forms of writing when samples of both are provided. Alternatively, it could be used to summarize differences in work that learners have already done.

- *Students chart the differences between reflective and essay/report-writing.* Instead of giving the learners Figure 10.1, they can be asked to discuss the differences and develop their own chart. Material such as this, developed by one cohort of learners can be useful as material to pass on to the next cohort. They could be asked to do the exercise once early in their reflective writing to facilitate their own learning and to review their initial attempts once again towards the end of the year/module/programme for the benefit of the next cohort.

The issues around the use of the first person – 'I'

- *The place of the first person.* Most learners will have learnt that they should not use the first person singular in an academic environment. They can be confused if they are suddenly being encouraged to use 'I'. The idea that the first person is permissible in an academic context can be difficult for staff too. It may be helpful here to talk about the manner in which knowledge is constructed and the relationship between our unique frames of reference and our attempts to be objective and how the use of the first person can be helpful in acknowledging this gap.

- *Learning from written expressive language.* It may also be worth noting that writing in the first person can be more powerful as a means of learning than formal writing. It can represent a form of expression that is closer to our current understandings (Moon, 1999b, Chapter 2) or it brings 'ownership' to expression. By 'training' students to write normally in formal academic language, we may be damaging their ability to learn. It can be useful to recognize that there are at least two roles for writing in study. The first and most usual is as a means of communication (as in formal reports or essays). The second is as a means of learning. It is this second form of writing that is advocated in reflective writing and it is probably not exploited enough in study. Learning from personal written language can be a point of discussion. It has particular relevance to the process of revision where often learners personalize notes.

Give examples of reflective writing – both good and poor

- *Samples of reflective writing (1).* (Resource 4) Learners find real examples of reflective writing helpful. Samples may be taken from other learners' work (with permission), but it may be from published reflective work (fiction or biography). Several sets of sample material are provided in the Resources section. These or similar samples may be useful at the beginning of a reflective writing initiative.

- *Samples of reflective writing (2)*. (Resources 5, 6 and 10) These resources provide examples of reflective writing to which we will refer several times in this chapter (see also Chapter 7). They consist of three and four accounts of the same event, written at different levels of reflectivity. They provide some criteria that attempt to distinguish between what might be called the levels of reflection. The criteria may be held back until after the accounts have been read, considered and discussed. At this first stage of presenting reflection, it is probably not useful to introduce more than the first three stages of 'The Park' and with undergraduates, the first two stages of 'The Presentation' and 'The Dance Lesson'. The later parts will then be an effective contrast at the second stage of deepening reflection. An effective manner of using these resources is to ask learners to read the accounts and attribute a mark for the relative quality of reflectivity in each. They are then asked for the criteria that lead them to this judgement. They can compare their criteria with those listed after the accounts (or the general framework – Resource 9 'The Dance Lesson'). The exercise works better with small groups where there can be discussion of reactions.

Generate discussions of learners' conceptions of reflection

- *Discussion of conceptions of reflection*. It is useful at some stage (perhaps as a spin-off from another activity – such as that in the previous paragraph) to encourage students to talk about what they think reflection is. This will provide an opportunity for misconceptions to come to light. There can be misconceptions due to the lack of vocabulary for 'reflection' in some languages. It may also become evident that some students consider that reflection is only used in an academic context when something has gone wrong, or when something could be improved. Learners have been known deliberately to produce self-depreciating material when asked to write reflectively because that is what they thought their tutor wanted (Salisbury, 1994).

Enable practice and opportunities for feedback

- *Subject matter for practice (1)* A good way of getting learners to write reflectively without too much difficulty is to ask them to reflect on their own performance in something. The performance might be in the past or in the present. They are asked in advance to come prepared to give a 5-minute talk that might be on a topic that is relevant to the actual module – something that they are going to have to think about anyway. They do the talk and straightaway write a reflective account of how their performance went, feelings, weaknesses and strengths, assessment against their expectations, relationships to previous similar situations, etc. The impact of this exercise can be increased if they write a brief descriptive account of their performance before they write reflectively.

There are several possibilities for providing feedback on a performance such as this:

- The tutor reads scripts and gives written feedback and maybe some generalized oral feedback to the whole group, perhaps providing examples of the best reflective writing.
- They are asked to consider the criteria that they might use to mark the scripts for evidence of reflection. These criteria might have been generated earlier from 'The Park' and the other exercises. They peer mark on the basis of these criteria.
- The group divides into subgroups and each subgroup passes all of the scripts to another subgroup. The subgroups then read the other group's material and identify examples of good practice to share with everyone (e.g., by highlighting in marker pen five or ten good examples of reflective writing from across all the scripts. Some scripts might have several areas highlighted and some none). To achieve this, the group will have to consider what is meant by reflective writing and will need to think about the criteria used for judgement.

- *Subject matter for practice (2)*. Rather than go through the process of learners giving brief presentations (as above), they could write reflectively on a recent assignment and the mark attributed to it; on their experience of the first few days on the module/programme (new learners); on the current level of their study skills, etc. It is useful to ask them all to write on the same subject or otherwise content tends to get in the way of considerations about the reflective process.

Give a starting exercise that eliminates the blank page

- *Avoiding the blank page*. Blank pages are threatening to many people (although they can be exciting to some). If learners are setting out on writing any ongoing reflective account like a learning journal, it can be helpful to them to have some reflective writing done before they know they have really started. This could be set as an exercise (as above) or it might be a preliminary exercise such as a set of questions relevant to the subject matter of the journal. The adoption of a loose-leaf formal journal is a basic necessity for this 'game'.
- *A framework of questions*. (Resource 7) One of the easiest ways of getting learners started on reflective writing is to use a series of questions that lead them into reflective writing. They can be encouraged to dispense with the structure as soon as they can manage to set their own structure for reflection, or feel sufficiently confident to manage without. Some will need the support for longer than others. Resource 7 provides a sample of some questions.

Support the further development of reflective writing with exercises/activities

- *Other exercises to expand reflective writing.* (Resource 8) There are plenty of activities and exercises available that can encourage learners to expand the range and variety of their reflective writing (e.g., in Moon 1999a, 1999b). The use of these exercises in occasional class situations can stimulate reflective consideration of specific topics. It may provide new ways of seeing issues or events and it will provide techniques to help them to deepen their reflection. Some of the particularly useful exercises entail the development of dialogues between the learner and an event or a project, or (in imagination) a person or organization (Moon, 1999b). It is usually easiest to start with a form of greeting, welcoming the chance to hold a dialogue, and then some words about the state of things as they exist at present. It is probably wise to encourage the imagined dialogues with real (but distant) people first, before going on to events or artifacts.

Set up situations in which learners can share their ideas

- *Develop situations in which learners can support each other.* Learners can be of great help and support to each other, not only in facilitating the learning of how to write reflectively, but also in improving the quality and range of their reflection itself. They could work:

  - in a group, sharing selected paragraphs or reading each other's work;
  - in pairs in the same way. The pairs should be self-selected and they could be stable for the duration of the task or set up for initial support or sporadically.

Expect to support some learners more than others

- *When learners still do not grasp the idea of reflection.* Some learners carry on saying that they are not clear about what is required in reflective writing. This is one of the reasons why it is so useful to have samples of reflective writing to hand. In addition, in a one-to-one situation, asking them to describe (orally) how they feel about a recent experience (module, placement, field-trip, semester, etc.) can prompt them into demonstrating reflective speech – from which the written alternative can be derived.
- *Peer support.* Organizing peer support may help those who are still in difficulty. The peer might be a learner of a previous year or one of the same cohort who is at ease with and aware of the processes of reflective writing. Peers can sometimes provide better support than teachers and once they have been through a process of reflective writing, it could be said that they are more expert in the process than are their teachers!

Be open about your need to learn about reflection as a form of learning and how you can improve your management of it

- *Learning curves.* Demonstrating that staff, as well as the learner, are on a learning curve when it comes to managing reflective tasks can facilitate the situation for everyone. Some suggestions are that:

  - a tutor might write a learning journal about the process of helping learners to learn reflectively – and share elements of it with the learners;
  - she might ask them for feedback on how the task could be better managed;
  - she might ask them to collaborate in the production of written feedback to her on the task and its management. This might occur after the first few weeks and then at a couple of times later in the process and at the end. In this kind of activity, there is benefit to both staff and learners.

Stage 2 Deepening reflective activities

Some learners will write profound reflective material without any further prompting. They may well be those who have written diaries and journals for some years. Other students will be able to deepen their writing by becoming aware of how to do it. For a variety of reasons, some will have difficulty in making progress.

The development of awareness of what is involved in deeper reflection seems to be important and this process will need to take into account the constructed nature of knowledge – enabling learners to start to understand, for example:

- that different people can see the same event in different ways;
- that events can be conceived differently by the same person if she views it with different frames of reference;
- that, for the same person, frames of reference may be different at different times;
- the role of emotions in guiding our conceptions of events or people;
- that different disciplines rely on different structures of knowledge and have different ways of working with knowledge.

In the same format as for Stage 1, we present approaches, suggestions and ideas that can facilitate the deepening of reflection (Stage 2). These are summarized in Figure 10.2 elaborated below.

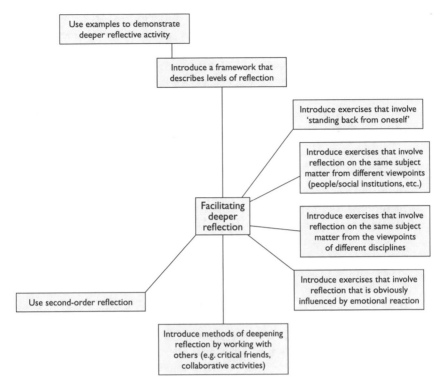

Figure 10.2 Facilitating deeper reflection

Use examples to demonstrate deeper reflective activity

- *Use examples to deepen reflection.* (Resources 5, 6 and 10) In the stage of presenting reflection, we suggested the use of material such as 'The Park', 'The Presentation' and 'The Dance Lesson'. The focus now would be on the fourth account in 'The Park' and the third accounts in the other two, and the use of the criteria that distinguish the deeper account to the more descriptive accounts. Learners could be asked to read all of the accounts and (before seeing the criteria) note the differences between the less and more profound levels of reflection demonstrated. Again, the effect of this kind of work is enhanced if there are opportunities for sharing views.

Introduce a framework that describes levels of reflection

- *A framework describing levels of reflection.* (Resource 9) This chapter is written broadly on the basis that there are different levels of reflectivity in reflective writing, though here the idea is applied to the stages of teaching students to write reflectively. One of the most widely known frameworks for tutors is that of Hatton and Smith (1995), which was prepared on the basis of written work presented by students. The introduction of a framework that describes the characteristics of levels of reflection is an important aid in developing awareness of the nature of deeper reflective writing for students at this stage. As a result of working within the broad framework of Hatton and Smith, a simplified form of reflective writing framework has been produced (Resource 9). Chapter 7 describes the background to this framework.

Introduce exercises that involve 'standing back from oneself'

- *An exercise on 'standing back' (1)*. 'Standing back from oneself' is like changing the camera lens in order to take a broader view of ourselves and the context in which we exist. When we are directly involved in an activity, the tendency is to describe immediate experience. But, for example, buying a drink for a friend in a pub involves the purchasing process but also the reason for being there is also the background to the behaviour. The event occurs in a context which is a workplace; there may be others involved, with different influences and considerations; the event may be governed by particular social norms; there are political and moral issues, and so on. Clearly, in any context only some of these broader issues will be relevant to the current reason for the reflection. Examples of writing that involves 'standing back from oneself' can be taken from Resources 5, 6 and 10. Topics that could be used to practise 'standing back' are:

  - preparing a meal;
  - settling down to study or a session of study;
  - finding a reference in the library;
  - a time when things went really well;
  - a time when things went wrong.

- *An exercise on 'standing back' (2)*. Another form of 'standing back from oneself' is to imagine someone telling one what to do 'over one's shoulder'. There are some interesting accounts of students improving their problems solving skills by doing written reflection as they solve problems in science, mathematics and engineering. The account can either involve a description of the procedures taken, with relevant commentary on the role of emotion, or it could be written from the point of view of a third person who is giving advice.

- *An exercise on 'standing back' (3)*. Another form of standing back from oneself is to view one's performance or abilities in an objective manner (i.e., in the third person). This may be a specific account (e.g., 'Jane's ability to write an essay') or it may relate to abilities within the context of reflection on an event. A bonus of this kind of exercise (and that above) is that it involves the consideration on one's own abilities (metacognitive awareness). Learners who are metacognitive tend to be the better students (see Chapter 6).

Introduce exercises that involve reflection on the same subject matter from different viewpoints of people/social institutions, etc.

- *Considering the same situation from different points of view.* In deeper reflection, it is important to recognize that different people see the same situation from different points of view. This is exemplified in Resource 6. Learners could be asked to reflect on an event that has occurred to them, which involves others and to write the account from others' points of view. Thus, an event in work experience in a shop might involve the points of view of a supervisor, customer, counter assistant, onlooker, and so on.
- *Considering one's work from different points of view.* Alternatively, learners may be asked to reflect on a piece of work that they have done from a personal standpoint, from the imagined point of view of the tutor who is marking the work and from the point of view of any relevant others (e.g., other learners, any others involved). Again, this kind of exercise develops metacognitive abilities (see above).

Introduce an exercise in which there is reflection on the same subject matter from viewpoints of different disciplines

- *Investigating the viewpoints of different disciplines (1).* Different disciplines view the same object in different ways. The differences may be greater than simply the focuses of the interest as the structure of the way of knowing in disciplines is different. Because most of us do not cross-disciplinary boundaries, we do not tend to be aware of these differences. A way of beginning to address this kind of issue in reflection is to ask learners to write about a single object from the point of view of different disciplines. For example, they could be asked to write about a storm from what the viewpoint of an artist, physicist, geographer, and so on.
- *Investigating the viewpoints of different disciplines (2).* An elaboration of this exercise is to ask learners to write about the understanding of an abstract concept from the viewpoint of different disciplines. For example, they could look at the idea of a 'petness' (as in a child's pet animal) from the point of view of practitioners in sociology, psychology, medical sciences, English, art, and so on.
- *Investigating the viewpoints of different disciplines (3).* A variation on the exercise above would be to take a concept from within the discipline of the learners, and ask them to view it from the standpoint of one or

more disciplines. For example, the concept of disability has meanings within medicine, sociology, psychology, architecture, physical education, and so on.

Introduce exercises that involve reflection that is influenced by emotional reactions to events

- *The role of emotions.* The role of emotion in its influence on learning is complex. Some people suggest that taking feelings into account is one of the main characteristics of reflective writing. Others (including this writer) suggest that it is possible to be reflective without emotion being the central issue. We can reflect, for example, on how the activities of a current government meets or does not meet our understanding of the political movement that it purports to represent. There would probably be an attempt here not to be too swayed by emotional reactions.
- *Learning how emotional state can distort events.* What is important about the role of emotion in reflection is to recognize how it can distort reflection. This point is well illustrated by reference to an anecdote. I decided to write down my feelings about a particular event that had occurred – it was a family argument. Normally I would have simply written about it reflectively in my journal that evening and then, as things moved on, might not have referred to it again. However, I was trying to find out more about my process of learning and I decided to go back to the same event and write on it for several days in succession. In the successive accounts, I found that I was viewing the event differently as my emotional reactions to it changed and eased. I realized that had I just written one account of the event, for example as part of an assessed learning journal, the reflection would have been very narrow, and very much influenced by the emotions of the moment of writing. Learners may choose to write reflectively on events at the end of a week or immediately after. They need to recognize that the time period can influence what is written.

  Learners could be asked to take an event in which they have been involved and work with it as described above, then to reflect on the role of their emotional reactions in affecting the reflective writing, and the learning that results.
- *Investigating the role of emotion in influencing reflection through use of fiction.* Alternatively such an exercise as that above can be done with a fictitious event – perhaps from literature.
- *The effect of mood on reflective writing.* It is not always the immediate emotions surrounding an event that will affect a piece of reflective writing. On different days, we may have different orientations to the world in general. Learners can be asked to consider how their general mood might affect the content of their reflection and how this relates to the 'accuracy' of reflective writing and learning. This can generate consideration of the notion of 'accuracy'. They could experiment with writing

reflectively about a simple event imagining that they are at odds or at ease with the day.

Introduce methods of deepening reflection by working with others e.g., critical friends, group activities, etc.

- *Work in groups*. Some of the best methods of deepening reflection involve working with others. The idea of work with others in itself will affect the nature of the material that will be written in the first place, and it is important that learners should recognize this. However, the effect may be less than the effect of tutors seeing or assessing reflective material. The groups will need to have common ideas about methods by which to deepen reflection and to see themselves as peer facilitators. The groups or pairs may work together over a period, learning how best to help each other by prompting and asking questions, querying frames of reference, and so on.

- *Model co-counselling*. One method of deepening reflection is to use techniques of co-counselling (Evison and Horobin, 1983; Moon, 1999b) where learners use sessions with a peer to explore issues before they write or reflect. The method of co-counselling involves pairs where each takes a turn of being first listener and then of speaker. There is an initial agreement between the students about the length of the sessions – ten minutes in each role is probably plenty to start with and as they become better at the technique, the time can be expanded. In the ten minutes the speaker chooses a subject and uses the time and the listening attention of the other to explore the subject. It might be 'what I have learned while in work experience placement', or 'how I feel about my study ability and what I need to do about it', and so on. The listener simply listens, encourages and prompts very briefly, helping the speaker in pursuit of her material. There is no conversation, and the focus is entirely on the speaker. This is a method, in effect, of people 'finding out for themselves what they think about something or what they have to say about it'. After the session, the speaker might want to write notes about what she has covered with help of the listener. Then reverse the roles. Partners may choose to remain constant over several sessions, or may choose to change. Afterwards, both write on what they have learned.

- *Critical friend*. The role of a 'critical friend' is similar to the above but we use the term here to describe a situation where students read the material that a colleague has actually written. Looking at each piece of work in turn, they prompt each other with questions that lead to further and deeper reflection on the writing – 'Why did you say that?', 'What did that mean to you?', 'How did you feel at that moment?', 'How do you think that X felt about that?', 'Do you think that Y saw it in the same way?', and so on. Both then re-write some aspects of their material. This is a form of second-order reflection (see below).

Use second-order reflection

- *The double entry journal design.* Second-order reflection is represented in any technique that requires a learner to look through previous reflective work and to write a deeper reflective overview. One of the most convenient ways to do this is the double entry journal method. Learners write only on one page of a double spread or on one half of a vertically divided page. They leave space blank until, at another time, they go through the initial material writing generating further comments that emerge from their more coherent overview of the initial work. The activity of revisiting material relates to a number of the techniques mentioned above. For example, they act as their own critical friend. They may also recognize the influences of particular emotional states or orientations that may have changed (see above).

Chapter 11

Assessment issues

Introduction

Assessment matters for more reasons than most people recognize. Most see it as a means of producing a mark for a piece of work or for a learner. In fact, it has a great deal to do with enhancing learning itself. In addition, assessment matters in the context of this book because it is particularly an issue of concern in this area of reflective and experiential learning. Indeed, it has been suggested that until the assessment issues of reflective and experiential learning are solved, these cannot be easily used as forms of learning in higher education. However, the main message of this chapter is that there is no more to assessing these less usual forms of learning than to assessing any other common task, such as the writing of an essay or an examination script. This is not because there is necessarily similarity between assessment methods such as essays and journals (O'Rourke, 1998). The similarity is at the level of the application to both of a set of principles of assessment. This chapter, therefore, is an account of the basic principles of assessment as they can be applied to reflective and experiential learning.

The chapter deals with both reflective and experiential learning in tandem. However, we must recognize that the most obvious way of assessing experiential learning is to ask the learner to demonstrate the ability that the learning has concerned. We can ask a teacher to demonstrate the management of a difficult class, or a nurse to demonstrate her ability to give an injection. Much of the experiential learning in higher education and professional development involves reflective learning through reflective writing, which is the element that is assessed. In these cases there are overlaps in the assessment method. However, even for the assessment of practical activity, the same principles apply.

In this chapter, we consider first the general principles of assessment and then focus attention on specific issues that arise in the process of assessing situations of experiential learning and those separate issues that relate to reflective writing or reflective learning. The last section of the chapter provides a list of assessment methods that might be used in a typical experiential learning situation (work experience placement).

Assessment in reflective and experiential learning

We first need to acknowledge the views of those who consider that reflective work should not be assessed (e.g., at undergraduate levels – Stewart and Richardson, 2000). More strategic learners will often not work on what is not assessed and an assessment process at least ensures that work is done. But to forego assessment is also to ignore the broader purposes of assessment. Certainly, at its worst, assessment is tacked onto the end of a programme and seen as something people just do because it is what happens in education. There is a tendency to associate the act of assessing with 'giving a mark', but we tend to muddle the attribution of marks with a number of other purposes for assessment. Some purposes or outcomes of assessment are:

- to give feedback to learners on their learning as well as on the reason for the mark (Mutch, 2003);
- the provision of information for the manager of learning on the learning and her management of it (in this case, supervisor, mentor, link person with the educational institution, etc.);
- for general quality assurance purposes;
- to indicate readiness for more advanced study;
- to focus learning;
- to motivate students to learn;
- to shape/direct learning;
- to require that students can apply or transfer their learning to unexpected situations. This may be an aspect of assessment that is not sufficiently exploited.

We also assess because learners expect us to assess. Often the simple attribution of pass/fail or pass/not yet pass would be sufficient (Rust, 2002), but it is learners who want to be graded, particularly where they are not certain about what it is that they should be doing.

We exploit the different purposes of assessment differently according to the nature of the subject matter and intended learning. Many uses of assessment in experiential learning, for example, focus on the enhancement and shaping of learning, and double as a means of attaining a mark. We return to this point below.

It would normally be desirable to look at assessment as a basic part of the design of reflective or experiential learning situations and not as a separate issue. This is important in these forms of learning because it is often not clear what the learner is expected to be able to learn. If the right thinking is done about assessment with assessment criteria properly developed, the right and proper thinking is likely to have been done about the development of the module. The separation of assessment from the learning perpetuates the tendency to see assessment as something added. Too frequently a pile of learning journals is handed in and the tutor is asking 'OK, How do I mark these?' It is too late at that stage to be thinking of how to mark. Building assessment into module design involves an ordered consideration of the learning expected (learning outcomes), in relation to standards (level) with this information related to expectations in terms of a chosen mode of assessment. The next section describes this sequence. It was written to support the design of modules in higher education, but the general principles will fit any learning situation. More detail, with plenty of examples, is provided in Moon (2002a) and Gosling and Moon (2001).

A map of curriculum design

Those developing assessment procedures in what might be construed as less unusual forms of learning in particular need to understand the structure of modules in order to understand how assessment 'fits in'. Too often the important linkages in the process are not articulated (e.g., between learning outcomes and assessment criteria). The aim of the module needs to be translated into learning outcomes in order to imply the assessment criteria, which are the basis for assessment. Figure 11.1, a map of curriculum design, depicts this.

The model is worked at the threshold, in other words, learning outcomes are written to denote the pass/fail point. Another way of putting this is that learners must achieve the learning outcomes or they fail this module or element of learning. This version of the map does not directly take account of grading. The map suggests that learning outcomes are developed as a result of thinking first about the aim for the learning or the aim. An aim is a teaching intention or a rationale for the curriculum or for the element of learning. It may provide an indication of context. For reflective or experiential learning, with no formal teaching, it is more likely to be written in terms of the coverage or content of the learning.

The standard of the learning outcomes is guided by reference, in higher education, to level descriptors, for example, those developed by SEEC (2003). A valuable extra step is to get subject specialists to translate the generic language of the level in which they are interested, into their own language, saying in it what they expect of their learners for this piece

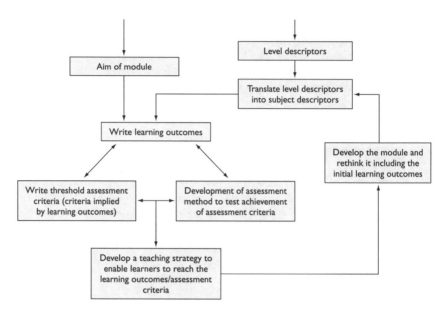

Figure 11.1 Basic map of module development

Source: Based on Moon (2002a)

of work. This activity facilitates the writing of well-considered learning outcomes. Learning outcomes imply assessment criteria. Assessment criteria can
be written in many different formats, but in general terms provide more detail
about the learning outcomes or they may describe what a learner must do in
order to achieve a particular grade. They may be developed directly from the
learning outcomes, or (as often happens) developed in relation to a chosen
assessment method.

An example of a learning outcome with assessment criteria might be:

> At the end of the work experience placement, the learners will be able
> to demonstrate an appropriate manner of dealing with a dissatisfied
> customer in the initial contact with the company.
>
> Assessment criteria might be:
>
> • The learner uses a polite and confident manner.
> • The learner rapidly can decide whether she can manage the subject
>   matter of the complaint in an appropriate manner herself – or
>   needs to refers the matter to others.
> • The subject matter is handled appropriately by the learner or is
>   handed on to a correctly identified other.

Or, another learning outcome:

The learner demonstrates her ability to give a presentation on what she has learnt in her placement.

The presentation demonstrates:

- adequate content: the development of her learning over the period of the placement
- competent process: it is given with confidence and clarity;

The learner can manage and respond to a series of questions or comments during or at the end of the presentation and so on, see Moon (2002a).

In whatever manner assessment criteria are presented, they need to be directly related to the learning outcomes. If the work is graded, learning outcomes and associated assessment criteria are written for the pass/fail point and other assessment criteria (grade criteria) are linked to marks or ranges of marks.

On the basis of the map, an assessment method is any manner in which the assessment criteria can effectively be tested. Too often assessment methods are picked on the basis of long-held habit, rather than a clear consideration of effectiveness both for those who assess and the learners. Too often concern about a method is given primacy over concern about assessment criteria. It seems to be the case that some assessment methods have acquired their own 'traditional' assessment criteria that may have little relevance to the actual learning outcomes being assessed. In this way learners can learn to do well because they are effective report-writers, regardless of the learning outcomes under question. Work experience placements may be assessed by a written report with little concern for the nature of learning to be demonstrated within the report.

In reflective and experiential learning, assessment methods may have much to do with the enhancement of learning. An assessment method needs to be effective for the assessment criteria being assessed, but must also be convenient and efficient for learner and assessor. We have said that often in reflective and experiential learning, the assessment method doubles as a method of enhancing learning itself. In this situation, it is particularly important to find an appropriate balance for the learning function and result of the assessment method with the effort for student and tutor and effectiveness as a 'marking instrument'.

In the rest of the map, the guidance that is given is designed to enable the learner to achieve the learning outcomes/assessment criteria. An important feature of any sequence that links assessment with learning outcomes and levels is that it is not seen as static – it is iterative. It is important to check round the cycle a number of times, modifying elements of it until there is consistency. The only element in the cycle that is not changeable is the level descriptors that indicate standard.

Another general principle of assessment is that everyone involved in the process understands every element of the design – standards (e.g., as level), the aim, what it is intended that should be learnt, the assessment criteria and method, and how it all fits together. This includes all tutors and, in particular, the learners themselves.

Assessment in reflective and/or experiential learning

We have shown in earlier chapters that in many situations, reflective learning is part of most experiential learning. However, an outcome of experiential learning may be the improved ability to do something and then the assessment task can be to ask learners to demonstrate the activity or provide evidence that something has been done (Brown, 1999). The assessment criteria will concern the quality of the evidenced activity or the activity itself and this is a relatively straightforward process. Often it is not possible to assess activity of individuals and, then, the assessment process may concern the reflective activity that links the initial learning and subsequent activity. This is usually expressed as reflective writing, though it may be demonstrated orally (Watton *et al.*, 2002). The focus of the remainder of this chapter is on the assessment of reflective activity within the context of reflective or experiential learning situations – and there are immediate issues of what to assess.

On knowing what to assess

Some experiential learning situations are set up in order that there can be learning about a specific subject matter. Often, however, they are set up as 'experiences' with only vague statements about what it is that should be learnt. This is often the case in work experience and other placement learning. We have said that we assess the learning outcome statements but that does not solve the problem of what to write into learning outcomes. There are, for example, many different forms of learning that can result from work experience (see list on p. 164). There is also much incidental learning, which may be assessed (Marsick and Watkins, 1990; Tomlinson, 1999) and it is important to recognize that assessment may be formative or summative. Formative assessment indicates to the learners how they are progressing (George and Cowan, 1999) while summative assessment is the end result of the process.

Without mediation in reflective and experiential learning, it is the learning outcomes and/or assessment criteria and task that tend to shape learners' deliberate learning. In a sense, these take the place of the curriculum in providing a guide to learning. It is particularly important, therefore, that much consideration is given to the kinds of learning assessed and how it relates to what it is anticipated that learners 'get out of' the whole experience.

There may be difficulty encountered in setting assessment criteria for some forms of experiential learning where different placements are used, since all learners need similar opportunities to learn what is to be assessed. This does not mean to say that all situations must be 'good' in the sense of being demonstrations of good practice. Given appropriate support and guidance, learners can also learn usefully from seeing poor practice; it is a matter of the guidance and identification of the learning outcomes.

When the learning activity is focused on reflective learning (for example, a learning journal), there is an early and important decision to be made that will be written into the learning outcomes – whether the concern is for the product or the process of the learning. The product of the learning is 'content' – what the learner can do or what she now knows or understands as a result of the reflective learning. In this case, the journal (or method chosen) is the means of developing the knowledge. However, increasingly it is being seen as important that learners, particularly those involved in professional learning, are able to engage in reflection on their practice (or progress). In this case, a learning journal may be used primarily as a means of developing the learner's capacity in reflective learning and it is the process that is important. Process and product would be expressed in separate learning outcomes, and would require separate assessment criteria. In fact, in many cases, reflective writing is used to engender learning of process and product at the same time but it is important that learners are clear about this. There are also implications for the kind of assessment method that is adopted.

Issues in the assessment of reflective learning

When the concern in reflective learning situations is the product of the learning, the role of the reflective learning (e.g., the journal – Moon, 1999b) is as a means of learning, and the assessment method can be any of the conventional means – essays, reports, presentations – even possibly examinations. The importance is that the assessment criteria are appropriate, and relate to the aim, level and learning outcomes.

The more interesting issues arise when the purpose of reflective work is that learners improve their ability to learn from reflection. The question now concerns the nature of assessment criteria that will demonstrate that the learner is able to reflect effectively. A difficulty here is that, as we have indicated, different people have different conceptions of reflection. In the development of learner work on reflection where the process is the prime concern, it is vital that tutors develop a common conception of reflection, and from that, seek common agreement about the criteria to be used.

Discussion of criteria for the process of reflection takes us back to Chapter 7 in which the depth dimension of reflection was discussed and Chapter 10 where the depth dimension of reflection is operationalized in the two-stage introduction of reflective activity to learners. The two-stage introduction is based on observations that superficial reflection does not seem to be as effective as a means of learning as deep reflection and that it is difficult to get learners to reflect at any depth. This two-stage approach, therefore, in itself, provides a basis for the development of assessment criteria. Materials from which assessment criteria can be developed more directly are the Map of Reflective Writing (Resource 1) and the Framework for Reflective Writing (Resource 9).

The usual method of assessing reflective learning using assessment criteria for process (see above) is to mark the actual reflective writing of learners. Typically they might be asked to write a learning journal or 'reflective pieces', and it is this actual work that is considered by the tutor. It is worth thinking about this. The reflective writing in a learning journal may be considered as an assessment method but often it is really more of an aid to learning. For example, often when it is used, reflective writing is the 'raw material' of learning. It can be at the equivalent stage to the notes that are taken before an essay is written, or lecture notes. You could almost say that the reflective writing of some learners is their 'personal curriculum' in a written form. We do not expect to assess learners' notes. We ask them to reprocess their notes into an essay or report or we test their learning from the notes in an examination. In this sense, if we assess the reflective writing directly, we are assessing only the relatively unprocessed (raw) material.

A convenient way of assessing reflective writing is, therefore, to ask learners to write a report or an essay or to use some other method (see below) that draws and quotes material from their reflective writing. They should be required to use this material either to support an argument or to respond to a question in a given title. A title might require students, for example, to assess the value of their reflective learning as evidenced in their learning journals, using evidence quoted the journals. Again, given a title, learning outcomes and agreed assessment criteria, there should not be too much difficulty in most tutors marking such material since it is a relatively conventional format. It may be useful to ask students to hand in their reflective writing as evidence that it has been completed in an appropriate manner and sometimes it is helpful to attribute a (very) few marks to the reflective writing itself. It is, however, the use of the 'reprocessed' (and therefore more valuable) material that is assessed in the essay/report. The requirement that learners reflect on their primary reflections is likely to yield deeper levels of reflection with improved learning. This is an important principle.

Other assessment methods for experiential and reflective learning (e.g., in a work experience placement)

We should encourage creativity and the use of imagination in the development of assessment methods. So long as process/product issues have been considered and assessment criteria have been developed from learning outcomes, any appropriate method of assessing the criteria can be used. As Henry said, 'Assessment methods used in experiential learning are as diverse as the activities' (1989, p. 34). There are many methods for assessing, for example, a work experience placement. They may test both process and product of learning or one or the other and most involve reflection (see list on p. 166).

Recognizing the experience of assessment

An important final point is that assessment is an experience in itself (Thorpe, 2000). It is a life experience and in particular, an experience that is part of being in a formal education situation. An effective manner of capitalizing on the learning that can occur in assessment situations can be in the use of peer assessment or self-assessment. Peer assessment and self-assessment are not assessment methods. An assessment method is chosen to be subjected to peer and self-assessment, with the selection of appropriate assessment criteria. More information about peer assessment and self-assessment are provided in Boud and Falchikov (1989), Boud (1995), Cowan (1998), Brown and Glasner (1999), and Mutch (2003).

Chapter 12

Enhancing reflective and experiential learning

Introduction

This chapter is a collection of further exercises, activities, ideas and suggested applications for the enhancement of reflective and experiential learning. The chapter adds to the collection of materials that were presented in a deliberate order in Chapter 10 but, of course, any of the Chapter 10 exercises can be used out of that context. Some of the exercises in this chapter are for individual use and some are for group or whole class work. Some of the material here is for the guidance of staff. As in Chapter 10, there is no attempt to distinguish between reflective and experiential learning. Any activity or exercise that enhances reflective learning will be useful to support experiential learning and any exercise given here that is more directly concerned with experiential learning will involve reflective learning anyway. In most of these activities, reflection is the means by which awareness of experience is recognized as knowledge and is made explicit and generalizable to other situations.

The sections in this chapter that relate to experiences do not have real boundaries, indeed, creative development of opportunities to practise reflective and experiential learning should be the aim. The use of the headings is a tidying-up device rather than any indication of how or where material *should* be used. As with earlier chapters, some of the actual material is presented in the Resources section.

The first section in this chapter covers the more common methods of supporting reflective and experiential learning. This section is deliberately brief. To use this chapter only to reiterate material already well explored elsewhere would be a waste of the opportunity to expand the range of ideas. There is much guidance in texts and on the Internet and the author has presented material of this type in previous books (see below).

The following section deals with the enhancement of reflective and experiential learning activities directly within the teaching situation. The next considers learning from current experience. This section is divided into two parts, the first of which covers work experience (and to some extent applies to other field and placement experiences). The other half of the section deals with the learning from other current experience. Corresponding to that there is a further section on learning from previous or past experiences.

There is a growing appreciation of the value of creativity and the use of imagination in formal education (Jackson, 2003). Perhaps it has been lost in the current attempts to document everything to be learnt – the next section considers the interaction between reflective and experiential learning and creative activities. Again, this is in two parts. The first relates to more general activities, the second to the use of story. To some extent the last section of the chapter also provides a means of enhancing creativity. It suggests a method of setting up a personal learning journal which incorporates a range of ways of working in order to draw past, present and creative experiences together.

The various exercises and activities included in this book focus on different aspects of the process of learning from reflective and experiential learning. All the exercises present the learner with aspects of external experience that she is expected to meet with her internal experience and thus develop further learning. The material of learning may be subject matter or it may concern the process of reflective learning itself. Some exercises present simple material, some present microcosms of the complexity of everyday existence. Some present pictures of 'reality' and some work in the world of imagination, though past, present and possible future all come to be processed by the learner's present internal experience. Some relate to the ordinary experiences that a professional might meet any time, and some exploit creative means whereby the deeper or less predictable experience can be brought to the fore for examination. The use of story or the deep journal is an example of the latter.

More usual means of supporting reflective and experiential learning

The activities in this section may overlap considerably. Hinett (2002) is a source of information about websites that discuss many of the topics below.

Learning journals, diaries, logs, notebooks, etc.

There are many names for the activity of recording reflective thought in a structured or unstructured but ongoing manner. There are also many ways of doing it, different purposes that can be fulfilled and different activities that will enhance the learning (Rainer, 1978; Young and Fulwiler, 1986;

Fulwiler, 1987; Holly, 1991; Moon, 1999b). The last section of this chapter is one illustration of a journal design.

Portfolios

The term 'portfolio' can be used for anything from a collection of work (e.g., drawings) to a learning journal with the odd article or set of lecture notes included. There is a great deal of literature on portfolios but it is important to bear in mind that there is no one thing called a portfolio and no one way of managing the activity of compiling one. For the same reason, no one reference will give a complete picture of the method but Jasper's work in nursing is well developed (Jasper, 1995, 1998).

Action learning sets

The aim of an action learning set is to enhance and support an individual's project through work with a set of others who will listen in order to support the action of the individual. Generally, in turn, each member of the set will have the opportunity for such support. The set would meet for an agreed number of sessions, and the expectation is that the project is achieved. The project could be a change in practice, or a particular activity. The technique is documented in McGill and Beaty (1992) and Brockbank and McGill (1998).

Human inquiry groups

Like action learning sets, these are groups that come together for a limited period to explore and research aspects of human behaviour or the condition of being human (Reason and Rowan, 1981).

Action research

This is a similar process to the techniques described above. The subject matter may be staff development or an issue in the workplace that affects the person who is engaged in the research. It involves a process of linking experience and the potential for change through reflection (Winter, 1989).

APEL – the accreditation of prior experiential learning

This is a means of awarding credit for prior experiential (non-certificated) learning. The learner is usually expected to demonstrate the learning from experience in a variety of manners. APEL as a process is often akin to learning from concurrent experience (see below) (Evans, 2000).

Personal development planning (PDP)

Professional development planning or profiling is a self-appraisal system being introduced in undergraduate programmes in the UK as a means of supporting the development of learning, employability skills and self-awareness. It usually consists of organized collection of evidence and reflection on the experiences of the programme and is often connected to the pastoral care system in an institution (Fullerton, 2002; or LTSN website www.ltsn.ac.uk/genericcentre and follow the links for PDP).

Peer and self-assessment

When learners assess their own or others' work they tend to become constructively critical about the processes of the work and the assessment of it. They learn from and about the experience of learning (Boud, 1995 and Cowan, 1998).

Problem-based learning (PBL)

Learners are given a problem to solve in a topic area, rather than the content knowledge about a topic. They have to seek the information sources required, and integrate the knowledge in order to solve the problem. PBL mimics the processes of naturalistic learning from experience. The approach is more common in professional development subjects (Savin-Baden, 2000), but forms of it can be used with any learners (Matthews *et al.*, 2002).

Enhancing reflective and experiential learning through teaching processes

There are different ways in which to learn from a lecture. One way is to listen and write notes that capture the structure of what is being said in a mechanical manner, without really thinking about what is being said. This is a surface approach to learning (see Chapter 1). Another way is to write the lecture notes while taking note of what is being said and perhaps getting as far as thinking about how the current material relates to what was said last week. Another way is to find the mind spinning into other related material, reflecting, wondering, questioning, putting asterisks into the notes to remind oneself to check or think more about an idea. This is starry-eyed, excited learning. It is not only the state of the learner and the nature of the material that determine a learner's reaction but the style of the teacher. Some teachers promote interest and questioning and some do not. It is not all a matter of personality – there are techniques to be learnt and it is important to remember that reflection is intimately connected with a deep approach to learning. Reading a book is a similar situation (Usher, 2000b). Some techniques that promote reflective learning are:

- 'Wait time' – wait time is the pauses between sentences, the moments after posing a rhetorical question; the pacing of phrases – it is time that allows a listener's brain to reflect or question during speech or a lecture. Tobin (1987) found that lecturers who used wait time well enabled better learning.
- Confronting learners with their misconceptions. The early chapters of this book indicate that we learn by distinguishing figure from ground – by making comparisons. Learners who are always taught the 'right' answer, or given the right techniques do not learn to make judgements (Fazey and Marton, 2002). They are helped if their misconceptions are pursued to the end, and not just corrected.
- A method of finding how learners see a topic is to ask them to draw concept maps. The maps of the teacher and peers may demonstrate differences in thinking and therefore material on which to reflect (Desler, 1990; Hadwin and Winne, 1996; Moon, 1999b).
- Explaining something and possibly then applying the idea to something else is an activity that distinguishes the learner who has taken a surface approach from one who has taken a deep approach. If learners know that they will be required to explain something, they are likely to adopt a deep approach to the learning of it. The requirement to explain calls on the ability to reflect and check the soundness of ideas (Chi *et al.*, 1989; Chi *et al.*, 1994).
- Styles of questioning in class and in assessment tasks can elicit reflection if they are open and set as problems to be considered. Often the simplest questions are the most difficult to answer and demand the most thought (Morgan and Saxon, 1991).
- Encourage reflection during problem solving. Selfe and Arbabi (1986) found that learners who had accompanied problem-solving activities in engineering with reflective accounts of their progress were more successful at solving subsequent problems.
- Use a notice-board with two sections – one for notices and one for reflective comment by staff or learners.

One of the most helpful ways of enabling learners in higher education levels to reflect and to learn from experience is to enable them to progress in their conception of the structure of knowledge (see Chapter 2). While they tend to see knowledge in terms of 'right or wrong', viewing the teacher as the expert who will pass on knowledge while they absorb it (i.e., in Baxter Magolda's (1992) absolutist stage, it is harder for them to recognize the need to reflect. Enabling them to progress in their understanding of learning will bring them to stages in which they will recognize that there are alternative interpretations that require reflection. The use of examples that are not initially in their discipline can be helpful in enabling them to begin to recognize that knowledge is constructed. Maps are a valuable material by which to demonstrate constructed knowledge. A map of an area is shown and learners are asked if it is a true representation of the area and to write down their response ('To what extent is this a true map of this area?'). They are then shown other maps of the same area that demonstrate that maps are constructed to show what the map-maker wants to show. They can be distorted, ignore features or can be constructed in a manner to make a point to those they want to influence. The ideas developed are then translated to the learner's own discipline with the aim of engendering a more questioning and reflective mode of working.

When encouraging the development of reflective learners, it is worth considering the conditions under which reflection is fostered. There are a number of qualities that have emerged from previous chapters in this book and from common experience that would seem to enhance the qualities of reflective and experiential learning. Some are:

- the willingness to engage in cognitive housekeeping (p. 27) – the reordering of one's conceptions on a topic;
- clarity of purpose – having an idea of what the end point of the exercise might be;
- self-management skills – the knowledge of how one best functions alone/with others and the ability to make good use of that knowledge (Chapter 3);
- linked to the above, an appropriate understanding of the role of emotion in reflective learning (Chapter 3);
- appropriate conceptions of knowledge and willingness to work with others' conceptions that may differ (Chapter 2);
- an awareness of the 'rules' of the relevant discipline or mode of operation;
- open-mindedness – a willingness to accommodate to new ways of thinking (Chapter 1);
- 'voice' – a willingness to reason for oneself and to express the results of the reasoning.

Learning from work experience and other current experience: 1 Work experience

It is important first to clarify terms. Work experience and work-based learning can be seen as the poles of a continuum of work-related learning. In work experience learners engage in placements that do not necessarily have anything to do with their discipline. The learner usually arranges the placement which may be paid or unpaid or voluntary and the focus of the experience is being at work or in the workplace and reflective activity is involved (Harvey *et al.*,1998; Watton *et al.*, 2002). In contrast, work-based learning describes situations in which the work activity is the curriculum (Portwood and Costley, 2000). Aspects of both types can be variously combined in a placement with, for example, projects that are related to the learner's discipline (Marshall and Cooper, 2001).

With increasing consciousness of employability skills and the advent of Foundation degrees (two-year degrees) in UK higher education with a mandatory element of work-related learning, work experience initiatives are increasing. However, full opportunities for the experience are not always taken. Miller *et al.* comment that too easily, 'work experience programmes . . . [come to] resemble old hotels that have undergone periodic refurbishment of an unsympathetic kind' (1991, p. 233). In this brief section, the aim is to point out some of the issues – the thinking points – that are usefully considered in setting up such situations for learners. Some of the principles are applicable to the learning in other placement situations within formal education.

A work experience module in a higher education programme involves learners in experiences that may not be unfamiliar, but that are very different from most academic modules. A learner might set up and work a placement in a newsagent shop for a short period of time (or it might be her normal workplace to support her finances). She is likely to have undergone an induction or briefing phase with a tutor, which will have provided topics and tasks to explore at work and write up. These will usually involve reflective writing in some form. There is also likely to be a final phase, with some sort of debriefing and sometimes a presentation on what she has learnt. Such modules are more likely to be at undergraduate levels, but may also be at Master's level (Watton and Collings, 2002).

The existence of work experience modules on programmes is usually justified in terms of employability skills but the potential for learning is far greater than the most generous definition of employability (Caley and Hendry, 2000). Whatever is the underlying intent for the work experience placement or for other placement experiences, an underpinning principle is that a process of reflection focuses the learning and enables it to be generalized to other situations. Some of the areas of potential learning in a work experience placement are as follows. A considered selection of these should be made more explicit in learning outcomes and thence assessment criteria (see Chapter 11):

- learning about work and workplace practices;
- learn how organizations 'work';
- learning communication skills and about working with people;
- learning about personal work behaviour patterns;
- learn to evaluate own performance;
- learn to work with feedback from others;
- learn about own career aspirations;

- project work;
- learning to learn from experience;
- learning self-management (Reeders, 2000);
- learning to use reflection and reflective practice;
- to gain employability skills/'key skills' not easily gained elsewhere in the curriculum (Little, 1998);
- development of self-confidence and willingness to take initiatives (Postle, 2000);
- to enhance orientation towards lifelong learning;
- to enable students to learn skills not easily embedded in the rest of the curriculum.

The learning may be discipline-related either through the nature of the work or through the nature of tasks set (see below). Some of the differences from the conventional academic activity (and therefore potential areas for important learning) are as follows:

- the learner manages her own learning;
- there is a different teacher–learner relationship (Tennant, 2000);
- there is no curriculum as such – the required material of learning may not be clearly identified. The learner may be required to identify it for herself with relatively little guidance;
- there are no academic texts from which to learn;
- the context is different from an academic context;
- there is usually emphasis on reflection – that may be a new experience.

Learning from work experience mimics everyday learning. It is disrupted and non-routine (Marsick and Watkins, 1990; Tennant, 1999), emotion is involved, variously enhancing and confusing learning processes (see Chapter 3; Eraut *et al.*, 1998; Boud and Walker, 1991). Much of the learning is incidental or informal, with figures and grounds continually changing (see Chapter 1). More fundamentally, the learner needs to learn that in the 'real world' there are different points of view for virtually any issue. She needs to learn to make judgements (Hager, 1999) by 'bringing alternative frames of reference to bear on the frames of reference with which one is presented' – learners engage with 'supercomplexity' in work (Barnett, 1999). Beckett sums the situation up: 'Humour, negotiation, anecdote and spontaneity are hallmarks of this kind of learning . . . Putting out spotfires, seizing the moment, catching the nuance and making something unique out of human sensibilities . . . are all part of this too (1999, p. 73).

Making something of this chaotic learning situation is confusing for a learner who is used to being 'fed' information in lectures. To enable her to make sense of specific parts of it, it is important that she is made aware of what the focus of the learning is to be or the placement becomes simply an opportunity for awareness-raising, rather than actual learning (Davies and Easterby-Smith, 1984, Ways in which the learning can be focused are:

- through the learning outcomes;
- through guidance at the induction/briefing session or within handouts;
- through focused opportunities for reflective learning (e.g., in discussion with tutors or other mentors);
- through the kinds of tasks provided to the learner (e.g., critical incidents on which to reflect);
- by implication from the assessment criteria in any assessment tasks given to the learner;
- by giving the learner tasks that directly apply what has been learnt from the placement (Mumford *et al.*, undated).

A useful concept for this process is that in these ways, there is a 'management' or 'shaping of subjectivity' (Usher and Solomon 1999, pp. 155, 157). The potential for choice of focus of the learning from experience that is indicated in this section demonstrates the need for careful focus on the kinds of learning that learners are expected to achieve.

It is not unusual, however, for a learner simply to take a work placement without much guidance as to the focus of learning, and be asked to write a report with vague learning outcomes and the indication that it will be marked like any other essay. Such a task is far too imprecise to focus reflection which, as we have indicated above, enables learning to be recognized and more easily applied elsewhere. Some of the unhelpful situations in work experience arise because there is not a clear understanding of how work experience differs from work-based learning (WBL). In WBL the focus is on the enhancement of disciplinary learning because the nature of the work is the curriculum.

There are a variety of ways in which learners can be asked to focus their learning in order that reflection on the experience may occur. It is useful that at least in some of these tasks, the idea of reflection is overt:

- the maintenance of a learning journal or a portfolio;
- reflection on critical incidents;
- a presentation on what has been learnt;
- analysis of strengths and weaknesses and related action planning (Watton and Collings, 2002);
- an essay or report on what has been learnt (preferably with references to excerpts from a learning journal or other reflective writing);
- self-awareness tools and exercises (e.g., questionnaires about learning patterns);
- a review of a book that relates the work experience to own discipline;
- short answer questions (half A4 sheet) of a 'why' or 'explain . . .' nature;
- a project that develops ideas further (group or individual);

- self-evaluation of a task performed (i.e., the task or the evaluation assessed);
- an article (e.g., for a newspaper) explaining something in the workplace;
- recommendation for improvement of some practice (a sensitive matter);
- an interview of the learner as a potential worker in the workplace;
- a story that involves thinking about learning in the placement (see later in this chapter);
- a request that students take a given theory and observe its application in the workplace;
- an oral examination;
- management of an informed discussion;
- a report on an event in the work situation (there may be ethical issues here);
- account of how discipline (i.e., subject) issues apply to the workplace;
- an identification of and rationale for projects that could be done in the workplace.

The need for reflection can be worked into most of these assessment tasks. As Chapter 11 makes clear, the tasks should test clear assessment criteria that are derived from the learning outcomes.

However, in using work experience within the context of a formal educational programme, there is a danger of 'trapping learners' understanding within their own work setting'. They may 'be unable to move beyond it. Their understandings and working knowledge become over-localized . . . and cannot transcend the present and the particular' (Boud, 2001, pp. 40–1). The lore of poor transfer of learning could be cited and questioned here (Tennant, 1999) but, as has been indicated (see Chapter 8) and Boud himself says, the experience of variation in learning enables learners to progress and apply learning to new situations (Fazey and Marton, 2002). In this sense the good practice is learning to learn but there are other ways in which work experience placements can be seen to relate, or more deliberately be related to the rest of the programme. For example:

- epistemological contrasts and similarities with the learner's own discipline can be drawn;
- learners can be asked deliberately to find ways in which the experience in work relates to their own discipline. There is chemistry in the burger bar, mathematics in the pub till, English in the work of the care assistant, etc. The relationship between home discipline and work experience might be explored in fiction (see later in this chapter);
- skills in the manipulation of knowledge are developed in the new context;
- there is useful emphasis on and development of reflective learning abilities that are now relevant to all programmes in personal development planning (see above).

This list can be seen as elements of a rationale for inclusion of work experience in an otherwise academic programme. They may be used to 'market' work experience to those academics who see it as irrelevant.

Finally, there are some practical matters about instituting work experience which need attention. Some are as follows:

- finding work placements;
- deciding how long the placement should be – it is the learning that emanates from the placement, not the placement length itself that relates to the credit attributed to it;
- sorting out health, safety and responsibility issues;
- helping learners to cope with a new learning environment;
- helping them to reflect (Chapter 10);
- getting the appropriate level of learning in the module and assessing appropriately (Moon, 2002a).

We can summarize by mentioning two important points here. The first is that reflective activities that focus on specific experiences in work are very important as a means of ensuring that the learning is 'captured'. Second, 'work experience' is not one thing. It is a mass of interweaving subjective experiences. To make good use of the situation requires careful guidance and directing of the anticipated learning those who plan the module.

Learning from current experience: 2 Other experience

Again, this section gives some brief notes about a diversity of ideas, most of which are new. There are other exercises of this kind in Moon (1999a, b). Most are individual but when a colleague can comment or ask further questions in a trusting environment, the reflection and learning can be more effective.

Methods for learning from informal and incidental experience (Resource 11)

This material is adapted from Marsick and Watkins (1990, pp. 226–7). The original version is presented at the end of their book as 'Strategies for Enhancing Informal and Incidental Learning'.

Scales and questionnaires

There are many scales and questionnaires presented in everything from weekly magazines to restricted-use psychological materials. Scales can be taken as measures of what they purport to measure but often they provide very useful material for reflection and reflective learning whether or not their outcomes are believed (e.g., learning style materials). Examples are Honey and Mumford (1992) and Redman (2001).

Deliberate learning from a personal experience

This exercise treats a discrete event as an experience from which to learn – like, for example, work experience. The inspiration results from a personal experience (see Introduction). In the early stages of thinking about this book when I was deeply involved in a work experience module, and wondering what the students were really learning from it, I went on a camping trip with a friend, and we took kayaks. Camping was familiar, as was kayaking, but the friend and the location were new. I recognized that this two-week period had something in common with the work experience placements. Much was familiar, but there were also new elements to the situation. I decided to write about the experience reflectively, looking for what I might have learnt. It was a fascinating experience on many levels, particularly when I went back to the task on several subsequent days. I noticed, for example, that how I recalled what I learnt changed over subsequent days. Initially, when it was easy to 're-enter' the experience of the holiday, it was not difficult to recognize what I had learnt. As days went by, it became more difficult and I seemed to be fishing around on the surface of the experience, without engaging with it. Perhaps the most interesting point to me is that the learning that I 'pulled out' and reflected upon in the first day or two and then remained accessible. I could think about it and generalize to other situations. It was as if that which was not pulled out from the whole experience early on became tied more tightly to its context and was and remained much less accessible. A similar observation has been made elsewhere and seems to be significant in the academic applications of learning from experience (Mason, 2000; Hoadley-Maidment, 2000).

Following the first experience, I repeated the exercise, this time choosing to work on an emotionally disturbing event. Again I learnt from doing the exercise, particularly from the writing on subsequent days. As the immediacy of the strong feelings subsided, I found that I construed the event in a different way. When we ask learners to write about an event only once, there is a loss of the richness of the real experience of reflection in which we turn events around and see them differently over a period of time. This observation demonstrated the need to be aware of levels of reflection, and the importance of the ability to engage with deeper levels where a learner reflects on the process of her own reflection. It raises many interesting issues about how we deal with learners' understanding of 'reality' – or in other words, their conceptions of knowledge (see Chapter 2 and Pardoe, 2000).

There are some very interesting examples of personal reflective projects such as these in the literature. We have already mentioned the work of Marion Milner, *On Not Being Able to Paint* (1957).

Record on the hour

A variation on the exercise above is to explore the nature of experience or of learning from experience by recording on the hour in a notebook. The focus could be 'what I have experienced' or 'what I have learnt'. After a day or two, there will be some interesting data and probably some new insights into day-to-day experience and the learning from that experience. It is interesting to consider how much of the learning is generalizable to other contexts and the effects on it of the recording and inevitable subsequent reflective processes.

Ask questions

Different forms of question demand different respondent behaviour. Morgan and Saxon (1991) suggest that the following kinds of questions encourage reflection:

- the development of supposition or hypothesis, e.g., 'I wonder what you will learn from that experience';
- questions that focus on feelings, e.g., 'How do you feel about that teacher's behaviour?'
- those that project into the future, e.g., 'How do you think you will react in that situation?'
- those that encourage critical judgements to be made, e.g., 'How can we justify this war?'

Learning to ask helpful and probing questions is a valuable skill. Learners need the same skills as teachers in this and can help each other in peer learning situations.

Use a metaphor

Morrow Lindberg (1983) used shells to generate thought processes about her life and experiences as she took walks on a beach. Each shell did no more than initiate a reflective process – each, though, in a different way. Not only the writing of this kind of material, but also the reading of it generate reflective and experiential learning as one compares and contrasts one's own experiences with those described. Everyone will have their own favourite books that generate a reflective mode. Some personal favourites are Hesse (1972), Storr (1988).

Construct exercises that challenge judgement and conceptions of knowledge

Exercises can be constructed in order to stimulate reflective judgement (King and Kitchener, 1994). Resource 12 is one such exercise. Use of material such as this in a group means that those making differing judgements will be exposed to each other and there can be some recognition that people are at different stages in their conceptions of the nature of knowledge (see Chapter 2). There will also be a recognition that, in real life, there may be no clear-cut solutions to problems. Reflective processes are involved in the identification of a 'best-in-the-circumstances' solution. In the exercise, group members are asked, individually, to rank the behaviour of each of the characters in the story from best to worst (Victoria, Albert, Fred, Archibald and George). They are asked to decide which of the characters is most responsible for the outcome of the story and which least responsible. Individuals are then asked to collaborate in small groups to create a joint response.

Dialogues techniques (Resource 8)

A major reason why activities such as those listed in this chapter can have a useful outcome is that they cause the learner to shift from one frame of reference to others – to recognize that there are 'two sides' to most arguments, for example. This is one of the reasons that so much learning is done in new relationships where there is a considerable effort to understand the other's frames of reference (Taylor, 1997). One of the most direct means of enabling this recognition on paper is by the use of dialogue techniques. Ira Progoff's work best exemplifies this, though others have used similar techniques, sometimes based on his work (Progoff, 1975; Rainer, 1978). A dialogue is like a play with two actors – the writer and another chosen because she is involved in a situation, or has insight into it. The writer introduces the issue under consideration in a short paragraph, and then writes words that would prompt dialogue (e.g., 'What do you think I should do . . . ?'). The writer then 'listens' to the imagined voice of the other, writing the words, then responding, and so on. Dialogues can travel over remarkable and unexpected territory and yield useful learning.

The most obvious 'other' in a dialogue is a known 'other' who is involved in a situation – though the 'other' may have a different point of view. However, the 'other' may be a figure of wisdom such as a philosopher or a religious figure.

Learning from past experience

In a sense, past experience becomes 'current' as soon as it is brought into the present because its nature is interpreted within the current context. Many of the techniques in the previous section can focus on the past but it is useful to note a few techniques that more specifically focus on past situations.

Dialogues (Resource 8)

Dialogues (see above) have the advantage that the imagined 'other' can be completely flexible in time and space and they therefore are a way of exploring past events as much as present events. The 'other' might be a real person who was 'there' or an (at the time, unseen) observer watching the past event . The 'other' could be an esteemed historical or religious figure.

Footprints (Resource 13)

This is a modification of Progoff's 'Stepping stones' exercise (Progoff, 1975). Since it may be useful to copy the details of it for learners, it is described in the Resources section. Footprints can be run as an individual exercise, but much is gained from a group approach as described.

Learning shifts

The different aspects of learning that have unfolded in the process of writing this book have engendered memories of occasions when I have had insights into aspects of my learning process. This has come about particularly since I have become interested in the development of conceptions of knowledge. An example is when, in a Philosophy of Education module I found my own reasoning valued! The identification of these 'learning shifts' is an exercise that is of use in itself as reflective learning, but also can yield valuable information about personal learning processes that can underpin further learning activity. It can be done on one occasion, perhaps using the 'footprints' techniques described in Resource 13, or it can be an ongoing exercise over a period of time. The incorporation of opportunities to share memories and insights increases the benefits of the exercise. It may also be helpful to introduce Baxter Magolda's framework as an initial exercise (Baxter Magolda, 1992, see Chapter 2).

Learning from creative activity: 1 General techniques

As this book is coming towards completion, there is a growing concern to encourage a more creative and imaginative approach to higher education (Dewulf and Baillie, 1999; Jackson, 2003). Representation of creative and imaginative activity is often based on reflective and experiential learning and in essence, a creative activity involves working with imagination, and imagination can be free from already known time and space. In this section we identify some activities that would be construed as creative, and demonstrate how they exploit, depend on and develop further the activities of reflective and experiential learning. One reason why such activities might not be used more commonly is because of the difficulty of assessment. As Chapter 11 points out, all assessment methods come down to a few simple rules that concern the recognition of assessment criteria.

An important point with which to begin this section is that we are not discussing expert work in poetry, art, drama and story writing and telling but the use of these forms of activity as a medium with which to make sense, or better or broader sense, of experiences.

Poetry (Resource 14)

There are many quotations about the nature of poetry. Essentially a poem is a capturing of an experience either to make greater sense of the experience for herself, or to communicate aspects of it to another. The poem in Resource 14 does exactly that. Writing a poem is an activity of experiential learning for the writer and the reader (Skelton, 1971). Ted Hughes illustrates the manner in which poetry writing entails the learning of something new. He describes the process as a 'special kind of excitement, the slightly mesmerised and quite involuntary concentration with which you make out the stirrings of a new poem in your mind, then the outline, then the mass and colour . . . the poem is a new species of creature, a new specimen of the life outside your own' (Hughes, 1967, p. 17). There are many exercises that enable the 'not-usually-poetic' to write and experience the reflective and learning processes involved (e.g., Hughes, 1967; Brownjohn 1981, 1982).

The use of the absurd

An absurd idea is an idea that is subject to mockery because it is outside the usual frames of reference. To work with the absurd is also to work freely with ideas, unconstrained by logic and reasoning. Since we have suggested that deeper reflective learning relies on being able to understand that there are different frames of reference for any subject matter and a sense of freedom to shift around ideas, it would seem that the absurd might have a use. One way of making use of the absurd in reflective and experiential learning is in action learning sets where a group of individuals have arranged to support each other in turn in dealing with a real-life issue (p. 160) (McGill and Beaty, 1992). When an individual's issue has been described, a 'mind-freeing' experience can be introduced in which there is a collection of two or three absurd solutions to the issue from each person before going on to the 'proper' processes. It will not be at all unusual to find that the best solution resides in the absurd.

Drama

There are many forms of drama and theatre that are designed to inspire reflective and experiential learning in the audience by the use of action and language in somewhat the same manner as poetry or the absurd (see above). In the most conventional form, participants watch and then respond to the presentation of an issue that is anticipated by the actors to stimulate thought, clarify, disturb and generally promote learning of a kind that could not just be 'told' (Beard and Wilson, 2002). In a more sophisticated form, the issue is taken from the audience present, and the actors improvise, creating an 'imaginary mirror'. The audience participates in directing the actors as they see the work unfold (Boal, 1995). In this theatre there is a conscious mixing of subject and objective representations (Jackson, 1995).

In other uses of drama to elucidate experience, the roles of audience, actors, observers and learners elide and the total involvement in the depiction of a situation is designed to be a learning and/or therapeutic experience. Sometimes the actors create a immobile 'scene' and sometimes they move through events. In this kind of work, it would be usual to have a facilitator.

Graphic depiction – cartoons and other forms of art

A cartoon is a graphic depiction of an experience, using elements of the absurd to push ideas towards extremes and thereby make points more clearly. A good cartoonist can throw back to a group of people images that epitomize their behaviour or events under discussion. In turn the cartoon leads to further learning or the generation of further reflection. Beard and Wilson (2002) describe the use of cartoons in work with companies.

Other forms of drawing enable learning. This is the basis of art therapy. Milner's work on 'not being able to paint' represents a detailed description of a learning process through and about art (Milner, 1957). Doodling might sometimes also have a related role.

Learning from creative activity: 2 Working with story

More clearly than some of the other creative activities mentioned above, stories have the ability to lift aspects of external experience from their context. Stories can be subjected to closer examination, experiment (imbued with different meanings in new contexts) and further development in fantasy. They can also act as mirrors, reflecting back to a person another's conception of what is perceived to be the first person's internal experience or a modification of it. Sometimes in a therapeutic situation, the subject is asked to tell her story and then, with support and reflective comment from the therapist, is encouraged to re-experience the imagined external experience in a different manner. The notion of reflecting back a perceived story in a clarified or modified form is similar to Boal's work with drama and this kind of work is in the tool box of many therapies (e.g., narrative and hypnotherapy) and many aspects of counselling (Egan, 1990)).

Work with story is very flexible and there is no one way to use it in facilitating the learning from reflection or experience. There are some excellent texts on working with story in the context of education or professional development. Examples are Bolton (1999), Winter *et al.* (1999) and McDrury and Alterio (2002). The first of these largely focuses on the use of stories in therapeutic contexts and the latter two on professional development. Story work is also being used in business and management (Beard and Wilson, 2002; Snowden, 2003).

Probably the barrier to story work in formal education is that it is seen as flippant and 'made up', and 'not real' unless it is located in formal literature, creative writing or some cultural studies. There are assumptions here that need to be discussed. Connelly and Clandinin said that 'study of narrative . . . is the study of the ways humans experience the world' and Bruner suggests that humans seem to actually have a 'readiness or predisposition to organise experience into a narrative form, into plot structures' (1990, p. 45). On this basis, any work with story is a common human means of working with experience and learning from it. In terms of learning (see Chapter 1), a story is an organized representation of the internal experience of the writer, and there are both recognized and freely created forms for the representation. There is apparently a hard division between what we call 'fact' and fiction, with only fact acceptable in formal education outside the studies mentioned above. Before turning to the fact/fiction 'divide', we can reiterate the point about the manner in which story relates to learning from experience. We have already suggested different forms of representation to provide the learner with different learning opportunities (Eisner, 1991). This idea can be applied in two ways. The first is to the form being represented in storywork (oral, written or in mime). Also it can be applied to the manner of organization – whether the story is presented as myth, fable, play short story, a true account, and so on.

When we approach story from the point of view of learning, the divide between fact and fiction – or 'non'-fact – decreases. Memory is a reconstruction in the light of current experience because it is selective. In other words, what we recall can be 'doubly' constructed. It is first constructed in the process of learning it in the first place, and then constructed again when we recall it in a particular context (Bruner, 1990). Bruner talks about the human capacity to 'alter the past in the light of the present' as well as our capacity to 'turn around on the past and alter the present in its light . . . Neither the past nor the present stays fixed in the light of this reflexivity' (ibid., p. 109).

Newman (1999) illustrates the point further when he talks about the experience of recalling an event and reconstructing it in several ways, each time investing it with a different interpretation. We are suggesting here, therefore, that what is presented as 'fact' is partly fiction only because it is selectively presented and reconstructed.

We can also say, like Winter et al., that 'fiction is only partly "invented"' (1999, p. 21), because any 'fiction' is made up of the experienced experiences of the story maker (teller/writer). A number of writers more overtly mix 'made up' and 'lived through' experiences. The authors cite Ashton-Warner (1985a, b). The work of Henry Williamson (e.g., The Pathway, 1933) is a similar example. Winter et al. have exploited this notion of mixing overt 'fact' and 'fiction' in their design of a technique of exploring professional experience in the 'patchwork' method which recognizes the learning that can emerge from processes of selection and interpretation of experience. The use of fiction and therefore imagination broadens people's ranges of perspective on a particular topic. Bolton makes a related point in suggesting that fiction takes people into 'different and deeper territories' and enables exploration of a 'wider range of material' (1999, pp. 215, 216). Similarly useful is her suggestion that the deliberate treatment of 'factual' stories as fiction can free the story-teller in her depiction of the story (Bolton, 1994).

A further and different view of the fact/fiction divide emerges in collaborative story-telling work (McDrury and Alterio, 2002), where a story-teller presents a story that is then expanded and reinterpreted by a group of listeners. In such cases, it could be said that the 'fact'/fiction divide is relevant only to the 'teller', and then only at the time of the first 'telling'. The original story will have been fictionalized by progressive representations and interpretations of it by the teller and the listeners. The final task is to fictionalize it in a manner that is useful for the teller and the listeners. So long as the story is plausible, for most participants it would matter little if the original story was fact or fiction. Sometimes more could be learnt from fiction because it can be entirely manipulated and designed to illustrate any point that is chosen, and can facilitate any relevant learning, depending on the skill of the presenter and the work of interpretation. Because fiction can relate to anything, and because people learn from hearing stories told, there is no limit to the learning that can emerge from story work. It is a matter of how the activity is defined and how then it is facilitated in order that the planned learning is achieved.

The task of the facilitator in using story could be characterized as a matter of finding the balance between suitable precision and encouragement of broad imagination, either of which will have different management implications. Such activity also confronts people's beliefs about what they can and cannot do ('I can't tell stories') and so it requires thoughtful introduction with due attention to the context. An early decision is whether the story activity is through the written or spoken word. This may depend on the context (e.g., class size). It is important in creative activities such as those described below, for the facilitator to be clear for herself and the learners about the aim and the learning outcomes of the session(s). It is not helpful if learners do not feel that the activity has proper purpose.

Learning that can form the focus of story work can concern:

- the subject matter of professional practice;
- personal functioning;
- different perspectives of viewing a situation;
- learning about conceptions of knowledge, e.g., through seeing the operation of differing perspectives and ill-structured situations;
- emotional learning and the role of emotion in different situations;
- the exploration of alternative actions;
- the passing on of cultural history (e.g., in a business or profession);
- the thinking through of a difficult issue;
- group or team work (when used as a collaborative exercise);
- preparation for and practice in advance of a difficult situation.

The writers mentioned at the beginning of this section provide a broad range of methods of using story. However, we present a few methods below, both as a general illustration and, in some cases, to illustrate particular purposes.

Developing one's own story

Being asked to write a story can be a difficult and often threatening activity for learners. There are, however, many ways of helping them to get started through structured exercises (McDrury and Alterio, 2002) and free writing (Bolton, 1994, 1999). A number of the exercises given in this chapter would also serve to lead learners towards their own stories. 'Footprints' is particularly effective as a means of generating story material, particularly since, by its nature, the subject matter is controlled by the facilitator (Resource 13). It can lead to oral or written stories and the first stories are 'told' in the process of the exercise without being identified as stories as such.

Person, time and place

This is another useful starter exercise which can be developed to fit a professional or workplace topic or can be 'free'. The group of learners is asked to write for two minutes on a person (known or unknown), then they are asked to write for two minutes about a place and, finally, they are asked to identify a time (time can be in historical terms, time of the day, season, etc.). The facilitator, at random, picks one learner's person, another learner's place and another person's time. Learners are asked to write about or develop a story about how the person comes to be in that place at that time, preferably with some kind of conclusion. The exercise can involve written or oral stories that are then written or developed. The stories can be developed by groups or individuals and the 'pick' of person, time and place can be focused on a topic or discipline.

Different perspectives

A story relevant to the material of learning is selected. It may be one that has been written by members of the group, or it may be story already published. Learners are asked to re-write the story in the voice of different character from the original. A typical pattern would be the choice of a story in the third person originally, rewritten as a first person story by one of the characters.

Writing in different roles

This is a development of the previous exercise but probably used to fulfil a different learning purpose. It has the advantage that it can be adapted to any discipline at all and it may have some its principal value in the sciences or maths where it might be more difficult to apply story work. A reaction or event of any kind at all is explained to the learners. Examples are a form of chemical reaction, a mathematical equation, a biological theory, a pattern in particle physics. One element of the event is identified and its story is told from its point of view. Thus, a chemical reaction is 'told' from the point of view of the molecule. 'x' tells its tale in the mathematical equation, and so on. No longer are the learners learning about the event from the outside, but now from the inside. There is some evidence that this kind of approach facilitates learning (Selfe and Arbarbi, 1986).

Creating scenarios

This exercise is developed from the idea of three exercises in the Resource section (Resources 5, 6 and 10) that illustrate the deepening of reflection (see Chapter 7). In this case, however, the learners write the initial scenario and then the subsequent two or three developments that represent increasing depths of reflection. They use the Generic Framework for Reflective Writing (Resource 9) as a guide. The purpose of the exercise is to enable learners to understand the factors that are involved in reflecting at deeper levels. It would be a useful exercise to use with learners who have been using a learning journal for a little while and who need to develop, improve and broaden their ability to reflect. The exercise could be done individually or in a group.

Collaborative story work

McDrury and Alterio (2002) provide extensive support for this kind of work. They suggest that there are generally three phases in a collaborative story situation. In the first stage, a suitable story with suitable subject matter is identified and told or written. A transcript is provided for other learners (or an audio-taped copy). They reflect individually on the story in the second stage and in the third stage, the group reconvenes and there is a pooling of individual reflections, and discussion on the perceptions of the story. There could, obviously, be further developments from this stage, such as 'different perspectives' activities (above).

Patchwork

Winter *et al.* (1999) present the patchwork approach which involves the integration of creative imagination; factual material and story. The different contents of the patchwork mean that experience (e.g., in a professional area) is shaped, but there is no attempt to conclude it. It is coherent but without conclusion, which is actually the nature of real experience if we recognize that we construct knowledge. Winter *et al.* describe the patchwork 'text' in the following way: 'The texts usually consist of five or six pieces of writing, each about a page or two long, sometimes with short linking commentaries' (ibid., p. 11) or sometimes including longer pieces.

Setting up a personal learning journal

The use of learning journals is the subject matter of Moon, 1999b and although journals have become much more common since the late 1990s in educational situations, not a great deal has changed. Indeed, this book is intended to deal with specifically identified issues that have emerged from the wider use of journals. These mainly concern a generation of greater understanding about helping learners to start to reflect (see Chapter 10) and the making of judgements about the quality of reflection. This is developed throughout this book, and in particular Chapter 7 on the deepening of reflection and in the development of the Generic Framework for Reflective Writing (Resource 9).

While the earlier work on learning journals provided many ideas and ways of structuring journals, it did not recommend a format that could support ongoing learning as well as the integration of learning from past experiences. Most journals are really only concerned with learning from present experience. The work of Progoff (1975) epitomizes the form of journal to which we refer, however, the format of the Intensive Journal is just too cumbersome for most people with busy lives. We therefore suggest a format of journal that draws on the work of Progoff and others, allows for the integration of learning from past experiences but which is easier to maintain.

In this deep learning journal there are three sections: Everyday Experience; Timespells and Workings. There are several important features of the journal apart from its structure.

- The journal needs to use loose-leaf paper so that pages can be or shifted at any point. This makes the use of the journal potentially more flexible. The size and design are personal choices (discussed in Moon, 1999b).
- While we refer to writing in the journal, drawing, doodling, typing and any other form of depiction is to be encouraged if it is meaningful. If the material is not in a format that fits a paper journal, there will need to be a reference to it (see below).
- Cross-referencing: this is an important feature of the journal and its use will become evident in the description of the sections below. Most cross-referencing will be done from the Workings section into Everyday Experience. For this reason, it is helpful if work in 'Workings' is dated and given a title (e.g., Dec 23rd Dream: no-one gives me a Christmas present). When a reference is made to this in Everyday Experiences, use a symbol to show that it is a reference to writing elsewhere. This might be an asterisk.
- Where there is something that is newly learnt – a 'learning', mark it. Again this can be a matter of choice. It might be mildly symbolic such as a light bulb, or the writing might be underlined or circled. Some journal writers might want to develop a theme for these 'learnings'. Joanna Field wrote notes on 'What makes me happy' (Field, 1952).

Everyday experience

This is the everyday writing – reflections on the day, mood, events – the material of most diaries although there is a greater orientation to the drawing of provisional 'learnings'. There is no need to write in it slavishly every day but unless it is completed fairly often, there will be no 'flow' to the journal.

Timespells

This section is inspired by Progoff's 'Period Log', though again it is simplified. It is based on the observation that the feeling of our lives does not usually run in a completely steady state. To use the metaphor of travel, we travel over a rocky period of time and then reach a flat and easy route where there is relaxation and peace. There is a sudden change and the pace speeds up, and so on. Life occurs in chunks. Within each 'chunk' we feel and experience broadly the same. The chunks might be a day or two, or a week or two or even months, but most people would experience changes within months. The characteristics of each spell are decided by the journal writer in retrospect.

We write in Timespells when there is a sense that there is a period of time to describe and the writing is more about the feelings and sense of the period than the events, even though events may have defined it. The writing might take place after some reflection on what that period has meant in our lives. Depicting it in cartoon or sketch – abstract or 'real' may help to make sense of the period alongside straightforward reflective writing.

When there are insights or 'learnings' that emerge from the writing in Timespells, these are cross-referenced in the Everyday Experience.

Workings

Workings is a section for any writing that is neither daily or period recording (which then fits in the first two sections described above). It will often be exercises such as those described earlier in this chapter – dialogues, the results of Footprints exercises, writing that occurs from asking questions, using metaphor, and so on. On the other hand, it may be a piece of reflection about a particular person or situation, or the description and work on a dream (Shohet, 1985; Reed, 1985). There are many more such exercises in Moon (1999b). These are cross-referenced to Everyday Experiences. This links the experience of a day with the decision to write in Workings, and what is written in Workings may relate to the experience of the day.

Conclusion, a hint and a recipe . . .

We conclude this work on the personal learning journal, this chapter on ways of enhancing reflective and experiential learning, and this whole book first of all with a hint given by a participant at a workshop: 'Sometimes there is a struggle to make time to reflect and to learn from experience. Make an appointment with yourself in your diary.'

The recipe stirs ideas of reflection, of learning from experience, of the value of story and metaphor, and personal development – indeed, the professional development of a wizard:

> Harry stared at the stone basin. The contents had returned to their original silvery white state, swirling and rippling beneath his gaze.
>
> 'What is it?' Harry asked shakily.
>
> 'This? It is called a pensieve', said Dumbledore. 'I sometimes find, and I am sure that you know the feeling, that I simply have too many thoughts and memories crammed into my mind.'
>
> 'Er,' said Harry, who couldn't truthfully say that he had ever felt anything of the sort.
>
> 'At these times,' said Dumbledore, indicating the stone basin, 'I use the pensieve. One simply siphons the excess thoughts from one's mind, pours them into the basin, and examines them at one's leisure. It becomes easier to spot patterns and links, you understand, when they are in this form.'
>
> (Rowling, 2000, pp. 518–19)

Resources

Introduction

On these pages are exercises, material for handouts and examples that are designed to support the introduction and use of reflective and experiential learning. Instructions for the use of these materials is given in the text, mainly in Chapter 10, with some further references in Chapter 12. Copyright restrictions have been waived, so these may be copied freely for use with learners.

Below the resources and their subject matter are listed with the page number that is their main reference in the text of the book.

Photocopiable
Resource

Resource 1

The processes of writing reflectively: a map of reflective writing

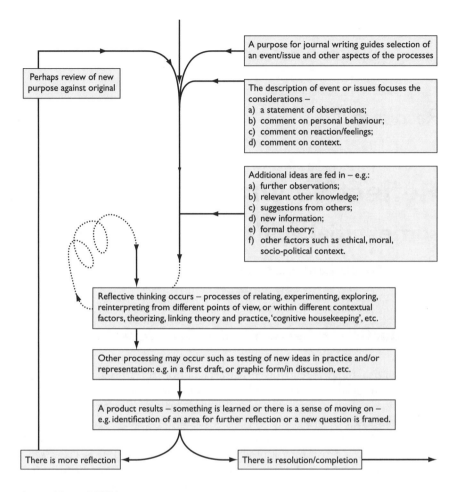

A purpose for journal writing guides selection of an event/issue and other aspects of the processes

Perhaps review of new purpose against original

The description of event or issues focuses the considerations –
a) a statement of observations;
b) comment on personal behaviour;
c) comment on reaction/feelings;
d) comment on context.

Additional ideas are fed in – e.g.:
a) further observations;
b) relevant other knowledge;
c) suggestions from others;
d) new information;
e) formal theory;
f) other factors such as ethical, moral, socio-political context.

Reflective thinking occurs – processes of relating, experimenting, exploring, reinterpreting from different points of view, or within different contextual factors, theorizing, linking theory and practice, 'cognitive housekeeping', etc.

Other processing may occur such as testing of new ideas in practice and/or representation: e.g. in a first draft, or graphic form/in discussion, etc.

A product results – something is learned or there is a sense of moving on – e.g. identification of an area for further reflection or a new question is framed.

There is more reflection

There is resolution/completion

Source: Moon (1999b)

Resource 2

Reflective writing:

some initial guidance for students

Jenny Moon, University of Exeter

Introduction: reflection and reflective writing

Reflection lies somewhere involved with the notion of learning and thinking. We reflect in order to learn something, or we learn as a result of reflecting. Reflective writing is the expression on paper/the screen of some of the mental processes of reflection. Other forms of expressing reflection are in speech, in film, in graphic portrayal, music, etc. The expression of reflection is not, however, a direct mirror of what happens in the head. It is a representation of that process within the chosen medium and reflection represented in writing, for example, will be different to that encompassed in a drawing. In other words, in making a representation of reflection, we shape and model the content of our reflection according to many influences. Factors that could shape your reflection into reflective writing might include:

- the reason why you are writing reflectively (personal reasons, e.g., in a diary or for academic purposes, etc.);
- whether others are going to see what you have written and who they are (e.g., no-one else; a tutor who will mark it; a tutor who will not mark it, friends, etc.);
- your emotional state at the time of writing, and your emotional reaction to what you are writing (e.g., a disturbing event that you do not want to think about or something you did well and want to enjoy in the rethinking process);

© RoutledgeFalmer (2004)

186

- related to the above, how safe you feel about the material and anyone seeing it;
- what you know about reflective writing and how able you are to engage in it (see below).

It is also worth noting that you will learn not only from the 'in the head' reflection but from the process of representing the reflection itself. Also, you will learn different things according to the manner in which you represent your reflection. For example, what you would learn from drawing a picture to represent reflections will differ from what you will learn in writing about the same content. It is a part of the process of writing reflectively to be as aware as possible of the influences that are shaping the writing that you actually do.

What is reflective writing?

We will start from what reflective writing is not. It is NOT:

- conveyance of information, instruction or argument in a report, essay or 'recipe';
- straightforward description, though there may be descriptive elements;
- a straightforward decision, e.g., about whether something is right or wrong, good or bad, etc.;
- simple problem solving like recalling how to get to the nearest station.

In the context of your higher education programme, reflective writing will usually have a purpose (e.g., you will be writing reflectively about something that you have to do or have done). It will usually involve the sorting out of bits of knowledge, ideas, feelings, awareness of how you are behaving and so on. It could be seen as a melting pot into which you put a number of thoughts, feelings, other forms of awareness, and perhaps new information. In the process of sorting it out in your head, and representing the sortings out on paper, you may either recognize that you have learnt something new or that you need to reflect more with, perhaps, further input. Your reflections need to come to some sort of end point, even if that is a statement of what you need to consider next.

It is also worth recognizing that reflective writing may be a means of becoming clearer about something. For example, you might use reflective writing to consider the kind of career direction that you might take. Into the 'melting pot' you might then 'put' ideas, information, feelings, other people's perspectives and advice. A metaphor for reflection or its expression in reflective writing in this context is 'cognitive housekeeping' to imply its nature as a sorting out, clarifying process.

From what has been said above, it will be obvious that reflection is not a straightforward and 'tidy' process itself. When you have to represent the process for someone else to read, you will inevitably tidy it up – but if a tutor is expecting reflective writing, she will not be looking for a dry 'single-track' account, or just a conclusion. It is also all right to use the first person – 'I' – in reflective writing.

Let us assume that you are reflecting on a presentation that you have just done in class. We said above that reflective writing is not a 'straightforward' description. You will probably have to describe what you are about to reflect on and perhaps relate it to the purpose for which you are reflecting. But reflection is more than that. You might want to evaluate your performance in the presentation, for example. This may be represented by you questioning yourself, perhaps challenging yourself. You may consider your reactions, and even the manner in which you have intially viewed the situation and written about it. Your writing may recognize that others may have different views of the same event. So with regard to the presentation, you might think about the performances of others, and so on.

Some subject matter for reflective writing

Reflective writing may apply to anything that is relatively complex. You might reflect on:

- how to go about your dissertation topic;
- how well you wrote an assignment;
- experiences gained in your part-time work;
- what your essay title means and how to go about writing it;
- how to present some project work;
- how you want to behave differently in some context;
- the way in which your non-work activities relate to the programme that you are on;
- the quality of a relationship with someone (to do with your programme or home or family, etc.);
- how well you got on in your programme last semester;
- your process in solving a difficult problem (e.g., in academic work);
- what you need to do to improve your study processes.

You will often find there to be unexpected rewards in working in this manner. You will find out things that you had not considered, you even find that your academic writing becomes more fluent; you may find that you can solve problems more easily when you have reflected on your processing of similar problems.

The quality of reflective writing

It is worth thinking about the quality of reflective writing as being on a continuum from rather superficial writings that are largely descriptive, to much deeper writings in which the questioning is more profound. Neither is necessarily right or wrong – they are just different. Reflective writing will need be 'pitched' according to the purpose for which the task is done. Those who are learning to become counsellors and need to question their motives for the way they work will require to take a much more profound approach, for example, than most others in higher education programmes. The challenge is at least to 'go beyond' descriptive writing.

A final note

'Reflection' is a word in everyday language but note that in some contexts it is a subject of academic study, with many books and papers devoted to it. The material in this paper is derived from three books (Moon, 1999a, 1999b, 2004), which provide an introduction to the literature for those who are interested in taking this further.

Moon, J. (1999a) *Reflection in Learning and Professional Development*, London: Kogan Page.

Moon, J. (1999b) *Learning Journals: A Handbook for Academics, Students and Professional Development*, London: Kogan Page.

Moon, J. (2004) *A Handbook of Reflective and Experiential Learning*, London, Routledge.

Resource 3

A comparison of reflective writing and report or essay writing

Jenny Moon, University of Exeter

Undergraduate report/essay writing	*Reflective writing*
The subject matter is likely to be clearly defined	The subject matter may be diffuse and ill-structured
The subject matter is not likely to be personal	The subject matter may be personal
The subject matter is likely to be given	The subject matter may be determined by the writer
The purpose of this kind of writing is set in advance, usually fairly precisely in a title/topic	There may be purpose, but it is more of the nature of a 'container' or direction, not a precise title that predicts the outcome
Most of the ideas drawn into an essay/a report will be predictable and will be determined by the subject matter	Ideas will be drawn into reflective writing from anywhere that the writer believes to be relevant. What is drawn in will be determined by the sense being forged by the writer

There will be a conclusion	There may be a conclusion in that something has been learnt, or there may be a recognition of further areas for reflection
Essays/reports are more likely to be 'one off' – finished and handed in	Reflective writing may be part of a process that takes place over a period of time
There is likely to be a clear structure of introduction, discussion and conclusion	There is not necessarily a clear structure other than some description at the beginning and some identification of progress made. Structures, such as questions to prompt reflective activity may be given
The writing style is likely to be relatively objective – probably without use of the first person	The writing style is likely to be relatively subjective, using the first person
An essay or report is usually intended to be a representation of learning	The intention underlying reflective writing is likely to be for the purpose of learning
An essay/a report is likely to be the product of a thinking process, tidily ordered	Reflective writing usually involves the process of thinking and learning, and it is therefore not necessarily 'tidy' in its ordering

Resource 4

Samples of reflective writing

Jenny Moon, University of Exeter

An experience in a work experience placement on a Business and Management programme (Level HE1): reasonably reflective writing

The placement is in the Black Bull in Grentown. The student, Barry, has been at the placement for only a few days. He has been asked to wait on the tables at lunchtime.

Today the pub was full and many people wanted lunch. I think that Mr Freddings (the manager) was a bit caught out because it had been very quiet the last few days and he had told two of the regular lunchtime staff not to bother to come in until later. I helped out in the kitchen this morning – washing up and doing some cleaning up. Jan, the cook, said that I would be needed to wait at the tables. I was a bit shocked because I had not done this before. I was embarrassed when she took me out and told me what to do in front of some of the customers, but I suppose I did need to know. I was left in a situation in which some customers knew that I am new to this, and others did not. On the whole, I decided to pretend that I had been doing it all my life. Jan told me how to write down what people order very quickly, and told me her type of shorthand which I have been trying

© RoutledgeFalmer (2004)

to use. On the whole it seems to work – I did make one or two mistakes when I had to go back to the customers and ask again what they wanted. One customer was really nice when this happened because she had seen me being taught what to do. Another, a bit later, was quite abrupt. I guess that I had become a little over-confident by then. I backed off and realized that I have a lot to learn even in this simple matter of taking orders and bringing out the food.

A bit later there was a difficult incident that I got involved in. There was a party of three women – I think that they work at the big company that makes furniture up the road. They had booked but were a bit late and, because it was quite busy by then, we had to tell them that they would have to wait for their meal for a bit. They grumbled and then ordered. Then it got really busy and cook could really hardly cope so it made it even longer that they had to wait. She asked me to go and tell them they would have to wait even longer. She told me what to say – to be polite but firm and not to get drawn into stuff about how they had booked – because, as she said, it was their fault because they were late. Anyway, the women treated me as if it was my fault. I fell apart a bit, not sure what to say apart from sorry lots of times. I got away and went back to the kitchen. By then Mr Freddings had come in and he and Jan had decided to offer the women some food that could be served up straight away. I wished they could have thought of it earlier. Again, I had to take out the message. The women were cross and made a huge fuss about not wanting the food on offer, and said how the pub had gone downhill and it used not to be like that. I just had to stand and listen and wished I had not pretended to have been there all my life. It all made me feel upset especially when, at last, grudgingly they said they would have the food.

I brought out their meals and now they were all smiles because they thought they had got a bargain because what they had been given was more expensive. They were nice to me then and left quite a tip. I think I learnt quite a bit about waiting all in a short time.

These are some of the things that I learnt from today [she lists 6 topics].

Reflection on study habits over the last semester: reasonably reflective writing

The student, Kerry, is in Level HE2 on a Biology programme. She has been asked to reflect on her progress in study in the previous semester by her tutor and to bring the piece she has written to the tutorial. This is part of the personal professional planning initiative in the university.

In the summer at the end of my first year of uni, I travelled all around Europe. I had always wanted to do that and felt that I had to come back before I was ready. I got back to uni two days late and I felt unsettled for a while after because it seemed that everyone had got into ruts of studying before I could. I missed a few lectures in the first two weeks – none of it seemed to have any meaning. I thought about leaving but my parents were wild when I said that so I thought I had better try to settle down.

We had lots of work to do at that stage for the first genetics module. You can't afford to get behind in that and I was behind. I had to go to Dr Spolan and tell him I couldn't do it. He was really helpful which made me feel a lot better. He said he knew several of us would have difficulty and set up a surgery with some of the postgraduate students. Mostly they were good, though sometimes they did not have much idea of just how hard I found it. Somehow they could not always explain. Anyway, I seem to have caught up now and passed the exam.

I think I have difficulty writing essays. I can't seem to organize my ideas in the way that tutors want. I think I have done it correctly and then get comments about there not being proper discussions and conclusions to what I write. I am not sure that anyone has ever told me how to write an essay – you just have to guess. I did buy a study skills book for science students and that helped me because it had examples, even from biology. It also helped me with referencing. I have always been confused about how much you can put down of someone else's work without it being plagiarism. I know we had some rules about plagiarism in the course handbook, but when you are in the middle of an essay, with a really relevant book in front of you, it seems difficult to see how to apply the rules. Can you, for example, put down quite a big chunk of someone else's work if it says exactly what you want to say yourself? It would have a reference put after it, of course. I think I need some help on this.

We have multiple choice questions for the first biology methods module. I was not sure how to revise for an exam like that. We ended up making up questions and testing each other on the answers. I did find that I did not seem to need to understand the ideas that were put over in the questions – I thought I could just guess at the kinds of questions and make sure that I had the answers. I did not do all that well in the exam so maybe I need to prepare differently – but I really don't know how to do it. I will need to ask.

Anyway, I think that deciding to stay on at uni was a good idea and as the term goes on, I feel more settled.

Reflection on a skills module: not very reflective writing

Jackie is on a Level HE1 Skills module. She has just given a presentation as part of that module and has been asked to assess how she got on in a reflective manner as part of the assessment of the module.

I have just done a presentation to our group. We were asked to choose any subject this time but next time we will be giving a presentation on a topic associated with our subject. I chose to talk about my adventure sailing holiday in Scotland. I was third to go. I was nervous because the last time I gave a presentation was at school and then I knew everyone well. This is a new module so I do not yet know people. There were fifteen of us, and the tutor.

I talked about the journey up to Scotland – and how we missed the train and then could not find the boat we were going on. People seemed to be listening. I talked about the first day of sailing. It was windy and I told them how I was a bit scared – then there were two days when we did not go anywhere because it was so rough. We then did get some sailing and went to several islands. There were adders on the islands so we had to wear boots if we walked on the heather. It made me very nervous about going onto the land.

I talked for the six minutes that was required. I fitted in most of what I had to say. I then had to ask if anyone had any questions. There were three questions. Sam asked how old the boat was and I told him that it was built in 1910. Beckie asked where we sailed from and Dr Smythe asked if we had to be the crew and pull ropes. I told him that we were the crew and that over the week I began to learn which ropes did what to the boat.

Then it was over. I think I did the presentation well and people listened. I do not think that I would do anything differently next time.

Resource 5

The Park:

an exercise in reflective writing

Jenny Moon, University of Exeter

Introduction

This is an account of an incident in a park. It is recounted by 'Annie' who was involved in the incident herself. It is written in different versions that demonstrate different levels of reflective writing. At the end of the accounts, there are notes on the criteria for the levels of reflection that each account portrays. You may not be given the notes until you have discussed your responses to the material.

The Park (I)

I went through the park the other day. The sun shone sometimes but large clouds floated across the sky in a breeze. It reminded me of a time that I was walking on St David's Head in Wales – when there was a hard and bright light and anything I looked at was bright. It was really quite hot – so much nicer than the day before, which was rainy. I went over to the children's playing field. I had not been there for a while and wanted to see the improvements. There were several children there and one, in particular, I noticed, was in too many clothes for the heat. The children were running about and this child became red in the face and began to slow down and then he sat. He must have been about 10. Some of the others called him

© RoutledgeFalmer (2004)

up again and he got to his feet. He stumbled into the game for a few moments, tripping once or twice. It seemed to me that he had just not got the energy to lift his feet. Eventually he stumbled down and did not get up but he was still moving and he shuffled into a half-sitting and half-lying position watching the other children and I think he was calling out to them. I don't know.

Anyway, I had to get on to get to the shop to buy some meat for the chilli that my children had asked me to make for their party. The twins had invited many friends round for an end-of-term celebration of the beginning of the summer holidays. They might think that they have cause to celebrate but it makes a lot more work for me when they are home. I find that their holiday time makes a lot more work.

It was the next day when the paper came through the door – in it there was a report of a child who had been taken seriously ill in the park the previous day. He was fighting for his life in hospital and they said that the seriousness of the situation was due to the delay before he was taken to hospital. The report commented on the fact that he had been lying unattended for half an hour before someone saw him. By then the other children had gone. It said that several passers-by might have seen him looking ill and even on the ground and the report went on to ask why passers-by do not take action when they see that something is wrong. The article was headed 'Why do they "Walk on by"?' I have been terribly upset since then. James says I should not worry – it is just a headline.

The Park (2)

I went to the park the other day. I was going to the supermarket to get some meat to make the chilli that I had promised the children. They were having one of their end-of-term celebrations with friends. I wonder what drew me to the playground and why I ended up standing and watching those children playing with a rough old football? I am not sure as I don't usually look at other people's children – I just did. Anyway there were a number of kids there. I noticed, in particular, one child who seemed to be very over-dressed for the weather. I try now to recall what he looked like – his face was red. He was a boy of around 10 – not unlike Charlie was at that age – maybe that is why I noticed him to start with when he was running around with the others. But then he was beginning to look distressed. I felt uneasy about him – sort of maternal but I did not do anything. What could I have done? I remember thinking, I had little time and the supermarket would get crowded. What a strange way of thinking, in the circumstances!

In retrospect, I wish I had acted. I ask myself what stopped me – but I don't know what I might have done at that point. Anyway he sat down, looking absolutely exhausted and as if he had no energy to do anything. A few moments later, the other children called him up to run about again. I felt more uneasy and watched as he got up and tried to run, then fell, ran again and fell and half-sat and half-lay. Still I did nothing more than look – what was going on with me?

Eventually I went on I tell myself now that it was really important to get to the shops. It was the next day when the paper came through the door that I had a real shock. In the paper there was a report of a child who had been taken seriously ill in the park the previous day. He was fighting for his life in the hospital and the situation was much more serious because there had been such a delay in getting help. The report commented on the fact that he had been lying, unattended, for half an hour or more. At first, I wondered why the other children had not been more responsible. The article went on to say that several passers-by might have seen him playing and looking ill and the report questioned why passers-by do not take action when they see that something is wrong.

The incident has affected me for some days but I do not know where to go or whom to tell. I do want to own up to my part in it to someone though.

The Park (3)

The incident happened in Ingle Park and it is very much still on my mind. There was a child playing with others. He looked hot and unfit and kept sitting down but the other children kept on getting him back up and making him play with them. I was on my way to the shop and only watched the children for a while before I walked on. Next day it was reported in the paper that the child had been taken to hospital seriously ill – very seriously ill. The report said that there were several passers-by in the park who had seen the child looking ill and who had done nothing. It was a scathing report about those who do not take action in such situations.

Reading the report, I felt dreadful and it has been very difficult to shift the feelings. I did not stop to see to the child because I told myself that I was on my way to the shops to buy food for a meal that I had to cook for the children's party – what do I mean that I *had to* cook it? Though I saw that the child was ill, I didn't do anything. It is hard to say what I was really thinking at the time – to what degree I was determined to go on with my day in the way I had planned it (the party really was not that important, was it?). Or did I genuinely not think that the boy was ill – but just over-dressed and a bit tired? To what extent did I try to make convenient excuses and to what extent was my action based on an attempt to really understand the situation? Looking back, I could have cut through my excuses at the time – rather than now.

I did not go over to the child and ask what was wrong but I should have done. I could have talked to the other children – and even got one of the other children to call for help. I am not sure if the help would have been ambulance or doctor at that stage – but it does not matter now. If he had been given help then, he might not be fighting for his life now.

It would be helpful to me if I could work out what I was really thinking and why I acted as I did. This event has really shaken me to my roots – more than I would have expected. It made me feel really guilty. I do not usually do wrong, in fact, I think of myself as a good person. This event is also making me think about actions in all sorts of areas of my life. It reminds me of some things in the past, as when my uncle died – but then again I don't really think that that is relevant – he was going to die anyway. My bad feelings then were due to sheer sadness and some irrational regrets that I did not visit him on the day before. Strangely it also reminds me of how bad I felt when Charlie was ill while we went on that anniversary weekend away. As I think more about Charlie being ill, I recognize that there are commonalities in the situations. I also keep wondering if I knew that boy . . .

The Park (4)

It happened in Ingle Park and this event is very much still on my mind. It feels significant. There was a child playing with others. He looked hot and unfit and kept sitting down but the other children kept on getting him back up and making him play with them. I was on my way to the shop and only watched the children for a while before I walked on. Next day it was reported in the paper that the child had been taken to hospital seriously ill – very seriously ill. The report said that there were several passers-by in the park who had seen the child looking ill and who had done nothing. It was a scathing report about those who do not take action in such a situation.

It was the report initially that made me think more deeply. It kept coming back into my mind and over the next few days I began to think of the situation in lots of different ways. Initially I considered my urge to get to the shop – regardless of the state of the boy. That was an easy way of excusing myself – to say that I had to get to the shop. Then I began to go through all of the agonizing as to whether I could have mis-read the situation and really thought that the boy was simply over-dressed or perhaps play-acting or trying to gain sympathy from me or the others. Could I have believed that the situation was all right? All of that thinking, I now notice, would also have let me off the hook – made it not my fault that I did not act at the time.

I talked with Tom about my reflections on the event – on the incident, on my thinking about it at the time and then immediately after. He observed that my sense of myself as a 'good person who always lends a helping hand when others need help' was put in some jeopardy by it all. At the time and immediately after, it might have been easier to avoid shaking my view of myself than to admit that I had avoided facing up to the situation and admitting that I had not acted as 'a good person'. With this hindsight, I notice that I can probably find it easier to admit that I am not always 'a good person' and that I made a mistake in retrospect rather than immediately after the event. I suspect that this may apply to other situations.

As I think about the situation now, I recall some more of the thoughts – or were they feelings mixed up with thoughts? I remember a sense at the time that this boy looked quite scruffy and reminded me of a child who used to play with Charlie. We did not feel happy during the brief period of their friendship because this boy was known as a bully and we were uneasy either that Charlie would end up being bullied, or that Charlie would learn to bully. Funnily enough, we were talking about this boy – I now remember – at the dinner table the night before. The conversation had reminded me of all of the agonizing about the children's friends at the time. The fleeting thought/feeling was possibly something like this – if this boy is like one I did not feel comfortable with – then maybe he deserves to get left in this way. Maybe he was a brother of the original child. I remember social psychology research along the lines of attributing blame to victims to justify their plight. Then, it might not have been anything to do with Charlie's friend.

So I can see how I looked at that event and perhaps interpreted it in a manner that was consistent with my emotional frame of mind at the time. Seeing the same events without that dinner-time conversation might have led me to see the whole thing in an entirely different manner and I might have acted differently. The significance of this whole event is chilling when I realize that my lack of action nearly resulted in his death – and it might have been because of an attitude that was formed years ago in relation to a different situation.

This has all made me think about how we view things. The way I saw this event at the time was quite different to the way I see it now – even these few days later. Writing an account at the time would have been different to the account, or several accounts, that I would write now. I cannot know what 'story' is 'true'. The bullying story may be one that I have constructed retrospectively – fabricated. Interestingly, I can believe that story completely.

The Park: comments on the quality of reflection in the accounts

See also Resource 9, which is a generic framework for reflective writing.

The Park (1)

This piece tells the story. Sometimes it mentions past experiences, sometimes anticipates the future but all in the context of the account of the story:

- There might be references to emotional state, but the role of the emotions on action is not explored.
- Ideas of others are mentioned but not elaborated or used to investigate the meaning of the events.
- The account is written only from one point of view – that of Annie.
- Generally ideas are presented in a sequence and are only linked by the story. They are not all relevant or focused.

In fact, you could hardly deem this to be reflective at all. It is very descriptive. It could be a reasonably written account of an event that could serve as a basis on which reflection might start, though it hardly signals any material for reflection – other than the last few words.

The Park (2)

In this account there is a description of the same events. There is very little addition of ideas from outside the event – reference to attitudes of others, or comments.

The account is more than a story though. It is focused on the event as if there is a big question to be asked and answered. In the questioning there is recognition of the worth of exploring the motives for behaviour but it does not go very far. In other words, asking the questions makes it more than a descriptive account, but the lack of attempt to respond to the questions means that there is little actual analysis of the events.

Annie is critical of her actions and, in her questions, signals this. The questioning of action does mean that Annie is standing back from the event to a small extent. There is a sense that she recognizes that this is a significant incident, with learning to be gained but the reflection does not go sufficiently deep to enable the learning to begin to occur.

The Park (3)

The description is succinct – just sufficient to raise the issues. Extraneous information is not added. It is not a story. The focus is on the attempt to reflect on the event and to learn from it. There is more of a sense of Annie standing back from the event in order to reflect better on her actions and in order to be more effectively critical.

There is more analysis of the situation and an evident understanding that it was not a simple situation – that there might be alternative explanations or actions that could be justified equally effectively.

The description could be said to be slightly narrow (see The Park (4)) as Annie is not acknowledging that there might be other ways of perceiving the situation – other points of view. She does not seem to recognize that her reflection is affected by her frame of reference at the time or now. It is possible, for example, that her experience with Charlie (last paragraph) – or her question about knowing the boy have influenced the manner in which she reacted. It might not just be a matter of linking up other events, but of going beyond and checking out the possibility that her frame of reference might have been affected by the prior experiences.

The Park (4)

(You may not have been given the fourth part of The Park.)

The account is succinct and to the point. There is some deep reflection here that is self-critical and questions the basis of the beliefs and values on which the behaviour was based.

- There is evidence of standing back from the event, of Annie treating herself as an object acting within the context.
- There is also an internal dialogue – a conversation with herself in which she proposes and further reflects on alternative explanations.
- She shows evidence of looking at the views of others (Tom) and of considering the alternative point of view, and learning from it.
- She recognizes the significance of the effect of passage of time on her reflection, e.g., that her personal frame of reference at the time may have influenced her actions and that a different frame of reference might have led to different results.
- She notices that the proximity of other, possibly unrelated events (the dinner-time conversation) has an effect either on her actual behaviour and her subsequent reflection or possibly on her reflective processes only. She notices that she can be said to be reconstructing the event in retrospect – creating a story around it that may not be 'true'.

- She recognizes that there may be no conclusion to this situation but that there are still things to be learnt from it.
- She has also been able to reflect on her own process of reflecting (acting metacognitively), recognizing that her process influenced the outcome.

Resource 6

The Presentation:

an exercise in reflective writing

Developed by Jenny Moon, University of Exeter

Introduction

This is an account of the experience of giving a presentation. It is written by Marianne who is in her first job after graduating. It is written in three different versions that demonstrate different levels of reflective writing. At the end of the accounts, there are notes on the criteria for the levels of reflection that each account portrays.

The Presentation (1)

I had to take an agenda item to the weekly team meeting in my third week of working at PIGG PLC. I had to talk about the project that I am on (creating a new database for the management information system). I had done a presentation before and then I relied on my acting skills. Despite the acting, I spent quite a bit of time preparing it in the way that I have seen others make similar presentations.

The presentation at the last team meeting, given by my colleague, went well – she used PowerPoint and I decided to use it too. I decided that a good presentation comes from good planning and having all the figures that anyone might request so I spent a long time in the preparation and I went in feeling confident.

© RoutledgeFalmer (2004)

However, I became nervous when I realized they were all waiting for me to speak and my nerves made my voice wobble. I did not know how to stop it. Early on, I noticed that people seemed not to understand what I was saying despite the PowerPoint. Using PowerPoint meant that people received my presentation both through what I was saying and what I had prepared on the slides. In a way that meant they got it twice but I noticed that Mrs Shaw (my boss) repeated bits of what I had said several times and once or twice answered questions for me. This made me feel uncomfortable. I felt it was quite patronising and I was upset. Later my colleagues said that she always does that. I was disappointed that my presentation did not seem to have gone well.

I thought about the presentation for several days and then talked with Mrs Shaw about the presentation (there was no-one else). She gave me a list of points for improvement next time. They included:

- putting less on PowerPoint;
- talking more slowly;
- calming myself down in some way.

I also have to write down the figures in a different way so that they can be understood better. She suggested that I should do a presentation to several of the team sometime next week so that I can improve my performance.

The Presentation (2)

I had to take an agenda item to the weekly team meeting in my third week of working at PIGG PLC. I had to talk about the project that I am on. I am creating a new database for the management information system. I had given a presentation before and that time I relied on my acting skills. I did realize that there were considerable differences between then and now, particularly in the situation (it was only fellow students and my tutor before). I was confident but I did spend quite a bit of time preparing. Because everyone else here uses PowerPoint, I felt I had better use it – though I realized that it was not for the best reasons. I also prepared lots of figures so that I could answer questions. I thought, at that stage, that any questions would involve requests for data. When I think back on the preparation that I did, I realize that I was desperately trying to prove that I could make a presentation as well as my colleague, who did the last one. I wanted to impress everyone. I had not realized there was so much to learn about presenting, and how much I needed to know about PowerPoint to use it properly.

When I set up the presentation in the meeting I tried to be calm but it did not work out. Early on PowerPoint went wrong and I began to panic. Trying to pretend that I was cool and confident made the situation worse because I did not admit my difficulties and ask for help. The more I spoke, the more my voice went wobbly. I realized, from the kinds of questions that the others asked, that they did not understand what I was saying. They were asking for clarification – not the figures. I felt worse when Mrs Shaw, my boss, started to answer questions for me. I felt flustered and even less able to cope.

As a result of this poor presentation, my self-esteem is low at work now. I had thought I was doing all right in the company. After a few days, I went to see Mrs Shaw and we talked it over. I still feel that her interventions did not help me. Interestingly, several of my colleagues commented that she always does that. It was probably her behaviour, more than anything else, that damaged my poise. Partly through talking over the presentation and the things that went wrong (but not, of course, her interventions), I can see several areas that I could improve. I need to know more about using Power-Point – and to practise with it. I recognize, also, that my old acting skills might have given me initial confidence, but I needed more than a clear voice, especially when I lost my way with PowerPoint. Relying on a mass of figures was not right either. It was not figures they wanted. In retrospect, I could have put the figures on a handout. I am hoping to have a chance to try with a presentation, practising with some of the team.

The Presentation (3)

I am writing this back in my office. It all happened two days ago.

Three weeks after I started at PIGG PLC I had to take an agenda item to the team meeting. I was required to report on my progress on the project on which I am working. I am developing a new database for the management information system of the company. I was immediately worried. I was scared about not saying the right things and not being able to answer questions properly. I did a presentation in my course at university and felt the same about it initially. I was thinking then, like this time, I could use my acting skills. Both times that was helpful in maintaining my confidence at first, at least. Though the fact that I was all right last time throughout the whole presentation may not have helped me this time!

I decided to use PowerPoint. I was not very happy about its use because I have seen it go wrong so often. However, I have not seen anyone else give a presentation here without using it – and learning to use PowerPoint would be valuable. I was not sure, when it came to the session, whether I really knew enough about running PowerPoint. (How do you know when you know enough about something? – dummy runs, I suppose, but I couldn't get the laptop when I wanted it.)

When it came to the presentation, I really wanted to do it well – as well as the presentations had been done the week before. Maybe I wanted too much to do well. Previous presentations have been interesting, informative and clear and I thought the handouts from them were good (I noticed that the best gave enough but not too much information).

In the event, the session was a disaster and has left me feeling uncomfortable in my work and I even worry about it at home. I need to think about why a simple presentation could have such an effect on me. The PowerPoint went wrong (I think I clicked on the wrong thing). My efforts to be calm and 'cool' failed and my voice went wobbly – that was, anyway, how it felt to me. My colleague actually said afterwards that I looked quite calm despite what I was feeling (I am not sure whether she meant it or was just trying to help me). When I think back to that moment, if I had thought that I still looked calm (despite what I felt), I could have regained the situation. As it was, it went from bad to worse and I know that my state became obvious because Mrs Shaw, my boss, began to answer the questions that people were asking for me.

I am thinking about the awful presentation again – it was this time last week. I am reading what I wrote earlier about it. Now I return to it, I do have a slightly different perspective. I think that it was not as bad as it felt at the time. Several of my colleagues told me afterwards that Mrs Shaw always steps in to answer questions like that and they commented that I handled her intrusion well. That is interesting. I need to do some thinking about how to act next time to prevent this interruption from happening or to deal with the situation when she starts*. I might look in the library for that book on assertiveness.

I have talked to Mrs Shaw now too. I notice that my confidence in her is not all that great while I am still feeling a bit cross. However, I am feeling more positive generally and I can begin to analyse what I could do better in the presentation. It is interesting to see the change in my attitude after a week. I need to think from the beginning about the process of giving a good presentation. I am not sure how helpful was my reliance on my acting skills*. Acting helped my voice to be stronger and better paced, but I was not just trying to put over someone else's lines but my own and I needed to be able to discuss matters in greater depth rather than just give the line*.

I probably will use PowerPoint again. I have had a look at the manual and it suggests that you treat it as a tool – not let it dominate and not use it as a means of presenting myself. That is what I think I was doing. I need to not only know how to use it, but I need to feel sufficiently confident in its use so I can retrieve the situation when things go wrong. That means understanding more than just the sequence of actions*.

As I write this, I am noticing how useful it is to go back over things I have written about before. I seem to be able to see the situation differently. The first time I wrote this, I felt that the presentation was dreadful and that I could not have done it differently. Then later I realized that there were things I did not know at the time (e.g., about Mrs Shaw and her habit of interrupting). I also recognize some of the areas in which I went wrong. At the time I could not see that. It was as if my low self-esteem got in the way. Knowing where I went wrong, and admitting the errors to myself give me a chance to improve next time – and perhaps to help Mrs Shaw to improve in her behaviour towards us!

*I have asterisked the points that I need to address in order to improve.

The Presentation: comments on the quality of reflection in the accounts

See also Resource 9, which is a generic framework for reflective writing.

The Presentation (1)

This account is descriptive and it contains little reflection:

- The account describes what happened, sometimes mentioning past experiences, sometimes anticipating the future but all in the context of an account of the event.
- There are some references to Marianne's emotional reactions, but she has not explored how the reactions relate to her behaviour.
- Ideas are taken up without questioning them or considering them in depth.
- The account is written only from Marianne's point of view.
- External information is mentioned but its impact on behaviour is not subject to consideration.
- Generally one point is made at a time and ideas are not linked.

The Presentation (2)

An account showing evidence of some reflection:

- There is description of the event, but where there are external ideas or information, the material is subjected to consideration and deliberation.

- The account shows some analysis.
- There is recognition of the worth of exploring motives for behaviour.
- There is willingness to be critical of action.
- Relevant and helpful detail is explored where it has value.
- There is recognition of the overall effect of the event on self – in other words, there is some 'standing back' from the event.

The account is written at one point in time. It does not, therefore, demonstrate the recognition that views can change with time and more reflection. In other words the account does not indicate a recognition that frames of reference affect the manner in which we reflect at a given time.

The Presentation (3)

This account shows quite deep reflection, and it does incorporate a recognition that the frame of reference with which an event is viewed can change:

- Self-questioning is evident (an 'internal dialogue' is set up at times) deliberating between different views of her own behaviour (different views of her own and others).
- Marianne takes into account the views and motives of others and considers these against her own.
- She recognizes how prior experience, thoughts (her own and other's) can interact with the production of her own behaviour.
- There is clear evidence of standing back from the event.
- She helps herself to learn from the experience by splitting off the reflective processes from the points she wants to learn (by an asterisk system).
- There is recognition that the personal frame of reference can change according to the emotional state in which it is written, the acquisition of new information, the review of ideas and the effect of time passing.

Resource 7

Questions to support reflective writing

Developed by Jenny Moon, University of Exeter

It can be useful to prompt the description of the subject matter of reflection in terms of a question such as:

What is the issue/event/topic/plan/project/task/period of time, etc. that is to be the subject matter of the reflection?

Questions to facilitate reflection

- From the description above, what is the issue/are the issues that could be addressed in reflective writing? These issues can be raised within the description or separately.
- Is there anything else you need to consider at the moment in terms of the context?
- What is the nature of the significance of this issue to you?
- How do you feel about it?
- How do your feelings relate to any action?
- Was it good/bad – and what are the implications?
- What do you need to do?
- What other information do you need (ideas, knowledge, opinion, etc.)?

- Are there previous instances of this event, issue arising that will help you to think more or differently about it?
- Are there others, or the views of others, who are relevant to this matter – and in what way?

Questions that are likely to be helpful in prompting more profound reflection

- Has the nature of your description of the issue/event etc. influenced the manner in which you have gone about the reflective writing?
- Is there relevant formal theory that you need to apply?
- How do your motives for and the context of the reflective writing affect the manner in which you have gone about the task?
- In what way might have you tackled the task differently if the context was not one of formal education (perhaps with assessment)?
- Is there another point of view that you could explore – are there alternative interpretations to consider?
- Are others seeing this issue from different points of view that may be helpful to you to explore?
- Does this issue relate to other contexts – reflection on which may be helpful?
- If you 'step back' from this issue, how does it look different?
- How do you judge your ability to reflect on this matter?
- Do you notice that your feelings about it have changed over time – or in the course of writing this – suggesting that your own frame of reference has changed?
- Are there ethical/moral/political wider social issues that you would want to explore?

Resource 8

Dialogue:

an exercise to develop reflective thinking and writing

Developed by Jenny Moon, University of Exeter

This is an imagined dialogue between Toni and a teacher, Mr Jaques, who inspired her and was helpful at school. Toni is using this exercise in the context of a learning journal in a Careers and Personal Development Planning module in her biology degree programme. She is trying to make up her mind what group of modules to choose for her final year studies. She 'seeks advice' from a teacher whom she remembers as being very helpful at school. She writes what she would ask and then 'listens' (in her imagination) for the response and the continuation of the conversation.

TONI   Hello, Mr Jaques, I haven't seen you for a long time – since I left school. You were really helpful to me at school. You always seemed to give me good advice, and I remember when you went through that essay and showed me how I could make it a lot better. I was always better at writing essays after that time. I seemed to understand what to do.

MR JAQUES   Hello, Toni, how are you getting on – is it some more help that you want? How can I help?

TONI   Yes, I need some help. I don't know what modules to take next year. I have to make a choice very soon. I am getting quite worried about it. I don't know how to make a choice.

MR JAQUES   OK, what are the choices?

TONI   I have a choice between going down the road of molecular biology modules with lots of lab work and the modules of ecology and the kind of field work types of modules.

MR JAQUES   Yes, I can see that there is quite a choice to make. I suppose the important question now is what you want to do when you have left university. You may want to make a career in biology and in that case the kinds of experience you have at this stage of your degree may be pretty influential in what you do.

TONI   That's what they said at careers a while ago. I have to say that I have been mainly thinking about what I want to do while I am here. It's quite hard to think about the future – though everyone keeps saying we should. I feel I have only just really settled here!

MR JAQUES   So what is the bigger picture? What do you see yourself doing?

TONI   Well, I don't know really – I did think that I might teach – and then I felt that I did not want to be shut in with lots of kids all day and wanted to work more with adults. I suppose I do like being outside quite a bit.

MR JAQUES   Do you see yourself in a lab?

TONI   Well, I like it sometimes – that is why the choice is so hard. I like being precise and working towards a measured result in an experiment – but that is only sometimes.

MR JAQUES   There are jobs where you might spend quite a bit of time in the field, but still need lab skills. Do you really have to go in one way or the other? Could you do some ecology modules and some that would equip you with lab skills? Then you might look for a job that combined the two, for example, agriculture or some aspects of ecology where lab work is relevant. It seems like a hard choice to make to go purely in one direction or the other at present.

TONI   Well, yes. You make me think that I should get some more information on careers and see what is possible that combines the two areas. I think you are right that I should be able to use both skills.

Resource 9

A Generic Framework for Reflective Writing

Developed by Jenny Moon, University of Exeter

Descriptive writing

This account is descriptive and it contains little reflection. It may tell a story but from one point of view at a time and generally one point at a time is made. Ideas tend to be linked by the sequence of the account/story rather than by meaning. The account describes what happened, sometimes mentioning past experiences, sometimes anticipating the future but all in the context of an account of the event:

- There may be references to emotional reactions but they are not explored and not related to behaviour.
- The account may relate to ideas or external information, but these are not considered or questioned and the possible impact on behaviour or the meaning of events is not mentioned.
- There is little attempt to focus on particular issues. Most points are made with similar weight.
- The writing could hardly be deemed to be reflective at all. It could be a reasonably written account of an event that would serve as a basis on which reflection might start, though a good description that precedes reflective accounts will tend to be more focused and to signal points and issues for further reflection.

Descriptive account with some reflection

This is a descripive account that signals points for reflection while not actually showing much reflection:

- The basic account is descriptive in the manner of description above. There is little addition of ideas from outside the event, reference to alternative viewpoints or attitudes to others, comment and so on. However, the account is more than just a story. It is focused on the event as if there is a big question or there are questions to be asked and answered. Points on which reflection could occur are signalled.
- The account may mention emotional reactions or be influenced by emotion. Any influence may be noted and possibly questioned.
- There is recognition of the worth of further exploring but it does not go very far. In other words, asking the questions makes it more than a descriptive account, but the lack of attempt to respond to the questions means that there is little actual analysis of the events.
- The questioning does begin to suggest a 'standing back from the event' in (usually) isolated areas of the account.
- There is a sense of recognition this is an incident from which learning can be gained, but the reflection does not go sufficiently deep to enable the learning to begin to occur.

Reflective writing (1)

- There is description but it is focused with particular aspects accentuated for reflective comment. There may be a sense that the material is being mulled around. It is no longer a straightforward account of an event, but it is definitely reflective.
- There is evidence of external ideas or information and where this occurs, the material is subjected to reflection.
- The account shows some analysis and there is recognition of the worth of exploring motives or reasons for behaviour.
- There is recognition of any emotional content, a questioning of its role and influence and an attempt to consider its significance in shaping the views presented.
- Where relevant, there is willingness to be critical of the action of self or others. There is likely to be some self-questioning and willingness also to recognize the overall effect of the event on self. In other words, there is some 'standing back' from the event.

- There may be recognition that things might look different from other perspectives, that views can change with time or the emotional state. The existence of several alternative points of view may be acknowledged but not analysed.
- In other words, in a relatively limited way the account may recognize that frames of reference affect the manner in which we reflect at a given time but it does not deal with this in a way that links it effectively to issues about the quality of personal judgement.

Reflective writing (2)

- Description now only serves the process of reflection, covering the issues for reflection and noting their context. There is clear evidence of standing back from an event and there is mulling over and internal dialogue.
- The account shows deep reflection, and it incorporates a recognition that the frame of reference with which an event is viewed can change.
- A metacognitive stance is taken (i.e., critical awareness of one's own processes of mental functioning – including reflection).
- The account probably recognizes that events exist in a historical or social context that may be influential on a person's reaction to them. In other words, multiple persectives are noted.
- Self-questioning is evident (an 'internal dialogue' is set up at times) deliberating between different views of personal behaviour and that of others.
- The view and motives of others are taken into account and considered against those of the writer.
- There is recognition that prior experience and thoughts (one's own and other's) can interact with the production of current behaviour.
- There is recognition of the role of emotion in shaping the ideas and recognition of the manner in which different emotional influences can frame the account in different ways.
- There is observation that there is learning to be gained from the experience and points for learning are noted.
- There is recognition that the personal frame of reference can change according to the emotional state in which it is written, the acquisition of new information, the review of ideas and the effect of time passing.

Resource 10

The Dance Lesson:

an exercise in reflective writing

Developed by Jenny Moon, University of Exeter

Introduction

These reflective accounts concern a lesson in dance. The teacher, Hanna, is working with Year 8 pupils in the first lesson of the day. The lesson is the fourth in a five-lesson unit of work based on street dance style. She has found that the children have been quite slow to learn. There are two state-mented children in the class, Ben and Jade. She has written other notes about her concerns about working with mixed ability groups and enabling the learning of all the children in the class. Jade and Ben have given rise to some difficulties in her teaching in previous classes, and the situation bothers her.

A dance lesson (1)

When I took the register today, I saw that there were several absences. This would cause difficulties since the pupils had been creating their dance in pairs. This would mean that those on their own would need to pair up and create a new duet, rapidly learning to co-operate with each other. Generally they were not a group of quick learners, and some had shown that they had particular difficulties in working together. I realized then that I could be in for some difficulties myself and wished I had planned better.

The two statemented pupils – Ben and Jade – worried me a bit as I could see that they were both distracted and lively this morning. As we started to warm up, a learning support assistant (LSA) came in. She acknowledged me briefly and then turned her attention to Jade.

I had decided to do simple fun activities for the warm-up – based on walking and travelling at different speeds. It meant that the pupils had to concentrate in order to vary the direction and speed of travel in response to my instructions. It all went well with everyone involved.

I developed the warm-up, repeating exercises and phrases that we had performed in previous lessons. Most pupils joined in and seemed to enjoy the simple repetitive patterns of movement but I noticed that Ben and Jade were already having problems, though a few moments later, to my relief, I noticed that Jade was beginning to settle down and had started to fall in with the patterns of the movements quite nicely. Ben, however, could not copy the movements and his concentration began to wander. Then he started to distract others. I focused my attention on him and praised him when he did things well. The LSA moved across to Ben, leaving Jade. She talked to him and gave him some encouragement but I could see that he was not able to listen to her.

By now, the rest of the class had picked up the repetitive movements. The lesson was, on the whole, going quite well at this stage. I introduced a more challenging phase by adding two new actions to the sequence and they danced in time to the music. By now Ben had really lost concentration and was running around in the space among the dancers. It was only 10 minutes into the lesson and his very public display of off-task behaviour could potentially throw everything off course again. Eventually, after just catching my eye, the LSA removed Ben from the room. I was not completely easy with this, but I do not know what else I might have done. I learnt afterwards from another colleague that he had been given sanctions which included a letter home to inform his parents of his poor behaviour. I felt guilty but it was a very difficult situation. I have been trying to think how it could have been different.

A dance lesson (2)

I want to consider a situation that arose in a potentially unsettled mixed ability class where I was teaching dance. The focus of the situation was Ben, one of two statemented pupils. The situation left me feeling guilty and inadequate as a teacher.

I began the lesson with slightly uneasy feelings. I noticed that there were several absences. The pupils had been creating their dance in pairs and with some of the partners absent, they would have to co-operate in new pairings. Co-operation was a problem for some. The children are mixed in their abilities and I had already been thinking that I need to develop strategies both to help individuals when they work outside their friendship groups and also where they need to create new material quickly. I began the lesson with these concerns and thoughts in mind.

I had started the warm-up when the learning support assistant came in to work with Jade, the other statemented pupil. It might have been helpful if she had come in just a few minutes before. Generally, however, things went well in the warm-up. I felt that I had got that right with simple and fun activities and because the skill level was low, everyone could join in and enjoy it. It really engaged them and this good start probably helped later when things got distracting.

The next stage also went well for most of the class. It was a development of the warm-up using exercises and phrases that had been mastered in previous lessons. Although I was a bit anxious about the lesson, fortunately I was patient and at their own pace nearly all of the class joined in. This too was a useful strategy. It was Jade and Ben who were having problems, though with the help of the LSA, Jade was beginning to settle. Ben was not. He found it difficult to copy the movements, seemed briefly to get frustrated, and then began to distract others, eventually running around in the spaces between the other pupils. The LSA left Jade and went to help him, while I tried as well as I could to carry on the class, moving into more challenging work.

Ben's behaviour did not improve and the LSA removed him from the room. Later I was informed that he had been given sanctions, including a letter to his parents about his poor behaviour.

I felt I had failed with this situation. I wanted to manage the behaviour of all of the children. There are several things that might have contributed to the situation. I started the class with a sense that I was not on top of the situation because of the new pairings – though in the end, I felt that things might have actually gone better because of that (I could look at this matter another time). I certainly did not need to worry about it. Also, the LSA came in late. She probably would not have seen that as a problem but for me it was. There is something about the three-way relationship – Ben, the LSA and me – and, in this situation, the LSA's work with Jade. Perhaps the LSA should have worked more with Ben from the start. Who made the decisions there and who should make them?

There is also something about the situation of dance being public – it is so obvious when pupils are off-task. Then there is Ben and his behaviour. I wonder how he felt about it all? Did he want to distract others? Was he really behaving 'poorly' – was his action deliberate, warranting sanctions or maybe just an overflow of energy?

I know a bit about Ben and his inability to hold concentration for more than a few minutes, but dance could be of help to him as a means of using his energy in a productive manner – that is if he could be enabled to stay engaged with the activity. What could I have done better?

I want to involve all of the pupils.

A dance lesson (3)

I want to reflect on the dance lesson with Year 8, and in particular on the situation that arose with Ben, though I think that there are wider issues to be considered than just Ben. The situation left me feeling guilty and inadequate as a teacher.

The class were doing some work in pairs. I felt uneasy that day because a number of children were absent and some would have to learn to co-operate with new partners who were not necessarily their choice. It is a mixed ability class, not always quick to learn or necessarily to be able to co-operate. I had already recognized the need to develop strategies:

- to help individuals to work outside their friendship groups;
- to create new material quickly.

Jade and Ben are statemented. As we started to warm up, a learning support assistant came in, specifically to help Jade.

The warm-up of simple fun activities seemed to engage all of the class and I was pleased with that. Then I added some of the repetitive exercises that we had done in previous classes. This stage also went well for most of the class. Although I was a bit anxious about the lesson, I kept on top of the feelings. I was patient and at their own pace nearly all of the class joined in. This too was a useful strategy. Managing to get most of the class engaged and listening to the music is really important for this group and I must not lose this point in relation to what then happened. At this stage, Jade and Ben were having problems, though with the help of the LSA, Jade was beginning to settle.

Ben found it difficult to copy the movements, seemed to get frustrated, and then began to distract others. By the time we were 10 minutes into the class, he was running around in the spaces between the other pupils – totally off-task. The LSA left Jade and went to help Ben. I moved into more challenging work in order to keep the other children engaged and active.

Eventually, the LSA removed Ben from the room. I later learned that his parents were sent a note about his poor behaviour and there were other sanctions.

I see myself as having failed to prevent this situation and I suspect that none of us gained from it. I notice that my feelings were made worse by the fact that I felt I had failed in front of the LSA. She may have felt that she had failed in front of me. (These feelings would be better discussed.) The children in the class had had their learning disrupted.

I think about being in Ben's shoes. How would he have seen it? Dance – a chance to have some space and be creative – it started with a bit of fun – so he might have felt that he could enjoy the fun. Ben would find it hard to move from what he would construe as pure 'fun' to a more serious activity. It is possible that the 'fun' works well for children who can change their focus of attention easily but not for some like Ben who cannot quickly shift, especially in the direction of more serious work. Also the other children often laugh at him when he clowns and since he does not have many friends, such attention from the others is rewarding. They did not actually laugh this time, I think because the music and repetitive movement took up their attention but he may have thought that they would have done. I suppose that he might have been all right if he had been guided by the LSA from the start but it was Jade who got the attention this time and he has to learn to manage without one-to-one attention sometimes.

Should I see Ben as a problem on his own or as an issue in the class as a whole including the LSA? I realize that we are only an element in an even larger situation when I consider what happened to Ben when he was removed from the class. His behaviour was construed as poor behaviour and sanctions were levied. I don't imagine that his parents were helped by receiving another letter about his poor behaviour – they know about it only too well. The sanctions will probably mean that I will have even more difficulties with Ben next time. At least I should have been involved in discussions about his behaviour in my class. I must mention this to the LSA and raise it as a more general issue when we discuss the role of LSAs next time. It is something about getting everyone pulling in the same direction.

I did feel particularly uneasy that day. I wonder if it was because I was tired from the late night. Things like this certainly are more of a burden when I feel tired. It is worth remembering that things might have looked different if I had felt fresh.

Anyway, it is worth trying to learn something from this situation and having a strategy better developed for when it happens next time. If I go further with the theme of 'getting everyone pulling in the same direction' . . . how could this be achieved?

- It would have been helpful if I had shared my concerns about the group with the LSA to start with.

- It would have been helpful to me if she had come in at the beginning of the class, and we could have both been forearmed with some tactics to work with Ben and Jade.
- I need to include in my planning strategies to deal with partner work when one person is away.
- Praise motivates those who are working well, I must remember to use that as a teaching strategy.
- There is something about the need for me to be involved in the discussion about the repercussions of Ben's behaviour. They have consequences for my later dealings with Ben.
- I have concerns about the actual kinds of sanctions levied. I need to follow this up.

Resource 11

Strategies for enhancing learning from everyday experience

This is an elaborated and rewritten version of material presented in Marsick and Watkins (1990, pp. 36–7) as 'Strategies for enhancing informal and incidental learning'.

1 Investigate metaphors and images

Our images and metaphors represent the theories on which we base our thinking and action. They act as an ordering and reference system. To understand how our processing of information works towards development of our personal systems of knowledge, we need to understand this system and the contents of it. Access to this understanding is either through reflection or by more direct observation of our actions and reactions in relation to events and objects. With greater understanding of the image/metaphor system that we use, we can reject it, modify it or retain it with greater understanding.

2 Recognize assumptions that we have made about people or situations

We have to make rapid assumptions about people and situations in order to manage in busy and everyday lives. These assumptions might not always be accurate but it is often easier to retain the original view despite evidence that it is not or is no longer appropriate. If, for example, a person is said to be difficult to get on with, to avoid cognitive dissonance, we may make assumptions about that person to justify the rumour, rather than judge her afresh. It is comfortable to have evidence that points in a consistent direction. These assumptions can be the subject of reflection. We thus reframe our view.

3 Question and challenge familiar situations

When a situation is new or unfamiliar, we are more able to question and challenge it in order to understand it. Familiar situations are apt to evoke automatic judgements and unconsidered responses. One means of reframing assumptions and reactions is to see situations as if it they are unfamiliar and to problematize them, asking naïve questions. One method of doing this is to describe the situation as if one were seeing it for the first time. It may be helpful to write about it in the present tense. Leave the writing for a day or two and then return to it and write down as many questions about it as you can think of (brainstorm for questions), not trying to answer them straight away – leaving it again for a day or two more. Another method is to work with another person who acts as a facilitator. You describe the event while the other simply listens. The other then asks questions, particularly naïve and simple questions. These two methods may be combined so that the facilitator reads a written account and prepares questions that may be written or oral.

4 Create a situation for review and reflection

Counselling and therapy are means of reviewing and reflecting on present and past events and their relationship to the future. People tend only to 'go into' therapy and counselling from a state of being down or negative, rather than use such deliberate tactics in order to reconsider and rethink work or home events that are apparently normal. Mentoring, self-help groups or learning groups can be situations for the opportunities to learn to see things in a different and transformative manner.

© RoutledgeFalmer (2004)

5 Listen to the views of others

There is often a tendency to assume that others see events, people and organizations in the same way as we do. Engineering situations in which people
can share attitudes enables the possibility of recognizing the range of view
that can exist. Discussion of perceptions of an event that has been experienced
by several people can be a helpful manner of eliciting such sharing. A start for
this work can be that everyone develops a concept map (see Chapter 10).

6 Take a wider view

There is a tendency to focus on the day-to-day events. It is possible to view
events at different levels of magnification. There is a tendency in thinking
about an event to easily become caught up in the detail of small points.
We could see this form of viewing as increased magnification. What we
manage less well is to see events in longer-term contexts. Without this perspective, we cannot see the patterns and cycles of events, or monitor the flow
of feelings. A method of working with this in reflective mode is to conceive of
periods of time in which life (emotions/events/relationships – the personal
aspects of life) have felt as if there is a common thread (e.g., a week, a
month). Think back over that time and write/draw or in other ways, depict
the characteristics of that period. Monitor every so often whether a period
continues or if there is a new period (based on Progoff, 1975).

Resource 12

An exercise on judgement

*Developed as the basis of other work by Jenny Moon,
University of Exeter*

Two lovers lived in towns that were separated by a large hot desert. One
was called Victoria and the other, Albert. Though they e-mailed each other
passionately, it was really Victoria who wanted to cross the desert to Albert
but the desert was too dry and hot for her to walk across it. One of her neigh-
bours, Fred, had an ancient Land Rover and she asked him to take her over to
Albert. He said he would do so if she gave him the gold bracelet that only
recently had been sent to her by Albert. She refused because she knew
Albert would be devastated if she was not wearing the bracelet and, besides,
it had belonged to his mother who was now dead. It could not be replaced.
So she went to her so-called friend Archibald and explained the situation but
he said he could not or would not help. She was now desperate and went
back to Fred and very sadly gave him her bracelet, which he took once he
had driven her over the desert and delivered her to Albert's house.

Victoria then had to explain the loss of the bracelet to Albert. Albert
responded furiously, telling her she could have no place in his life. In despera-
tion, she called one of his friends, George, on her mobile. George was deeply
saddened at the situation and marched straight round to Albert's house and
beat him up. Victoria watched this process with delight.

Resource 13

Footprints

This exercise is devised by Jenny Moon, modified from an original idea in Progoff (1975).

Rationale

This exercise is modified from the 'Stepping stones' exercise of Progoff (1975). The principal aim of the exercise is to 'jog' or as Progoff says 'loosen' memory about a particular topic. Any topic at all can be the subject matter, for example, it can enable the exploration by individuals and groups of experiences such as 'being a learner' or the development of capacities such as 'skills', and so on.

The exercise is particularly valuable for:

- exploring experiences or experiences of something (such as 'learning', feeling 'cared for' or 'teaching'). The topic might be the subject of current or future work for example, in learning journals;
- expanding personal perspectives on some topic or issue;
- finding subject matter for story writing – for creative writing or for professional development or other academic purposes;
- the generation of subject matter for personal skills exercises such as the giving of presentations;
- enabling the sharing of ideas in a group about a specific topic;
- group development. For shy or uninvolved participants in a group it provides a situation in which everyone will have a turn to make an oral

contribution from written notes about familiar material in a light and usually creative atmosphere.

It is an enjoyable and usually enlightening exercise that tends to generate good feeling and energy. It can serve to energise a group after lunch, for example. It can be run many times even on the same topic because beyond the obvious first few memories that a person retrieves on a topic, different memories will emerge on different occasions. This is an interesting aspect of the exploration involved.

The equipment needed is a paper and pen each. To do this exercise properly takes around 40 minutes and it can be done with large numbers with space enough to form small (self-managed) groups and to be able to hear each other speak within those groups.

The exercise

After the introduction of the topic to be explored, the first part of the exercise is the individual writing of a number of lists, each of about seven items. Participants are asked to list around seven memories of the chosen topic in chronological order – so they are asked to start with the earliest memory and then to move forward towards their present age in sequence. They are asked to write a phrase, or a few words on the paper that will enable them to recall the memory later (e.g., 'The time when I learnt to ride a bike'). They should be reassured that they will not be asked to reveal to anyone anything that they do not want to say.

While the lists are being written, it is likely that memories will occur that are previous in sequence to where participants have reached in their current list and they are told to hold onto that memory for the next list. In this way, over a period of 10 to 15 minutes, participants write a series of lists.

Sometimes people will begin to talk about their memories before or as they write them. They should be dissuaded from talking. A calm and meditative atmosphere works best. It is very rewarding at this stage of the exercise. The lively part of the exercise is for the second part of sharing memories.

The list-writing is stopped after what seems to be a reasonable period as judged from watching the behaviour of the participants. Nearly all should have written at least two lists. Participants are then asked to form into groups of around six. Within the group and in turn each participant briefly shares the details of one of her memories from the lists written. There is no need to be chronological – the memory can be drawn from any time. Depending on circumstances, it is wise to ask participants to limit their sharing to a set time such as 4 minutes each to start with. This guards against 'long-windedness'. Once each member of the group has shared one memory, there might be a second round – and more.

This stage of the exercise tends to involve good listening, and often merriment as diverse memories are shared. The rationale for this element of the exercise is that as the memories of others are unearthed, they will stimulate new memories in each individual, in this way, generating many more memories than would have been achieved in the first stage of the exercise. The new memories may be quite unexpected (and sometimes a quick private note may be made of them).

After a period of sharing memories, the group is asked to disperse again and individuals are asked to return to their lists and again put the new memories that have emerged as a result of the sharing, into lists, as before. Getting groups to break up at this stage can be difficult.

The outcome of this exercise for each individual will be a series of recollections about the topic chosen. Some may be memories that have not been considered for a long time. Depending on the purpose of the exercise, one of the memories may be developed into a story, presentation or an issue for further reflection in a learning journal (for example). Alternatively, the whole list may be taken as an expression of personal experience to be explored further in the same or other contexts.

Instructions to give at the beginning:

- The topic is given by the facilitator.
- The task is to write lists of around seven memories of the topic, in chronological order.
- When memories arise that do not fit into the current sequence, they are used to seed another list where they are put into the correct chronological order.
- No-one else will see the lists, and no-one will be asked to share anything that she does not wish to share.
- After a period of time, the list writing will stop and participants will be asked to share memories, in turn, in a group. The idea of this is that other people's memories will generate new memories for the individual.
- For vulnerable groups and/or some topics that might be explored, it may be useful to say that the exercise could give rise to uncomfortable memories, and in this case a member of staff is available afterwards for consultation. However, because the material shared is totally under the control of individuals, this is not a likely event.

Resource 14

Poetry as a form of capturing experience

The Pub Singer

He took the seat, fresh-faced, took to the spotlight.
He shuffled and settled – then with long fingers
And the work of strings, forged glittering streams of sound.

They looked. They listened. For one moment
He had them. For a moment, the fire held back its flicker.
It was a sensitive birth to which they gave those seconds.

He took them among byways and flowers of new love,
Drew ships sailing on cut glass seas. Words were threads
Of life that danced a fine line between delight and the dark.

And in the half-dark, the half-pissed resumed their chatter.
There was a rise of laughter, voices, a spill of coins
Across the bar; glass chinked in the beery air.

Now his ships roared by as powerboats. His words
Thundered on highways obliterating flowers.

Three claps went with him as he slipped from the light,
The ships sunk and words hanging off their lines.

(Jenny Moon, 2003)

Glossary

accommodation   the process of modification of new material of learning or current cognitive structure (qv) in a learning process that results in change of conceptions (i.e., understanding or state of knowledge). Accommodation follows the process of assimilation (qv).

appresentation   the process in which an element of an external experience stimulates a more complete or richer internal experience of the 'whole' of that thing on the basis of the prior experience of it. For example, seeing a familiar face triggers an internal experience of the whole person.

assimilation   the processing of new material of learning such that learning occurs. The process of assimilation is guided by the current internal experience (prior experiences in current state of cognitive structure (qv)) of the object of learning, and any given current purposes for the learning. In meaningful learning, assimilation is accompanied by the process of accommodation (qv).

cognitive structure – the network of concepts, emotions, knowledge, experiences, beliefs, etc. that guides a person's functioning at a particular time.

conception of (structure of) knowledge   this term relates to a suggested developmental sequence of increasing understanding of the nature of knowledge generally from the concept of there being only right and wrong ideas to the acceptance of the constructed nature of knowledge.

constructivism   a theoretical position in education/psychology that holds that in the process of learning, an individual constructs a view of an object through the processes of accommodation (qv) and assimilation (qv) giving rise to a cognitive structure (qv) that is unique and that guides the processes of further learning. In this way, the individual has a unique view of the world based on her own processes of learning.

distinction of figure from the ground   being able to discern the appropriate cues for learning for a particular purpose from other 'background' or non-relevant stimuli.

external experience the relevant experience of an object/idea (material of learning (qv)) that is to be learnt by the learner at a given moment. See also internal experience.

frame of reference the 'beam' of awareness or attention that is directed by the learner within a learning situation. Within that focus, the distinction of specific figures from ground (qv) is made. Frame of reference may concern the object of learning or the conceptions used by the learner to interpret the learning situation.

ill-structured ill-structured problems have no 'right or wrong' answer, but require reasoning and personal judgement. Ethical issues provide a good example.

internal experience the cognitive structure or sum of prior experiences relevant to an object within a particular context and at a particular time. Internal experience may be the material of learning for reflective learning.

learning and teaching These words have separate meanings. Learning refers solely to the action of a learner and concerns the processing of information both from outside the learner (external experience – qv) and a reprocessing of ideas already possessed by the learner (working with internal experience – qv). Learning may or may not imply action. Teaching, and other words such as instruction, indicate the action of another to make learning easier or more appropriate for the learner through guidance or through presentation of a simplified or helpfully sequenced version of the material of teaching (qv). Mediation of learning experience (qv) is a generic term used for this process in this book.

learning challenge the challenge that a learning task effects for the learner.

level descriptors these are guides to the level of learning expected to be attained by learners at a particular stage in formal education. The SEEC (qv) descriptors are commonly in use and cover post-16 levels in English, Welsh and Northern Irish education.

material of learning – material that is learnt (see learning and teaching) by a learner.

material of teaching material that is taught (see learning and teaching) by a teacher.

mediation of learning experience any form of secondary experience in which the material of teaching is simplified or recodified to create a more certain situation for a learner or to challenge the learner and thereby improve her learning.

relevance a concept that concerns the noticing and perception of the appropriate elements in current external experience for the current learning purposes.

representation of learning the manner in which learning is demonstrated or utilized in, for example, action, in written tasks, orally, etc. We assess the representation of learning, not learning itself.

SEEC Southern English Consortium for Credit Accumulation and Transfer.

teaching   See learning and teaching.

teaching challenge   the challenge for the teacher in conveying the material clearly and appropriately to a learner, taking account of the current state of the learner's knowledge. The same material of teaching may pose more or less of a learning challenge to different learners. See 'learning challenge'.

variation   the change in experience which can prompt new learning. Variation provides new material of learning – in order for there to be new learning, there needs to be variation in the experience. On this basis, learning is a process of experiencing variation and choosing to accommodate to that variation.

Bibliography

Andresen, L., Boud, D. and Cohen, R. (2000) 'Experience-based learning', in *Understanding Adult Education and Training*, Sydney: Allen and Unwin, pp. 225–39.

Angelo, T. and Cross, K. (1990) *Classroom Assessment Techniques*, San Francisco: Jossey-Bass.

Ashton-Warner, S. (1985a) *Spinster*, London: Virago.

Ashton-Warner, S. (1985b) *Teacher*, London: Virago.

Atkins, S. and Murphy, K. (1993) 'Reflection: a review of the literature', *Journal of Advanced Nursing*, 18, 1188–92.

Atkinson, T. and Claxton, G. (2002) *The Intuitive Practitioner*, Milton Keynes: Open University Press.

Ausubel, D. (1960) 'The use of advance organisers in the learning and retention of meaningful verbal material', *Journal of Educational Psychology*, 51, 267–72.

Ausubel, D. and Robinson, F. (1969) *School Learning*, London: Holt, Rhinehart and Winston.

Bannister, D. and Fransella, F. (1974) *Inquiring Man*, Harmondsworth: Penguin.

Barnett, R. (1997) *Higher Education: A Critical Business*, Milton Keynes: SRHE/Open University Press.

Barnett, R. (1999) 'Learning to work and working to learn', in D. Boud and J. Garrick (eds) *Understanding Learning at Work*, London: Routledge.

Baxter Magolda, M. (1992) *Knowing and Reasoning in College Students: Gender-related Patterns in Students, Intellectual Development*, San Francisco: Jossey-Bass.

Baxter Magolda, M. (1994) 'Post-college experiences and epistemology', *Review of Higher Education*, 18 (1), 25–44.

Baxter Magolda, M. (1996) 'Epistemological development in graduate and professional education', *Review of Higher Education*, 19 (3), 283–304.

Beard, C. and Wilson, J. (2002) *The Power of Experiential Learning*, London: Kogan Page.

Beaty, E., Dall'Alba, G. and Marton, F. (1997) 'The personal experience of learners in higher education: changing views and enduring perspectives', in A. Sutherland (ed.) *Adult Learning: A Reader*, London: Kogan Page.

Beckett, D. (1999) 'Past the guru and up the garden path: the new organic management learning', in D. Boud and J. Garrick (eds) *Understanding Learning at Work*, London: Routledge.

Belenky, M., Clinchy, B., Goldberger, R. and Tarule, J. (1986) *Women's Ways of Knowing*, New York: Basic Books.

Bennett, N., Dunne, E. and Carre, C. (2000) *Skill Development in Higher Education and Employment*, Milton Keynes: SRHE/Open University Press.

Biggs, J. (1993) 'From theory to practice: a cognitive systems approach', *Higher Education Research and Development*, 12, 73–85.

Biggs, J. (1999) *Teaching for Quality Learning at University*, Buckingham: SRHE.

Biggs, J. and Collis, K. (1982) *Evaluating the Quality of Learning*, New York: Academic Press.

Boal, A. (1995) *'The Rainbow of Desire': The Boal Method of Theatre and Therapy*, London: Routledge.

Bolton, G. (1994) 'Stories at work: fictional–critical writing as a means of professional development', *British Educational Research Journal*, 20 (1), 55–68.

Bolton, G. (1999) *The Therapeutic Potential of Creative Writing*, London: Jessica Kingsley.

Boreham, N. (1987) 'Learning from experience in diagnostic problem-solving', in J. Richardson, M. Eysenck and D. Warren Piper (eds) *Student Learning: Research in Education and Cognitive Psychology*, Milton Keynes: SRHE/Open University Press.

Boud, D. (1995) *Enhancing Learning Through Self Assessment*, London: Kogan Page.

Boud, D. (2001) 'Knowledge at work: issues of learning', in D. Boud and N. Soloman (eds) *Work-based Learning*, Milton Keynes: SRHE/Open University Press, pp. 34–43.

Boud, D., Cohen, R. and Walker, D. (2000) 'Understanding learning from experience', in D. Boud, R. Cohen and D. Walker (eds) *Using Experience for Learning*, Milton Keynes: SRHE/Open University Press, pp. 1–18.

Boud, D. and Falchikov, N. (1989) 'Qualitative studies of student self-assessment in higher education: a critical analysis of findings', *Higher Education*, 18 (5), 529–49.

Boud, D. and Garrick, J. (1999) *Understanding Learning at Work*, London: Routledge.

Boud, D., Keogh, R. and Walker, D. (1985) *Reflection: Turning Experience into Learning*, London: Kogan Page.

Boud, D. and Miller, N. (1996) *Working with Experience*, London: Routledge.

Boud, D. and Walker, D. (1991) *Experience and Learning; Reflection at Work*, Geelong: Deakin University Press.

Boud, D. and Walker, D. (1998) 'Promoting reflection in professional courses: the challenge of context', *Studies in Higher Education*, 23(2), 191–206.

Boud, D. and Walker, D. (2000) 'Barriers to experience', in D. Boud, R. Cohen and D. Walker (eds) *Using Experience for Learning*, Milton Keynes: SRHE/Open University Press, pp. 73–86.

Bourner, T. and Flowers, S. (undated) 'Teaching and learning methods in higher education: a glimpse of the future', http://www.bbk.ac.uk/asd/bourne.htm (accessed February 2003).

Bowden, J. and Marton, F. (1998) *The University of Learning: Beyond Quality and Competence in Higher Education*, London: Kogan Page.

Boyd, E. and Fales, A. (1983) 'Reflective learning: key to learning from experience', *Journal of Human Psychology*, 23, (2) 94–117.

Boydell, T. (1976) *Experiential Learning*, Manchester: University of Manchester Press.

Brah, A. and Hoy, J. (1989) 'Experiential learning: a new orthodoxy?', in S. Warner Weil and I. McGill (eds) *Making Sense of Experiential Learning*, Milton Keynes: SRHE/Open University Press.

Brew, A. (2000) 'Unlearning through experience', in D. Boud, R. Cohen and D. Walker (eds) *Using Experience for Learning*, Milton Keynes: SRHE/Open University Press.

Brockbank, A. and McGill, I. (1998) *Facilitating Reflective Learning in Higher Education*, Milton Keynes: SRHE/Open University Press.

Brown, S. (1999) 'Assessing practice', in S. Brown and A. Glasner (eds) *Assessment Matters in Higher Education*, Milton Keynes: SRHE/Open University Press.

Brown, S. and Glasner, A. (eds) (1999) *Assessment Matters in Higher Education*, Milton Keynes: SRHE/Open University Press.

Brownjohn, S. (1981) *Does it Have to Rhyme?* Sevenoaks: Hodder and Stoughton.

Brownjohn, S. (1982) *What Rhymes with Secret?* Sevenoaks: Hodder and Stoughton.

Bruner, J. (1990) *Acts of Meaning*, Cambridge, MA: Harvard University Press.

Burnard, P. (1991) *Experiential Learning in Action*, Avebury: Ashgate.

Burns, S. and Bulman, C. (eds) (2000) *Reflective Practice in Nursing*, 2nd edn, Oxford: Blackwell Science.

Caley, L. and Hendry, E. (2000) *Frameworks for Effective Work-related Learning*, Cambridge: University of Cambridge Press.

Candy, P. (1991) *Self Direction for Lifelong Learners*, San Francisco: Jossey-Bass.

Carey, S. (1988) 'Reorganisation of knowledge in the course of acquisition', in S. Strauss (ed.) *Ontology, Phylogeny and Historical Development*, Norwood, NJ: Ablex Publishing, pp. 1–27.

Carlson, R. (1997) *Experienced Cognition*, Hillsdale, NJ: Lawrence Erlbaum Associates.

Carter, R. (1985) 'A taxonomy of objectives for professional education', *Studies in Higher Education*, 10 (2), 135 .

Cell, E. (1984) *Learning to Learn from Experience*, Albany, NY: State University of New York Press.

Chi, M., Bassock, M., Lewis, M., Reimann, P. and Glaser R. (1989) 'Self-explanations: how students study and use examples in learning to solve problems', *Cognitive Science*, 13, 145–82.

Chi, M., de Leeuw, N., Chiu, M. and LaVancher, C. (1994) 'Eliciting self-explanations improves understanding', *Cognitive Science*, 18, 439–77.

Chickering, A. (1977) *Experience and Learning*, New York: Change Magazine Press.

Claxton, G. (2000) *The Intuitive Practitioner*, Milton Keynes: Open University Press.

Coffield, F. (1998) 'Introduction: new forms of learning in the workplace', in F. Coffield, *Learning at Work*, London: The Policy Press.

Collings, J. and Watton, P. (2001) *JEWELS Project: Learning through Independent Work Experience: Final Report*, JEWELS@exeter.ac.uk

Connelly, F. and Clandinin, D. (1990) 'Stories of experience and narrative inquiry', *Educational Researcher*, 19 (4) 2–14.

Cowan, J. (1998) *On Becoming an Innovative University Teacher*, Milton Keynes: SRHE/Open University Press.

Criticos, C. (1989) 'Media, praxis and empowerment', in S. Warner Weil and I. McGill (eds) *Making Sense of Experiential Learning*, Milton Keynes: SRHE/Open University Press.

Criticos, C. (2000) 'Experiential learning and social transformation for a post-apartheid learning future', in D. Boud, R. Cohen and D. Walker (eds) *Using Experience for Learning*, Milton Keynes: SRHE.

Csikszentmihalyi, M. (1990) *Flow: The Psychology of Optimal Experience*, New York: Harper and Row.

Cunningham, P. (1983) 'Helping students to extract meaning from experience', in R. Smith (ed.) *Helping Adults to Learn How to Learn: New Directions for Continuing Education*, San Francisco: Jossey-Bass.

Dart, B. (1997) 'Helping students to extract meaning from experience', in R. Smith (ed.) *Helping Adults to Learn How to Learn: New Directions for Continuing Education*, San Francisco: Jossey-Bass.

Dart, B., Boulton-Lewis, G., Brownlee, J. and McCrindle, A. (1998) 'Change in knowledge of learning and teaching through journal writing', *Research Papers in Education* 13 (3), 291–318.

Davies, J. and Easterby-Smith, M. (1984) 'Learning and developing from work experiences', *Journal of Management Studies*, 21 (2), 167–83.

Davies, L. (2001) Personal communication.

Dennison, B. and Kirk, R. (1990) *Do, Review, Learn, Apply*, Oxford: Blackwell.

Denzin, N. and Lincoln, Y. (2000) *Handbook of Qualitative Research*, London: Sage Publications.

Desler, D. (1990) 'Conceptual mapping: drawing charts of the mind', in J. Mezirow (ed.) *Fostering Critical Reflection in Adulthood*, San Francisco: Jossey-Bass.

Dewey, J. (1938) *Experience and Education*, New York: Collier.

Dewulf, S. and Baillie, C. (1999) *Creativity in Art, Science, and Engineering: How to Foster Creativity*, London: Imperial College of Science.

Donaldson, M. (1992) *Human Minds: An Exploration*, Harmondsworth: Penguin.

Edelman, G. (1992) *Bright Air, Brilliant Fire: On the Matter of Mind*, London: Penguin.

Egan, G. (1990) *The Skilled Helper*, Pacific Grove, CA: Brooks and Cole.

Eisner, E. (1982) *Cognition and Curriculum: A Basis for Deciding What to Teach*, New York: Longman.

Eisner, E. (1991) 'Forms of understanding and the future of education', *Educational Researcher* 22, 5–11.

Elbow, P. (1973) *Writing without Teachers*, New York: Oxford University Press.

Entwistle, N. (1988) *Styles of Learning*, Edinburgh: David Fulton.

Entwistle, N. (1996) 'Recent research on student learning and the learning environment', in J. Tait and P. Knight (eds) *The Management of the Learning Environment*, London: SEDA/Kogan Page.

Entwistle, N. and Entwistle, A. (1992) 'Experience of understanding in revising for degree examinations', *Learning and Instruction*, 2, 1–22.

Entwistle, N. and Entwistle, A. (1997) 'Revision and the experience of understanding', in F. Marton, D. Hounsell and N. Entwistle (eds) *The Experience of Learning*, Edinburgh: Scottish Academic Press.

Entwistle, N. and Ramsden, P. (1983) *Understanding Student Learning*, Beckenham: Croom Helm.

Entwistle, N., McCune, V. and Hounsell, D. (2002) *Approaches to Studying and Perceptions of University Teaching-Learning Environments: Concepts, Measures and Preliminary Findings*, ETL Project (ESRC), Occasional Report 1, September.

Entwistle N. and Walker, P. (2002) 'Strategic alertness and expanded awareness within sophisticated conceptions of teaching', in N. Hativa and P. Goodyear (eds)

Teacher Thinking, Beliefs and Knowledge in Higher Education, Dordrecht: Kluwer Academic Publishers, pp. 15–39.

Epstein, S. (1993) *Constructive Thinking* Westport, CT: Praeger.

Eraut, M. (1994) *Developing Professional Knowledge and Competence*, London: Falmer Press.

Eraut, M. (1999) 'Non-formal learning, implicit learning and tacit knowledge', in F. Coffield (ed.) *Informal Learning*, London: The Polity Press.

Eraut, M. (2000) 'Non-formal learning, implicit learning and tacit knowledge in professional work', in F. Coffield (Ed.) *The Necessity of Informal Learning*, London: The Polity Press, pp. 12–31.

Eraut, M., Alderton, J. and Senker, P. (1998) 'Learning from other people at work', in F. Coffield (ed.) *Learning at Work*, London: The Polity Press.

Ertmer, P. and Newby, T. (1996) 'The expert learner: strategic, self-regulated and reflective', *Instructional Science*, 24, 1–24.

Evans, N. (1992) 'Linking personal learning and public recognition', in J. Mulligan and C. Griffin (eds) *Empowerment through Experiential Learning*, London: Kogan Page, pp. 85–93.

Evans, N. (2000) *Experiential Learning Around the World: Employability and the Global Economy*, London: Jessica Kingsley.

Evison, R. and Horobin R. (1983) *How to Change Yourself and Your World: A Manual of Co-counselling*, Sheffield: Co-counselling Phoenix.

Fazey, J. and Marton, F. (2002) 'Understanding the space of experiential variation', *Active Learning in Higher Education*, 3 (3), 234–50.

Fenwick, T. (2000) 'Expanding conceptions of experiential learning: a review of five contemporary perspectives on cognition', *Adult Education Quarterly*, 50 (4), 243–72.

Ferry, N. and Ross-Gordon, J. (1998) 'An inquiry into Schön's epistemology of practice: exploring links between experiencing and workplace practice', *Adult Education Quarterly*, 48, 98–112.

Festinger, L. (1957) *A Theory of Cognitive Dissonance*, Stanford, CA: Stanford University Press.

Field, M. (1952) *A Life of One's Own*, Harmondsworth: Penguin.

Flavell, J. (1979) 'Metacognitive aspects of problem-solving behaviour', in L. Resnick (ed.) *The Nature of Intelligence*, Hillsdale, NJ: Lawrence Erlbaum.

Fraser, W. (1995) *Learning from Experience*, Leicester: NIACE.

Friere, P, (1970) *Pedagogy of the Oppressed*, Harmondsworth: Penguin.

Fullerton, H. (2002) 'Moving forward: linking work experience to progress files and personal development planning', in P. Watton, J. Collings and J. Moon (eds) *Work Experience: An Evolving Picture*, SEDA Paper 114, Birmingham: SEDA.

Fulwiler, T. (1987) *The Journal Book*, Portsmouth: Heinemann.

Gardner, H. (1983) *Frames of Mind*, New York: Basic Books.

George, J. and Cowan, J. (1999) *A Handbook of Techniques for Formative Evaluation*, London: Kogan Page.

Gibbs, G. (1988) *Learning by Doing: A Guide to Teaching and Learning Methods*, Birmingham: SCED.

Goleman, D. (1995) *Emotional Intelligence*, New York: Bantam Books.

Goleman, D. (1998) *Working with Emotional Intelligence*, London: Bloomsbury.

Gosling, D. and Moon, J. (2001) *How to Write Learning Outcomes and Assessment Criteria*, London: SEEC Office, University of East London.

Green, A. (1995) 'Experiential learning and teaching – a critical evaluation of an enquiry which used phenomenological method', *Nurse Education Today*, 15, 420–6.

Greenaway, R. (2003) 'Reviewing skills training', www.reviewing.co.uk (accessed November 2003).

Greeno, J. (1997) 'On claims that answer the wrong questions', *Educational Researcher*, 26 (1), 5–17.

Griffin, C. (1992) 'Absorbing experiential learning', in J. Mulligan, and C. Griffin (eds) *Empowerment through Experiential Learning*, London: Kogan Page, pp. 31–36.

Hadwin, A. and Winne, P. (1996) 'Study strategies have meager support: a review, with recommendations for implementation', *Journal of Higher Education*, 67 (6), 1–17.

Hager, P. (1999) 'Finding a good theory of workplace learning', in D. Boud and J. Garrick (eds) *Understanding Learning at Work*, London: Routledge.

Harrison, R. (1991) *Training and Development*, London: Institute of Personnel Management.

Hart, M. (1990) 'Liberation through consciousness-raising', in J. Mezirow and associates (eds) *Fostering Critical Reflection in Adulthood: A Guide to Transformative and Emancipatory Learning*, San Francisco: Jossey-Bass.

Hartland, J. (1982) *Medical and Dental Hypnosis*, London: Bailliere and Tindall.

Harvey, L., Geall, V. and Moon, S. (1998) *Work Experience: Expanding Opportunities for Undergraduates*, Birmingham: UCE, Centre for Research into Quality.

Harvey L. and Knight, P. (1996) *Transforming Higher Education*, Milton Keynes: SRHE/Open University Press.

Hatton, N. and Smith, D. (1995) 'Reflection in teacher education – towards definition and implementation', *Teaching and Teacher Education*, 11 (1), 33–49.

Heller, A. (1984) *Everyday Learning*, London: Routledge.

Henry, J. (1989) 'Meaning and practice in experiential learning', in S. Warner Weil and I. McGill (eds) *Making Sense of Experiential Learning*, Milton Keynes: SRHE/Open University Press.

Henze, R. (1992) *Informal Teaching and Learning: A Study of Everyday Cognition in a Greek Community*, Hillsdale, NJ: Lawrence Erlbaum.

Heron, J, (1989) *The Facilitator's Handbook*, London: Kogan Page.

Heron, J. (1992) 'The politics of facilitation: balancing facilitator authority and learner autonomy', in J. Mulligan and C. Griffin (eds) *Empowerment through Experiential Learning*, London: Kogan Page, pp. 66–75.

Hesse, H. (1972) *Wandering*, London: Pan Books.

Hettich, P. (1976) 'The journal, an autobiographical approach to learning', *Teaching of Psychology*, 3 (2), 60–1.

Hettich, P. (1990) 'Journal writing, old fare or nouvelle cuisine?, *Teaching of Psychology*, 17 (1), 36–9.

Hinett, K. (2002) 'Improving learning though reflection', parts I and II, ILTHE members sites, http://www.ilt.ac.uk

Hinett, K. (2003) 'Improving learning through reflection', parts I and II, http://www.ilt.ac.uk (accessed April 2003)

Hoadley-Maidment, E. (2000) 'From personal experience to reflective practitioner', in M. Lea and B. Stierer (eds) *Student Writing in Higher Education*, Milton Keynes: SRHE/Open University Press.

Holly, M. (1991) *Keeping a Personal-Professional Journal*, Victoria: Deakin University Press.

Honey, P. and Mumford, A, (1992) *Manual of Learning Styles*, Maidenhead: Honey Publications.

Houle, C. (1976) 'Deep traditions of experiential learning', in M. Keeton (ed.) *Experiential Learning, Rationale, Characteristics and Assessment*, San Francisco: Jossey-Bass.

Hounsell, D. (1977) 'Contrasting conceptions of essay-writing', in F. Martin, D. Hounsell and N. Entwistle (eds) *The Experience of Learning*, Edinburgh: Academic Press.

Hughes, T. (1967) *Poetry in the Making*, London: Faber and Faber.

Hutton, M. (1989) 'Learning from action: a conceptual framework', in S. Warner Weil and M. McGill (eds) *Making Sense of Experiential Learning*, Milton Keynes: SRHE/Open University Press, pp. 50–9.

Jackson, A. (1995) 'Translator's introduction', in A.H. Boal (ed.) *'The Rainbow of Desire': The Boal Method of Theatre and Therapy*, London: Routledge.

Jackson, N. (2003) 'Nurturing creativity through an imaginative curriculum', e-mail communication to the Imaginative Curriculum Project, LTSN Generic Centre.

Jarvis, P. (1987) *Adult Learning in the Social Context*, London: Croom Helm.

Jarvis, P. (1992) *The Paradoxes of Learning*, San Francisco: Jossey-Bass.

Jasper, M. (1995) 'The portfolio workbook as a strategy for student-centred nursing', *Nurse Education Today*, 15, 446–51.

Jasper, M. (1998) 'Assessing and improving student outcomes through reflective writing', in C. Rust (ed.) *Improving Student Learning, Improving Student Learning Outcomes*, Oxford: OSCLD, Oxford Brookes University, pp. 1–15.

Jones, J. (2002) 'Reflective learning: helping learners and teachers to see more clearly: the learner's perspective', *Learning and Teaching*, 2 (2), 4–6.

Kelly, G. (1955) *The Psychology of Personal Construct Theory*, Neew York: Norton.

Kember, D. (1996) 'The intention to memorise and understand: another approach to learning', *Higher Education*, 31, 341–54.

Kember, D., Jones, A., Loke, A., McKay, J., Sinclair, K., Harrison, J., Webb, C., Wong, M. and Yeung, E. (1999) 'Determining the level of reflective thinking from student's written journals using a coding scheme based on Mezirow', *International Journal of Lifelong Learning*, 18 (1), 18–30.

Kember, D., Leung, D. with Jones, A., Loke, A., McKay, J., Harrison, T., Webb, C., Wong, F. and Yeung, E. (2000) 'Development of a questionnaire to measure the level of reflective thinking', *Assessment and Evaluation in Higher Education*, 25 (4), 370–80.

Kim, H. (1999) 'Critical reflective inquiry for knowledge development in nursing practice', *Journal of Advanced Nursing*, 29 (5), 1205–12.

King, P. and Kitchener, K. (1994) *Developing Reflective Judgement*, San Francisco: Jossey-Bass.

Knowles, M. (1980) *The Modern Practice of Adult Education*, Chicago: Follet.

Knowles Z., Borrie, A. and Stewart, M. (2001) 'Embedding reflection within a degree programme', *Learning and Teaching Press*, 1 (2), 8–10.

Kolb, D. (1984) *Experiential Learning as the Science of Learning and Development*, Englewood Cliffs, NJ: Prentice Hall.

Kolb, D. and Fry R. (1975) 'Toward an applied theory of experiential learning', in C. Cooper (ed.) *Theories of Group Processes*, New York: John Wiley and Sons.

Kuhn, D., Amsel, E. and O'Loughlin, M. (1988) *The Development of Scientific Thinking Skills*, London: Academic Press.

Laski, M. (1961) *Ecstasy*, London: Cresset Press.

Laurillard, D. (1993) *Rethinking University Teaching*, London: Routledge.

Lave, J. and Wenger, E. (1991) *Situated Learning, Legitimate Peripheral Participation*, Cambridge: Cambridge University Press.

Lawlor, M. and Handley, P. (1996) *The Creative Trainer*, Maidenhead: McGraw-Hill.

Lennon, K. and Whitford, M. (1994) *Knowing the Difference: Feminist Perspectives in Epistemology*, London: Routledge.

Lewis, M. (1990) 'Thinking and feeling in the elephant's tail', in M. Schwebel, C. Maher and N. Fagley (eds) *Promoting Cognitive Growth over the Lifetime*, Hillsdale, NJ: Lawrence Erlbaum, pp. 89–110.

Little, B. (1998) *Developing Key Skills through Work Placement*, London: Quality Support Centre.

Lowy, A. (2002) 'Reflective practice and web-based learning', *Learning and Teaching Press*, 1 (2), 10–11.

Lucas, B. (2001) *Power Up Your Mind*, London: Nicholas Brealey.

Lyons, J. (1999) 'Reflective education for professional practice: discovering knowledge from experience', *Nurse Education Today*, 19, 29–34.

McAlpine, L. and Weston, C. (2002) 'Reflection: improving teaching and students learning', in N. Hativa and P. Goodyear (eds) *Teacher Thinking, Beliefs and Knowledge in Higher Education*, Dordrecht: Kluwer Academic Publishers, pp. 59–77.

McDrury, J. and Alterio, M. (2002) *Learning through Storytelling*, Palmerston, New Zealand: Dunmore Press.

McGill, I and Beaty, L. (1992) *Action Learning*, London: Kogan Page.

McGill, I. and Warner Weil, S. (1989) 'Continuing the dialogue: new possibilities for experiential learning', in S. Warner Weil and I. McGill (eds) *Making Sense of Experiential Learning*, Milton Keynes: SRHE/Open University Press, pp. 245–74.

Mackintosh, C. (1998) 'Reflection: a flawed strategy for the nursing profession', *Nurse Education Today*, 18, 553–7.

Marshall, I. and Cooper, L. (2001) 'Earning academic credit for part-time work', in D. Boud and N. Soloman (eds) *Work-based Learning*, Milton Keynes: SRHE/Open University Press, pp. 184–200.

Marsick, V. and Watkins K. (1990) *Informal and Incidental Learning in the Workplace*, London: Routledge.

Marton, F. (1994) 'Phenonemography', in T. Husen and N. Postlethwaite (eds) *International Encyclopedia of Education*, Oxford: Pergamon, pp. 4424–9.

Marton, F. and Booth, S. (1997) *Learning and Awareness*, Hillsdale, NJ: Lawrence Erlbaum Associates.

Marton, F. and Saljo, R. (1984) 'Approaches to learning', in F. Marton, D. Hounsell and N. Entwistle (eds) *The Experience of Learning*, Edinburgh: Scottish Academic Press.

Marton, F., Hounsell, D. and Entwistle, N. (1997) *The Experience of Learning*, Edinburgh: Scottish Academic Press.

Mason, J. (2000) 'Learning from experience in mathematics', in D. Boud, R. Cohen and D.Walker (eds) *Using Experience for Learning*, Milton Keynes: SRHE/Open University Press.

Matthews, N., Nicholls, J., Corcoran, M. and Moylan, T. (2002) 'Adapting problem-based learning to non-vocational modules', *Learning and Teaching Press*, 2 (2), 16–18.

Meyers, C. (1986) *Teaching Students to Think Critically*, San Francisco: Jossey-Bass.

Mezirow, J. (1981) 'A critical theory of adult learning and education', *Adult Education*, 32 (1), 3–24.

Mezirow, J. (1991) *Transformative Dimensions of Adult Learning*, San Francisco: Jossey-Bass.

Mezirow, J. (1998) 'On critical reflection', *Adult Education Quarterly*, 48 (3), 185–99.

Michelson, E. (1996) 'Carnival, paranoia and experiential learning', *Studies in the Education of Adults*, 31 (2), 140–54.

Miller, A., Watts, A. and Jamieson, I. (1991) *Rethinking Work Experience*, London: Falmer.

Miller, C. and Parlett, M. (1974) *Up to the Mark*, Milton Keynes: SRHE/Open University Press.

Milner, M. (1957) *On Not Being Able to Paint*, London: Heinemann.

Milner, M. (1987) *Eternity's Sunrise: A Way of Keeping a Diary*, London: Virago.

Moon, J. (1999a) *Reflection in Learning and Professional Development*, London: Kogan Page.

Moon, J. (1999b) *Learning Journals: A Handbook for Academics, Students and Professional Development*, London: Kogan Page.

Moon, J. (2001a) *Short Courses and Workshops: Improving the Impact of Learning and Professional Development*, London: Kogan Page.

Moon, J. (2001b) 'Reflection in higher education learning'– a working paper commissioned by Norman Jackson for Personal Development Planning area of the LTSN website (www.ltsn.ac.uk/genericcentre/projects/pdp). Separately on the same site is an abbreviated version 'A Guide for Busy Academics', No. 4 Learning through reflection.

Moon, J. (2002a) *The Module and Programme Development Handbook: Linking Levels, Learning Outcomes and Assessment* London: Kogan Page.

Moon, J. (2002b) 'The academic rationale for work experience', in P. Watton, J. Collings and J. Moon (eds) *Work Experience: An Evolving Picture*, SEDA Paper 114, Birmingham: SEDA, pp. 57–61.

Moon, J. (2002c) 'Issues in the introduction of reflective writing to students – recording achievement', web-based journal – www. Recordingachievement.org.uk (members' section).

Moon, J. (2003) (In preparation) 'Reflection and employability', paper for LTSN website (www.LTSN.ac.uk /generic centre – follow links for employability).

Morgan, A. (1995) *Improving Your Students' Learning: Reflections on the Experience of Study*, London: Kogan Page.

Morgan, N. and Saxon, S. (1991) *Teaching Questioning and Learning*, London: Routledge.

Morrow Lindberg, A. (1983) *Gift from the Sea*, New York: Pantheon Books.

Mortiboys, A. (2002) *The Emotionally Intelligent Lecturer*, SEDA Special Paper 12, Birmingham: SEDA.

Mulligan, J. (1992) 'Internal processors in experiential learning', in J. Mulligan and C. Griffin (eds) *Empowerment through Experiential Learning*, London: Kogan Page.

Mulligan, J. (2000) 'Activating internal processes in experiential learning', in D. Boud, R. Cohen and D. Walker (eds) *Using Experience for Learning*, Milton Keynes: SRHE/Open University Press.

Mumford, A., Robinson, G. and Stradling, D. (undated) *Developing Directors*, London: MSC.

Mutch, A. (2003) 'Exploring the practice of feedback to students', *Active Learning in Higher Education*, 4 (1), 24–38.

Newman, M. (1999) *Maeler's Regard*, Sydney: Stewart Victor Publishing.

Noble, M. (2002) 'Accrediting experience', paper given at NUCCAT Annual Conference, November, 2002.

Odum, E. (1968) *Ecology*, New York: Holt, Rhinehard and Winston.

O'Reilly, D. (1989) 'On being an educational fantasy engineer: incoherence, "The Individual", and independent study', in S. Warner Weil and I. McGill (eds) *Making Sense of Experiential Learning*, Milton Keynes: SRHE/Open University Press.

O'Rourke, R. (1998) 'The learning journal: from chaos to coherence', *Assessment and Evaluation in Higher Education*, 23 (4), 403–14.

Pardoe, S. (2000) 'A question of attribution: the indeterminacy of learning from experience', in M. Lea and B. Stierer (eds) *Student Writing in Higher Education*, Milton Keynes: SRHE/Open University Press, pp. 123–45.

Perry, W. (1970) *Forms of Intellectual and Academic Developments in the College Years*, New York: Holt, Rhinehart and Winston.

Peters, R. (1966) *Ethics and Education*, London: George Allen and Unwin.

Piaget, J. (1971) *Biology and Knowledge*, Edinburgh: Edinburgh University Press.

Polanyi, M. (1969) *Knowing and Being*, edited by M. Grene, Chicago: University of Chicago Press.

Portwood, D. and Costley, C. (2000) *Work-based Learning and the University: New Perspectives and Practices*, SEDA paper 109, Birmingham: SEDA.

Postle, D. (2000) 'Putting the heart back into learning', in D. Boud, R. Cohen and D. Walker (eds) *Using Experience for Learning*, Milton Keynes: SRHE/Open University Press.

Progoff, I. (1975) *At an Intensive Journal Workshop*, London: Dialogue House Library.

Progoff, I. (1980) *The Process of Practice Mediation*, New York: Dialogue House Library.

Prosser, M. and Miller, R. (1989) 'The how and what of learning physics', *The European Journal of the Psychology of Education*, 4, 513–28.

Race, P. (2002) 'Evidencing reflection – putting the "w", into reflection', ESCALATE, LTSN, http://www.escalate.ac.uk/exchange/Reflection (accessed March 2003).

Rainer, T. (1978) *The New Diary*, Los Angeles: J.B. Tarcher Inc.

Ramsden, P. (1992) *Learning to Teach in Higher Education*, London: Routledge.

Reason, P. and Rowan, J. (1981) *Human Inquiry*, Chichester: Wiley.

Redman, W. (2001) 'Check your emotional health', http://www.innerbalancing.ca/resources/article19htm (accessed May 2003).

Reed, H. (1985) *Getting Help from Your Dreams*, Virginia Beach, Virginia: Inner Vision.

Reeders, E. (2000) 'Scholarly practice in work-based learning: fitting the glass slipper', *Higher Education Research and Development*, 19 (2), 205–16.

Reif, F. and Larkin, J. (1991) 'Cognition in scientific and everyday domains: comparison and learning implications', *Journal of Research in Science Teaching*, 28 (9), 733–59.

Rider, R. and Rayner, S. (1998) *Cognitive Styles and Learning Strategies*, London: David Fulton.

Rogers, C. (1969) *Freedom to Learn*, Columbus, OH: Charles E. Merrill.

Rose, C. (1985) *Accelerated Learning*, Great Missenden: Topaz Publishing.

Ross, D. (1989) 'First steps in developing a reflective approach', *Journal of Teacher*, 40 (2), 22–30.

Rowland, S. (2000) *The Enquiring University Teacher*, Milton Keynes: SRHE/Open University Press.

Rowling, J. (2000) *Harry Potter and the Goblet of Fire*, London: Bloomsbury.

Rumsey, T. (1996) *Not Just Games: Strategic use of Experiential Learning to Drive Business Results*, Dubuque: Kendall/Hunt Publishing Company.

Rust, C. (2002) 'The impact of assessment on student learning: how can research literature practically help to inform the development of departmental assessment strategies?', *Active Learning in Higher Education*, 3 (2), 128–44.

Ryan, A. (2001) *Feminist Ways of Knowing*, Leicester: NIACE.

Saddington, J. (1992) 'Learner experience: a rich resource for learning', in J. Mulligan and C. Griffin (eds) *Empowerment through Experiential Learning*, London: Kogan Page, pp. 37–49 .

Sadler-Smith, E. (1997) 'Learning styles: frameworks and instruments', *Educational Psychology*, 17, 51–63.

Salisbury, J. (1994) 'Becoming qualified – an ethnography of a post-experience teacher-training course', PhD thesis, University of Wales, Cardiff.

Saljo, R. (1979) *Learning in the Learner's Perspective 1: Some Common-Sense Conceptions, Reports from the Department of Education*, Goteborg: Goteborg University, No. 76.

Salmon, P. (1989) 'Personal stances in learning', in S. Warner Weil and M. McGill (eds) *Making Sense of Experiential Learning*, Milton Keynes: SRHE/Open University Press, pp. 230–44.

Salmon, P. (1995) *Psychology in the Classroom*, London: Cassell.

Saunders, S. (undated) 'Experiential learning theory: is it valid or hype? http://www.usd.edu-knorum/learningpapers/experiential.html (accessed May 2002).

Savin-Baden, M. (2000) *Problem-Based Learning in Higher Education*, Milton Keynes: SRHE/Open University Press.

Schön, D. (1983) *The Reflective Practitioner*, San Francisco: Jossey-Bass.

Schön, D. (1987) *Educating Reflective Practitioners*, San Francisco: Jossey-Bass.

SEEC (2003) *Credit Level Descriptors*, SEEC Office, London: UEL.

Selfe, C. and Arbabi, F. (1986) 'Writing to learn Engineering students journals', in A. Young and T. Fulwiler (eds) *Writing Across the Disciplines*, Upper Montclair, NJ: Boynton/Cook.

Seller, A. (1994) 'Should the feminist philosopher stay at home?', in K. Lennon and M. Whitford (eds) *Knowing the Difference, Feminist Perspectives in Epistemology*, London: Routledge, pp. 230–48.

Shohet, R. (1985) *Dream Sharing*, Wellingborough: Turnstone Press.

Skelton, R. (1971) *The Practice of Poetry*, London: Heinemann Educational.

Snowden, D. (2003 – in preparation) 'Narrative patterns – the perils and possibilities of using story in organisations', in E. Lesser and K. Prusak (eds) *Creating Value with Knowledge*.

Songer, N. and Linn, M. (1991) 'How do students' views of science influence knowledge integration?', *Journal of Research in Science Teaching*, 28 (9), 761–84.

Sparker-Langer, G. and Colton, A. (1991) 'Synthesis of research on teachers' reflective thinking', *Educational Leadership*, March, 37–44.

Sparkes-Langer, G., Simmons, J., Pasch, M., Colton, A, and Stako, A, (1990) 'Reflective pedagogical thinking: how can we promote and measure it?', *Journal of Teacher Education*, 41, 23–32.

Steinaker, N. and Bell, R. (1979) *The Experiential Taxonomy: A New Approach to Teaching and Learning*, New York: Academic Press.

Steiner, G. (1998) *Learning: Nineteen Scenarios from Everyday Life*, Cambridge: Cambridge University Press.

Stewart M. (2002) 'Encouraging reflective practice', *Learning and Teaching Press*, Spring 1 (2), 4–6.

Stewart, S. and Richardson, B. (2000) 'Reflection and its place in the curriculum on an undergraduate course: should it be assessed?, *Assessment and Evaluation in Higher Education*, 25 (4), 369–86.

Storr, A. (1988) *Solitude*, London: Flamingo Press.

Sutherland, P. (1997) 'Experiential learning and constructivism', in P. Sutherland (ed.) *Adult Learning: A Reader*, London: Kogan Page, pp. 82–93.

Svensson, L. (1997) 'Learning and organising knowledge', in F. Marton, D. Hounsell and N. Entwistle (eds) *The Experience of Learning*, Edinburgh: Scottish Academic Press.

Taylor C. and White, S. (2000) *Practising Reflectivity in Health and Welfare*, Milton Keynes: Open University Press.

Taylor, E. (1997) 'Building upon the theoretical debate: a critical review of the empirical studies of Mezirow's transformative learning theory', *Adult Education Quarterly*, 48 (1), 34–59.

Tennant, M. (1999) 'Is learning transferable?', in D. Boud and J. Garrick (eds) *Understanding Learning at Work*, London: Routledge, pp. 165–79.

Tennant, M. (2000) 'Learning to work, working to learn: theories of situational education', in C. Symes and J. McIntyre (eds) *Working Knowledge*, Milton Keynes: SRHE/Open University Press.

Thorpe, M. (2000) 'Experiential learning at a distance', in D. Boud, R. Cohen and D. Walker (eds) *Using Experience for Learning*, Milton Keynes: SRHE/Open University Press, pp. 199–112.

Tobin, K. (1987) 'The role of wait time in higher cognitive learning', *Review of Educational Research*, 57 (1), 69–75.

Tomlinson, P. (1999) 'Continuous reflection and implicit learning – towards a balance in teacher preparation', *Oxford Review of Education*, 25 (4), 533–44.

Torbert, W. (1972) *Learning from Experience: Towards Consciousness*, New York: Columbia University Press.

Trigwell, K. and Prosser, M. (1999) *Understanding Learning and Teaching*, Milton Keynes: SRHE/Open University Press.

Tumin, M. (1976) 'Valid and invalid rationales', in M. Keeton, *Experiential Learning: Rationale, Characteristics and Assessment*, San Francisco: Jossey-Bass.

Usher, R. (2000a) 'Imposing structure, enabling play', in C. Symes and J. McIntyre (eds) *Working Knowledge: The New Vocationalism and Higher Education*, Milton Keynes: SRHE/Open University Press.

Usher, R. (2000b) 'Experiential learning or learning from experience: does it make a difference?, in D. Boud, R. Cohen and D. Walker (eds) *Using Experience for Learning* Milton Keynes: SRHE/Open University Press, pp. 169–80.

Usher, R. and Edwards, R. (1994) *Post-modernism and Education* London: Routledge.

Usher, R. and Soloman, N. (1999) 'Experiential learning and the shaping of subjectivity in the work-place', *Studies in the Education of Adults*, 31 (2), 155–63.

Van Manen, M. (1977) 'Linking ways of knowing and ways of teaching', *Curriculum Inquiry*, 6, 205–8.

Van Rossum, E. and Schenk, S. (1984) 'The relationship between learning conception, study strategy and learning outcome', *British Journal of Educational Psychology*, 54, 73–83.

Vygotsky, L. (1978) *Mind in Society: The Development of Higher Psychological Processes*, Cambridge, MA: Harvard University Press.

Wallace, M. (1996) 'When is experiential learning not experiential learning?', in G. Claxton, T. Atkinson, M. Osborn and M. Wallace (eds) *Liberating the Learner*, London: Routledge.

Ward, A. (1999) 'The "matching principle" – designing for process in professional education, *Social Work Education*, 18 (2), 161–69.

Warner Weil, S. and McGill, I. (1989a) 'A framework for making sense of experiential learning', in S. Warner Weil and M. McGill (eds) *Making Sense of Learning*, Milton Keynes: SRHE/Open University Press, pp. 3–24.

Warner Weil, S. and McGill, I. (1989b) *Making Sense of Experiential Learning*, Milton Keynes: SRHE/Open University Press.

Watton, P. and Collings, J. (2002) 'Developing a framework for independent work experience', in P. Watton, J. Collings and J. Moon (eds) *Independent Work Experience: an evolving picture*, SEDA Paper 114, Birmingham: SEDA.

Watton, P., Collings J. and Moon, J. (2002) *Independent Work Experience: An Evolving Picture*, SEDA Paper, 114, Birmingham: SEDA.

Wedman J. and Martin, M. (1986) 'Exploring the development of reflective thinking through journal writing', *Reading Improvement*,23 (1), 68–71.

West, H. and Pines, A. (1985) *Cognitive Structure and Conceptual Change*, New York: Academic Press.

Wilkes, A. (1997) *Knowledge in Minds: Individual and Collective Processes in Cognition*, London: Psychology Press.

Williamson, H. (1933) *The Pathway*, London: Faber and Faber.

Wilson, E. (1998) *Consilience*, London: Little, Brown and Company.

Winitzky, N. and Kauchak, D. (1997) 'Constructivism in teacher education: applying cognitive theory to teacher learning', in V. Richardson (ed.) *Constructivist Teacher Education*, London: Falmer Press.

Winter, R. (1989) *Learning from Experience: Principles and Practices of Action Research*, London: Falmer Press.

Winter, R., Buck, A. and Sobiechowska, P. (1999) *Professional Experiences and the Investigative Imagination*, London: Routledge.

Young, A. and Fulwiler, T. (1986) *Writing across the Disciplines*, Upper Montclair, NJ: Boynton/Cook.

Zsambok, C. and Klein, G. (1997) *Naturalistic Decision-Making*, Hillsdale, NJ: Lawrence Erlbaum Associates.

Zuber-Skerritt, O. (1992) *Professional Development in Higher Education: A Theoretical Framework for Action Research*, London: Kogan Page.

Index

248

ILTHE, 4
imagination, 117, 119, 157, 159, 173
informal learning (see learning,
  incidental)
inhibition of learning (see learning –
  inhibition)
instruction (see facilitation of learning)
intellectual space, 86
intelligences (Gardner's work), 46
intention to understand, 58–68
interdisciplinarity, 134, 145
internal experience
introduction of reflective activities,
  133–42

journals, vii, 2–4, 51, 124, 134, 140,
  148, 149, 155, 159–60, 166,
  179–81, 229
judgement exercise, Resource 12

King, P. and Kitchener, K., 5, 32–43,
  56–7, 99, 171
knowledge, 34–43, 48–54, 71
Kolb, D., 3, 13, 72, 104–20, 121

language, 11–12
learning: appresentation, 23, 72–3,
  glossary 231; architecture of
  variation, 29, 124; 'building bricks'
  view of, 11, 16–17; accelerated,
  49–54; and teaching, 12–13,
  glossary 232; challenge, 14, 87,
  129–30, glossary 232; facilitation of,
  13–14; figure/ground, 11, 24–31,
  72–3, glossary 231; from work
  experience, viii, 3; incidental, 15,
  54, 120, 128, 154, 168, 223,
  Resource 11; inhibition of, 49–54;
  journals (see journals); logs (see
  journals); material of, 13, 18, 19,
  23–31, 90–2; mediation of, 6,
  71–78, 123, 154, glossary 232;
  network view of, 11, 24–31; non-
  reflective, 92; outcomes, 166, 112,
  151, 164, 168; ownership, 86, 138;
  pace of, 88; relevance, 26–31, 90–2,
  glossary 232; situated, 20–1, 118;
  shifts, 172; styles, 114; to learn,
  30–46; transfer, 118; upgrading of,

85–7; variation, 26–31, 72–3,
  glossary 232; vocabulary for, 11–15
lecture, lecture notes, 161
level descriptors, 32, 39, glossary 232
levels of reflective writing (see
  reflection, depth)
limiting factors, 60

management of variation (see
  'architecture of variation')
map of reflective writing, 185–6
Marton, F. and Booth, S., 4, 11, 20,
  23, 59–68, 75, 101
Master's level, 40, 94, 110, 164
material of learning (see learning –
  material of)
material of learning (see teaching,
  material of)
material of teaching (see learning,
  material of)
material of teaching (see teaching –
  material of)
meaning, 11–31
meaningfulness (see meaning)
mediation of learning (see learning –
  mediation)
mediation of learning (see learning,
  mediation)
memory, 112, 175
menstrual cycle, 93
metacognition, 89, 100, 145
metaphor, 174–9

module design, 151
mood (see emotional state)
music, 28, 49

narrative, 174–179
NVQ's, 75
non-reflective learning (see learning –
  non-reflective)
notice board, 162
nursing, 80–2, 109, 122

ownership of learning (see learning –
  ownership)

patchwork text (see story – patchwork)
PBL (see problem-based learning)